Business Model Innovation

For a while now Allan Afuah has been a leading thinker in the areas of business model development, innovation management, and strategic analysis. In his most recent book on business model innovations, he takes us to the next important level of strategic thinking for twenty first century enterprise—the nexus of business model development and innovation, where companies both create and capture value by coming up with novel and original business recipes. Professor Afuah's book provides a comprehensive coverage of the topics that are relevant to this subject, and includes both useful analytical tools as well as many concrete illustrations of how these ideas have been applied. Any business leader who is interested in understanding the importance of inventive business models and how they can be designed should read this book.

—*Ira Ginsberg, Professor, New York University*
Stern School of Business, USA

As we move deeper into the 21st century with its environment characterized by accelerating technological change, uncertainty, and complexity, business model innovation has become the hottest topic in strategy. In Business Model Innovation, Allan Afuah delivers a fresh paradigm that allows managers to leverage new ways of conducting business to gain and sustain a competitive advantage. Compelling, insightful, and practical.

—*Frank T. Rothaermel, The Russell and Nancy McDonough*
Chair, Professor & Sloan Industry Studies Fellow,
Georgia Institute of Technology, USA

Allan Afuah unfailingly captures attention with his outstanding work. This time he offers an astonishing new book that explains Business Model Innovation. Exploiting his superior scholarship, he explores recent phenomena and shows how they relate to business models. His discussion of Business Model Innovations highlights not only what happens now (e.g. Long Tail, Social Media, Crowd-sourcing) but also how companies can, with the right capabilities, capture and create value tomorrow. Close to practice, each chapter features case studies and the book closes with implications and helpful applications. This exceptional work deserves your undivided attention.

—*Patrick Reinmoeller, Professor,*
Cranfield University School of Management, UK

Rooted in strategic management research, *Business Model Innovation* explores the concepts, tools, and techniques that enable organizations to gain and/or maintain a competitive advantage in the face of technological innovation, globalization, and an increasingly knowledge-intensive economy. The book investigates how organizations can use innovations in business models to take advantage of entrepreneurial opportunities from:

- Crowdsourcing and open innovation
- Long tails
- Social media
- Disruptive technologies
- Less-is-more innovations
- Network effects
- Scarcity of complementary capabilities

The book also looks at the ways firms can use innovations in business models to exploit or defend against threats. With twelve supplementary cases to help readers apply the concepts and techniques, this book is a must-have for anyone looking to understand the fundamentals of business model innovation.

Allan Afuah obtained his PhD from MIT and is Associate Professor of Strategy at the Ross School of Business at the University of Michigan. Professor Afuah's honors include *Academy of Management Review* (*AMR*) winner of Best Article Award for the year 2012 for his paper, "Crowdsourcing as a solution to distant search" which he co-authored with Christopher Tucci. *AMR* is No. 1 out of 172 management journals and No. 1 out of 116 business journals in the world.

Business Model Innovation
Concepts, Analysis, and Cases

Allan Afuah

NEW YORK AND LONDON

First published 2014
by Routledge
711 Third Avenue, New York, NY 10017

and by Routledge
2 Park Square, Milton Park, Abingdon, Oxon OX14 4RN

Routledge is an imprint of the Taylor & Francis Group, an informa business

Library of Congress Cataloging in Publication Data
Afuah, Allan.
    Business model innovation: concepts, analysis, and cases/Allan Afuah.
    pages cm
    Includes bibliographical references and index.
    1. Strategic planning—Mathematical models. 2. Industrial management—Mathematical
    models. I. Title.
    HD30.28.A3467 2014
    658.4'012—dc23
    2013035835

ISBN: 978-0-415-81739-4 (hbk)
ISBN: 978-0-415-81740-0 (pbk)
ISBN: 978-0-203-58458-3 (ebk)

Typeset in Minion
by Florence Production, Stoodleigh, Devon, UK

Printed and bound in the United States of America by Edwards Brothers Malloy, Inc.

To every family that has been kind enough to welcome a foreign student to its home.

To my grandmother, Veronica Masang-Namang Nkweta, and the Bamboutos highlands which she tilled to feed me.

CONTENTS

FIGURES

TABLES

EXHIBITS

PREFACE

Good theory enables us to explain, predict, plan, and execute. In the words of Kurt Lewin, "nothing is quite so practical as a good theory". The theory of gravity enabled human beings to explain why things fall down, predict what the gravitational pull on the surface of the moon would be, plan how to land a person on the moon, and execute the plans to get to the moon.

Yes, social science theories may not have the precision of the theories of physics. However, strategic management scholars have drawn on social sciences to develop theories that explain why some industries or firms are more profitable than others, predict the impact of technological innovation on industry and firm profitability, explain and predict the impact of a firm's capabilities on its performance, suggest what good plans for using or building capabilities should look like, and how to execute strategies or plans. These theories include the competitive positioning or product-market-position view, resource-based view, dynamic capabilities, social network theory, evolutionary economics, agency theory, institutional theory, resource dependence theory, and transaction costs economics.

Business Model Innovation: Concepts, Analysis, and Cases is about drawing on some of these theories to explain and predict the relationships among a business model, its profitability, and the environment in which the model is conceived and executed. These explanations and predictions help managers better create and execute profitable business models. More importantly, the book is about using management theory to explain and predict *how* and *why* firms can gain and/or maintain a competitive advantage in the face of technological innovation, globalization, and an increasingly knowledge-intensive economy. In particular, the book is about using business model innovations to exploit the opportunities and threats in phenomenon such as crowdsourcing, social media, the long tail, less-is-more innovations, disruptive technologies, and scarce resources.

Yes, the principles of economics have not changed and may not need to change to be effectively used in exploring the so-called new economy. Yes, some of the phenomena—e.g. crowdsourcing, long tail, and social media—have been around for centuries or more. However, technological innovation, the shift to knowledge economies, and globalization have created an environment in which we can better understand the opportunities and threats in the phenomena and how to better exploit the opportunities and/or defend against the threats.

Because the book is about the concepts, tools, and techniques for generating and executing high-performing business models, it should be useful to anyone—manager, scholar, entrepreneur, or venture capitalist—who wants to contribute to creating or capturing value whether in a for-profit or nonprofit organization.

WHAT IS UNIQUE ABOUT THE BOOK

By drawing on strategic management theories and the comprehensive research that has been performed in other areas of management, *Business Model Innovation*:

- Reduces the components of a business model to five comprehensive yet parsimonious building blocks.
- Synthesizes a practical framework (the VARIM)—that is rooted in both the resource-based *and* product-market-position views—for assessing the profitability potential of a business model, product, resource, brand, activities, and any other capability.
- Provides a comprehensive description of the characteristics of seven phenomena whose impact on management and entrepreneurial activity is growing rapidly in the face of technological innovation, globalization, and an increasingly knowledge-intensive economy: Crowdsourcing, social media, the long tail, disruptive technologies, network effects, less-is-more innovations, and scarcity of capabilities.
- Offers a detailed analysis of the impact of each of these phenomena—crowd-sourcing, social media, and so on—on an organization's business models.
- Is centrally focused on performance, especially profitability.
- Is peppered with examples throughout.
- Has the latest cases that illustrate the application of the core concepts, tools, and techniques of the book.

NON-UNIQUE FEATURES OF THE BOOK

In addition to the above unique features, *Business Model Innovation* also:

- Explores what value creation and capture are all about especially in the face of innovation.
- Explains first-mover advantages and disadvantages.
- Revisits an organization's system of activities as capabilities.

ORGANIZATION OF THE BOOK

Befittingly, *Business Model Innovation* is organized as follows. Part I, which is made up of two chapters, is the introduction. Chapter 1 defines business models and business model innovation, and then explores five comprehensive yet parsimonious building blocks of a business model. The chapter also explores four types of business model innovations and suggests how a firm can paint a portrait of a business model.

Because business models and strategic management are about performance, it is critical to be able to tell whether one has a winner or a loser when generating or executing a business model. Therefore, Chapter 2 is dedicated to assessing the profitability potential of a business model in its various forms. The model can also be used to assess the profitability potential of products, capabilities, activities, strategies, business units, and so on.

Part II explores the opportunities and threats that firms face when conceiving of, generating, and implementing business model innovations. The first chapter in Part II, Chapter 3, explores what the long tail is all about and its potential as a source of innovation for business models. Chapter 4 explains crowdsourcing and open innovation, pointing out their potential impact on business model innovations. Chapter 5 introduces social media and explores the potential opportunities and threats that they present to business model innovation. Chapter 6 is about a phenomenon called less-is-more innovations and its impact on business model innovation. It is about why more is not always better, and what that means to business model innovations. Chapter 7, the last chapter in Part II, is about disruptive technologies, an extremely useful but often misunderstood concept.

Part III explores the strengths and weaknesses of the firms that must conceive of, generate, and execute business models in the face of the opportunities and threats of Part II. Since capabilities are the core of any business model, Chapter 8 is dedicated to the resources and activities that make up capabilities—to explaining what they are all about. Chapter 9 explores value creation and capture—how the activities and resources of Chapter 8 are used to create and capture value. Moving first or being a follower has some implications that can be critical in the face of an innovation. Therefore, Chapter 10 is dedicated to first-mover advantages and *dis*advantages. No matter how promising, a business model innovation will not amount to much if it is not well executed. Therefore, Chapter 11 is dedicated to implementation of business model innovations.

For a course in which students have not yet taken a core course in strategy, it may be good to go through Part III before Part II since the former contains some of the fundamental strategy concepts that are needed to understand Part II.

Part IV gets into the application of some of the business model innovation concepts to globalization and growth. Thus, Chapter 12 is about globalization and its implications for business model innovation.

Part V consists of cases of firms with interesting business model innovations.

ROOTS OF THE BOOK

Business Model Innovation started out as a revision of *Strategic Innovation: New Game Strategies for Competitive Advantage*, but in implementing the suggestions made by the professors, managers, and students who had used *Strategic Innovation*, I quickly realized that a new book had emerged—a book centered around innovations in business models rather than strategies. That book is *Business Model Innovations.*

Allan Afuah
Ann Arbor, Michigan
August 8, 2013

ACKNOWLEDGMENTS

I would like to thank the Routledge anonymous reviewers, adopters of *Strategic Innovation*, students, and managers whose critique of *Strategic Innovation* enabled me to write *Business Model Innovation*. Their suggestions were extremely valuable to me throughout the process of researching and writing this book.

I continue to owe a huge debt of gratitude to my professors and mentors at MIT. They introduced me to the subject of strategic innovation, and to the virtues of patience and tolerance. I am forever grateful to them. Some of my students at the Stephen M. Ross School of Business at the University of Michigan gave me very useful feedback when I pre-tested the concepts of *Business Model Innovation*. Some of the cases in Part V of the book were written by some of my MBA students under my supervision. In particular, I would like to thank Nung Yoo (Chris), Shana Anderson, and Steve Harutunian for excellent research assistance. Shana Anderson and Steven Harutunian also co-authored some of the cases in Part V of the book.

Special thanks go to Michael and Mary Kay Hallman for the funding that enabled me to explore the topic of business model innovation with more freedom and dedication.

Finally, I would like to thank Sharon Golan, Routledge Editor for business books, for a great editorial job. The chapter on social media was Sharon's suggestion, and it fit in beautifully with the other building blocks of the book.

Part I

Introduction

1

INTRODUCTION TO
BUSINESS MODEL INNOVATIONS

Reading this chapter should provide you with the conceptual and analytical tools to:

- Define business models and business model innovation.
- Understand the components of a business model.
- Describe different types of business model innovations (regular, resource-building, position-building, and revolutionary).

INTRODUCTION

Consider the following business examples.

When Goldcorp, a Canadian gold mining company, had difficulties striking gold on its Red Lake, Canada property, it turned to the world to help it find the gold. It offered prizes totaling $575,000 to anyone from anywhere in the world that could analyze its banks of geological survey data and suggest where to find the gold. Fractal Graphics, an Australian company, won the top prize of $105,000. More importantly, the contest yielded targets that were so productive that the firm started producing 504,000 ounces of gold per year, at a cost of $59 per ounce, compared to the pre-contest annual rate of 53,000 ounces at a cost of $360 per ounce.[1] Remarkable!

With a market value of over $160 billion for most of 2008, Google was one of the most valuable companies in the world. Its net income in 2007 was $4.2 billion on sales of $16.6 billion, giving it a net profit margin of 25.4 percent, one of the highest of any company of its size. This was a remarkable performance for a company that only four years earlier, in 2002, had revenues of $439 million and a net income of $99 million in a struggling dotcom industry.

These extraordinary stories are not limited to high-tech businesses. In 2006, Threadless, an online T-shirt company founded in 2000, had profits of $6 million on revenues of $18 million, from T-shirts that had been designed, marketed, and bought by members of the public. Such a high rate of profitability made the firm one of the most profitable in the T-shirt business.

In 2007, Pfizer's Lipitor was the world's best-selling drug with sales of $12.7 billion, more than twice its nearest competitor's sales (Plavix, with $5.9 billion). This was the third year in a row that Lipitor had topped the best-seller list. One of the most telling things about Lipitor is that it was the fifth cholesterol drug in its category (statins) in a pharmaceuticals industry where the third or fourth product in a category usually has little chance of surviving, let alone of becoming the best seller in the world.

BUSINESS MODEL INNOVATION

At the core of each of these fascinating success stories is a business model innovation. To define a business model innovation, we first define a business model and an innovation. A *business model* is a framework or recipe for making money—for creating and capturing value.[2] Innovation is about doing things differently from the norm. Therefore, a *business model innovation* is a framework or recipe for creating and capturing value by doing things differently.[3] It is often about changing the rules of the game. For example, rather than keep its databanks of geological survey data on its Red Lake, Ontario, Canada property secret, and struggle to pinpoint the location of gold on the property, Goldcorp made the data available to the public and challenged the world to locate the gold. Goldcorp was looking to the public, rather than to its employees or a designated contractor, to solve its problem. Only the winners—those who produced desirable results—were paid. Contrast this with the situation in which employees or designated contractors are paid whether or not they succeed in locating the gold.

Business model innovation does not have to involve leapfrogging competitors with products that have better product characteristics than competitors'. In fact, some of the more interesting business model innovations are those in which firms cut back some product/service characteristics that have come to be considered sacred cows by some customers. For example, when Nintendo offered the Wii, it deliberately used much cheaper three-year-old microprocessor and graphics technologies, rather than trying to outmuscle Microsoft and Sony, which used the latest and fastest but much more expensive technologies which many avid gamers had come to expect in each new generation of game consoles. The Wii had other features that appealed more to non-avid gamers, such as the ability to play games that also enabled people to get some physical exercise.

More importantly, some of the most profitable business model innovations have little to do with a product. The story of the Xerox 914 photocopier is an astonishing example.[4] The 914 copier was a good new copier but was going to cost so much if sold outright that Xerox was advised by consulting firms to shelve it because of the machine's economics. However, the machine's sales and profitability shot through the roof when Xerox decided to lease the machines rather than sell them.

The winner in the face of business model innovation can be the firm that moved first to change the rules of the game, or a firm that came in later and pursued a better business model. Google was neither the first to introduce search engines nor the first to introduce sponsored ads (paid listings). However, it played the new game very well. It was better at business model innovation and therefore was more successful at monetizing search engines. To understand business model innovation, it is important to first understand what business models are all about, starting with the five building blocks of any business model.[5] (For more details on how these five components were derived, please see the Appendix at the end of this chapter.)

Components of a Business Model

The components of a business model are shown in Figure 1.1. Before we explore each of these components in detail, a word about the rationale behind the components and the linkages between them is in order. Recall that a business model is about making money, and money comes from customers. For customers to buy from a firm, the firm must offer them something that satisfies their needs—that is, the firm must offer the right *customer value proposition*. However, the right customer value proposition to the wrong customers will do the firm little good. Therefore, a firm may be better off targeting the type of *market segment* whose needs it can satisfy, and that has many customers with a high willingness to pay.

A *revenue model* is the structure through which a firm monetizes the value proposition that it offers customers. The wrong revenue model can leave money on the table or drive customers away. If a firm starts making money by targeting a high willingness-to-pay market segment with the right customer value proposition and revenue model, competitors are likely to want to imitate the firm so as to make profits also. Thus, part of a firm's business model is its *growth model* in which the firm figures out how to grow profitably even as competitors try to imitate it. Finally, delivering customer value proposition to the target market segment, and so on, requires the right *capabilities*—the right resources/assets and the activities that use the resources/assets to create and capture value. We now explore each component in more detail (Figure 1.1).[6]

Customer Value Proposition

A firm's value proposition to customers consists of those things that the firm and its products/services can do for customers to solve their problems and/or satisfy their needs better than competitors. It answers the question: What is so compelling, engaging, rewarding, or delightful to customers about what a firm has to offer them that will attract customers from competitors or from the sidelines? It's about the benefits that a firm

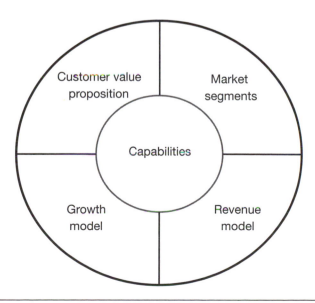

Figure 1.1 Components of a business model

and its products offer customers and how much these customers perceive the benefits as valuable. The right customer value proposition meets customers' needs and/or solves a problem for them, and provides them with a reason to buy from you rather than your competitors. Note that customers do not always know, *ex ante*, what they need in a product or service. For example, many customers did not know that they needed touch screens and Internet access in their cell phones until the iPhone was introduced to them. Few knew how much the Internet would change their lives until it did. Thus, part of a customer value proposition may involve helping customers to discover their own latent needs for products/services.

A firm's customer value proposition depends on not only its products/services and their attributes, but also on its reputation/image and the other assets that it controls such as relationships with customers. For example, a car enthusiast may buy a car not only because it handles well on the road, but also because it is a BMW or Lexus. A brand-minded customer may buy a product because it is sold in one store rather than another. Effectively, customer value proposition is rooted not only in products and services but also in other assets such as brands, access to distribution channels, and so on.

Market Segment

Money comes from customers and a firm needs to know what these customers want, how many of them there are, their willingness to pay, and how profitable it will be serving these customers. The market segment component is about the groups of customers to whom a value proposition is being offered or should be offered, how many customers there are in each group, their willingness to pay, and the attractiveness of each group. The larger the market size, the higher would be the likelihood of more revenues. And the higher the willingness of customers to pay, the better a firm's chances of obtaining high prices for the benefits offered to customers. The market segment component of a business model is also about the quality and quantity of the coopetitors—of the suppliers, customers, complementors, competitors, and any other institution with which the firm has to cooperate to create value and compete to capture value.[7] From a cooperation point of view, a firm can work with knowledgeable customers, suppliers, governments, complementors, and even rivals to co-create products, thereby better meeting customers' needs and increasing the number of high willingness-to-pay customers. From a competition angle, a market segment—with customers and suppliers who have bargaining power over the firm, that experiences high rivalry, and that is rife with high threats of substitutes and potential new entry—is likely to be less profitable than one in which competitive forces are low.[8] That is, a market segment in which industry forces are weak (attractive segment) is more likely to be profitable for the firm than one in which the forces are strong (an unattractive segment). Just as important is what the firm does to improve its position within the market segment, whether the market is attractive or not. A firm's customer value proposition contributes immensely to its position in a market segment.[9]

Segmentation can be by the type of customers and their preferences, type of product being offered, demographics, geography, willingness to pay, distribution channels, and the type of relationships that a firm has with its customers. Segmentation results in different types of market segments: niche market, mass market, and multi-sided market.[10] For example, a multi-sided market segment is one in which two or more groups of customers are interrelated and the firm makes money by facilitating that interaction.[11] For example, a credit card market is a two-sided market since cardholders are on one side and merchants on the other. The more cardholders that own a particular credit card, the better off would be the merchants that accept that particular card and, of course, the better off would be the credit card company.

Note that, because many customers often do not know their needs, *ex ante*, in the face of some innovations, the entrepreneur may have to work with them—especially so-called lead users—to help them discover their needs.[12] Also note that the attraction of a market segment to a firm is a function of not only the product/services that meet the segment's needs but also of the firm's other assets such as the firm's access to distribution channels, brand name reputation, and relationships with customers that the firm needs to profit from the segment.

Revenue Model

The revenue model component is about how many customers get to pay how much for what product/service, when and how. It is about getting as many of the customers who like the value proposition as possible to pay a price that is close to their reservation prices without driving them away. (A customer's reservation price for a product is the highest price that the customer is willing to pay for the product.) Making money starts with revenues. Without revenues, no amount of cost cutting would amount to anything good. Revenue models are what are sometimes referred to in the popular press as "business models." Types of revenue models include: advertising, razor-blade or razor-and-blade, brokerage, subscription, freemium, leasing, licensing, asset sale, loss leader, bait-and-hook, usage fee, cash and carry, recurring revenues, and so on.[13] In Google's advertising model, for example, it has two sets of customers: those who conduct searches, and those who advertise. Google has to deliver compelling value to both sets of customers but only one of them pays Google directly. In general, each revenue model has advantages and disadvantages that can make or break a business. For example, in the razor-and-blade model, a firm sells products (e.g. razors) at very low prices but sells a complementary product (blades) at higher prices and/or more often. Kodak used the razor-blade model in its film-based photography business and it worked beautifully. However, the firm failed miserably when it tried to apply the same model to digital photography.[14]

Since price is such an important component of revenues, a firm's pricing model is usually a critical part of its revenue model. Because pricing determines how much a customer gets to pay for the customer value proposition, getting the price right has one of the most direct impacts on revenues. Too high a price can drive customers away, possibly to competitors or substitutes. Too low a price—without any strategic motives—unnecessarily leaves money on the table. Types of pricing models include: Auction pricing, posted pricing, cost-plus, skimming, tiered pricing, value pricing, limit pricing, bundling, give-away, loss-leader, and two-part tariff.

Sources of revenues can also be critical. Many car dealers make their money from servicing cars and not from selling them. In fact, one reason why IBM was able to turn around after years of decline was because it decided to also focus on services as a key source of revenue rather than focus only on products. In 2013, a reasonable fraction of Ryanair's profits came from onboard sales, advertising, hotel, and car rental referral—that is, the airline's revenues came from more than just air tickets.

The ideal revenue model would get as many of the customers—who find the customer value proposition compelling—as possible to pay prices that are as close to their reservation prices as possible without driving customers away.

A firm's revenue and pricing models depend on the customer value proposition, market segments, growth model, and capabilities components of the business model. For example, a firm in a market segment with little or no competition and with customers who have a high willingness to pay can afford to charge high prices.

Growth Model

The primary question in the growth model component of a business model is: How can a firm grow *profitably*? Most businesses want to grow. However, growing for growth's sake without profitability or a strategic path to profits is irresponsible. The growth component of a business model is about what a firm has to do to increase the number of customers, increase willingness to pay, keep prices close to customers' reservation prices while keeping costs low. This can be very difficult because, once a firm offers the right customers the right value and starts making money, its coopetitors are likely to want a piece of the action. Suppliers may demand higher prices for the firm's inputs or push to start delivering inputs with lower quality, thereby increasing costs or forcing the firm to ship lower quality products to its customers. Customers may want lower prices or demand higher quality products.

More importantly, competitors (incumbents and potential new entrants alike) may want to imitate or leapfrog the firm, forcing it to lower its prices or raise its costs. Macro-environmental factors such as shortages resulting from higher demand or government regulations may increase the cost of inputs. In some countries, the government may step in, demanding that prices be lowered. What is even more important than the reaction of coopetitors is that major events such as technological change can disrupt the basis of business models, giving rivals, suppliers, and customers an advantage. For example, the Internet turned the business models of many newspapers and other traditional media upside down, eroding the basis for their profitability. An important part of a business model is finding ways to maintain or grow revenue levels relative to competitors, and keeping costs low or driving them even lower relative to revenues.

Maintaining higher revenues. Three strategies can help a firm stem erosion of its revenues and grow profitably.[15] First, a firm can pursue a *block* strategy in which it defends its position in the market vigorously even as it tries to win over more customers. It can do so proactively or in response to competitors' moves. For example, when a pharmaceutical company applies for and obtains a patent for a new drug, it is making a proactive move to block others from legally replicating the drug. If a firm sues someone for violating its intellectual property, or retaliates in some other way, it is making a blocking move in response to being challenged. Second, a firm can pursue a *run* strategy in which it is one of the first to innovate and before competitors have had a chance to become a significant threat, it has already moved on to something better by innovating again. That is, in a run strategy, a firm grows by growing the market. For example, since the 1980s, Intel has often introduced a new generation of its microprocessors before sales of an existing generation have peaked.[16] When Apple introduced the iPod, then the iPhone, and then the iPad, it was pursuing a run strategy. As proved by Apple and Intel, a run strategy is one of the best approaches to grow profitably.

The third strategic move that a firm can take is to *team up* with one or more coopetitors. (Recall that coopetitors are the suppliers, customers, complementors, competitors, and any other institution with which a firm has to cooperate to create value and compete to capture it.) Firms usually team up through strategic alliances, acquisitions, joint ventures, licensing, and venture capital participation. Teaming up can enable a firm to share valuable and rare complementary assets enabling the team to attain and prolong profitability. For example, Pixar teamed up with Disney—first through a strategic alliance and later, an acquisition—and each party brought something to the table. Pixar brought digital animation technology to the team while Disney brought its valuable, rare, and difficult-to-imitate-or-substitute brand name in animation movies, merchandising might, theme parks, distribution channels, and story-telling competence to the team. In the face of an innovation, teaming up to go far growth-wise is reminiscent of the African proverb, "If you want to go fast, go alone. If you want to go far, go together." Many firms pursue some combination of the *block, run* or *team-up* strategies in parallel or series over time.[17]

Cost structure. The other component of profits—that a firm must pay attention to as it grows—are the costs that are incurred in offering customers the right value proposition, targeting and meeting the needs of the right market segments, pursuing the right revenue models, and acquiring the relevant underpinning capabilities. There are two types of costs that a firm has to worry about: production and transaction costs. Production costs—made up of fixed costs, variable costs, marginal costs, and sunk costs—are the costs that go into conceiving, designing, and manufacturing a product or delivering a service. Transaction costs are the costs associated with (1) searching and acquiring information about inputs, (2) the contracting associated with value creation and capture activities, and (3) the monitoring and enforcement of contracts/agreements. The profile of these costs is the cost structure of the business model.[18]

Keeping costs low is important, but it is even more important for a cost-driven business model than for a differentiation-driven one. In a cost-driven business model, a firm's competitive advantage comes from positioning itself as a low-cost provider. Wal-Mart's business model is cost-driven. In a differentiation-driven business model (sometimes called value-driven business models), a firm's competitive advantage comes from being a product differentiator. Apple's business model is differentiation-driven. In any case, it is critical to ensure that as a firm grows or faces other challenges, its costs do not rise faster than its revenues.

Of course, growth depends very much on the underlying capabilities. To pursue a block strategy, a firm needs to have difficult-to-imitate-or-substitute capabilities. To pursue a run strategy, a firm needs to have what it takes to innovate. Not everyone who wants to pursue a run strategy can do so. Apple had Steve Jobs, a strong brand, and distinctive design capabilities that were critical to the firm's run strategy. To successfully pursue a team-up strategy, each member of the team has to bring valuable complementary capabilities to the table.

Capabilities

As already hinted above, capabilities are central to every business model.[19] For example, at the core of every entrepreneur's business model are the people, including the entrepreneur, who must obtain financing for the venture and deliver its first products. At the core of Google's business model are search capabilities that enable it to deliver searches that are perceived as very dependable by many customers, software that enables the firm to serve the needs of the long tail of its customers, the many tools that it offers its apps developers, copyrights to its look-and-feel, and so on. An important part of an entrepreneur's challenge is to build the capabilities to take advantage of any opportunities to offer better customer value propositions, find attractive market segments whose needs it can satisfy, increase the number of high-willingness-to-pay customers in an existing market or move to new markets, look for better revenue models or improve an existing one, implement better pricing models, or pursue profitable growth.

Capabilities consist of *resources* and *activities*. Resources or assets are what a firm *owns* or *has access* to, while activities are what it *does*. Activities transform resources into value created and/or captured. How much value is created and captured depends on the quality of the resources.[20] Resources include brands, people, equipment, products, culture, financing, knowledge, patents, copyrights, trademarks, trade secrets, relationships with coopetitors in an ecosystem, distribution channels, shelf space, position in a network or vis-à-vis coopetitors, installed base, and so on. More recent research suggests that a firm's social capital can be just as important in a business model as other resources.[21] For example, a firm can use its ties (relationships) to members of its social network to locate and acquire vital information during business model generation or execution.[22]

How much value is created and captured also depends on *which* activities are performed to build and/or transform the resources, *who* performs the activities, *when* they are performed, *where* they are performed, and *how* they are performed.[23] All the activities of a value chain, value network, and value shop are candidates.[24] That means all activities from vertical integration (forwards and backwards) and alliances to the seemingly mundane ones such as accounts receivable are candidates. One of the best examples of how the choice of seemingly unimportant activities can impact the value created and/or captured comes from the founding of Genentech. Its founders went to venture capital heavyweight Kleiner Perkins and asked for about $3 million, most of which was to go towards buying capital equipment to perform the pioneering research in gene-splicing—to produce proteins—that would lead to the production of human insulin and a lot more. By convincing the founders to outsource some of the work to existing scientific laboratories, Kleiner Perkins was able to reduce the amount needed to $250,000, making the investment in the venture more plausible.

More specifically, activities are the instruments that a firm uses to build and/or transform resources into value created and captured. For example, firms advertise to build brands or leverage brands to enhance the value perceived in products by customers, use access to distribution channels to get products to customers, transform knowledge embodied in patents into new products, transform designs into products, use pricing activities to capture more consumer surplus by leveraging their positions vis-à-vis coopetitors, network with suppliers to keep input costs low, and so on. Increasingly, firms also take the right actions to build and take advantage of large dependable networks/platforms.[25]

Effectively, capabilities consist of the resources/assets and the activities that use these resources to create and capture value—to offer the right customer value proposition, target the right market segments, promote the profitability of revenue models, and enable the firm to grow profitably.

Business Model as a System

In general, a business model is a system with components and linkages between them—that is, a system with interrelated components.[26] However, the interrelationships are not symmetric since one component—capabilities—drives the other four components. One advantage to the systems nature of a business model is that although it may be easy to imitate a few components of a business model, it can be difficult to replicate all components and the linkages between them.[27] This difficulty in replicating a business model can be an asset to a firm that wants to pursue a block strategy. One disadvantage is that a firm can also get trapped in its own business model even as competitors leapfrog the business model using a disruptive technology, eroding its competitive advantage.[28]

Finally, it is important to note that a business *model* has the core ingredients of a business *plan*. That is, although the structure of the business plan that one entrepreneur or manager would present when seeking venture capital can vary considerably from the plan presented by the next entrepreneur, the *plan* still has the core components of a business *model*. Somewhere in a business plan—explicitly stated or embedded in other elements—there is usually a customer value proposition, a market that is being addressed by the customer value proposition, the revenue model (including the pricing model and sources of revenues), a growth model, and the capabilities—especially the people and funding—needed to execute the plan profitably. (Note that because a business model is a system whose components interact, there is likely to be overlap when analyzing a business model using these components as a framework.)

The Innovation Difference

So far, we have explored the components of a business model—any business model. The question now is: What does business model *innovation* mean as far as these components are concerned? Business model innovation is about doing things differently—about *change*. It is often about changing the rules of the game—slightly or radically—to make money. These changes are often about creating and/or taking advantage of opportunities to better create and capture value. The changes can be manifested in one or more of the components of a business model. Many innovations involve a new customer value proposition that is compelling enough to attract customers from competitors' products or from the sidelines. This compelling customer value proposition can come from new ideas/capabilities or a re/combination of existing ideas/capabilities. For example, Apple's iPod business model changed the rules of the game in the way people could now buy music—through its iTunes music store—and the relationships between MP3 player makers and music label companies. In its iPhone business model, Apple's App Store, access to the Internet, and relationships with chip suppliers also changed the rules of the game. Nintendo's Wii business model changed the rules of the game in video game consoles. Ford's innovative assembly line model also changed the rules of the game, starting with the model-T.

The *innovation* in the business model can also be in the way a market is addressed. For example, in the 1990s and early 2000s, Dell changed the rules of the game in the PC industry with its build-to-order and direct sales models. It can also be in the revenue model. For example, as we saw earlier, it was Xerox's decision to lease rather than sell its Xerox 914 that may have enabled the company to climb to the top of the photocopy-machine business, earning the right for its name to become a verb—to Xerox something.[29] Sponsored ads revolutionized advertising in the search world and enabled Google to rise to prominence.

A common mistake that firms often make during innovation is to focus on one component of a business model and forget about the innovation's potential impact on other components. Consider the case of Kodak again. In film-based photography, Kodak pursued a razor-and-blade revenue model that worked incredibly well.[30] It sold cameras at relatively low prices and made most of its money from film, chemicals, and paper. In the face of the digital photograph, Kodak developed digital technology but did not know how to deal with the razor-and-blade revenue model that had worked so well with film-based photographs. The result was that Kodak's new business model failed, and may have ushered Kodak into bankruptcy.

Effectively, a firm that pursues a business model innovation is better off looking carefully at which components should change by design, and what changes are triggered by these designed changes. Some of the questions that can help a firm better identify changes in different components of a business model and the potential impact on business model profitability are:

- *Customer value proposition*: What is so compelling about the customer value proposition of the new business model (relative to the old one) that would attract customers from competitors or from the sidelines?
- *Market segments*: How many customers does the innovation attract? How many of these customers are from growing the market and how many are from existing markets? What is their willingness to pay? Is the new market any more attractive than the existing one?
- *Revenue models*: Does the business model innovation create an opportunity for new profitable revenue models, and/or change old revenue models? Does the business model innovation require a new pricing strategy?
- *Growth model*: How can the firm grow *profitably*?
- *Capabilities*: Does the firm have the capabilities needed to deliver superior customer value proposition to many high-willingness-to-pay customers, pursue the right revenue and growth models? To what extent do a firm's existing capabilities help or hurt what it needs to do to succeed with the new business model from the innovation?

TYPES OF BUSINESS MODEL INNOVATIONS

An important question for firms in the face of a business model innovation is: To what extent are the rules of the game changed by the innovation?[31] That is, how game-changing is the business model innovation? Are the rules of the game changed so much that old ways of doing things are no longer effective? One approach to understanding the degree to which the rules of the game have changed in a business model innovation is to use two important strategy variables.[32] The first variable is the degree to which existing products/services are rendered noncompetitive as a result of the innovation. The idea here is that if the rules of the game change radically, the new business model is likely to be such that products/services that are rooted in the old business model will no longer be competitive in the market addressed with the new business model. The second variable is the degree to which existing capabilities are rendered obsolete by the new business model. If the rules of the game in a new business model change drastically, the capabilities needed to pursue the new business model may be so different that existing capabilities are rendered obsolete (of no use in pursuing the new model). For example, the rules of the game changed so much from film-based photography to digital photography that film-based capabilities were rendered obsolete.[33] These two variables are shown in the two-by-two matrix of Figure 1.2.

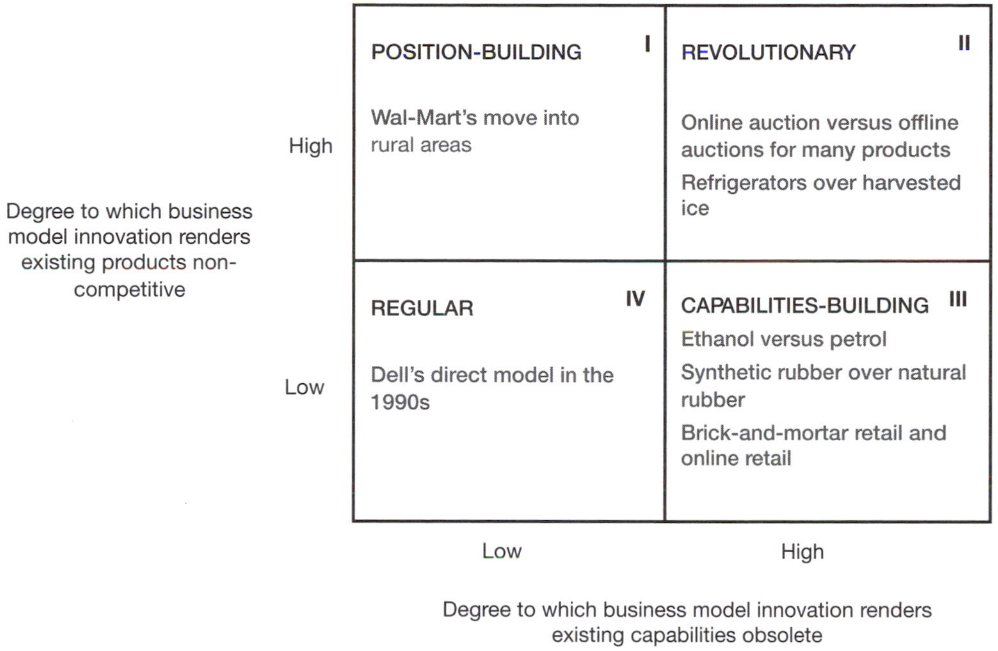

	POSITION-BUILDING I	REVOLUTIONARY II
High	Wal-Mart's move into rural areas	Online auction versus offline auctions for many products Refrigerators over harvested ice
Low	REGULAR IV Dell's direct model in the 1990s	CAPABILITIES-BUILDING III Ethanol versus petrol Synthetic rubber over natural rubber Brick-and-mortar retail and online retail

Degree to which business model innovation renders existing products non-competitive

Low   High

Degree to which business model innovation renders existing capabilities obsolete

Figure 1.2 Types of business model innovation

The four quadrants of the two-by-two matrix represent different types of business model innovation. The degree to which the rules of the game change increases as one moves from the origin of the graph to the top right corner. In a *regular* business model innovation, there is little or no change in the rules of the game.[34] The biggest changes in the rules of the game are in a *revolutionary* business model innovation since it renders existing products non-competitive and existing capabilities obsolete (Figure 1.2). Changes in the rules of the game are about the same in *position-building* and *capabilities-building* model innovations. We now discuss all four types in more detail.

Regular

In a *regular* business model innovation, a firm uses existing capabilities—e.g. value chain activities and underpinning resources—to build the new business model. The business model is such that existing products in the market remain competitive. That is, products rooted in a regular business model may take some market share from those that use the old model, but the latter remain profitable enough to be a competitive force in the market. The business model pursued by Dell in the 1990s when it introduced its build-to-order direct model was a regular business model innovation. Rather than pass through distributors to sell its computers, Dell sold directly to customers who could order their computers directly from Dell, specifying what they wanted in their computers. Dell did some things differently but the capabilities that it used were not radically different from those needed for the indirect model. More importantly, the business model was such that computer makers such as Compaq and HP who sold through distributors were still competitive.

Capabilities-building

In a *capabilities-building* business model innovation, the capabilities that are needed in the new model to create and capture value are radically different from those of the old model (Figure 1.2).[35] However, products that are rooted in older business models are still competitive. Changes in the rules of the game are largely capabilities-related. We describe such a business model as capabilities-building because the capabilities needed to pursue the model need to be built from scratch or to be acquired in some other way. For example, a firm that pursues energy from renewable resources is pursuing a capabilities-building business model innovation since it needs to develop new capabilities that are very different from petroleum-based business models. Consider the pursuit of ethanol as a fuel for cars. Making ethanol—especially from cane sugar, sugar beat, corn, or sweet potatoes—requires very different capabilities from those used to drill, pump out, transport, and refine petrol to get gasoline for use in cars. However, both fuels coexist in the market. Thus, a renewable energy business model is capabilities-building.

Another example of a capabilities-building business model is the use of synthetic rubber (made from oil) and natural rubber from trees to make and sell tires. Making synthetic rubber from petroleum is very different from tapping sap from trees in tropical forests and turning it into rubber. Synthetic rubber was an innovation over natural rubber and required capabilities-building business models. Natural rubber remained competitive in many markets.

A more familiar example in developed countries is brick-and-mortar versus online retail. The capabilities needed for one are radically different from those needed for the other and yet both coexist and are doing well.

Position-building

In a *position-building* business model innovation, products/services rooted in the new business model render products/services rooted in old business models non-competitive (Figure 1.2). However, the capabilities that underpin the new business model are primarily the same as the capabilities that underpin the old business model or build on them. We describe this model as position-building because it renders existing products noncompetitive. Wal-Mart's business model when it moved into small towns in the United States was a position-building business model. The capabilities on which the company's business model was rooted were largely the same as, or built on, those that underpinned incumbent retailers' business models. However, Wal-Mart's business model rendered many small businesses in these small towns noncompetitive since these competitors could not offer customers the cost savings offered by Wal-Mart.

Revolutionary

In a *revolutionary* business model innovation, the core capabilities that underpin the new model are so different from those that underpin the old business model that these old capabilities are largely useless for pursuing the new business model.[36] Products that are rooted in the old business models are also rendered obsolete. A revolutionary business model redefines what creating and capturing value in a market is all about while overturning the way value chain activities were performed before. The rules of the game are changed both capabilities-wise and market-wise. It is the most game changing of all the business model innovations. Examples of revolutionary business model innovations include the business models pursued by online auctions firms such as eBay. Online auctions require radically different capabilities from offline auctions and, for many products, offline auctions business models are no longer competitive. The business models pursued by makers of the refrigerators that replaced harvested ice as a cooling device were also revolutionary.

Dynamics and Application

It is important to note that the classification of business model innovations in Figure 1.2 is at a point in time. The figure assumes that business model innovations are static —that is, once a business model innovation is regular, it remains regular forever. However, many business model innovations that start out as regular can quickly become position-building, capabilities-building, or revolutionary. In fact, disruptive technologies usually start out as regular or capabilities-building innovations before becoming position-building or revolutionary. One can show the evolution of a business model innovation in Figure 1.2 by adding dates to show when the innovation was regular, position-building, capabilities-building, or revolutionary. An organization can also use Figure 1.2 to plot its progress relative to its competitors in a business model innovation that is evolving.

THE EXTERNAL ENVIRONMENT AND BUSINESS MODEL INNOVATION

Entrepreneurs and firms do not pursue their business models in a vacuum. They operate in ecosystems made up of an industry environment, and an overarching macro environment (Figure 1.3). An industry ecosystem is made up of the suppliers, customers, complementors, competitors, substitutes, and other institutions with which the firm has to cooperate to create value and compete to capture the value created.[37] The macro-environment is made up of the political/legal, economic, social/demographic, technological, and natural environments (PESTN). Firms usually pursue business model innovation when they want to take advantage of the opportunities and threats of their environments. These opportunities and threats may come in the form of phenomena such as disruptive technologies, less-is-more innovations, crowd-sourcing, social media, and the long tail (Figure 1.3). The opportunities and threats could also come from factors such as government regulations.

BUSINESS MODEL DISCOVERY PROCESS TO GENERATE A PORTRAIT

A business model discovery process is a procedure in which groups of people set out to discover and describe—using the building blocks of a business model—how a firm creates and captures value.[38] It is the process of painting a portrait of the business model. The process depends on whether the firm already has a business model or not. We consider both cases.

Business Model Already Exists

If a firm already has a business model, then the task is one of uncovering it. This may sound trivial but it's not. One reason is because very few employees—including the CEO—know everything that they need to know about every component of their business models.

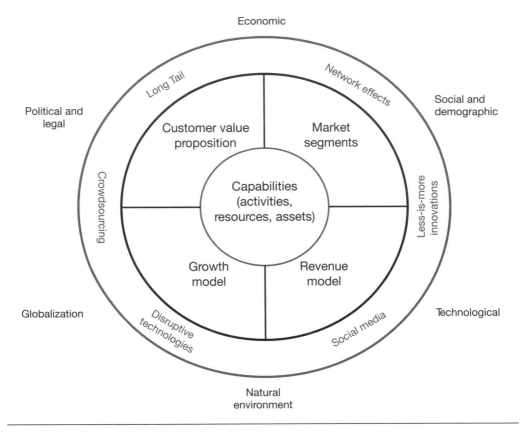

Figure 1.3 A business model innovation's environment

The idea here is not so much to make judgments about whether the firm is doing the right thing or not, as it is to detail what is going on within each of the building blocks of the model. The task is "to call them as you see them." After painting an accurate portrait of its business model, a firm can then appraise the model to determine what is good or bad about the model and what the firm can do to reinforce the good while changing the bad.

The process is simple but the payoff can be huge. Each group gathers around a board or any other surface on which post-it notes can be posted. Every participant's ideas about each of the five components of the business model are posted in the appropriate component box for everyone to examine, learn from (discover what's new), and contribute to. Towards the end of the process, the groups can vote or seek the help of experts to decide what belongs in the model and what does not—that is, what is part of the firm's value creation and capture activities and what is not.

Increasingly, such processes are taking place via social media such as wikis in which participants can include anyone from anywhere who wants to participate. In any case, diverse groups are more likely to paint an accurate portrait of the model than homogeneous ones. This is particularly true of revolutionary business model innovations than regular, position-building, or capabilities-building ones.

The first mistake that is easy for a firm to make in undertaking a business model discovery process—in painting the business model portrait—is to start making judgments about what the group sees. Such judgments can turn potential eager participants into very defensive participants, especially if the participants are from the firm whose business model is being described. When the portrait has been painted, a different group at a different time can make the judgments using a framework such as the VARIM framework that we will explore in Chapter 2. The second mistake is to generate a long laundry list of items in each component, many of which are not important. The process should be such that what gets into the portrait is comprehensive and yet parsimonious. That is, it (the process) should not leave out something that should be in the model but make sure that items that should not be there are not. One way to assure parsimony and comprehensiveness is to have an outsider—such as a consultant that is familiar with the industry and can look at the firm with an outsider's lens—be present as an observer. The third mistake in generating a portrait of a business model is to relegate the whole process to one person. In many companies, not even the CEO knows everything that is going on in all the five building blocks of a business model.

No Business Model Exists

Many start-ups and entrepreneurs do not yet have business models. Therefore, one cannot paint a portrait of what one does not have. Consequently, the task here is to try to determine what should go into the model. In that case, one can make judgments about what should go into the new model and what should not. One of the best ways to do this is to use the VARIM model of Chapter 2. Alternatively, the group can use the business model innovation questions that we saw earlier. These are paraphrased below:

- *Customer value proposition*: What is so compelling about the start-up's customer value proposition that will attract customers from competitors or from the sidelines?
- *Market segments*: How many customers does the start-up expect to attract? How many of these customers are expected to be from growing the market and how many are expected to be from existing markets? What is the willingness to pay of each group? How attractive is the market expected to be?
- *Revenue models*: Will the new business model innovation create an opportunity for new profitable revenue models? Will the firm have an opportunity to pursue better pricing strategies?
- *Growth model*: How can the firm grow *profitably*?
- *Capabilities*: Does the start-up have access to—or can it acquire—the capabilities needed to deliver superior customer value proposition to many high-willingness-to-pay customers, pursue the right revenue and growth models?

By answering these questions, a diverse group can help generate a business model for a start-up.

NONPROFIT BUSINESS MODELS

Because we defined a business model as a framework or recipe for making money, the phrase "nonprofit business models" may sound like an oxymoron. However, a closer look at what nonprofits do suggests the contrary. Nonprofits usually have two kinds of customers: donors and clients. Nonprofits have to raise money from donors and use it to serve clients. Donors usually have many nonprofits competing for their money. Therefore, for any donor to choose one nonprofit over another, the nonprofit must offer something that the donor cannot get from competing nonprofits. The nonprofit also needs to keep its costs down. Thus, each nonprofit needs to offer its customers (clients and donors) something that they value—a value proposition. Market segments can be a function of geography, demographics, the type of service offered to clients, and so on. A visible difference is in pricing where many nonprofits do not set "prices" but depend on donors to donate what they like. This is not to say that some for-profits cannot use a donation-pricing model. The point here is that nonprofits need business models as much as for-profits. In fact, the main distinction between a for-profit and nonprofits is that for-profits redistribute the difference between revenues and costs to shareholders whereas nonprofits reinvest theirs in serving clients.

Nonprofits need to pay attention to their business models so as to better offer their clients the benefits that they value and convince donors to keep donating. If nonprofits doze at the wheel and the benefits become stale or costs become too high, entrepreneurs can move in with for-profit or nonprofit business model innovations. A case in point is higher education in the United States where the cost of obtaining an undergraduate degree has become very high. Professor Vance Fried of Oklahoma State University has long proposed a higher education model in which graduates obtain their high quality education but at very low cost.[39] In one scenario, Professor Fried showed that an undergraduate in the United States could obtain a first-class education for as little as $6,700 a year compared to $25,900 in public research universities, or $51,500 in a private university.[40] Many for-profit start-ups have targeted the higher education market in the United States with new business model innovations that draw on some of Professor Fried's ideas, hoping to disrupt existing high-cost models.

KEY TAKEAWAYS

- A business model is a framework or recipe for making money—for creating and capturing value. Innovation is about doing things differently from the norm. Therefore, a *business model innovation* is a framework or recipe for creating and capturing value by doing **things** differently.

- Components of business model include:
  - *Customer value proposition*: Consists of those things that the firm and its products/ services can do for customers to solve their problems and/or satisfy their needs better than competitors. It answers the question: What is so compelling, engaging, rewarding or delightful to customers about what a firm has to offer them that will attract these customers from competitors or from the sidelines?
  - *Market segments*: Is about the groups of customers to whom a value proposition is being offered or should be offered, how many customers there are in each group, their willingness to pay, and the attractiveness of each market segment.
  - *Revenue models*: The revenue model component is about how many customers get to pay how much for what product/service, when and how.
  - *Growth model*: Answers the question: How can a firm grow *profitably*?

- *Capabilities*: Capabilities consist of *resources* and *activities*. Resources or assets are what a firm *owns* or *has access* to, while activities are what it *does*. Activities transform resources into value created and/or captured. How much value is created and captured depends on the quality of the resources. It also depends on *which* activities are performed to build and/or transform the resources, *who* performs the activities, *when* they are performed, *where* they are performed and *how* they are performed.

- A business model innovation can come through a change in any of the components of a business model.

- Business model innovations can be grouped into four:
  - In a *regular* business model innovation, a firm uses existing capabilities—e.g. value chain activities and underpinning resources—to build the new business model. The business model is also such that existing products in the market remain competitive.
  - In a *capabilities-building* business model innovation, the capabilities that are needed in the new model to create and capture value are radically different from those of the old model and need to be built or acquired (Figure 1.2). However, products that are rooted in older business models are still competitive.
  - In a *position-building* business model innovation, products/services rooted in the new business model render products/services rooted in older business models non-competitive (Figure 1.2). However, the capabilities that underpin the new business model are primarily the same as the capabilities that underpin the old business model.
  - In a *revolutionary* business model innovation, the core capabilities that underpin the new model are so different from those that underpin the old business model that these old capabilities are largely useless for making the new product. Products that are rooted in the old business models are also rendered noncompetitive.

- Since business models do not operate in a vacuum, their competitive environments as well as their macro-environments can also have a huge impact on the profitability of business models. The conditions that enable phenomenon such as crowdsourcing, the long tail, social media, less-is-more innovations, and disruptive technologies to thrive, can play a critical role in a firm's business model.

- How can one uncover a firm's business model? By having diverse groups of employees and coopetitors undertake a process of exploration and discovery in which they collectively paint a portrait of the model. No attempt is made to judge the model. Trying to make judgments may make many contributors defensive and less likely to contribute to painting a true picture of the business model, especially if the contributors are employees. What if it's a start-up and no business model exists? Use the VARIM model of Chapter 2 or the following questions to generate the new model. *Customer value proposition*: What is so compelling about the start-up's customer value proposition that will attract customers from competitors or from the sidelines? *Market segments*: How many customers does the start-up expect to attract? How many of these customers are expected to be from growing the market and how many are expected to be from existing markets? What is the willingness to pay of each group? *Revenue models*: Will the new business model innovation create an opportunity for new profitable revenue models? Will the firm have an opportunity to pursue better pricing strategies? *Growth model*: How can the firm grow profitably? *Capabilities:* Does the start-up have access to—or can it acquire—the capabilities needed to deliver superior customer value proposition to many high-willingness-to-pay customers, pursue the right revenue and growth models?

• Nonprofits need business model principles as much as for-profit organizations.

APPENDIX: DERIVING THE BUSINESS MODEL BUILDING BLOCKS

How did I arrive at the five components of a business model? From a Google search of "business models" and "business model" on July 20, 2013, I went through the top 20 most cited publications. From these publications, I chose the top two management journals and the top two books—as ranked by the number of citations—that not only explicitly featured a business model as having components, but also explored each component in some detail. I then drew on recent review articles on the resource-based view of the firm, the competitive positioning view, and the dynamic capabilities view to determine which of the components from the different publications were components of a larger component called "capabilities" as suggested by these theories. The other components fell in place. Table 1.1 shows the five components in the first column. For more details, please see the working paper by the author.[41]

KEY WORDS

Activities	Capabilities	Position-building
Business model	Capabilities-building	innovation
Business model	innovation	Regular innovation
innovation	Customer value	Resources
Business model portrait	proposition	Revolutionary innovation

QUESTIONS

1. Construct a business model portrait of a business at a firm where you would like to work.

2. Construct a business model for a firm or nonprofit that you would like to start.

3. How would you determine whether the model in (1) or (2) is a winner or a loser?

Table 1.1 Integrating the components of a business model

This book's components	Afuah and Tucci, (2001)[1]	Chesbrough and Rosenbloom (2002)[2]	Morris, Schindehutte and Allen (2006)[3]	Osterwalder, Pigneur (2010)[4]
Customer value proposition	Customer value	Value proposition	Factors related to offering Competitive strategy factors	Value proposition
Market segments	Scope	Market segment	Customer factors Economic factors	Customer segments
Revenue model	Revenue sources Price		Economic factors	Revenue streams
Growth model	Sustainability	Cost structure and profit potential	Growth/exit factors	Cost structure
Capabilities	Connected activities Implementation Capabilities	Value chain Position within value network Competitive strategy	Internal capability factors Competitive strategy factors	Key resources Key activities Key partnerships Customer relationships Channels

Notes
1. Afuah, A., & Tucci, C. L. (2001). *Internet business models and strategies: Text and cases*. New York: McGraw-Hill (pp. 80–81).
2. Chesbrough, H. W., & Rosenbloom, R. S. (2002). The role of the business model in capturing value from innovation: Evidence from Xerox Corporation's technology spinoff companies. *Industrial and Corporate Change*, 11(3), 529–555 (pp. 533–634).
3. Morris, M., Schindehutte, M., & Allen, J. (2005). The entrepreneur's business model: Toward a unified perspective. *Journal of Business Research*, 58(6), 726–735 (pp. 729–731).
4. Osterwalder, A., & Pigneur, Y. (2010). *Business model generation*. Wiley: New York (p. 17).

NOTES

1   Tapscott, D., & Williams, A. D. (2006). *Wikinomics: How Mass Collaboration Changes Everything*. New York: Penguin Books.
    Tischler, L. (2002). He struck gold on the net (really). *Fast Company*. Retrieved April 29, 2010, from www.fastcompany.com/magazine/59/mcewen.html.

2   See the following for more definitions of business models: Johnson, M. W., Christensen, C. C., & Kagermann, H. (2008). Reinventing your business model. *Harvard Business Review*, 86(12), 50–59. Amit, R., & Zott, C. (2001). Value creation in e-business. *Strategic Management Journal*, 22(6–7), 493-520. Baden-Fuller, C., & Morgan, M. S. (2010). Business models as models. *Long Range Planning*, 43(2–3), 156–171. Timmers, P. (1998). Business models for electronic markets. *Electronic Markets*, 8(2), 3–8. Zott, C., & Amit, R. (2010). Designing your future business model: An activity system perspective. *Long Range Planning*, 43(2–3), 216–226. Teece, D. J. (2010). Business models, business strategy and innovation. *Long Range Planning*, 43(2–3), 172–194.

3   For more on business model innovation, please see: Chesbrough, H. W. (2010). Business model innovation: Opportunities and barriers. *Long Range Planning*, 43(2–3): 354–363. Yip, G. (2004). Using strategy to change your business model. *Business Strategy Review*, 15(2), 17–24. Osterwalder, A., & Pigneur, Y. (2010). *Business Model Generation*. Wiley: New York. Sosna, M., Trevinyo-Rodríguez, R. N., & Velamuri, S. R. (2010). Business models innovation through trial-and-error learning: The Naturhouse case. *Long Range Planning*, 43(2–3), 383–407. McGrath, R. G. (2010). Business models: A discovery driven approach. Long Range Planning, 43(2–3), 247–261. Gambardella, A., & McGahan, A. M. (2010). Business model innovation:

General purpose technologies and their implications for industry structure. *Long Range Planning*, 43(2–3), 262–271.

4   Chesbrough, H. W., & Rosenbloom, R. S. (2002). The role of the business model in capturing value from innovation: Evidence from Xerox Corporation's technology spin-off companies. *Industrial and Corporate Change*, 11(3), 529–555.

5   For more on the components of a business model, please see: Zott, C., Amit, R., & Massa, L. (2011). The business model: Recent developments and future research. *Journal of Management*, 37(4), 1019–1042. Bonaccorsi, A., Giannangeli, S., & Rossi, C. (2006). Entry strategies under competing standards: Hybrid business models in the open source software industry. *Management Science*, 52(7), 1085–1098. Morris, M., Schindehutte, M., & Allen, J. (2005). The entrepreneur's business model: Toward a unified perspective. *Journal of Business Research*, 58(6), 726–735. Casadesus-Masanell, R., & Ricart, J. E. (2010). From strategy to business models and to tactics. *Long Range Planning*, 43(2–3), 195–215. Clemons, E. K. (2009). Business models for monetizing internet applications and websites: Experience, theory and predictions. *Journal of Management Information Systems*, 26(2), 15–41. Magretta, J. (2002). Why business models matter. *Harvard Business Review*, 80(5), 86–92. Markides, C., & Charitou, C. D. (2004). Competing with dual business models: A contingency approach. *Academy of Management Executive*, 18(3): 22–36.

6   Afuah, A. N. (2004). *Business Models: A Strategic Management Approach*. McGraw-Hill: New York.

7   Brandenburger, A., & Nalebuff, B. (1996). *Co-opetition*. New York: Double Day.
Afuah, A. N. (2000). How much do your co-opetitors' capabilities matter in the face of technological change? *Strategic Management Journal*, March, Special Issue, 21, 387–404.

8   Porter, M. E. (1985). *Competitive Advantage: Creating and Sustaining Superior Performance*. New York: Free Press.

9   Porter, M. E. (1985). *Competitive Advantage: Creating and Sustaining Superior Performance*. New York: Free Press.

10 Afuah, A., & Tucci, C. L. (2001). *Internet Business Models and Strategies: Text and Cases*. New York: McGraw-Hill. Chesbrough, H. W., & Rosenbloom, R. S. (2002). The role of the business model in capturing value from innovation: Evidence from Xerox Corporation's technology spin-off companies. *Industrial and Corporate Change*, 11(3), 529–555. Osterwalder, A., & Pigneur, Y. (2010). *Business Model Generation*. New York: Wiley.

11 Parker, G., & Van Alstyne, M. (2005). Two-sided network effects: A theory of information product design. *Management Science*, 51(10), 1494–1504. Brousseau, E., & Penard, T. (2006). The economics of digital business models: A framework for analyzing the economics of platforms. *Review of Network Economics*, 6(2), 81–110. Eisenmann, T. R., Parker, G., & van Alstyne, M. (2006). Strategies for two-sided markets. *Harvard Business Review*, 84(10), 92–101.

12 von Hippel, E. (2005). *Democratizing Innovation*. Cambridge, MA: MIT Press.

13 Clemons, E. K. (2009). Business models for monetizing internet applications and websites: Experience, theory and predictions. *Journal of Management Information Systems*, 26(2), 15–41. Rappa, M. (2001). Business models on the web: Managing the digital enterprise. Retrieved July 31, 2013 from digitalenterprise.org/models/models.html.

14 Tripsas, M. (2009). Technology, identity, and inertia through the lens of "The Digital Photography Company". *Organization Science*, 20(2), 441–460.

15 Afuah, A. N. (2003). *Innovation Management: Strategies, Implementation, and Profits*. New York: Oxford University Press. Afuah, A. N. (1999). Strategies to turn adversity into profits. *Sloan Management Review*, 40(2), 99–109.

16 Afuah, A. N. (2003). *Innovation Management: Strategies, Implementation, and Profits*. New York: Oxford University Press. Afuah, A. N. (1999). Strategies to turn adversity into profits. *Sloan Management Review*, 40(2), 99–109.

17 Afuah, A. N. (2003). *Innovation Management: Strategies, Implementation, and Profits*. New York: Oxford University Press. Afuah, A. N. (1999). Strategies to turn adversity into profits. *Sloan Management Review*, 40(2), 99–109.

18 Williamson, O. E. (2002). The theory of the firm as governance structure: From choice to contract. *Journal of Economic Perspectives*, 16(3), 171–195.

19 Barney, J. B. (1991). Firm resources and sustained competitive advantage. *Journal of Management*, 17(1), 99–120. Peteraf, M. A. (1993). The cornerstones of competitive advantage: A resource-based view. *Strategic Management Journal*, 14(3), 179–191. Barney, J. B., & Hesterly, W. S. (2011). *Strategic Management and Competitive Advantage: Concepts*. Upper Saddle River, NJ: Pearson Education. Penrose, E. T. (1959). *The Theory of the Growth of the Firm*. New York: Wiley. Amit, R., & Schoemaker, P. J. H. (1993). Strategic assets and organizational rent. *Strategic Management Journal*, 14(1), 33–46. Mahoney, J. T., & Pandian, J. R. (1992). The resource-based view within the conversation of strategic management. *Strategic Management Journal*,

15(5), 363–380. Teece, D. J., Pisano, G., & Shuen, A. (1997). Dynamic capabilities and strategic management. *Strategic Management Journal*, 18(7), 509–533. Eisenhardt, K. M., & Martin, J. A. (2000). Dynamic capabilities: What are they? *Strategic Management Journal*, 22(10–11), 1105–1121.

20 Afuah, A. N. (2002). Mapping technological capabilities into product markets and competitive advantage: The case of cholesterol drugs. *Strategic Management Journal*, 23(2), 171–179. Henderson, R. M., & Cockburn, I. (1994). Measuring competence? Exploring firm effects in pharmaceutical research. *Strategic Management Journal*, 15 (Winter special issue), 63–84.

21 Rost, K. (2011). The strength of strong ties in the creation of innovation. *Research Policy*, 40(4), 588–604. Reagans, R., & McEvily, B. (2003). Network structure and knowledge transfer: the effects of cohesion and range. *Administrative Science Quarterly*, 48(2), 240–267. Perry-Smith, J. E., & Shalley, C. E. (2003). The social side of creativity: A static and dynamic social network perspective. *Academy of Management Review*, 28(1), 89–106. Adler, P. S., & Kwon, S. W. (2002). Social capital: prospects for a new concept. *Academy of Management Review*, 27(1), 17–40. Burt, R. S. (1997). The contingent value of social capital. *Administrative Sciences Quarterly*, 42(2), 339–365. Zott, C., & Amit, R. (2009). The business model as the engine of network-based strategies. In P. R. Kleindorfer & Y. J Wind (eds.), *The Network Challenge*: 259–275. Upper Saddle River, NJ: Wharton School Publishing. Atuahene-Gima, K., & Murray, J. Y. (2007). Exploratory and exploitative learning in new product development: A social capital perspective on new technology ventures in China. *Journal of International Marketing*, 15(2), 1–29.

22 Hansen, M. T. (1999). The search-transfer problem: The role of weak ties in sharing knowledge across organizational subunits. *Administrative Sciences Quarterly*, 44(1), 82–111. Afuah, A. N. (2013). Are network effects all about size? The role of structure and conduct. *Strategic Management Journal*, 34(3), 257–273.

23 Afuah, A. (2004). *Business Models: A Strategic Management Approach*. New York: Irwin/McGraw-Hill. Zott, C., & Amit, R. (2010). Designing your future business model: An activity system perspective. *Long Range Planning*, 43(2–3), 216–226. Amit, R., & Zott, C. (2001). Value creation in e-business. *Strategic Management Journal*, 22(6–7), 493–520. Zott, C., & Amit, R. (2007). Business model design and the performance of entrepreneurial firms. *Organization Science*, 18(2), 181–199.

24 Stabell, C. B., & Fjeldstad, O. D. (1998). Configuring value for competitive advantage: On chains, shops, and networks. *Strategic Management Journal*, 19(5), 413–437.

25 Sheremata, W. A. (2004). Competing through innovation in network markets: Strategies for challengers. *Academy of Management Review*, 29(3), 359–377. Schilling, M. A. (2002). Technology success and failure in winner-take-all markets: The impact of learning orientation, timing, and network effects. *Academy of Management Journal*, 45(2), 387–398. Gawer, A., & Cusumano, M. A. (2008). How companies become platform leaders. *MIT Sloan Management Review*, 49(2), 28–35.

26 Zott, C., & Amit, R. (2007). Business model design and the performance of entrepreneurial firms. *Organization Science*, 18(2), 181–199. Zott, C., & Amit, R. (2008). The fit between product market strategy and business model: Implications for firm performance. *Strategic Management Journal*, 29(1), 1–26.

27 Rivkin, J. (2000). Imitation of complex strategies. *Management Science*, 46(6), 824–844. Porter, M. E. (1996). What is strategy?, *Harvard Business Review*, 74(6), 61–78.

28 Leonard-Barton, D. (1992). Core capabilities and core rigidities: a paradox in managing new product development. *Strategic Management Journal*, 13 (Summer Special Issue), 111–125. Gargiulo, M., & Benassi, M. (2000). Trapped in your own net: Network cohesion, structural holes, and the adaptation of social capital. *Organization Science*, 11(2), 183–196. Uzzi, B. (1997). Social structure and competition in interfirm networks: The paradox of embeddedness. *Administrative Science Quarterly*, 42(1), 35–67. Atuahene-Gima, K. (2005). Resolving the capability-rigidity paradox in new product innovation. *Journal of Marketing*, 69(4), 61–83.

29 Chesbrough, H. W., & Rosenbloom, R. S. (2002). The role of the business model in capturing value from innovation: Evidence from Xerox Corporation's technology spin-off companies. *Industrial and Corporate Change*, 11(3), 529–555.

30 Tripsas, M., & Gavetti, G. (2000). Capabilities, cognition, and inertia: Evidence from digital imaging. *Strategic Management Journal*, 21(10–11), 1147–1161.
Tripsas, M. (2009). Technology, identity, and inertia through the lens of "The Digital Photography Company". *Organization Science*, 20(2), 441–460.

31 The rest of what follows draws heavily from Chapter 1 of: Afuah, A. N. (2009). *Strategic Innovation: New Game Strategies for Competitive Advantage*. New York: Routledge.

32 These two variables come from the two major views of strategy: The competitive positioning (product–market–positions) view and the resource-based view. See, for example: Porter, M. E. (1996). What is strategy? *Harvard Business Review*, 74(6), 61–78. Peteraf, M. A., & Barney, J. B. (2003). Unraveling the resource-based tangle. *Managerial and Decision Economics*, 24(4), 309–323.

33 Tripsas, M. (2009). Technology, identity, and inertia through the lens of "The Digital Photography Company". *Organization Science*, 20(2), 441–460.

34   This terminology builds on the classifications in the seminal paper: Abernathy, W., & Clark, K. B. (1985). Mapping the winds of creative destruction. *Research Policy*, 14(1), 3–22.

35   Tushman, M. L., & Anderson, P. (1986). Technological discontinuities and organizational environments. *Administrative Science Quarterly*, 31(3), 439–465.

36   Tushman, M. L., & Anderson, P. (1986). Technological discontinuities and organizational environments. *Administrative Science Quarterly*, 31(3), 439–465. Hill, C. W. L., & Rothaermel. T. T. (2003). The performance of incumbent firms in the face of radical technological innovation. *Academy of Management Review*. 28(2), 257–274. Henderson, R., & Clark, K. B. (1990). Architectural innovation: The reconfiguration of existing product technologies and the failure of established firms. *Administrative Sciences Quarterly*, 35(1): 9–30.

37   Afuah, A. N. (2000). How much do your co-opetitors' capabilities matter in the face of technological change? *Strategic Management Journal,* March, Special Issue, 21, 387–404.

38   This process is similar to the business model canvas process detailed by Professor Yves Pigneur of the University of Lausanne and Dr. Alexander Osterwalder Strategyzer. However, there are some important differences between the two processes that we will point out as we go along. See: Osterwalder, A., & Pigneur, Y. (2010). *Business Model Generation.* New York: Wiley.

39   Fried, V. (2011). Federal higher education policy and the profitable nonprofits. *Policy Analysis*, 678, Cato Institute. Fried, V. (2011). Opportunities for efficiency and innovation: A primer on how to cut college costs. *Future of American Education Project.* American Enterprise Institute.

40   *The Economist.* (2011). How to make college cheaper. Retrieved August 4, 2013, from www.economist.com/node/18926009?story_id=18926009.

41   Afuah, A. N. (2013). The theoretical basis of a framework for assessing the profitability potential of a business model. Working paper, Stephen M. Ross School of Business at the University of Michigan.

2

APPRAISING THE PROFITABILITY POTENTIAL
OF BUSINESS MODEL INNOVATIONS

Reading this chapter should provide you with the conceptual and analytical tools to:

- Understand the rationale behind the value, adaptability, rareness, inimitability, and monetization (VARIM) framework.
- Appraise the profitability potential of a business model.
- Extend the use of the VARIM framework to assessing the profitability potential of key products, resources, activities, strategies, business model units, new businesses, and so on.

INTRODUCTION

In Chapter 1, we explored the basic building blocks of a business model and very briefly discussed how an organization can construct a portrait of an existing business model or generate a new one. Now, the question is: How can an organization tell if the business model that it has generated—or any other business model—is a winner or loser? In this chapter, we answer this question by presenting a framework for assessing the profitability potential of a business model or business model innovation.

THE VARIM FRAMEWORK

The components of the VARIM (value, adaptability, rareness, inimitability, and monetization) framework for appraising the profitability potential of a business model are shown in Figure 2.1. The model is derived from three strategic management theories—the resource-based view of the firm, the competitive positioning (product-market-position) view, and the dynamic capabilities view—that have explored those attributes of capabilities that determine profitability.[1] According to these theories, four characteristics of a capability determine the expected profitability of its owner or those who have access to it: *value*, *adaptability*, *rareness*, and *inimitability*. Since, as we saw in Chapter 1, capabilities are central to a business model, we can use these four characteristics to measure the profitability potential of a business model. That is, we can assess the profitability potential of a business model by exploring the extent to which each of these characteristics of the model—*value, adaptability, rareness,* and *inimitability*—contributes to profitability.[2] More specifically, we assess the contribution of each attribute to profitability by answering the following questions:

Value: Does the business model offer benefits that customers perceive as valuable to them?

Adaptability: Is the business model—or core parts of it—cost-effectively reconfigurable or re-deployable to offer benefits that customers perceive as valuable to them?

Rareness: Is the firm the only one that offers the customer benefits? If not, is the firm's level of the benefits higher than that of competitors?

Inimitability: Are the benefits difficult for other firms to imitate, substitute, or leapfrog?

Monetization: Does the firm make, or stand to make, money from offering the benefits to customers?

These components of the VARIM framework are shown in Figure 2.1 and explored in more detail below. Briefly, however, here is the rational behind the model.

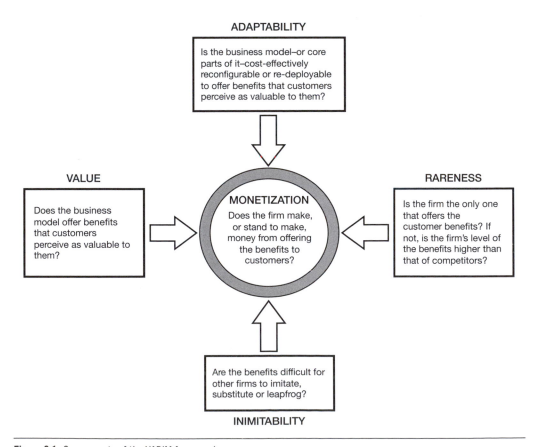

Figure 2.1 Components of the VARIM framework

Rationale Behind the VARIM Framework

Since a business model is a framework for making money, and money comes from customers, a business model must offer customers benefits that they find valuable enough to want to pay for. Hence, we have the *value* component that assesses the extent to which the business model offers benefits that customers find valuable. In an ever-changing world, a business model must be flexible enough to meet changing customer needs, address new markets, meet other challenges such as technological innovation and so on. That leads to the *adaptability* component of the framework—the extent to which the business model—or core parts of it—are cost-effectively reconfigurable or re-deployable to offer benefits that customers perceive as valuable to them, especially in the face of change.[3]

Offering customers benefits that they value is critical. However, if everyone can offer the same benefits, then there may be no reason why customers should bring their money to your firm when they could get the same benefits from anyone else perhaps for a lot less. The *rareness* component of the appraisal framework ascertains that the customer benefits that the firm offers are scarce enough for customers to keep buying from the firm. Just as important, benefits that are scarce today may not be tomorrow if they can be imitated, substituted, or leapfrogged. Hence, we have the *inimitability* component that is about the degree to which customer benefits are difficult to imitate, substitute, or leapfrog. Finally, being the only one that can offer customers what they value is no guarantee that one will make money. To make money, a firm must also price the benefits well, pursue the right sources of revenues, be well positioned in an attractive market, and so on. For example, if a firm sets its prices too high, it may unnecessarily drive away too many customers. If it sets its prices too low without any strategic motive, the firm may be needlessly leaving money on the table. Hence, we have the *monetization* component of the VARIM framework. We now explore each component in detail.

Value

Money comes from customers and they will continue to buy a product only if it meets their needs. Therefore, a necessary condition for making money in a market is to offer customers benefits that they perceive as valuable to them. Hence, the question: Does the business model offer benefits that customers perceive as valuable *to them*? If the answer is "yes," the firm may want to reinforce what it has been doing as far as offering customers what they want is concerned. If "no," the firm may need to take the necessary actions to turn things around. Measures of the extent to which a business model offers benefits that customers perceive as valuable include: Customer satisfaction and loyalty, market share, benefits offered to customers relative to competitors' offerings, and reputation/image as perceived by customers (Table 2.1).[4]

For two reasons, these measures may need to be complemented or replaced with more appropriate ones. First, a firm that is still in its infancy—such as a start-up—may not even have a product, let alone customers who know what they want enough to judge the firm and grade it. Second, collecting and interpreting the data for these measures may not be reliable. Therefore, we need to look beneath these measures to see what drives them—what enables a business model to offer customers benefits that they find valuable. The degree to which customers find benefits valuable is a function of the quality of the underpinning capabilities—of the resources and activities that underpin the benefits. That is, the quality of the resources that a firm owns or has access to, and of the system

Table 2.1 Examples of VARIM framework assessment measures for business models

Component	Key question	Measures (examples)
Value	Does the business model offer benefits that customers perceive as valuable to them?	• Customer satisfaction and loyalty • Market share • Benefits offered to customers relative to competitors' offerings • Reputation/image as perceived by customers • Quality of resources • Quality of activities
Adaptability	Is the business model—or core parts of it—cost-effectively reconfigurable or redeployable to offer benefits that customers perceive as valuable to them?	• Number and diversity of new products (benefits) offered by firm • Level of "improvement" in the benefits that customers perceive • Revenues from new products • Flexibility of valuable capabilities
Rareness	Is the firm the only one that offers the customer benefits? If not, is the firm's level of the benefits higher than that of competitors?	• Number of competitors or firms with substitute products • Level of the benefits from firm compared to those from competitors
Inimitability	Are the benefits difficult for other firms to imitate, substitute, or leapfrog?	• Number of imitators • Inimitability of resources • Inimitability of activities
Monetization	Does the firm make, or stand to make money from offering the benefits to customers?	• Return on sales or any other measure of profitability • Right pricing • Importance and value of complementary assets • Number of customers with a high willingness to pay • Number and quality of sources of revenues • Cost structure • Industry attractiveness and firm's positioning in it

of activities that it performs can speak volumes about the quality of the benefits that it is likely to offer customers.

Quality of Resources

A pharmaceutical start-up—with founders who have highly cited patents or that have a record of successfully starting new companies—has a better chance of successfully discovering a new drug to cure diseases than a start-up without such founders. A luxury brand is more likely to appeal to a market segment with high-willingness-to-pay customers than a nonluxury one. A business model with a subscription revenue model is more likely to work if the firm's reputation is high enough for potential customers to trust that the firm will not run away with their money when they subscribe to its services. If the product that they are buying exhibits network effects, customers are more likely to gravitate to the firm with the largest network since the larger a network, the more valuable that it is likely to become to each member of the network. For example, a word processor is more valuable to every member of a network if it can be opened, read, and modified by everyone rather than by only a few members.

Quality of Activities

The quality of the activities that a firm performs can signal the type of customer benefits that can be expected from the business model. The activities of an airline that operates only out of secondary airports rather than primary congested ones, flies only one type of airplane—Boeing 737s or Airbus A320s—rather than a mix of airplanes, and cultivates a low-cost culture among its employees, are consistent with a low-cost strategy and therefore the airline is more likely to appeal to frugal customers than to nonprice conscious ones.[5]

The ability of a business model to take advantage of industry value drivers can also result in improved customer benefits, and therefore can be used as a measure of the extent to which the business model can offer benefits that customers find valuable. An industry value driver is an industry-specific factor that stands to have a substantial impact on the benefits that customers want or the cost of offering the benefits, the quality and number of such customers, or any other driver of profitability. For example, in offline retail, location is an industry value driver because it determines the number and type of customers who shop there, the type of employees who may want to work there, the number and types of competitors, the cost of operations, the type and number of customers, the cost of retail space, the type of services that can be offered, and the prices that can be set. Thus, a firm that chooses the right location is taking advantage of industry value drivers. Wal-Mart was taking advantage of industry value drivers when it moved to small towns in the southwestern United States to keep its costs low and build a loyal customer base.

One reason why Nintendo Wii's business model worked beautifully was because it took advantage of a key industry value driver in microchips: the fact that prices of microchips drop rapidly. Thus, when Nintendo used three-year-old chips for its console, it was paying prices that were more than 70 percent lower than the prices paid by Sony and Microsoft for the latest chips that they used in their own consoles. Nintendo's console cost so much less than its competitors' consoles that it was able to sell it at a profit while its competitors sold their consoles at a loss hoping to make money in games and online gaming.

Adaptability

In an age of globalization and rapid technological change, customers' needs can change, a firm can discover foreign customers that it wants to serve, and technological innovation can usher superior methods for offering superior benefits to customers. The adaptability component of the VARIM framework is about the extent to which a business model can be adapted to satisfy customers' new needs, especially in the face of change. More specifically, the adaptability component is about the question: Is the business model—or core parts of it—cost-effectively reconfigurable or redeployable to offer benefits that customers perceive as valuable to them?

Since capabilities are at the core of a business model, we can obtain a lot of useful information about the adaptability of a firm's business model by exploring the adaptability of its capabilities.[6] We start with resources. Resources such as brands, distribution channels, and shelf space often can be used across different products, and generations of the same product. Some technology resources can also be used across different generations of products until a so-called competence-destroying innovation renders the resources obsolete. Yet others—such as computer or device-operating systems—can be ported across platforms. In some cases, a capability can be redeployed in different markets. A popular example is Honda's engine capabilities that are used in Honda cars, lawn mowers, motorcycles, generators, all terrain vehicles, marine vehicles, and so on.

Like resources, many value chain activities can be reconfigured and/or redeployed across different products or generations of the same product. For example, the design activities at Apple that have made its products easy to use over the years, have cut across different generations of products and across product lines.

So far, we have discussed how high adaptability of the capabilities that are at the core of a business model can improve the profitability potential of the model. However, in the face of some changes, some capabilities cannot be cost-effectively redeployed or reconfigured to contribute to value creation and capture—they are rendered obsolete. More importantly, in the face of some innovations, not only are capabilities rendered obsolete, they can also become a handicap.[7] For example, when Netflix attacked Blockbuster's brick-and-mortar movie-rental business model with an online one, Blockbuster decided to respond with an online model of its own. However, Blockbuster's brick-and-mortar stores—that had been an asset in its brick-and-mortar business model—became a bottleneck in the online one designed to fight Netflix. The retail stores cost way too much for Blockbuster to compete cost-effectively with Netflix which had no need for the costly retail stores. Blockbuster eventually went bankrupt.

Another example goes back to the days of Dell and Compaq in the PC business. In its profitable build-to-order direct model, Dell sold directly to customers. This was in contrast to Compaq, which had a build-to-stock model and sold through distributors—a valuable capability to Compaq. When Compaq decided to drop its build-to-stock model and pursue a build-to-order model, thereby selling PCs directly to customers, its distributors said Compaq could not have it both ways—if Compaq sold directly to customers, the distributors would not carry any of its products. Compaq had to drop the strategy for fear of losing all the revenues that were coming in through distribution, and that may have led to its demise.

In yet another example, Kodak's razor-and-blade revenue model that worked beautifully when it was king in the chemical/film photography era, handicapped the firm's efforts to create and capture value in the face of digital photography.[8] The hurdles from the razor-and-blade revenue model may have led to Kodak's bankruptcy.

Effectively, in assessing the profitability potential of a business model, the question to ask under the adaptability criteria is: Is the business model—or core parts of it—cost-effectively reconfigurable or redeployable to offer benefits that customers perceive as valuable to them? If the answer is "yes," the firm may want to reinforce the core elements of the business model. If the answer is "no," the firm may also want to know if the business model's capabilities handicap value creation and capture, and take the necessary action to remedy the predicament.

On a more superficial level, three measures of adaptability that can be used are: (1) the number and diversity of new products (benefits) that the firm has been able to offer, (2) the level of "improvement" in the benefits that customers perceive, and (3) revenues from new products. Note that the word "improvement" is in quotes because improvement to some customers can mean deemphasized or fewer attributes. Beyond these measures are those that are about the flexibility of capabilities.[9]

Rareness

Although business models that are valuable and have high adaptability can offer customers what they want—even in the face of major change—the firm is not likely to make much money if many other firms offer the same benefits to customers. However, if the firm's business model is the only one that offers customers what they want, the firm can make money since it has no competition and customers will gravitate towards it. If other firms offer the same benefits but the firm's level of the benefits is higher, the firm can still make money since it can use its benefits advantage over competitors to attract customers. If the difference between the level of benefits from the firm and those from competitors is very small but there are only a few other competitors, a firm can still make money if it has the right strategy. Witness the case of the carbonated soft drink industry where Coke and Pepsi have done extremely well over the years.

Effectively, an important question to explore in assessing the profitability potential of a business model is: Is the firm the only one that offers the customer benefits? If not, is the firm's level of the benefits higher than that of competitors? The answer to this question can be obtained by simply counting the number of other firms that offer the benefits or substitutes, and observing the difference in the levels of benefits offered by each competitor and substitute. A "yes" answer suggests that the likelihood of the business model being profitable is high, and therefore the firm may want to reinforce those aspects of the business model that give it the benefits edge. If the answer is "no," the firm may want to take the necessary competitive measures to improve the benefits that it offers customers.

Inimitability

If a firm's business model is such that it can offer customers rare benefits that they value, and the adaptability of the model is high, the firm will continue to make money only as long as the benefits are not imitated, substituted, or leapfrogged. That is, the inimitability, nonsubstitutability and leapfrogging of benefits offered are also important factors that a firm must look out for. Two of the biggest sources of imitation, leapfrogging, and substitutability are technological innovation and globalization. Witness the many technological innovations that have disrupted the competitive advantage of established firms. Given these threats, a critical question to ask, in assessing the profitability potential of a business model is: Are the benefits difficult for other firms to imitate, substitute, or leapfrog? If the answer is "yes," the firm is likely to make money and may want to reinforce the relevant activities of the business model. If the answer is "no," the firm may want to explore the possibility of pursuing better alternatives. In pursuing these alternatives, it is important to know that imitation may not always be bad. Often, some competitors can help grow the market and profits. Witness the case of Coke and Pepsi.

Beyond counting the imitators and substitutes, a firm can also analyze the capabilities that underpin the customer benefits to understand the extent to which they can be imitated, substituted, or leapfrogged. We consider the case when the benefits emanate from resources and when they come from activities. Benefits that come directly from protected intellectual property as well as complex relationships can be difficult to imitate. For example, the microcode that underpins Microsoft's products and the look-and-feel of many of these products are protected by copyright and trademark laws. Microsoft also has difficult-to-imitate relationships with many PC makers, some handheld device makers, owners of other platforms on which its software runs, and the huge network of people and businesses that have, over the years, learned how to use its software while accumulating switching costs.

If the benefits which customers value come from a system of activities, such a system can be very difficult to imitate if it has many interacting elements.[10] Also, a firm that patents heavily and retaliates against anyone who attempts to violate its intellectual property signals to potential imitators that it will fight any violators.[11]

Monetization

Although offering customers benefits that better meet their needs than those from competitors is a necessary condition for a business model to be profitable, it is not a sufficient condition. Several other factors impact profitability.[12] First, setting the right price for the benefits that customers want is critical. If a firm sets its prices too low without a strategic motive, it is likely to leave money on the table. If it sets the prices too high, it may unnecessarily drive many customers away. Therefore, to make money, a firm also needs a good pricing strategy. Second, a firm needs to have many customers with a high willingness to pay. Simple arithmetic suggests that having many customers who are willing to pay high prices is a good thing. Third, choosing a revenue model that is consistent with the other components of a business model increases the likelihood of higher profitability. For example, a subscription revenue model is more likely to work for a firm if the firm's reputation is high enough for potential customers to trust that the firm will not run away with their money when they subscribe to its services. Fourth, if the cost of offering the benefits that customers want and of performing the other value creation and capture activities is high, the firm might not make money. Thus, a firm may need to take the necessary measures to keep its costs low for its business model to be profitable. Fifth, a firm needs the right complementary assets.

Finally, if a firm is not well positioned in an attractive industry, its coopetitors may capture an undue share of the value created, reducing the firm's profits.[13] For example, if suppliers have enough bargaining power over a firm, they can extract a lot of the profits that the firm makes by charging higher prices for the firm's inputs, raising its costs. If customers have bargaining power over a firm, they can reduce the firm's revenues by forcing it to charge lower prices or to increase its cost of goods sold.

Effectively, an important part of capturing the value created is answering the question: Does the firm make or stand to make money from offering the benefits to customers? At a high level, one can answer this question by using measures of profitability that range from return-on-sales to return-on-capital. Beyond these measures, a firm can determine whether the firm has the right pricing strategy, has many customers with a high willingness to pay, has high quality sources of revenues, has a low-cost structure, and is well positioned in an attractive industry (Table 2.1). From these answers a firm can determine what to do to improve the business model and/or reinforce what it is already doing well.

EXAMPLE 1: AN APPRAISAL OF GOOGLE'S SEARCH BUSINESS MODEL IN 2013

Suppose you have been asked to appraise Google's business model. What would you do? If you already know what Google's business model is, you can go straight to the appraisal. Otherwise, you may want to start by generating a Google business model portrait before moving on to the appraisal.

Google's Business Model Portrait

Using the business model discovery process that was described in Chapter 1, you can generate Google's business model portrait. Recall that in a business model discovery process, the business model portrait is painted without any attempts to make judgments about whether the model is a winner or loser. Such a portrait for Google is shown in Figure 2.2.

An Appraisal of Google's Business Model

The profitability potential of Google's business model is assessed using the VARIM framework.

Value: Does Google's search business model offer benefits that customers perceive as valuable to them? Yes. In 2013, Google offered something compelling to its different groups of customers in its search business. To Internet users who performed searches, Google offered search results—of text, audio, video, blogs, news, and maps—that were perceived as fast, relevant, and comprehensive. Advertisers valued the potential to bid for and pay for key search words that they perceived as relevant to searchers. Advertisers' links were displayed above, below, or alongside search results sometimes under the heading "sponsored ads."

Google's customers also valued the network effects from the firm's two-sided network of searchers and advertisers. The more people that performed searches on a site, the higher the likelihood of someone clicking on an ad, making the network more valuable to advertisers. Additionally, the higher the number of advertisers, the higher the likelihood

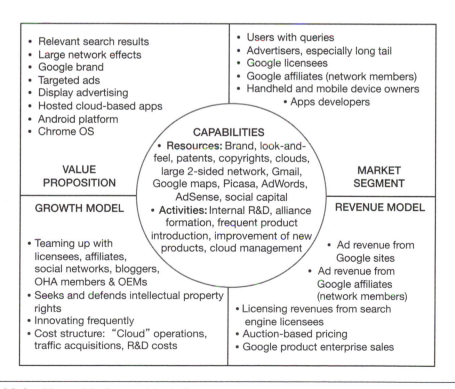

Figure 2.2 Google's search business model portrait

of a shopper finding what s/he wanted, making the website more valuable to online shoppers. (It was believed that 70 percent of online purchases originated from searches[14] while 40 percent of Web searches were for information about a product or service provider.[15])

Google's search engine was also used by affiliates—called Network Members by Google—to power sponsored ads (paid listing advertising). People visiting these websites could conduct searches of the affiliate's content using the engine from Google. Paid-listing ads appeared on an affiliate's site just as on Google's own site. Advertisers paid the affiliate and the affiliate paid Google a fraction of the advertising fees. Finally, Google licensed its search engine to organizations that used it to conduct their own searches.

To what extent were these benefits from Google perceived by customers as valuable? In 2013, Google had 67 percent of the search market compared to 17 percent for Microsoft and 11.8 percent for Yahoo. Its brand was second only to Apple's in the rankings of the world's top 100 most valuable brands. Its customer satisfaction rating was very high. To many customers, its name, Google, had become the verb "to search" as in "to conduct" online search, much the same as to make a hard copy of something had become synonymous with "to Xerox" many years earlier.

Beyond these more direct measures of how much Google's search business model contributed to the benefits that its customers perceived as valuable, there were other less quantifiable measures. For example, three industry value drivers in the search engine market are the speed with which search results are returned, how relevant the results returned are to the query made, and the comprehensiveness of searches. Google took advantage of these value drivers by developing algorithms such as PageRank that enabled its search engines to deliver fast search results that were perceived as relevant.

The look-and-feel of the firm's website also contributed to attracting customers. Since Google also pursued the long tail of customers, it was able to reach many more customers who would ordinarily not have advertised in a brick-and-mortar world. The overall effect was that Google was reaching many more advertisers, some of which had a higher willingness to pay.

Adaptability: Is Google's search business model—or core parts of it—cost-effectively reconfigurable or redeployable to offer benefits that customers perceive as valuable to them? Yes. Google was constantly innovating in its search business, improving different search algorithms, porting its products to different platforms, and experimenting with different types of advertising. For example, Google's PageRank and AdSense capabilities were redeployed repeatedly in different parts of Google's search business model over time to deliver new services that increased the benefits that customers perceived in Google's searches and the effectiveness of the ads that advertisers placed with Google. The firm was also able to successfully reconfigure and/or redeploy some of the knowledge accumulated in search and advertising for desktop computers to mobile devices, rapidly increasing its revenues in search. The firm's brand, look-and-feel, and relationships with customers had been successfully redeployed to different platforms and different markets.

Google had also been innovative in other ways that enabled its engineers to introduce new products in different areas. For example, by performing activities such as encouraging its engineers to use 20 percent of their time to work on projects of their own choosing, Google may have spurred more innovation in diverse areas. Finally, Google also entered other businesses with the goal of preemptively preventing or delaying other firms from moving into its search market space. However, it remained to be seen which of these capabilities the firm could successfully reconfigure or redeploy in the face of major changes such as radical technological innovation.

Rareness: Is Google the only one that offers the customer benefits? If not, is Google's level of the benefits higher than that of its competitors? No and Yes. In 2013, Google was not the only one with a search business model that could deliver benefits that customers considered valuable. Microsoft and Yahoo claimed to deliver similar benefits to customers. However, its level of the capabilities appeared to be higher than that of competitors. For example, many customers perceived Google's searches as being more reliable than those of its competitors. As mentioned earlier, in 2012, as many as 67 percent of online searchers used Google.

Inimitability: Are the benefits offered by Google's search business model difficult for other firms to imitate, substitute, or leapfrog? Yes and No. In 2013, Microsoft and Yahoo offered comparable customer benefits but Google's level of the benefits was higher. One reason why few firms came close to replicating or leapfrogging the value offered by Google was the intellectual property protection that the firm enjoyed, and the complexity of the system of activities that the firm performed. For example, the copyrights, patents, trademarks, and trade secrets that underpinned Google's look-and-feel, brand, and algorithms together with the credible threat of retaliation that the company posed, made replication of its business model difficult. To imitate the value that Google offered customers, one would have to imitate not only the firm's key resources, but one would also have to imitate the system of activities that it performed to build resources and/or translate them into benefits that customers want.

Another difficult-to-imitate resource was its large two-sided network of users and advertisers, and the relationships between them and Google. Merchants who had embedded AdWords self-service into their business models and routines were accumulating switching costs. Those affiliates who used Google's search engine and AdSense software had also built switching costs. Some of the largest switching costs were in Gmail. Once an individual got used to a mail system and had lots of past emails in an email account, it became more difficult moving to another account and starting all over again. Switching costs for users who went to Google just to conduct searches were a lot lower. However, when built, switching costs at its social networking site, Google+ promised to stick more since they involved building social relationships in a large network and storing personal blogs, documents, photos, and videos in Google's cloud.

Monetization: Does Google make or stand to make money from offering the benefits to customers? Yes. In 2012, Google's overall profit margins in search were 63 percent, with advertising making up 94.6 percent of the company's total revenues. Google's advertising revenue year-to-year growth rate was 20 percent.[16]

Beyond offering customers benefits that they valued, Google did other things well enough to make money. Google's search business revenue model was advertising. People who conducted searches did not pay but advertisers did. It used different versions of sponsored ads in which potential advertisers bid for key words that could be displayed above, alongside or below search results when a user conducted a search. When a customer clicked on a key word in the sponsored ad, the customer was redirected to the advertiser who had won the bid for the key word. The company utilized different types of sponsored ad models. In so-called pay-per-click (PPC)—also called cost-per-click (CPC)—the advertiser paid only if a customer actually clicked on the key word. Contrast that with display or banner ads where the advertiser paid for the time that users had looked at the ad.

Google's search business had four major sources of revenue: advertising on Google's site, advertising on affiliates' sites, licensing fees, and advertising on mobile devices. Google dominated in the first three sources of revenue and appeared to be on its way to overtaking Twitter in the fourth.

Auction pricing is one of the best ways to get as close as possible to each customer's maximum willingness to pay (reservation price). Thus, by having advertisers bid for key words through an auction, Google was taking advantage of its position in the markets to set prices that were as close as possible to customers' reservation prices.

Advertisers included those who placed adds on Google's own site or on third-party affiliates' sites, on computers, and mobile devices. These advertisers were very diverse. However, Google had an unusually high number of very small advertisers—in the so-called long tail of advertisers—who would ordinarily not advertise in the brick-and-mortar world. Although the revenues from each of these small advertisers were small, the total revenue from that long tail was large, and Google could cost-effectively serve the long tail using self-serve programs such as AdWords. There was also a licensee market—the organizations that licensed Google's search engine.

Google's cost structure was not transparent. However, some of the measures that it took early in its life considerably reduced its costs. First, by being a second mover in search engines and sponsored ads, Google was able to save on the costs that first movers had to incur to reduce market and technological uncertainty. Second, at its inception, Google used Intel microprocessor-based commodity servers that, at the time, were a lot cheaper but slower than proprietary servers from IBM, Sun Microsystems, and HP. (Intel microprocessor-based servers eventually more than caught up in speed as the cost dropped even more.) Since servers consumed large amounts of electricity while generating a lot of heat, Google located its servers in cold places with cheaper sources of electricity—a practice that would be followed years later by firms that wanted to build what had become known as "clouds" of servers. However, Google could do more to reduce its costs.

As far as the attractiveness of the search industry was concerned, the threat of new entrants and substitutes to Google's advantage in the search business was low, rivalry was not high, and its suppliers and buyers did not have that much power. That is, the search business was an attractive market for Google. However, the high technology business was such that one could never be comfortable for long in it. This is the sentiment that Andy Grove, former CEO of Intel, expressed in his book entitled *Only the Paranoid Survive.*

THE INNOVATION COMPONENT

So far, we have used the VARIM framework to appraise a business model. The question is, how about a business model *innovation*? The word "innovation" can refer to what is being done differently or to the outcome of doing things differently. Thus, a business model innovation can mean what is being done differently in the model, or it can mean the new business model that is the result of doing things differently. If a business model innovation means the latter, then we can appraise it using the VARIM framework. If innovation means the former, then the business model before and the one after the changes can be evaluated using the VARIM framework, and the difference between the two outcomes would represent the innovation in the model.

OTHER APPLICATIONS OF THE VARIM FRAMEWORK

Since the VARIM framework is rooted in the characteristics of capabilities, it can be used to evaluate components of capabilities and entities that depend on capabilities. For example, the framework can be used to assess the profitability potential of brands, products, patents, and human resources. It can also be used to evaluate activities such as R&D, alliances, marketing, and so on. To illustrate how the model can be used on something other than a business model, we explore its application to products.

Products

To use the VARIM framework to evaluate the profitability potential of a product, we reword the questions slightly:

- **Value:** Does the product offer benefits that customers perceive as valuable to them?
- **Adaptability:** Is the product cost-effectively reconfigurable or redeployable to offer benefits that customers perceive as valuable to them?
- **Rareness:** Is the product the only one that offers the customer benefits? If not, is the product's level of the benefits higher than that of competitors' products?
- **Inimitability:** Are the benefits difficult for other firms to imitate, substitute, or leapfrog?
- **Monetization:** Does the firm make, or stand to make, money from offering the benefits to customers?

To illustrate how to use VARIM for analyzing the profitability potential of a product, we use the example of Botox.

Example: Botox in 2012

Botox was the trade name given by Allergan to its botulinum toxin. It was used to treat wrinkles. In 2002, Botox was approved by the United States Food and Drug Administration (FDA) for treating wrinkles in the United States. By June 2013, it had been approved for treatment of more than 26 different conditions—from migraine prevention to urinary incontinence—in at least 85 countries. Its biggest use was still for treating wrinkles where the effects wore off in about six months and customers had to go back for another procedure with Botox.

Value: Does Botox offer benefits that customers perceive as valuable to them? Yes. For Botox to be approved by the US Food and Drug Administration (FDA) and health authorities in other countries for use to treat the 26 conditions in 85 countries, Botox must have made a significant contribution towards treating the conditions. Note that Botox had three sets of "customers": the FDA and doctors who chose drugs on behalf of patients, and the patients themselves. More specifically, the millions of people who went for Botox sessions (and parties) were testimony to the product providing customers with benefits that they value.

Adaptability: Is Botox cost-effectively reconfigurable or re-deployable to offer benefits that customers perceive as valuable to them? Yes. As demonstrated by the many health conditions for which Botox was approved, the drug could be reconfigured and/or redeployed to make significant contributions in different markets. (If a drug were approved for use to treat a particular disease, it could not be marketed for use in other applications until it had successfully gone through another lengthy approval process.)

Rareness: Is Botox the only one that offers the customer benefits? If not, is the product's level of the benefits higher than that of competitors' products? No and Yes. In 2013, Botox had two competitors in two other botulinum toxins that had been approved for use to remove wrinkles in the US: Dysport (also known as Reloxin) and Xeomin. Additionally, so-called dermal fillers were also used to treat wrinkles. However, these competing or substitute products were not perceived to be as good as Botox in meeting the needs of wrinkle sufferers and the many other conditions that Botox was approved for. More importantly, there were not enough competitors to reduce the monopolistic power enjoyed by these firms in different markets. In fact, in many of the other 25 approved uses of Botox, it was the only effective drug.

Inimitability: Is Botox difficult for other firms to imitate, substitute, or leapfrog? Yes. To keep the knowledge that underpinned Botox a secret, Allergan chose not to patent it. (In the US, the owner of a patent was usually given exclusive usage of the invention or discovery for some duration in exchange for revealing the associated knowledge.) Thus, it was difficult to imitate Botox. However, as we saw above, at least two firms succeeded in introducing competing products. Nevertheless, Botox was still perceived as having better quality than competitors' products. In the future, more firms were likely to imitate Botox. Besides, substitutes—including cosmetic surgery—existed. Additionally, in an age of technological innovation, there was always the possibility that new technologies might leapfrog Botox. However, given how important people's faces are to them, especially those who want wrinkles removed from them, it was very unlikely that Botox users and their doctors would switch to competitors unless there were very compelling reasons. Besides, Botox had lots of long-term data on its use while the new drugs did not.

Monetization: Does Allergan make, or stand to make, money from offering the benefits to customers? Yes. As of 2013, Allergan had built a strong brand in Botox and won many followers among customers who went to their doctors and asked for Botox. Consequently, the firm had power over doctors. There was little rivalry especially in the new markets where Botox had just gained FDA approval for new indications. It was estimated that, in 2002, a vial of Botox cost Allergan $40 and the company sold it to doctors for $400. Doctors charged their customers about $2,800 for injecting the one vial.[17] Effectively, Botox was well positioned in the wrinkle market and Allergan took advantage of the position to make money. Students are usually divided on whether Allergan was taking advantage of a pricing strategy called *skimming* that is common in pharmaceuticals. (In a skimming pricing strategy, a firm sets its prices very high in markets that are price inelastic and there is no competition, so as to extract as much consumer surplus as possible.) When competitors eventually enter, an incumbent can lower its prices (but not with the intention of driving out competitors). Those students who believe that the price was high believe that Botox was skimming and therefore pursuing the right strategy. Those who believe the price was too low, argue that it should have been raised to be consistent with skimming.

When Might one Apply the VARIM Framework?

The question is, when would one want to analyze the profitability potential of a business model, product, or brand, and therefore need to use the VARIM framework?

Compare Outcomes During Business Model Innovation

When an organization is generating a business model, it needs some way to evaluate the model to know what else to add or subtract, and when to stop. It needs to be able to compare the profitability potential of the old business model and the expected potential of the new business model. The VARIM framework can help. In general, the framework can be used to compare the profitability potential of business strategies, business units, brands, products, corporate strategies, technologies, R&D strategies, partnerships, acquisitions, market segments, and so on, under different scenarios.

Making Major Decisions

Entrepreneurs, venture capitalists, investors, and other stakeholders of a firm may be interested in understanding the profitability potential of any business model innovation that the firm wants to pursue. To the extent that the adage "You can't manage what you can't measure" is true, each stakeholder needs some measure of how well the business model is doing or should do so as to play his/her role better. When making major decisions about what activities to perform, what capabilities to build or leverage, and which components of a business model to focus on, a manager needs to know which alternatives contribute the most to value creation and capture and how. Appraising the profitability potential of each alternative business model can help a firm make more informed decisions about what should go into the model.

Organizing Platform for Data

Like most strategy frameworks, from the Growth/Share matrix to a Porter's Five Forces, the VARIM can be an excellent organizing platform for displaying data, making it easier for managers to wrap their minds around issues and questions for meetings, conferencing and so on.

Strategic Planning

Strategic planning usually starts with a strategic analysis. A firm needs to know where it is—especially relative to competitors—so as to know where it wants to go and how to get there. That is, before engaging in a strategic planning process, a firm needs to first understand its existing business model/strategy and profitability potential. A VARIM analysis can help in analyzing the profitability potential of existing business models/strategies under different scenarios, and those of its competitors.

Understanding Competitors

An analysis of competitors ought to include a comparison of competitors' business models, not just products or likely strategic moves. Such a comparison also entails a need for the appraisal of each competitor's business model.

Managing Nonprofits

Note that the VARIM framework can be used to assess the potential of nonprofit organizations. Yes, nonprofits! Why? As we saw in Chapter 1, nonprofits still have to create value—do something that their donors and clients perceive as valuable without exceeding the cost of offering the benefits. They also have to bring in money and keep their costs low—that is, they have to "capture" value. The primary difference between a for-profit and a nonprofit is that for-profit organizations, sooner or later, redistribute profits to the owners of the firm, but nonprofit organizations reinvest "profits" in the people that the organization is chartered to serve. If nonprofits do not create value, donors will take their money to other nonprofits that can do so. The VARIM framework is about value creation and capture, and can therefore be used by any organization to appraise its potential to create and capture value.

Relationship Between the VARIM and VRIO Framework

We conclude this chapter by taking a look at the similarities and differences between the VARIM and VRIO frameworks, where VRIO stands for value, rarity, imitability, and organization (VRIO). The VRIO framework was developed by Professors Jay Barney and William Hesterly of the University of Utah, based on earlier seminal research conducted by Professor Jay Barney and other scholars in the resource-based view of the firm.[18] Some of the similarities and differences between the VRIO and VARIM are displayed in Table 2.2.[19] In the VRIO, if a firm has a resource that is valuable, rare, costly to imitate, and the firm is organized to take advantage of the resource, the firm is likely to have a sustainable competitive advantage.[20] Both frameworks are rooted in the resource-based view of the firm. However, the VARIM also draws on the positioning view of strategy—also referred to as the competitive positioning or product-market-position view—pioneered by Professor Michael Porter of Harvard University.[21] The M in VARIM includes the contribution of a firm's positioning in its industry to its profitability.

Another difference between the two frameworks is in the level of analysis. Even though three of the variables—value, rareness, and inimitability—have the same name and roots, the questions asked are different. As an example, consider the variable "Value".

Table 2.2 Similarities and differences between the VRIO and VARIM frameworks

VARIM		VRIO	
Value	Does the business model offer benefits that customers perceive as valuable to them?	Value	"Is the firm able to exploit an opportunity or neutralize an external threat with the resource/capability?"
Adaptability	Is the business model—or core parts of it—cost-effectively reconfigurable or redeployable to offer benefits that customers perceive as valuable to them?	Not applicable	Not applicable
Rareness	Is the firm the only one that offers the customer benefits? If not, is the firm's level of the benefits higher than that of competitors?	Rare	"Is control of the resource/capability in the hands of a relative few?"
Inimitability	Are the benefits difficult for other firms to imitate, substitute or leapfrog?	Imitable	"Is it difficult to imitate, and will there be significant cost disadvantage to a firm trying to obtain, develop, or duplicate the resource/capability?"
Monetization	Does the firm make, or stand to make, money from offering the benefits to customers?	Organization	"Is the firm organized, ready, and able to exploit the resource/capability?

In the VRIO, the question is, "Is the firm able to exploit an opportunity or neutralize an external threat with the resource/capability?" while in the VARIM, the question is more specific: "Does the business model offer benefits that customers perceive as valuable to them?" Finally, the VARIM has an extra variable that the VRIO does not: Adaptability. This variable is derived from the dynamic capabilities view[22] of strategy to more directly address "change" via the question: "Is the business model—or core parts of it—cost-effectively reconfigurable or redeployable to offer benefits that customers perceive as valuable to them?" This component is critical, especially because it also highlights the fact that capabilities that were once useful can become huge bottlenecks in the face of some changes. That can be very bad news for incumbents who face revolutionary business model innovations.

KEY TAKEAWAYS

- For many reasons—one of which is because "You can't manage what you can't measure"—managers often need to be able to assess the profitability potential of a business model.

- The VARIM (value, adaptability, rareness, inimitability, and monetization) framework can be used to appraise the profitability potential of business models, products, brands, key personnel, R&D activities, patent, alliances, groups, and so on.

- To assess the profitability potential of a business model, the questions asked are:
  - **Value**: Does the business model offer benefits that customers perceive as valuable to them?
  - **Adaptability**: Is the business model—or core parts of it—cost-effectively reconfigurable or redeployable to offer benefits that customers perceive as valuable to them?
  - **Rareness**: Is the firm the only one that offers the customer benefits? If not, is the firm's level of the benefits higher than that of competitors?
  - **Inimitability**: Are the benefits difficult for other firms to imitate, substitute, or leapfrog?
  - **Monetization**: Does the firm make, or stand to make, money from offering the benefits to customers?

- The VARIM model is derived from three strategic management theories—the resource-based view of the firm, the competitive positioning (product-market-position) view, and the dynamic capabilities view.

- Assessing the profitability potential of a business model innovation usually means assessing the profitability potential of the new business model that has the innovation changes incorporated.

- To use the VARIM framework to evaluate the profitability potential of a product, we use the following questions that are only slightly different from those for a business model:
  - **Value**: Does the product offer benefits that customers perceive as valuable to them?

- **Adaptability**: Is the product cost-effectively reconfigurable or re-deployable to offer benefits that customers perceive as valuable to them?
- **Rareness**: Is the product the only one that offers the customer benefits? If not, is the product's level of the benefits higher than that of competitors' products?
- **Inimitability**: Are the benefits difficult for other firms to imitate, substitute, or leapfrog?
- **Monetization**: Does the firm make, or stand to make, money from offering the benefits to customers?

NOTES

1   This framework builds on the seminal work in this area done by:
    Barney, J. B. (1991). Firm resources and sustained competitive advantage. *Journal of Management*, 17(1), 99–120. Peteraf, M. A. (1993). The cornerstones of competitive advantage: A resource-based view. *Strategic Management Journal*, 14(3), 179–191. Barney, J. B., & Hesterly, W. S. (2011). *Strategic Management and Competitive Advantage: Concepts*. Upper Saddle River, NJ: Pearson Education. Penrose, E. T. (1959). *The Theory of the Growth of the Firm*. New York: Wiley. Amit, R., & Schoemaker, P. J. H. (1993). Strategic assets and organizational rent. *Strategic Management Journal*, 14(1), 33–46. Mahoney, J. T., & Pandian, J. R. (1992). The resource-based view within the conversation of strategic management. *Strategic Management Journal*, 15(5), 363–380. Teece, D. J., Pisano, G., & Shuen, A. (1997). Dynamic capabilities and strategic management. *Strategic Management Journal*, 18(7), 509–533. Eisenhardt, K. M., & Martin, J. A. (2000). Dynamic capabilities: What are they? *Strategic Management Journal*, 22(10–11), 1105–1121.
2   For more details, please see Afuah, A. N. (2013). The theoretical basis for a framework for appraising the profitability potential of a business model innovation. Working paper, Stephen M. Ross School of Business at the University of Michigan.
3   Helfat, C. E., & Winter, S. G. (2011). Untangling dynamic and operational capabilities: Strategy for the (n)ever-changing world. *Strategic Management Journal*, 32(11), 1243–1250. Teece, D. J., Pisano, G., & Shuen, A. (1997). Dynamic capabilities and strategic management. *Strategic Management Journal*, 18(7), 509–533. Eisenhardt, K. M., & Martin, J. A. (2000). Dynamic capabilities: What are they? *Strategic Management Journal*, 22(10–11), 1105–1121. Helfat, C. E. (1997). Know-how and asset complementarity and dynamic capability accumulation: the case of R&D. *Strategic Management Journal*, 18(5), 339–360. Foster, R. N., & Kaplan, S. (2001). *Creative Destruction: Why Companies that are Built to Last Underperform the Market and How to Successfully Transform Them*. New York: Doubleday/Currency.
4   For more measures, see Kaplan, R. S., & Norton, D. P. (1996). Using the balanced scorecard as a strategic management system, *Harvard Business Review* 74(1), 75–85.
5   Porter, M. E. (1996). What is Strategy? *Harvard Business Review*, 74(6), 61–78.
6   Helfat, C. E., & Winter, S. G. (2011). Untangling dynamic and operational capabilities: Strategy for the (n)ever-changing world. *Strategic Management Journal*, 32(11), 1243–1250. Teece, D. J., Pisano, G., & Shuen, A. (1997). Dynamic capabilities and strategic management. *Strategic Management Journal*, 18(7), 509–533. Eisenhardt, K. M., & Martin, J. A. (2000). Dynamic capabilities: What are they? *Strategic Management Journal*, 22(10–11), 1105–1121. Helfat, C. E. (1997). Know-how and asset complementarity and dynamic capability accumulation: the case of R&D. *Strategic Management Journal*, 18(5), 339–360. Døving, E., & Gooderham, P. N. (2008). Dynamic capabilities as antecedents of the scope of related diversification: The case of small firm accountancy practices. *Strategic Management Journal*, 29(8): 841–857. Zott, C. (2003). Dynamic capabilities and the emergence of intraindustry differential firm performance: Insights from a simulation study. *Strategic Management Journal*, 24(1), 97–125. Teece, D. J. (2007). Explicating dynamic capabilities: The nature and microfoundations of (sustainable) enterprise performance. *Strategic Management Journal*, 28(13), 1319–1350. Sirmon, D. G., Hitt, M. A., & Ireland, R. D. (2007). Managing firm resources in dynamic environments to create value: Looking inside the black box. *Academy of Management Review*, 32(1), 273–292.
7   Leonard-Barton, D. (1992). Core capabilities and core rigidities: a paradox in managing new product development. *Strategic Management Journal*, 13 (Summer Special Issue), 111–125. Gargiulo, M. & Benassi, M. (2000). Trapped in your own net: Network cohesion, structural holes, and the adaptation of social capital. *Organization Science*, 11(2), 183–196. Uzzi, B. (1997). Social structure and competition in interfirm networks: The paradox of embeddedness. *Administrative Science Quarterly*, 42(1), 35–67. Atuahene-Gima, K. (2005). Resolving the capability-rigidity paradox in new product innovation. *Journal of Marketing*, 69(4), 61–83.

8   Tripsas, M. (2009). Technology, identity, and inertia through the lens of "The Digital Photography Company". *Organization Science*, 20(2), 441–460. Tripsas, M. & Gavetti, G. (2000). Capabilities, cognition, and inertia: Evidence from digital imaging. *Strategic Management Journal*, 21(10–11), 1147–1161.

9   Research in this area is still ongoing.

10 Rivkin, J. W. (2000). Imitation of complex strategies. *Management Science*, 46(6), 824-844. Porter, M. E. (1996). What is Strategy? *Harvard Business Review*, 74(6), 61–78.

11 Chen, M-J., Lin, H-C., & Michel, J. G. (2010). Navigating in a hypercompetitive environment: the roles of action aggressiveness and TMT integration. *Strategic Management Journal*, 31(13), 1410–1430.

12 Afuah, A. N. (2013). The theoretical basis for a framework for appraising the profitability potential of a business model innovation. Working paper, Stephen M. Ross School of Business at the University of Michigan.

13 Porter, M. E. (1996). What is strategy? *Harvard Business Review*, 74(6), 61–78.

14 Norris, S. (2003, November 1). Search engine consolidation, Revolution. Retrieved June 12, 2013 from www.brandrepublic.com/news/193503/

15 Bartley, C., & Weinstein, S. (November 4, 2003). High growth in search creates opportunities for niche players. *Pacific Crest Securities*, 2.

16 Accessed July 4, 2013 from http://investor.google.com/financial/tables.html.

17 Creager, E. (2002). Move over, Tupperware: Botox injections are the latest thing at home parties. Retrieved September 14, 2007 from www.woai.com/guides/beauty/story.aspx?content_id=16358daf-d7db-4ade-a757-9e8d7cf30212.

18 Barney, J. B., & Hesterly, W. S. (2011). *Strategic Management and Competitive Advantage: Concepts*. Upper Saddle River, NJ: Pearson Education. VRIO variables are derived from: Barney, J. B. (1991). Firm resources and sustained competitive advantage. *Journal of Management*, 17(1), 99–120. Peteraf, M. A. (1993). The cornerstones of competitive advantage: A resource-based view. *Strategic Management Journal*, 14(2), 179–199. Barney, J. B., & Hesterly, W. S. (2011). *Strategic Management and Competitive Advantage: Concepts*. Upper Saddle River, NJ: Pearson Education. Penrose, E.T., (1959). *The Theory of the Growth of the Firm*. New York: Wiley. Amit, R., & Schoemaker, P. J. H. 1993. Strategic assets and organizational rent. *Strategic Management Journal*, 14(1), 33–46. Mahoney, J. T., & Pandian, J. R. (1992). The resource-based view within the conversation of strategic management. *Strategic Management Journal*, 15(5), 363–380.

19 Afuah, A. N. (2013). The theoretical basis for a framework for appraising the profitability potential of a business model innovation. Working paper, Stephen M. Ross School of Business at the University of Michigan.

20 Barney, J. B., & Hesterly, W. S. (2011). *Strategic Management and Competitive Advantage: Concepts*. Upper Saddle River, NJ: Pearson Education.

21 Porter, M. E. (1996). What is strategy? *Harvard Business Review*, 74(6), 61–78. Porter, M. E. (1985). *Competitive Advantage: Creating and Sustaining Superior Performance*. New York: Free Press.

22 Helfat, C. E., & Winter, S. G. (2011). Untangling dynamic and operational capabilities: strategy for the (n)ever-changing world. *Strategic Management Journal*, 32(11), 1243–1250. Teece, D. J., Pisano, G., & Shuen, A. (1997). Dynamic capabilities and strategic management. *Strategic Management Journal*, 18(7), 509–533. Eisenhardt, K. M., & Martin, J. A. (2000). Dynamic capabilities: What are they? *Strategic Management Journal*, 22(10–11), 1105–1121. Helfat, C. E. (1997). Know-how and asset complementarity and dynamic capability accumulation: the case of R&D. *Strategic Management Journal*, 18(5), 339–360.

Part II

Opportunities and Threats

3

THE LONG TAIL AND
BUSINESS MODEL INNOVATION

Reading this chapter should provide you with the conceptual and analytical tools to:

- Understand the long tail concept.
- Explore how a firm can make money from a long tail.
- Understand that the long tail is not limited to the Internet and products.
- Begin to understand the impact of the long tail on business model innovation.
- Begin to understand the strategic significance of the long tail.

INTRODUCTION

Every year, hundreds of movies are released, but only a few of them become box office hits or blockbusters. Each of the hits accounts for hundreds of millions of dollars in revenues while many of the nonhits each account for little or nothing. Every year, thousands of books are published, but only a select few make the bestseller list. In the music industry, only a few songs go on to become hits. In all three cases, a few blockbusters, hits, or bestsellers are each responsible for millions of dollars in sales while the great majority of the products each account for only thousands or fewer dollars. This behavior can be captured by the graph of Figure 3.1 in which the vertical axis represents the sales while the horizontal axis captures the products (movies, books, songs) that bring in the revenues. As one progresses along the horizontal axis away from the origin to the right, sales start out high but tail off as one moves further away from the origin. Effectively, the graph has a *long tail* to the right and a *short head* to the left. This phenomenon in which a few get most of the action while many get very little is not limited to product sales. In the Internet, a few blogs each get thousands of visitors while thousands of other blogs get a few hits each. In a book like this one, a few words like "the" are used frequently while many others such as "consequently" are seldom used. In many countries, 80 percent of the wealth is owned by less than 10 percent of the population.

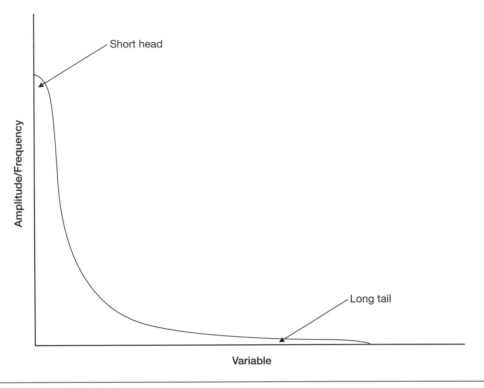

Figure 3.1 A long tail distribution

CHRIS ANDERSON AND THE LONG TAIL

Although, for centuries, the long tail phenomenon has been described by statisticians using the graph of Figure 3.1 and given names such as Pareto Law, Pareto Principle, 80/20 rule, heavy tail, power-law tail, and Pareto, it was Chris Anderson, Editor-in-Chief of *Wired* magazine and former correspondent for *The Economist*, who used the term *long tail* to explain why, by taking advantage of the Internet's properties—such as its near-infinite shelf space—a firm could make money by selling small quantities of very many one-of-a-kind products rather than selling many units each of a small number of hits.[1] He had read an MIT working paper by Professors Erik Brynjolfsson, Jeffrey Hu, and Michael Smith, one of whose findings was that a significant portion of Amazon.com's sales came from obscure book titles that were not found in brick-and-mortar stores.[2] After more research, Chris Anderson noted that:

- A significant fraction of eBay's revenues come from selling small volumes of many hard-to-find (one-of-a-kind) items.
- A large number of the DVD titles that Netflix rent out are nonblockbusters that are not found in brick-and-mortar stores.
- Most of Google's revenues come from the many obscure customers who spend small amounts on advertising rather than from a few large advertisers who spent huge amounts, as brick-and-mortar advertisers.

These are all instances of long tail distributions in which firms had used the Internet to make money by aggregating the niches of the tails of the distributions. Effectively, with the Internet, many products in the long tail can jointly make up a market share that is as large as, if not larger than, that of the relatively fewer hits and blockbusters in the short head.[3] To understand why and when the long tail may offer an opportunity for profitable business model innovations, let us explore the rationale behind the long tail phenomenon.

THE PHENOMENON

Rationale for the Long Tail of Products

The question is: Why do some products become hits, bestsellers, or blockbusters while others end up languishing in the long tail? That is, how do we explain the shape of the long tail distribution for the products of Figure 3.1? Beyond the attributes of the products, there are three reasons why a few products usually do very well, forming the short head of a distribution, while many products can languish in the long tail:

1. The high cost and scarcity of distribution channels and shelf space.
2. Customers' cognitive limitations and difficulties in making choices.
3. Customer heterogeneity, and the high cost of and difficulties in meeting the individual unique needs of all customers.

High Cost and Scarcity of Distribution Channels and Shelf Space
First, shelf space and distribution channels for many products are limited, especially in the offline world. That is, the cost of providing the space to display products in an offline world is very high, and so are the inventory carrying costs for distributors who decide to carry too many products. Thus, even if a producer were to try to offer products that satisfy the unique needs of everyone, there would not be enough space on shelves to display all such differentiated products cost effectively. There just isn't enough room in stores or in distribution channels to hold everything for everyone at affordable costs. Moreover, without access to everyone, most producers would not be able to reach every customer to find out what their needs are so as to incorporate them in each customer's product. Effectively, shelf space and distribution channels are a scarce resource and a barrier to entry for many products. Therefore, the few products that have access to these scarce resources have a good chance of becoming bestsellers or hits. Those products that do not have access to the scarce sources are more likely to end up in the long tail or off the distribution.

Customers' Cognitive Limitations and Difficulties in Making Choices
Even if there were enough shelf space to carry all the products that satisfy all individual needs, most customers would have a difficult time choosing from the huge variety. Given human cognitive limitations, it can be a frustrating experience choosing between five similar products, let alone hundreds or thousands. Think about how difficult it can be choosing between the cars that you can afford. Because of this cognitive limitation of many customers, some of them end up buying the mass-produced and mass-marketed products that may not be what they really need.

Customer Heterogeneity, and the Difficulties and High Cost of Meeting Individual Unique Needs

No two people have identical tastes (with the exception of some identical twins). Thus, it would be nice if each product were custom-made to meet the unique needs of each individual. However, doing so would be exorbitantly expensive for some products. Imagine how much it would cost in 2013 if a pharmaceutical company had to develop and produce a drug for each patient since each patient's physiology differs from that of other patients. Thus, most firms would rather mass produce one product and mass market it to as many customers as possible. Doing so enables them to enjoy the benefits of economies of scale that usually come from specialization in designing, producing, marketing, promoting, and selling one product for many customers. If the one product that is mass produced and mass marketed wins, it can become a hit. Losers languish in the long tail or outside the distribution.

For these three reasons, a limited number of products are produced and mass marketed, and some go on to occupy the limited shelf space and distribution channels. Some of these products gain wide acceptance and end up in the short head of the distribution while others are relegated to the long tail.

Then Comes the Internet and Other Innovations

Information technology (IT) innovations have changed some of the reasons why products in the short head do so much better than those in the long tail. This change potentially alters the long tail distribution. How? Because of the tremendous amounts of improvements in the cost-performance of computer hardware, software, and the Internet, websites can represent shelf space for many products. Thus, a bookstore or any other retailer can have millions of items on display on its online store shelves rather than the thousands that are possible in an offline world. Digital products like music and movies can also be distributed electronically. Additionally, search engines, online reviews, online community chats in social networks, software that makes suggestions using buyers' past purchases, and blogs can help consumers choose from the many available choices.

Moreover, because IT gives more producers and customers more low-cost access to each other, producers have an opportunity to find out more about customers and work with them to offer products that more closely match individual needs. Because of the low cost of interactions, firms can afford to sell to very small customers that they would ordinarily not pay attention to. That is one reason why, for example, Google could afford to sell advertising to many very small advertisers. It developed self-serve software that many of these advertisers could use to "interact" with the company. Firms and their customers also have more tools that they can use for lower cost customization of products.

Effectively, the Internet's and other IT innovation's properties—low-cost shelf space and distribution-channel tool for making better purchase choices, and a lower cost tool for producers to better meet customer needs—have mitigated some of the reasons why some products were relegated to the long tail. Products that may never have found themselves on offline shelves can now find their way on to electronic shelves. For example, rare books that were not in demand enough to be put on offline shelves can now be listed on an online shop at negligible costs. Available software also helps consumers choose products that better meet their individual tastes from the many available products. Thus, products that would ordinarily have languished in the long tail may find their way to people with diverse tastes who want them. The Internet not only extends the tail, but it also thickens it (Figure 3.2)[4].

Beyond the Internet and Revenues: Some Long Tail Cases

So far, our exploration of the long tail has been limited to Chris Anderson's original idea. That is, we have limited our exploration to long tail distributions in which the vertical axis is revenues or sales, the horizontal axis is a product or some variant of it, and the innovation to exploit the long tail is the Internet.[5] However, the idea can be extended to any case in which the vertical axis is a desirable dependent variable while the horizontal axis is the independent variable that drives the desirable dependent variable, and an *innovation* is used to change the factors that created the low values of the tail. As the following examples illustrate, there is an opportunity to *take advantage of the long tail using many innovations*—technological and nontechnological.

Botox and Cosmetic Surgery

Cosmetic surgery is the use of surgical or medical procedures to enhance the appearance of a person. In the United States, the best surgeons performed the most surgeries and made the most money while the less good surgeons and generalist doctors made very little money from surgery. Thus, great surgeons were in the short head while the less good surgeons and general practitioners were in the long tail of the cosmetic surgery Pareto distribution. (In the distribution, the Y-axis could be the revenues and the X-axis would be the type of physician.) Then came an innovation called Botox, whose

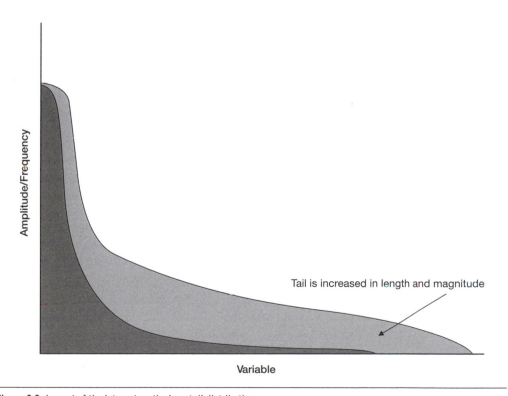

Figure 3.2 Impact of the Internet on the long tail distribution

approval by the FDA in April 2002 for use in cosmetic procedures promised to change all of that.[6] A Botox procedure involved injecting the substance into the wrinkle, frowning line, or targeted area using a fine gauge needle. The procedure lasted a few minutes, there was no surgery or anesthesia needed, and the patient could return to work the same day. More importantly, any doctor could apply it—that is, the procedure was not limited to surgeons. Thus, the less good surgeons and general practitioners who were in the long tail of the cosmetic surgery distribution could now earn more money from the cosmetic procedures using Botox than they did before Botox.

Cell Phones in Developing Countries

Before wireless cell phones, most villages and small towns in developing countries had little or no phone services. Only fixed-line telephones were available and because it was very costly to lay the wires (cabling) and associated equipment to low population centers, it was very uneconomical to offer phone services to rural areas. (Government-mandated monopoly phone companies were also very inefficient.) Thus, many communities had no phone service. If a person in one of these underserved areas wanted to make a phone call, he or she would go to a small town and make the phone call there. Thus, the number of phone calls made by people in cities was very large relative to that made by people from villages or small towns. Effectively, phone service for villagers was in the long tail of each country's phone system. Cell phone service changed all of that. Because wireless phone services did not require wires, the cost of cabling was no longer a large constraint. Moreover, government monopolies were eliminated and competition introduced in many countries. Suddenly, not only did phone service in rural areas increase considerably, the service in cities also increased. Thus, both the short head and long tail phone service increased.

Discount Retailing in Rural Areas

Before Wal-Mart moved into rural areas of the Southwestern United States, sales of most products in rural areas were at the long tail of discount retailing. Most discount retailing sales were at large discount stores built in large cities. Occasionally, people from the rural areas would drive the long distance to cities to buy some of what they needed or use catalogs from the likes of Sears to order products. Wal-Mart's strategy was to saturate contiguous small towns with small stores. Thus, by aggregating the sales in many small stores, Wal-Mart was able to generate the volumes that its competitors generated by building large stores in big cities, and more. It also adopted the latest in information technology at the time, built a first-class logistics system, established the Wal-Mart low-cost culture, grew in size, and so on.

Internet and Political Contributions in the US

Prior to the Internet, most political contributions—especially contributions to presidential candidates—were made by a few influential donors who made large contributions at fundraising dinners, dances, and other gatherings. Organizations such as unions could also raise money for candidates using their mailing lists or meetings. Many small donors who could have contributed were largely in the long tail of donations since each of them donated little or nothing. The problem was that there was no cost-effective way of aggregating all these small donations. The advent of the Internet changed all that.

The Internet not only increased the amplitude of the tail but extended it since many more small donors made more contributions. By appealing to these small donors, candidates such as a certain Senator Barack Obama were able to raise huge amounts of donations from ordinary Americans. He would become President of the United States of America.

Internet and User Innovation

For years now, Professor Eric von Hippel of MIT has argued that users and suppliers can be as good a source of product innovations as manufacturers of products.[7] Each user, for example, could make improvements to a product that other users and the manufacturer could or would not. Many of these user innovations have always languished in the long tail of innovations. With the Internet and other innovations, manufacturers can aggregate these user innovations and develop products that offer customers better benefits that they find more valuable.

Microfinancing

In many developing countries, a few rich people or businesses get most of the loans from banks, credit unions, and other major lenders. The large majority has no access to financing and when it does, interest rates are extremely high. This large majority can be said to be in the long tail of loans. Very small potential lenders can also be said to be in the long tail of lenders too, since they do not have enough money to lend to large borrowers. Microfinancing is an innovation that tackles these two long tails. It makes small loans available to poor people in developing countries at reasonable interest rates. When aggregated, these microloans can be large enough for big lenders to enter the business. Also, potential small lenders can get into the business of lending.

Organic Foods at the Long Tail of Foods

For a long time in developed countries, conventional foods (crops and animals) have been at the short head of foods while organic foods have been at the long tail. Organic crops are grown without using artificial fertilizers, conventional pesticides, human waste, or sewage sludge, while organic animals are grown without the use of growth hormones and routine use of antibiotics. Neither food is processed with ionizing radiation or food additives, and in some countries, they cannot be genetically altered. Producers of organic foods emphasize the conservation of soil and water as well as the use of renewable resources. Because conventional foods do not have these constraints, and the benefits of organic foods were not widely understood, most of the foods grown were conventional. The availability of organic foods tended to be limited to what local farmers could grow and sell in their local farmers' market or cooperative. They did not enjoy the economies of scale of conventional foods.

In 1978, Whole Foods Markets was founded to sell organic foods. It took advantage of the growing awareness of the health and environmental benefits of organic foods, and built many organic and natural foods stores in the United States. Whole Foods and its competitors increased the share of organic foods in the communities in which they built stores. Effectively, they increased the sales of organic foods—the products that had languished in the long tail of groceries.

Printing and the Written Word

Before printing, all works were handwritten and duplicating such works was manual, and therefore very expensive and time-consuming. Thus, only the privileged, such as kings, monks, and priests, had access to written information. Ordinary people were in the long tail of the written word since they had little or no access to it. Only the very rich or those who could afford to go to a library could read. However, it was the invention of the printing press that changed all that. It made a lot of the written word available to the masses. Thus the amount of learning from books by ordinary people, when added, rivaled or surpassed that of kings, priests, and other well-placed people.

Radio and TV Broadcasting

Before Radio and TV, news reception was available largely to people in cities who were close enough to each other to spread news by word of mouth, or get it from city theatres. Some of the news also spread via newspapers. Many villages and small cities were in the long tail of news. TV and radio changed all that since people in these small villages and towns with TV could now have access to news before it had become history.

Videotape Recorders and Blockbuster

Although Netflix's use of the Internet to erode Blockbuster Inc.'s competitive advantage is a classic example of a firm exploiting the long tail to displace an incumbent, Blockbuster actually attained its own competitive advantage by taking advantage of a new technology to exploit the long tail. That new technology was the home videotape recorder. Before home videotape recorders, people had to go to theatres to see movies or hope that the movie would appear on TV some day. (A select few people had their own projectors at home.) Moreover, when a movie was released, it had a few days to prove itself. After a few weeks in theatres, movies would be relegated to storage, unless a TV station came calling.

Sony introduced the home videotape recorder (Betamax format) in 1975 and in 1977 George Atkinson launched the first video rental store called Video Station, in Los Angeles.[8] Blockbuster Video was founded in 1985 to also rent out videocassettes for people to play in the comfort of their own homes. Suddenly each person with a videotape recorder who lived near a video rental store could turn his or her house into a theatre. The choices for each customer increased considerably from the ten or so movies that were available in one's local theatre, to the thousands of movies that were available in a rental store. The result was that sales of both the hits in the short head and the non-hits in the long tail increased. How? First, people who wanted to watch hits after they were out of theatres could now watch them again, at home, thereby increasing the sales of hits.

Second, nonhits that did not do well in theatres or had never even entered theatres could also be watched at home. This increased sales of the long tail. Third, some movies, such as adult entertainment movies that would never have been allowed in many theatres, could now be played in homes. This also increased sales of movies from the long tail. There were also some changes in the vertical chain. First, some moviemakers bypassed the theatres and went straight to the video store or to end-customers. Many makers of adult movies could now sell their movies directly to consumers with video recorders. At a later time, DVDs, the Internet, and movies on demand also offered opportunities to exploit long tail effects.

IMPLICATIONS FOR MANAGERS

So what does all this information about the long tail mean to a manager? Before answering this question, let us recap the short version of the long tail story so far. In many situations, there are likely to be a few hits, blockbusters, high-frequency, or high-amplitude occurrences that occupy the short head of a distribution—the so-called 20 percent that get 80 percent of the action of the Pareto 20/80 rule. The nonhits, nonblockbuster, low-amplitude, or low-frequency occurrences occupy the long tail—the so-called 80 percent that see only 20 percent of the action. Underpinning the long tail shape are usually some key factors—both technological and non-technological. Therefore, an innovation that changes the effect of these factors can shake up the (long tail) distribution, enabling the 20 percent to see more action. Thus, a firm that incorporates such an innovation in its business model increases its chances of profiting from the long tail.

Note that the long tail effect is not limited to revenues (on the Y-axis) and market niches (on the X-axis), and to the Internet as the innovation. Rather, it applies to any phenomenon that is expressed as a long tail distribution in which the Y-axis is a desirable variable. For example, the long tail effect applies to a plot of employee productivity versus types of employees, where a few employees are very productive and very many of them add little or no value to the firm. The question is: How can you, as a manager, help your firm exploit the long tail effect? You can improve your firm's chances of profiting from the long tail by going through the following steps:

- Identify the long tail distributions in each component of your existing or planned business model.
- Assess the profitability potential of the business model, for example, using the VARIM framework.
- Based on the analysis, take a decision on what to do with the business model.

To illustrate these three steps, we use the case of the iTunes Music Store (iTMS).

The iTunes Music Store in 2013

The iTunes Music Store was launched on the Mac on April 28, 2003, and in the first week alone, customers bought one million songs. In October, a Windows version of the software was launched and in just three and a half days, over one million copies of it were downloaded, and over one million songs purchased through the store.[9] Later that year, *TIME Magazine* declared iTunes Music Store "the coolest invention of 2003."[10] Music from the store could be played without difficulty only in iTunes or on Apple's iPods. However, the songs could be burnt on to a CD and then played on another digital audio player.

Apple also developed its FairPlay digital rights management (DRM) system that protected songs from piracy. When protected songs were purchased from the iTunes Store, they were encoded with FairPlay which digitally prevented users from playing the files on unauthorized computers. By 2007, iTunes had two primary functions: It was used for (1) organizing and playing music and video files, for interfacing with the iTunes Music Store (iTMS) to purchase digital music and movie files, and (2) interfacing with the iPod to record and play music and video.[11] Effectively, iTunes, in conjunction with iPod and iTunes Music Stores enabled users to access millions of songs, make a choice of what to purchase, back up songs on to DVDs and CDs, copy files to a digital audio player, download and play podcasts, organize music into playlists, and so on.

In February 2006, iTunes sold its one-billionth song, and later that year, in September, it started selling full-length feature movies. By January 2007, it had sold 2 billion songs, 50 million TV episodes, and 1.3 million feature-length films. In 2008, Apple introduced movie rentals on iTunes. In July 2008, the App Store was introduced, and later, in October, iTunes went high definition. The following year, in January 2009, all iTunes songs sold were DRM-free.

Initially, customers paid $0.99 for each song purchased in the iTunes store: $0.65 of the $0.99 went to the record label while distribution collected $0.25.[12] Apple was therefore left with about 9 cents. Later, the record labels fought and got an increase in the price of each song. Digital albums sold for $10.[13]

Question: To what extent was Apple exploiting the long tail effect?

The Long Tail Distributions in the iTunes Business Model

The impact of long tail effects on each component of a business model is shown in F igure 3.3.

Customer Value Proposition

Before the iTunes Music Store, only music hits or new releases were sold legally, while nonhits and most oldies were relegated to oblivion in the long tail or pirated online.

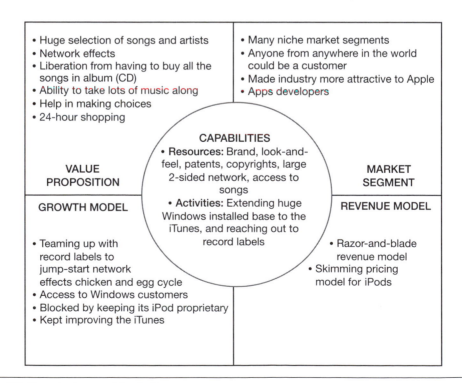

Figure 3.3 iTunes business model portrait

Nonblockbuster or old movies and TV episodes suffered the same fate. The combination of the Internet, MP3 technology, and other information technologies constituted the innovation that made exploitation of the long tails possible. The combination (1) made infinite shelf space and distribution channels available for music at much lower costs, (2) enabled more low-cost and effective access between producers and customers since offline record stores could be bypassed, and (3) offered customers better ways of choosing between the many songs available.

Importantly, people could buy the singles that they wanted rather than being forced to buy albums full of songs that they did not like just so that they could have the single. One could buy that single and take it away in one's "cool" iPod jogging, something that one could not do with a CD. Besides, customers could shop 24 hours a day, seven days a week, from anywhere in the world, and could test-play portions of any song on iTunes.

Before iTunes, a few very good artists sold most of the songs while very many artists sold few or no songs. Most of the music sold also tended to be of a few genres and from a few countries in the world. iTunes also changed that. Just about any artist from anywhere in the world could get their songs listed on iTunes, increasing the chances of selling the song. The result was increased supply.

Market Segments

Before the iTunes store, most music sales were to the few people who just happened to like what had emerged as the hits or new releases by crowned artists. Potential customers with more unique tastes were kept out of the legal market—relegated to the long tail. Apple's iTunes also changed all that. Customers from anywhere in the world could go to iTunes for music and while there, the site could help them find what they wanted by making suggestions. They could see the ratings of songs or use social networking to help them make their choices. Effectively, iTunes aggregated demand from many niches— geographic, demographic, nationalistic, and other orientations—to form a much larger market.

iTunes also changed the co-opetitive forces in the market. Recall that the market segment component of a business model is also about the quality and quantity of coopetitors—of the suppliers, customers, complementors, competitors, and any other institution with which a firm has to cooperate to create value and compete to capture value. Before iTunes, the powerful record label companies had difficulties dealing with music piracy. By developing the FairPlay digital rights management (DRM) system that protected songs from piracy, Apple reduced the fear of piracy by record labels and musicians. Thus, Apple could enter agreements with these record companies, giving it the right to sell their songs online. By demonstrating to the recording companies that it could protect their intellectual property from online piracy and cooperating with them, Apple was also effectively dampening their bargaining power. Record labels could sit by and watch their music being pirated for free or work with Apple so that it could pay them 65 cents per song *at no cost* to the labels.

The agreements also reduced the amount of rivalry that Apple could have faced from other makers of MP3 players. Finally, prior to iTunes being made available to Windows users, most of Apple's sales came from its hard-core fans, followed by others who just happened to be Apple computer users; windows users were largely in Apple's long tail of customers. By making sure that iTunes could run on Windows machines, Apple was able to reach out to the long tail of Windows users and that paid off.

Revenue Model

Apple used a razor-and-blade revenue model in which it made very little from music sales—9 cents out of 99 cents per song—but made a lot of money from the iPod. Record labels were forced to abandon the practice of bundling in which one good song would anchor a bunch of bad songs in one album at the high price of an album. For iPods, Apple practiced skimming in which it charged very high prices for those who had to have the product early and a lot less after competition moved in and its own costs had dropped.

Growth Model

Apple used a combination of team-up, run, and block strategies that helped it grow profitably.[14] By teaming up with the record labels and making its iTunes store available to Windows users, Apple was able to jump-start the critical indirect network effects chicken-and-egg cycle. How? The huge library of songs from record labels attracted many customers. These customers—many of them from the Windows camp—in turn, attracted more artists and record labels that wanted their songs exposed to Apple's many customers. That increased sales. The firm also kept improving the store and introducing newer generations of iPods. Just as important, it kept its iPod proprietary to make the razor-and-blade model work. Apple was ready to retaliate against anyone who violated its trademarks or any of its other intellectual properties and agreements.

Capabilities

Recall that capabilities are both what a firm owns and what it has access to, and include both resources as well as the activities that are used to build and/or transform resources into profits. The resources that underpinned Apple's iTunes included the software and virtual logistics infrastructure for the store, the intellectual property that underpinned the firm's look-and-feel, capacity to produce sleek designs, and very intuitive operating systems. Activities included the alliances with the record labels that gave iTunes access to the huge libraries of songs. Also, by making sure that its iPod worked on the Windows platform, Apple was instantaneously adding hundreds of millions of Windows users to its potential customer base. Finally, iTunes itself was a two-sided network with iPod owners on one side and producers of songs on the other.

Assessing the Profitability Potential of the iTunes Business Model

Having highlighted the effect of the long tail on each component of the business model, we now find out what that means to profitability. Yes, it is nice to know that iTunes had a wonderful value proposition. The question is, does iTunes make money and why? For answers, we assess the resulting model's profitability potential using the VARIM model (Figure 3.4).

Value: Does the iTunes business model offer benefits that customers perceive as valuable to them? Yes. The billions of songs sold on iTunes, Apple's market share of MP3 players (iPods), the huge selection of songs from the long tail (niches) of songs, and the increase in Apple's image (and other fortunes) following its introduction of iTunes were all testimony to the benefits that customers perceived as valuable in iTunes. Beyond these more superficial measures was the quality of the capabilities (resources and activities) that underpinned iTunes. Recall that the extent to which a firm's activities take advantage of industry value drivers is one measure of the quality of the activities.

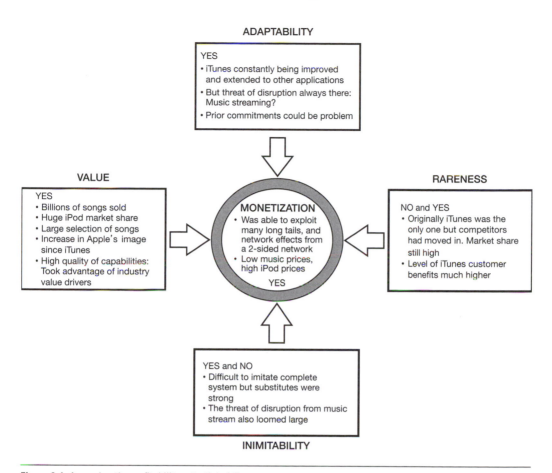

ADAPTABILITY

YES
• iTunes constantly being improved and extended to other applications
• But threat of disruption always there: Music streaming?
• Prior commitments could be problem

VALUE

YES
• Billions of songs sold
• Huge iPod market share
• Large selection of songs
• Increase in Apple's image since iTunes
• High quality of capabilities: Took advantage of industry value drivers

MONETIZATION
• Was able to exploit many long tails, and network effects from a 2-sided network
• Low music prices, high iPod prices
YES

RARENESS

NO and YES
• Originally iTunes was the only one but competitors had moved in. Market share still high
• Level of iTunes customer benefits much higher

YES and NO
• Difficult to imitate complete system but substitutes were strong
• The threat of disruption from music stream also loomed large

INIMITABILITY

Figure 3.4 Assessing the profitability potential of iTunes

Apple took advantage of two critical online music industry value drivers: protecting artists' intellectual property, and building a large two-sided network. Apple's FairPlay digital rights management (DRM) software assured record labels and artists that music sold through the iTunes would not be pirated. Its alliance with the record labels and artists, and its extension of iTunes access to Windows users helped build a huge valuable two-sided network.

Adaptability: Is the iTunes business model—or core parts of it—cost-effectively reconfigurable or redeployable—to offer benefits that customers perceive as valuable to them? Yes. The App Store for the iPhone built on iTunes' technology. The iPhone also used a razor-and-blade revenue model in which most of the apps were free and Apple received 30 percent of the few that were not free, but charged high prices for iPhones. Apple also employed the strategies used to cut deals with record labels to negotiate deals with full-feature videos, TV episodes, and movie rentals. Just as important, parts of the iTunes technology were extendable to many other Apple applications—it was a platform for other business model components. However, it was difficult to tell if, in the face of technological changes or business models rooted in streaming music, Apple's iTunes business model could be cost-effectively reconfigured or redeployed to offer streaming benefits that customers want. More importantly, Apple may be prevented by prior relationships with its coopetitors from wholehearted pursuit of streaming.

Rareness: Is the firm the only one that offers the customer benefits? If not, is the firm's level of the benefits higher than that of competitors? No and Yes. iTunes was not the only one to offer the customer benefits. In 2013, it had competitors such as Amazon MP3, Google Music, Rhapsody, Pandora, and Spotify, but iTunes still commanded a 63 percent market share.[15] iTunes' level of benefits was perceived to be higher than that of competitors because it was believed to have a larger music selection, larger network effects from its two-sided network, larger installed base of people with music libraries built with Apple products, sleek iPod and iPhone designs, and good relationships with coopetitors.

Inimitability: Is the value difficult for other firms to imitate, substitute or leapfrog? Yes and No. Replicating the iTunes business model and offering the same benefits as Apple might be difficult given the capabilities needed to offer customers the level of benefits that iTunes offered. However, substitutes were strong. More importantly, a business model rooted in streaming music or another technology might be disruptive to the iTunes model, rendering the iTune business model obsolete.

Monetization: Does Apple make money from offering the benefits to customers? Yes. Apple made a lot of money from iTunes, most of it indirectly (Figure 3.4). Apple's iTunes business model was a beautiful example of how to make money from the long tail when network effects are involved. By teaming up with record labels and artists, Apple was able to reach both the long tail of songs as well as the long tail of artists, leading to a huge selection of music. The huge selection of music had the potential to also reach out to many customers in the long tail. Apple facilitated access to these long-tail customers by expanding to the Windows installed base where the needs of some of the hundreds of millions of Windows users could be met by the huge selection of songs.

Apple's pricing strategy was also consistent with its razor-and-blade revenue model, enabling the firm to exploit network and long tail effects. How? Apple set the price of each song at 99 cents, from which the music labels would get 65 cents, distribution would get 25 cents, and Apple only 9 cents. This would cost the record labels nothing. The alternative for music label companies was to keep getting nothing while their music was being pirated. The 9 cents constituted a very low profit margin for Apple, but the margins on iPods were a lot larger. More importantly, the low prices brought in many customers who attracted more songs from record labels and artists, while enabling Apple to sell very many iPods at high prices.

Prior to iTunes, music labels and other content providers had huge bargaining power in their ecosystems. For example, record labels could stream music directly to customers and sell music on CDs, although CD demand was dropping. Thus, Apple's teaming up with music labels and the enlargement of its customer base with the inclusion of Windows users tempered some of music labels' power.

Effectively, Apple went into an unattractive market and through the right business model innovative activities, made the market attractive for itself and made lots of money. It was able to aggregate small amounts of revenues from many niche markets by selling a huge selection of many types of music at low prices—it exploited the long tail of music to build a large network of customers from different long tails of customers, many of whom wanted iPods. It then sold its iPods at high prices, making lots of money.

From this analysis, what should Apple do about iTunes? As we saw in Chapter 2, the most important thing about a VARIM analysis is about identifying what is right and reinforcing it while correcting what is not right. Most of what Apple did was right—teaming up, innovating, blocking, building a two-sided network, pricing strategically, and the choice of a revenue model—and it should reinforce that. However, we do not know much about what the firm is doing to keep its costs down. Even as a product differentiator, Apple may still want to keep its costs as low as possible. More importantly, music streaming may be a disruptive technology in the making for Apple, and therefore it may want to pay more attention to it.

KEY TAKEAWAYS

- In many markets, there are likely to be a few hit or blockbuster products/services, and many nonhits. The hits occupy the so-called short head while the nonhits occupy the long tail of a distribution that has been called names such as Pareto Law, Pareto Principle, 80/20 rule, heavy tail, power-law tail, Pareto tails, and long tail.

- Chris Anderson was the first to use the name *long tail* in business to describe the nonhits that end up in the long tail (niches) of each distribution and how, with the Internet, a firm could make money from the tail. He argued that in the face of the Internet, the combined sales of the many products in the long tail can be equal to, if not more than, sales of the relatively fewer hits in the short head. Thus, by using the right innovation to aggregate these nonhits, a firm may be able to make as much money from them as it could from hits, if not more.

- The Internet, for example, drastically reduces the cost of distribution and shelf space for some products, facilitates consumer choices, and makes it possible to better meet more different kinds of consumer tastes. Thus, firms can use the Internet to improve sales of products that once languished in the long tail.

- Chris Anderson's idea was about a long tail distribution in which the vertical axis is revenues or sales, the horizontal axis is a product or some variant of it, and the innovation to exploit the long tail is the Internet.

- This book argues that the long tail idea can be extended to any case in which the vertical axis is a desirable dependent variable while the horizontal axis is the independent variable that drives the desirable dependent variable, and any *innovation* is used to change the factors that created the low values of the tail. This is illustrated by a few examples:
  - Botox and cosmetic surgery;
  - cell phones;
  - discount retailing in rural areas;
  - Internet and political contributions;
  - Internet and user innovations;
  - micro-financing;
  - organic food stores;
  - printing press;

      –   radio and TV broadcasting;
      –   video tape-recorders.

- To take advantage of what we know about the long tail, you, as a manager, should:
  1. Identify the long tail distributions in each component of your existing or planned business model.
  2. Assess the profitability potential of the business model, for example, using the VARIM framework.
  3. Take the appropriate decision, using information from the assessment of the profitability potential.

- Apple's iTunes business model was used as an example to illustrate how to build a business model portrait and use a VARIM framework to assess the profitability potential of the model.

NOTES

1   Anderson, C. (2006). *The Long Tail: Why the Future of Business is Selling Less of More.* New York: Random House Business Books.

2   Brynjolfsson, E., Hu, Y., & Smith, M. D. (2003). Consumer surplus in the digital economy: Estimating the value of increased product variety at online booksellers. *Management Science,* 49(11), 1580–1596.

3   See similar arguments by Shirky, C. (2003, February 8). Power laws, weblogs and inequality. Retrieved July 9, 2008, from www.shirky.com/writings/powerlaw_weblog.html.

4   Brynjolfsson, E., Hu, Y., & Simester, D. (2006). Goodbye pareto principle, hello long tail: The effect of search costs on the concentration of product sales. Retrieved July 9, 2008, from http://papers.ssrn.com/ sol3/papers.cfm?abstract_id=953587. See also Brynjolfsson, E., Hu, Y., & Smith, M. D. (2003). Consumer surplus in the digital economy: Estimating the value of increased product variety at online booksellers. *Management Science,* 49(11), 1580–1596.

5   See also Elderse, A. (2008). Should you invest in the long tail? *Harvard Business Review,* 86(7/8), 88–96.

6   Agarwal, A., Johnson, M., Link, T., Patel, S., Stone, J., & Tsuchida, K. (2006). *Botox's Makeover.* Ann Arbor, MI: Ross School of Business, University of Michigan.

7   von Hippel, E. (2005). *Democratizing Innovation.* Cambridge, MA: MIT Press.

8   Film History of the 1970s. (n.d.). Retrieved December 10, 2007, from www.filmsite.org/70sintro.html

9   One Million Copies of iTunes for Windows Software Downloaded in Three and a Half Days. (2003). Retrieved September 15, 2007, from www.apple.com/pr/library/2003/oct/20itunes.html

10   Taylor, C. (2003). The 99 cent solution. Retrieved December 7, 2007, from www.time.com/time/2003/ inventions/invmusic.html

11   Apple. (2013). iPod + iTunes Timeline. Retrieved July 9, 2013, from www.apple.com/pr/products/ipodhistory

12   Taylor, C. (2003). The 99 cent solution. Retrieved December 7, 2007, from www.time.com/time/2003/ inventions/invmusic.html

13   Covert, A. (2013, April 25). A decade of iTunes singles killed the music industry. Retrieved July 9, 2013, from http://money.cnn.com/2013/04/25/technology/itunes-music-decline/index.html

14   Afuah, A. N. (1999). Strategies to turn adversity into profits. *Sloan Management Review,* 40(2), 99–109.

15   Covert, A. (2013, April 25). A decade of iTunes singles killed the music industry. Retrieved July 9, 2013, from http://money.cnn.com/2013/04/25/technology/itunes-music-decline/index.html

4

CROWDSOURCING AND
OPEN INNOVATION

Reading this chapter should provide you with the conceptual and analytical tools to:

- Understand the fundamentals of crowdsourcing.
- Understand the impact of crowdsourcing on a business model.
- Understand the relationship between open innovation and crowdsourcing.

INTRODUCTION

Some of the most fascinating innovation stories of the 2000s were about crowdsourcing. In 2008, rather than have its own employees translate its site from English to different languages, or contract the task to what it believed were some of the best translators around, Facebook turned to its users—the public—for help. Anyone who wanted to translate could help. The website was translated to French in 24 hours and to Spanish in two weeks.[1] By the end of 2010, the website had been translated from English to 70 different languages, helping the firm land one billion registered members. Just as remarkable is Goldcorp's story. In the late 1990s, the company encountered difficulties pinpointing the location of Gold on its property in Red Lake, Ontario, Canada and decided to turn to the public for help.[2] Against its geologists' advice, Goldcorp made its exploration databases available online to the public and offered cash prizes to anyone who could tell it where on its property it could find the gold. From the solutions that it received, Goldcorp struck enough gold to improve its value from $100 million to over $9 billion in a few years.

These two stories are examples of *crowdsourcing*, a form of open innovation. An agent (organization, team, nation, or person) is said to be crowdsourcing a task when—rather than perform the task by itself or outsource it to a designated contract supplier—the agent outsources the task to the public in the form of an open call.[3] Members of the public self-select to perform the task without any *ex ante* contracts. To illustrate this definition, take the Facebook translation case again. The firm could have built an internal translation group to translate the site or signed a contract with a chosen translation house to perform the tasks but it did not. Rather, Facebook outsourced the problem to the public in the form of an open call to anyone who wanted to perform the task. It did not choose those who self-selected to translate the site and they did not sign any *ex ante* contracts with Facebook to undertake the translation. (Throughout this chapter, we will refer to a firm, individual, or country that needs a solution to a problem as the seeker, and whoever solves the problem as the solver.)

Early research results from scholars have been just as fascinating as the Goldcorp and Facebook stories. For example, after analyzing 166 science challenges involving over 12,000 scientists, Professor Lars Jeppesen of Bocconi University and Professor Karim Lakhani of the Harvard Business School found that, "The provision of a winning solution was positively related to increasing distance between the solver's field of technical expertise and the focal field of the problem. Female solvers—known to be in the "outer circle" of the scientific establishment performed significantly better than men in developing successful solutions."[4]

These remarkable examples are not limited to crowdsourcing targeted at helping for-profit organizations better create and capture value. Many crowdsourcing projects are designed to create value for nonprofit organizations. For example, the United States' Library of Congress faced a challenge: how to identify people in its collections of old photographs. It turned to members of Flickr—a photo-sharing site—for help. Distant relatives and acquaintances identified hundreds of people in the photographs almost instantly.[5] At the peak of the Darfur conflict, Aegus Trust—an anti-genocide organization—developed a website called *Wanted for War Crimes* that let anyone from anywhere in the world report sightings of people suspected of war crimes in connection with the Darfur conflict by indicating the sightings on Google Maps.[6]

Wikipedia, the largest online encyclopedia, is another example of crowdsourcing at work. Rather than having its own employees research and write all encyclopedia entries, or outsourcing the tasks to designated contractors, Wikipedia depends on the public to self-select and perform the tasks. Anyone from anywhere in the world is welcome to research and make entries on any subject. In a form of crowdsourcing called crowd-funding, many individuals pool small amounts of money to raise relatively large sums to fund causes or businesses that would ordinarily not be funded at all or be funded by a few donors or investors.

BACK TO THE FUTURE

Although the examples listed so far can give the reader the impression that crowdsourcing is a recent phenomenon ushered by the Internet, its use to solve problems dates back by centuries, if not millennia, before the Internet. Crowdsourcing's history can be thought of as having three eras: grand challenges, open source, and IT-based.

Three Eras

In the era of grand challenges, governments and nonprofit organizations faced fundamental problems whose solutions they believed would have broad and lasting positive effects on society. These governments could neither solve the problems nor know to whom the problems could be contracted. So they turned to crowdsourcing. For example, in 1714, the British Government offered a cash prize—called the Longitude Prize—to anyone who would solve a critical problem at the time: Figure out an elegant way to determine the position of ships in the sea.[7] A clockmaker by the name of John Harrison won the prize. Clearly, if the government had decided to contract the problem to what it considered the greatest minds in maritime problem-solving at the time, there is a good chance that a clockmaker would not have been one of them.

In 1810, in an attempt to stop English cotton fabrics from entering France, the French Government (Napoleon) offered a prize of 1 million francs (about $3,870,000 in 2013)—also called the Prize for a Flax Machine—to anyone who could invent the best machine for spinning flax. A Frenchman named Philippe de Girard invented the machine but was never paid. He took his invention elsewhere. In the second half of the 18th century, when sugar was precious and had to be imported into Europe, the Dutch Society for the Encouragement of Agriculture offered the Prize for Sugar from Native Plants to anyone who would extract sugar from native plants. RJ Brouwer won the prize and collected the money.

In the open source era of crowdsourcing, volunteers worked as communities to develop software whose underpinning source code was open so that anyone could make useful improvements to it.[8] The resulting software (program) and underpinning source code were free. One of the questions that fascinated management scholars was why people—some of whom held down demanding full-time jobs—would spend so much time working for no pay to develop software that would be given away, for free. It turns out that many participants worked on open source software projects to signal their skills to potential employers, accumulate skills for future jobs, affirm their belief that software should be free, build or reaffirm their status in their communities, make a difference in the world, or work on the free software just for the fun of it.[9] Later, the open source concept extended to hardware and non-computer products.[10]

The low cost and availability of the Internet and other information technologies such as handheld devices ushered in an era in which problems could be far more easily broadcast to crowds anywhere in the world, solvers could more easily collaborate with other solvers, and crowds could be used to evaluate solutions from other crowds. That meant not only could more government challenges be broadcast to more diverse potential solvers all over the world, but also organizations and individuals could take advantage of the Internet to get their own problems solved using (1) challenge-type crowdsourcing in which there were many competing solutions from solvers and the winner collected a prize, or (2) open source-type crowdsourcing in which there was only one solution on which many solvers collectively worked to perfect the solution.

Types of Crowdsourcing

Because research in crowdsourcing was just taking off in 2013, the terminology in the field was still fluid and confusing.[11] For example, anecdotal examples of crowdsourcing included crowdfunding, crowdvoting, crowdsearching, and so on. From a problem-solving point of view—and consistent with the short history of crowdsourcing outlined above—these different types of crowdsourcing can be divided into two groups: tournament-based and collaboration-based.[12] In tournament-based crowdsourcing, many solutions from solvers compete for a prize that the winner(s) collects. Grand challenges such as the Longitude Prize and the Prize for the Flax Machine all fall in this category. So do Threadless' T-shirt design contest and Goldcorp's challenge to have someone tell it where to find gold on its goldmine.

In collaboration-based crowdsourcing, there is one solution on which members of the crowd collectively work to deliver the highest value solution that they can. Wikipedia and Facebook's translation project fall in this category. So does so-called crowdfunding in which individuals collectively self-select to contribute money to finance a project. Crowdvoting is used to describe the process in which a crowd votes to choose a winning solution, and can be tournament-based or collaboration-based. Crowdsearching refers to the process of getting a crowd to find something, and can be used in tournament-based or collaboration-based crowdsourcing.

THE CROWDSOURCING PROCESS

As a process, crowdsourcing has four major steps: problem delineation and prize determination for broadcast, self-selection of potential solvers to solve the problem, evaluation of solutions, and reception and implementation of solution.

Problem Delineation and Prize Setting for Broadcast to Crowd

Once a seeker decides to crowdsource a problem, it must delineate and transform it into a language that the crowd can understand before broadcasting it to the crowd.[13] The problem can be to design a new product/building, optimize a new software algorithm, translate documents, capture a criminal, isolate a chemical compound with specific properties, refine software to test a new chip, invent a new machine, and so on.[14] In transforming the problem, care must be taken to insure that it can be transmitted to the crowd and that the crowd can understand it well enough to deliver the best solution possible. Care must also be taken not to unwillingly give away too much information about the seeker's strategic moves, or information that makes it easier for competitors to violate the seeker's intellectual property.

Then there is the prize or reward that must be set right. Too low a reward may not motivate enough members of the crowd to self-select to solve the problem, and too high a reward leaves money on the table and may send the wrong signal to employees who would rather solve the problem internally. The size of the reward or prize depends on the estimated value of the solution and the extent to which solving the problem has some of the non-monetary benefits that have been shown to attract solvers.

Self-selection of Potential Solvers to Solve the Problem

The next step is for some members of the crowd to self-select to solve the problem. The seeker has no direct control over this step. However, whether potential solvers engage in solving the problem depends on the prize and the non-monetary motivating factors of the problem. Recall that some solvers can self-select to solve a problem because it is fun, they can improve their standing within their communities, they can signal their skills to future employers, they want to make a difference in the world, and so on.

Solution Evaluation

Once solutions are ready, they must be evaluated and a winner chosen. For two reasons, this stage can be as challenging as solving the problem, and may require another crowd to evaluate the solutions. First, there can be a lot of uncertainty about what the solution should be. For example, if the problem is to design a new car for some market, it is difficult to tell what potential customers in the crowd want until they have had a chance to look at the design. In that case, it may be better to have the would-be customers evaluate the designs. Second, the solutions may be too complex or there may be too many solutions to be cost-effectively evaluated. The evaluation process has to be cleverly designed.

Reception and Implementation of Solution

Finally, the seeker's organization must receive the solutions to problems and effectively incorporate them into its value creation and capture activities. There are potential pitfalls that a seeker must look out for in bringing in outsourced solutions. First, the seeker's employees may have a not-invented-here-syndrome (NIHS), a culture in which solutions from the outside are not objectively considered for the resources they needed to succeed.[15] Second, if the solutions from the outside are very different, the seeker may not have the absorptive capacity (related knowledge) to acquire and incorporate them into internal value creation and capture activities, since it takes related knowledge to absorb new knowledge. Third, since crowdsourcing can deliver superior solutions more quickly at lower cost than internal groups, some employees may see crowdsourcing as a threat to their jobs and wages.

ADVANTAGES AND DISADVANTAGES OF CROWDSOURCING

To understand the impact of crowdsourcing on a business model—which is our ultimate goal in this chapter—it is important to understand both the advantages and disadvantages of crowdsourcing. We explore both.

Advantages of Crowdsourcing

Access to a Talent Pool with Knowledge that has More Depth and Breadth
Bill Joy, co-founder of Sun Microsystems put it best when he said, "The smartest people in the world do not work for you." No organization—no matter how rich and powerful—can hire and successfully motivate all the world's brightest workers. Besides, since human beings are cognitively limited, many organizations necessarily have to specialize in some field so as to be efficient in solving problems in that field. In a world of increasing globalization and technological change, there are going to be times when a firm has a problem whose solution requires (1) a higher level of knowledge than the firm has or (2) knowledge from a field that is different from the firm's field. Effectively, there are always going to be very many people outside every firm who can do a better job at solving many problems than the firm. Crowdsourcing has the advantage that organizations can use it to tap this huge outside talent pool.

Higher Probability of Obtaining a Higher-value Solution at Lower Cost
In tournament-based crowdsourcing, the seeker gets to pay only for the best solutions. The solvers (in the crowd) whose solution does not win incur the costs. That is, the seeker does not have to pay for the deadwood. Thus, the seeker can get high value solutions at very low cost. The larger the crowd to which a problem has been broadcast, the higher will be the probability that a seeker will obtain a high-value solution. For some problems, crowdsourcing offers one of the best chances of superior bang for the buck.

Can Be a Good Recruiting Tool

Recall that one of the reasons why some solvers participate in crowdsourcing is to signal their skills to potential employers.[16] Thus, crowdsourcing can be an excellent tool for recruiting. No amount of interviewing can tell a recruiter as much about a job candidate's ability to solve problems as seeing the candidate solve problems similar to those that s/he would be solving if s/he were hired. In the Goldcorp case that we saw in the introduction of this chapter, ten of the semifinalists in the tournament that solved Goldcorp's problem ended up being hired by Goldcorp.[17] Many of the other contestants went to work for other miners.

Obtain Solutions to Problems that Only Crowds Can Solve

Some problems are such that only crowds can solve. Recall the Library of Congress example in which relatives and acquaintances were able to identify people in the Library's collections of old photographs. Only a crowd containing relatives and acquaintances—not employees of the Library of Congress or contractors—has the dispersed knowledge needed to solve this problem. Only a crowd of volunteers can build the type of rich encyclopedia that Wikipedia has built at a cost that is low enough for it to be given away.

Solution May Already Exist

In some cases, the solution to a problem may already exist somewhere in the crowd, or someone is already very close to solving the problem. In such a case, crowdsourcing not only saves time and money, but it can save the firm time and the travails of reinventing the wheel.

Free Up Management Talent

If a firm decides to solve a problem internally, it usually has to manage the process. If the firm outsources the problem to a designated contractor, it may have to manage the relationship with the suppliers. However, with crowdsourcing, a firm need worry only about receiving a winning solution and paying for it. There is no need to worry about failed solutions and their costs.

Opportunity for Seeker to Signal its Strategy to Its Coopetitors

By outsourcing a task to the public, a seeker is signaling to its coopetitors that it is going to engage in some activities. For example, if a seeker's competitors introduce a new product and the seeker wants its loyal customers to know that it is working on a similar or better product, it can crowdsource some of the tasks associated with its own version of the product. In so doing, the seeker is telling its loyal customers not to switch to its competitors, since it has a newer and better product around the corner. That is, a firm can use crowdsourcing as a marketing tool to get out information about its products.

Disadvantages of Crowdsourcing

Crowdsourcing also has *dis*advantages. First, since there are no *ex ante* written contracts or nondisclosure agreements in crowdsourcing, it is more difficult for a seeker to protect its intellectual property when it opens up to a crowd during crowdsourcing. Seekers expose themselves to more opportunistic behavior when they crowdsource problems. Second, there is always the risk that no one in the crowd will self-select to solve the problem, or that those who self-select to solve the problem are no good. This can leave the seeker with no solution whatsoever. Third, crowdsourcing may not be suitable for tasks that require tacit knowledge since it is difficult to encode and broadcast such knowledge to a crowd. Tacit knowledge is best transferred in person through learning-by-doing and by experiencing. Additionally, crowdsourcing may not be ideal for long and complex tasks such as designing and building an airplane. Such tasks require monitoring, continuous motivation, and other long-term commitments.

Fourth, it may be difficult to integrate the outsourced solution into the seeker's organization and/or products/services.[18] For example, an organization without the absorptive capacity—related knowledge—may not be able to value, bring in, and incorporate the solution into its value creation and capture activities. Fifth, an organization that depends too much on crowdsourcing may eventually not have the absorptive capacity to value, bring in, and use external knowledge to create and capture value. Sixth, opportunistic competitors can target seekers' problems with malicious solutions that they know will not work.

Some of these disadvantages can be eliminated or alleviated through the right organizational arrangements.[19] Thus, fascinatingly, crowdsourcing disadvantages are opportunities for entrepreneurs to start-up businesses to solve the problems associated with the disadvantages. InnoCentive's business model is designed to solve some of these problems. For example, because it acts as an intermediary between seekers and solvers, InnoCentive can hide a seeker's identity, thereby reducing the chances that competitors will find out its strategic moves. InnoCentive can also help seekers delineate and present problems in such a way that solvers can understand.

IMPACT OF CROWDSOURCING ON BUSINESS MODELS

Given the advantages and disadvantages of crowdsourcing, the question is, "What is its impact on business models?" To answer this question, we go through each of the five components of a business model. Recall from Chapter 1 that a business model has five components: customer value proposition, market segments, revenue model, growth model, and capabilities. Crowdsourcing has the potential to alter most of these components.

To make the discussion more tractable, we will use the case of Threadless to illustrate the concepts. The T-shirt company was founded in 2000 and rather than build an internal group to design its T-shirts or contract the design to carefully chosen designated designers, it crowdsourced the design. Anyone from anywhere could submit a T-shirt design. Members of the public—many of them T-shirt customers—voted for the best design. In 2013, winners were chosen every week and received cash payments of anywhere from $250 to $2,000 depending on the design and royalties of 3–20 percent contingent on the number of products sold with the design.[20]

Customer Value Proposition

Recall that the customer value proposition component of a business model is about offering customers benefits that they perceive as valuable enough to attract them from competitors or the sidelines. Crowdsourcing is about obtaining high value solutions to problems so as to offer customers benefits that they perceive as valuable to them. In tournament-based crowdsourcing, for example, high-value solutions are chosen and the seeker does not have to pay for failed solutions. Thus, the seeker can use the high-value solutions to deliver a product/service with higher quality, lower cost, and better timing to its own customers. Just as important, if the same crowd that designs a product and/or evaluates it to pick a winner is made up of customers, the chances that the final product will meet the needs of customers improve drastically.[21] Consider our Threadless example. Many of the judges in its T-shirt design contests are its customers. Thus, these customers pick what they want before it is manufactured, and they save on the search costs of looking for T-shirts to buy. Threadless gets a high-value design, does not pay for non-winners, and does not have to conduct marketing research since it already knows which T-shirts its customers want. What is more, these benefits cost Threadless almost nothing.

Market Segments

Recall that the *market segment* component is about the groups of customers to whom a value proposition is being offered or should be offered, how many of them there are, their willingness to pay, and the attractiveness of the market. If customers form part of the crowd that solves and evaluates problems, there is a high likelihood that the solution will better reflect customers' needs than if there were no customers in the crowd. Additionally, since in tournament-based crowdsourcing only the highest-value solutions are selected, the customers who choose the winning solution are likely to be choosing the solutions that they value the most. This increases the willingness of customers to pay, and the number of customers that want the product. A Threadless customer who voted for a design has a higher willingness to pay for the design than it does for another design.

Just as important is the fact that the high-value solution from crowdsourcing can also enable the seeker to occupy empty market spaces—also variously called sweet spots, white spaces, blue oceans, or uncontested markets—even if temporarily so. This gives the firm an attractive market in which it can make monopolistic profits until competitors move in. Since the members of a crowd that solve a problem for a seeker can also solve the same problem for other seekers, there is a good chance that someone will imitate, substitute, or leapfrog the solution. Just as important, the runners up in tournament-based crowdsourcing can take their solutions to the seeker's competitors. Effectively, imitation can be high.

Revenue Sources

For sources of revenues, we consider three kinds of players in crowdsourcing: seekers, solvers, and the intermediaries who sometimes mediate between seekers and solvers.

Seekers

A seeker's sources of revenues are determined by the products or services that utilize the solutions and the rest of the seeker's business model. However, since crowdsourcing can increase customers' willingness to pay, the seeker has a wider price range over which it can set its price without exceeding customers maximum willingness to pay. This increases pricing flexibility. For example, in a blade-and-razor revenue model, the higher the willingness of customers to pay for the "blade," the more that the firm can charge even less for the "razor."

In some business models, pricing is counter-intuitive. For example, in 2013, Quirky charged a fee for all ideas submitted by contestants so as to reduce the number of really bad ideas and jokes.

Solvers

Solvers are paid prizes. In some cases, solvers are paid a fraction of the sales that the seeker makes from selling the final product/service that incorporates their solutions. In our Threadless example, T-shirt design contest winners are paid upfront cash plus royalties. At Quirky, solvers whose designs are selected by the firm are paid royalties from future sales of the products that embody their designs.[22] Some solvers are "paid" by the employment that they get after showing off their skills in solving the problem, by the gains in status in their community, by the satisfaction for making a difference in their community or the world, and by what they have learnt in the process of solving the problem. Recall the Goldcorp example in which ten of the semifinalists in the tournament to pinpoint the location of gold on the firm's property ended up being hired by Goldcorp.

Intermediaries

Intermediaries can raise revenues by charging listing fees for problems displayed on their platform for solvers to solve. They could also charge commissions on the prizes that are paid to winners. An alternative is to get a share of future cash flows from the solution. In 2012, InnoCentive, a crowdsourcing intermediary, charged seekers for listing their problems on its site for solvers to see. The firm also charged commissions on the prizes paid to winners. However, it did not collect a share of seekers' future earnings from the solutions that passed through it.

Growth Model

Recall that the growth component of a business model is about growing profitably—growing while maintaining high prices and keeping costs low. Also recall that there are three major strategies for pursuing growth profitably: blocking, running, and teaming up.[23] Crowdsourcing impacts all three strategies. As argued above, crowdsourcing increases imitability of the solution since competitors can get the same crowd as the seeker to solve problems. Therefore, blocking as far as solutions are concerned is less efficient with crowdsourcing. However, if a seeker has valuable, difficult-to-imitate complementary assets, it can use them to defend its product market position. A run strategy is more consistent with crowdsourcing than a block. Recall that in a run strategy, a firm is always innovating so that by the time imitators catch up with one of its innovations, it has already moved on by innovating. A seeker can use the same crowd or different crowds to stay ahead of the innovation curve.

Teaming up is also very consistent with crowdsourcing. A seeker can team up with its customers to co-create products. That's what Threadless did when it got its customers to be part of the team that evaluates its T-shirt designs. If customers form part of the crowd that solves a problem and/or evaluates solutions, the chances of growing profitably are higher. Why? As noted above, when customers participate in solving problems or evaluating solutions, their willingness to pay is likely to rise, and there is likely to be a decrease in market uncertainty. The net result is that revenues go up while costs drop. During crowdsourcing, a seeker can also team up to obtain access to complementary assets.

Effectively, during crowdsourcing, a seeker can pursue all three strategies to help it grow profitably. It can use a block strategy to defend complementary capabilities associated with the solution, pursue a team-up strategy to obtain higher value solutions at lower costs, and follow a run strategy in which it uses crowdsourcing to stay ahead of competitors. Of course, the firm also has to make sure that it has the right cost structure as it pursues these strategies.

Capabilities

Crowdsourcing impacts capabilities in three major ways. First, research in technological innovation suggests that to profit from a solution, a seeker needs both the solution and complementary assets such as distribution channels, shelf space, brand, relationships with coopetitors, marketing, and manufacturing.[24] As stated above, crowdsourcing increases the chances of imitation, substitution, or leapfrogging of solutions. Therefore, a seeker's profitability from a solution depends on the degree to which it has access to difficult-to-imitate-or-substitute complementary assets. That is, as crowdsourcing becomes more and more popular, valuable, difficult-to-imitate-or-substitute complementary assets are likely to become more and more important. Second, apart from getting a higher-value solution at lower cost, the seeker does not have to allocate resources to market uncertainty-related activities when customers are part of the crowd that solves problems and/or evaluates solutions. Threadless already knows how much customers like a T-shirt before it manufactures the shirt since many of those who judge its T-shirt contests are its customers. That reduces the cost of market research and forecasting. Third, when a problem is crowdsourced, the seeker's employees who could have solved the problem have to perform another task. A problem arises if there is no other attractive task for the displaced solvers to perform. This can be problematic for the seeker.

WHY CROWDSOURCING HAS BECOME MUCH MORE IMPORTANT

As we saw at the beginning of this chapter, the use of crowdsourcing to solve problems has been around since at least the 1700s. In fact, crowdsourcing was being used to solve major challenges before businesses started conducting formal in-house R&D. The question is: why is crowdsourcing growing so much more in importance and scale now?

Technological Innovation

Growth in technological innovations such as cell phones, computers, social media, and the Internet greatly facilitate the delineation, broadcast, and reception of problems. That means anyone anywhere in the world can participate in crowdsourcing contests. This participation by diverse solvers increases the chances that high-value solutions for problems will be found. The same innovations—for example, social media—also make it possible for solvers to cooperate on crowdsourcing projects. Witness Wikipedia and the public's contributions to solving crime.

Globalization

More globalization has increased not only competition, but also the number and diversity of the markets that firms can serve. Not only are product life cycles shorter, but more new products have to be developed to serve both established and new diverse markets. Clearly, few organizations can solve all their own problems in the face of such demands. Since crowdsourcing can deliver higher-value solutions in a shorter time than alternatives, it may be just what the doctor ordered in the face of increased globalization.

A Shift to Knowledge Economies in Developed Countries

In developed economies, there have been dramatic shifts from brick-and-mortar economies to knowledge ones. For example, most of the value added in developing and selling the iPhone is knowledge-based—only less than 2 percent of the value added is manual labor. Therefore, many of the problems that need to be solved can be broadcast to potential solvers and the solutions transmitted back electronically. This increases the chances that a problem can be crowdsourced successfully.

Increase in the Number of Potential Solvers

The number of potential solvers increases every day as more and more people are educated, become richer, and can afford to live where they want and do what they like. That means the best car designer may not be in Detroit, LA, or Stuttgart but somewhere else in the world. He or she could even be on retirement in Australia, South Africa, Florida, or California. Jobs go to people, not people to jobs.

As people become richer and many products become cheaper relative to incomes, the cost of equipment for solving some problems drops enough to make potential solvers out of many crowds. Take, for example, the cost of cameras, cell phones, computers, and access to networks (the telephone and the Internet) that makes them readily available to many people. Pictures taken by crowds during major events can provide useful information in solving crimes during the events.

THE LONG TAIL AND CROWDSOURCING

In an annual Academy of Management conference in Chicago in 2009, Dr. Duayne Spradlin, CEO of InnoCentive, argued that his firm—known to session attendees as a crowdsourcing and open innovation start-up with a large community of solvers and seekers—was actually in the long tail business.[25] To understand why he was right, consider the long tail distribution of Figure 4.1. The vertical axis captures the revenues that are derived from solved problems while the horizontal axis represents problems. A few problems that were solved well generated lots of revenues while many problems that were not solved well or were never solved generated little or no revenues. The firm could get InnoCentive's community of solvers to solve the problems in the long tail. By aggregating the revenues from the many problems in the long tail—that it could not solve well before or could never solve—the firm can make as much money as, if not more money than in the short head of hits.

The vertical axis could also represent solutions while the horizontal axis represents individuals (Figure 4.2). Some individuals solve many problems because they find the problems interesting, engaging, motivating, and are well paid. Others are not as challenged or rewarded by the problems that they face and therefore are not as productive and therefore languish in the long tail of problem-solving. By joining InnoCentive's community of solvers, these solvers may be able to find the challenging and rewarding problems that will make them more productive. A solver can find enough such problems to keep him or her happy.

Finally, the vertical axis can also be the number of problems solved at a firm while the horizontal axis represents the types of solvers (Figure 4.3). The firm gets most of its problems solved by its employees and expert consultants in its field who are hired every now and then to solve some problems. However, since, as Bill Joy said, "the smartest

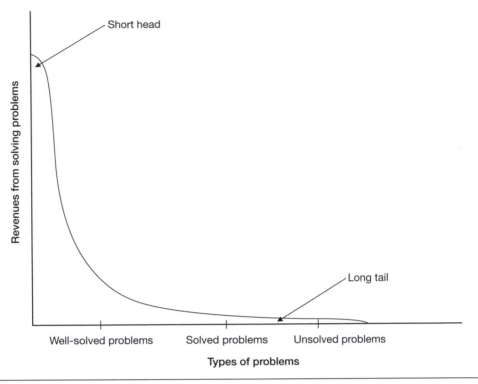

Figure 4.1 Seeker's view of the relationship between the long tail and crowdsourcing

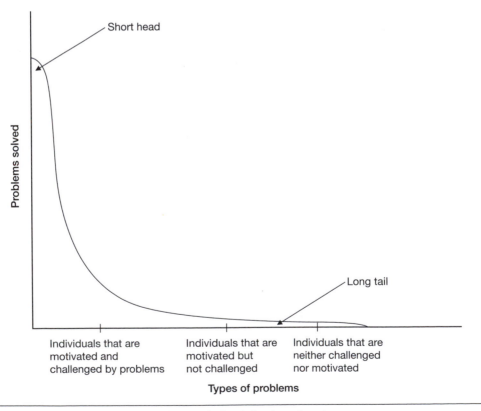

Figure 4.2 Solver's view of the relationship between the long tail and crowdsourcing

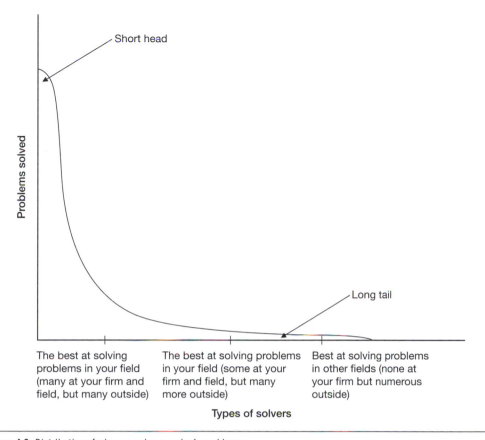

Figure 4.3 Distribution of who can solve a seeker's problems

people in the world do not work for you," there are many others outside the firm and its select group of consultants who could solve some of its problems. By reaching out to a crowd of diverse solvers from different parts of the long tail—such as InnoCentive's community of solvers—a firm can get better solutions to some of its problems. In fact, it can get some problems solved that it could never have solved even with the help of the expert consultants in its field.

CROWDSOURCING IS NOT FOR ALL PROBLEMS

If crowdsourcing is as wonderful as the examples in this chapter demonstrate, why is it not being used a lot more often? Research in this area of crowdsourcing is still in its infancy even though the practice has been around forever.[26] Until the prevalence of the Internet and other information technologies, the biggest hurdle to crowdsourcing was the technology to delineate and broadcast a problem to solvers. With the Internet, scholars are also finding out that crowdsourcing is not for all problems.[27] If a problem is too tacit to be delineated and broadcast or requires a considerable amount of interaction between the seeker and solver to solve, crowdsourcing might not yield the type of high-value, low-cost solution that is to be expected of crowdsourcing. If a seeker has intellectual property that must be protected and crowdsourcing jeopardizes the protection, the seeker may be better off not crowdsourcing.

OPEN INNOVATION

The phrase "to Xerox" something has become so popular that some students actually think Xerox, the company, got its name from the verb to Xerox or to copy. However, it was Xerox's copier innovations that earned it the verb. More importantly, what many students do not know is that Xerox's R&D arm, the Palo Alto Research Center (PARC), is also credited with inventing laser printing, personal computers, the computer mouse, graphical user interface (or windows to many), Ethernet local area networking, object-oriented programming, ubiquitous computing, and the pdf file format.[28] What is even more remarkable is how little Xerox has profited from all these inventions. It earns almost nothing from the hundreds of billions of dollars that its inventions generate every year. This raises an interesting question: What could Xerox have done to better profit from its inventions?

One answer to this question is that Xerox could have profited a lot more from its inventions if it had practiced *open innovation*. Professor Henry Chesbrough of the University of California, Berkeley who coined the phrase "open innovation" defined it as "the use of purposive inflows and outflows of knowledge to accelerate internal innovation, and expand the markets for external use of innovation, respectively."[29]

There are two parts to the rationale behind open innovation. First, since human beings are cognitively limited, no firm can know everything. Recall the Bill Joy adage that "the smartest people in the world do not work for you." Therefore, during innovation or other value-adding activities, a firm is not likely to have all the knowledge that it needs to deliver winners. Thus, such a firm may be better off bringing in some ideas from outside to complement or replace internal ideas. Somewhat counterintuitively, a firm may also need to open up some ideas for use by outsiders rather than keep them proprietary. Second, and just as important, complementary assets such as distribution channels, shelf-space, manufacturing, marketing, relationships with customers, and brand name reputation that are critical to commercializing inventions can be rare and difficult to acquire. Therefore, an inventor that does not have such complementary assets may be better off teaming up with someone who has them. Teaming up can be through licensing, strategic alliances, joint ventures or acquisitions.

Effectively, according to the open innovation hypothesis, Xerox could have made a lot of money from its inventions if it had been more open to outside ideas, to opening up rather than keeping its ideas proprietary, and to teaming up with firms that had the right complementary assets for commercializing its inventions, or using its own complementary assets to commercialize others' inventions. This purposive knowledge inflows/outflows and the use of internal and external paths to market has been the subject of research in technological innovation since at least the 1960s.[30]

Knowledge Inflows
During the value creation and capture activities that innovation entails, firms often need knowledge from outside their boundaries to complement or replace their existing stocks.

Success in acquiring and using this outside knowledge to create and capture value depends on the depth and breadth of search for the knowledge, absorptive capacity, information filters, people and culture, and the external environment.

Breadth and Depth of Search

Since the smartest people in the world do not work for any one firm, there is a good chance that smart people are distributed across geographies, nationalities, demographics, professions, and fields of expertise. Therefore, when searching for knowledge to solve problems, it might pay to cast a wide net so as to reach as many of these smart people as possible. In their study of UK manufacturers, Professors Keld Laursen of Copenhagen Business School and Ammon Salter of Imperial College London found that being more open to external knowledge sources is indeed positively related to firm performance.[31] However, the relationship is curvilinear (inverted U-shape) in that performance increases with the number of diverse outside sources up to some point. At that point, performance starts falling as more sources are added. In other words, there are diminishing returns to reaching out to many sources for knowledge. The diminishing returns are primarily from the increased cost of adding more sources to the value creation and capture process. For example, by adding too many sources, a firm may be getting out of the zones where its existing absorptive capacity, cognitive frames, and problem-solving routines are useful to one where it needs to rebuild these capabilities—a process that can be disruptive and costly.[32]

Absorptive Capacity

According to Professors Wesley Cohen of Duke University and Dan Levinthal of the University of Pennsylvania, absorptive capacity is "a firm's ability to recognize the value of new information, assimilate it, and apply it to commercial ends."[33] The idea here is that it takes related knowledge to be able to recognize, evaluate, acquire, bring in and use the acquired knowledge to create and capture value.[34] For example, a firm without the right depth and breath of knowledge in biology will have a difficult time acquiring and using biotech patents to develop new drugs. Effectively, for good knowledge inflows, a firm needs to have the right absorptive capacity.

Information Filters

Like absorptive capacity, information filters can play a critical role in shaping purposive knowledge inflows. Firms are bombarded with all kinds of information all the time and must use information filters to keep out what they do not need while letting in what they need. These information filters consist of cognitive frames—a set of beliefs, givens or assumptions about what information is worth using to create and capture value—that act as lenses through which a firm evaluates outside information.[35] They are also made up of everyday routines that keep out certain types of information while letting others in. Without the right information filters, a firm will keep out good useful information and bring in bad information, negatively impacting value creation and capture. During radical technological changes, information filters can become a bottleneck.[36] Thus, that may be one reason why during some radical changes, a firm may be better off crowdsourcing some problems.

People and Culture

The roles that people play in a firm also determine the quality and type of purposive knowledge inflows. One of these roles is that of gatekeepers and boundary spanners. A gatekeeper is a person who can act as a transducer between information transmitting and receiving entities because it has the right ties to both communities, and understands the communication codes (jargon) of both. Gatekeepers often play a critical role in shaping the type of information that is transferred, how it is transferred, and how much of it is transferred, especially in the face of an innovation. An organization's culture—the set of values, norms, and beliefs that are shared by employees—can also play a critical role in what information is allowed to flow into a firm. If information or the act of obtaining it is against an organization's values—what is important to the organization—the information is not likely to get into the organization and be effectively used to create and capture value.

External environment

A firm's ecosystem of suppliers, complementors, customers, competitors, potential new entrants, substitute products, and the overarching macro-environment also influence knowledge inflows.[37] Research in the area of management of technology has demonstrated that customers, suppliers, and complementors are sometimes the ones that innovate, not producers.[38] Therefore, a producer stands to gain by finding ways to obtain some of the knowledge from these coopetitors. Beyond innovation information, a firm may need information from suppliers about its inputs, from customers about their needs, and so on. The overarching macro-environment made up of political/legal, economic, sociological/demographic, technological, and natural environments also impacts knowledge inflows. For example, during a radical technological innovation in which a firm's resources have been rendered obsolete, the firm may have to obtain most of the new knowledge that it needs from the outside. For example, when digital photography rendered most of Kodak's chemical photography capabilities obsolete, the firm had to open up its boundaries as much as possible to learn everything that it could about digital photography.[39]

Knowledge Outflows

Pursuing knowledge inflows makes sense because a firm learns and accumulates valuable knowledge in the process. But how about doing the opposite—pursuing knowledge outflows? More specifically: why would a firm want to purposively open up its technology to the outside and let outsiders have it rather than keeping it proprietary? There are four major reasons why firms pursue or encourage knowledge outflows.

Object of Exchange

When firms acquire knowledge, they often trade some of what they have for what they want. The process can be informal or formal. In informal know-how trading, engineers or scientists from one firm trade knowledge with engineers and scientists from other firms without any formal agreements, especially when they believe that doing so does not hurt their firms.[40] Formal know-how trading usually takes place in the form of strategic alliances in which firms enter formal agreements to learn from each other.[41]

Gain Access to Complementary Assets

To profit from an invention, a firm needs complementary assets/capabilities such as distribution channels, shelf space, marketing, brand, manufacturing, and relationships with customers.[42] Many inventors often have neither the right complementary assets nor the money to acquire them. Even when inventors have money, the complementary assets that they need may be rare, inimitable, immobile, or not-for-sale. Such inventors use their inventions as currency to gain access to the complementary assets.

Win a Standard

In industries where standards are important, a firm may want to open up its technology so as to attract the critical mass of firms that can help its technology dominate the industry, becoming the standard. For example, Google made its Android operating system for touchscreen devices open to members of the Open Handset Alliance (OHA). The idea was that members of the alliance would produce compatible handsets (phones, tablets, etc.) that ran the same apps. The more firms that joined the alliance and produced compatible handsets, the more apps that would be written to run on the platform, and the more customers that would be attracted to handsets from the alliance. The more customers that gravitated towards an alliance's handsets, the more members that were likely to be attracted to the alliance. Such a positive feedback loop has helped alliances with compatible products dominate their industries. For example, by making its personal computer (PC) technology open (non-proprietary) IBM allowed competitors to produce compatible PCs attracting even more customers to add to IBM's large installed base. This large number of customers attracted more software firms to develop applications for the PC. Having many software applications developed for the PC then attracted even more customers and so on. These events helped the PC quickly emerge as the standard. Members of the ecosystem that evolved around the standard—later called the Wintel camp—such as Intel and Microsoft would go on to profit immensely from the standard.

To Expand a Downstream Market or Improve the Quality
of an Upstream One

A firm can develop a technology for downstream markets and give it away so as to expand the market for its products that are used as inputs in the downstream market. For example, to accelerate the adoption by PC makers of each new generation of its microprocessors, Intel used to develop new PCs that used its new microprocessors, well before PC makers. The firm would then make the PC technology open to anyone who wanted to make PCs using its new microprocessors, but made sure that it kept its microprocessor technology proprietary. Since Intel was in the business of supplying the microchips that go into PCs and other systems, it was expanding the downstream market for the PCs that used its chips.

A fast-food chain that moves to a developing country may have to improve or establish the upstream market that supplies the food that it needs for its restaurants. For example, the chain can establish potato farms and teach as many nationals as possible how to produce the type of high quality potatoes upstream that it needs for its downstream restaurants. That is, a firm can give away a technology that it has developed to be used by its suppliers to improve the quality of its inputs.

KEY TAKEAWAYS

- An agent (organization, team, nation or person) is said to be crowdsouring a task when—rather than performing the task by itself or outsourcing it to a designated contract supplier—the agent outsources the task to the public in the form of an open call.

- Although the Internet and other information technologies have enabled more people to take advantage of crowdsourcing, the idea of outsourcing a problem to the public in the form of an open call has been around since at least the 1700s.

- Crowdsourcing enables seekers in an inner circle to reach out to everyone, including potential solvers in outer circles.

- Crowdsourcing can be grouped into tournament-based and collaboration-based.

- In tournament-based crowdsourcing, many solutions from solvers compete for a prize that the winner(s) collects. Examples include grand challenges such as the Longitude Prize, as well as non-grand challenges such as the Goldcorp challenge that helped Goldcorp better pinpoint gold on its property.

- As a process, crowdsourcing has four major steps:
    - delineation, prize setting, and broadcast of the problem;
    - self-selection of potential solvers to solve the problem;
    - solution evaluation;
    - reception and implementation of solution by seeker.

- The advantages of crowdsourcing include:
    - access to a talent pool with knowledge that has more depth and breadth;
    - higher probability of obtaining a higher-value solution;
    - opportunity to signal strategy to coopetitors;
    - obtaining solutions to problems that only crowds can solve;
    - access to a solution that already exists somewhere and not having to reinvent the wheel;
    - freeing up management resources to work on something else.

- Disadvantages include:
    - It is more difficult for seeker to protect its intellectual property.
    - Seeker risks not getting any solution at all.
    - Crowdsourcing may not be suitable for tasks that rest on tacit knowledge.
    - It may be difficult to integrate solution back into seeker's products and organization.
    - Crowdsourcing exposes seeker to more opportunistic behavior.

- Note that many of these disadvantages can be eliminated or alleviated through the right organizational arrangements such as the use of intermediaries. In 2013, InnoCentive did just that.

- The increase in the prevalence of crowdsourcing can be attributed to technological innovation, globalization, a shift from brick-and-mortar to knowledge economies in the developed world, and an increase in the number of potential solvers.

- Crowdsourcing potentially can significantly change business model innovation:
  - *Customer value proposition*: crowdsourcing can drastically change customer value proposition by delivering the highest value possible to customers at very low prices.
  - *Market segments*: crowdsourcing can increase customers' willingness to pay. It can also take a firm into an uncontested market in which it can make monopoly profits until competitors move it.
  - *Revenue sources*: there are three different cases to consider: seekers, solvers, and intermediaries. Seekers can collect higher prices because of the higher willingness to pay from high-value solutions. They can also charge solvers a fee. Solvers can collect the prize, a share of future cash flows, or nonmonetary rewards. Intermediaries can collect listing fees, commissions on prizes paid, and a share of future cash flows from the solution.
  - *Growth model*: crowdsourcing can support all three growth strategies: blocking with complementary assets, teaming up with coopetitors to obtain higher solution values, and running through innovative crowdsourcing. Teaming up and running also keep costs down.
  - *Capabilities*: Crowdsourcing increases the likelihood of imitation, and therefore having valuable, rare, difficult-to-imitate complementary assets becomes even more important. Crowdsourcing can also save on market research costs but may displace some critical resources such as people.

- The relationship between crowdsourcing and the long tail is so strong that a crowdsourcing firm can be said to be in the long tail business.

- Not all problems can be crowdsourced profitably. Tacit problems, those that require interaction between seeker and solver, and those with intellectual property that needs to be protected are not likely to do well during crowdsourcing.

- The phrases "open innovation" was coined by Professor Chesbrough and refers to letting ideas flow in and out of a firm during innovation, and commercializing inventions through one's capabilities and those of outsiders. Such inflows/outflows result in better performance.

- Knowledge inflows depend on a firm's absorptive capacity, information filters, organizational culture and people, how wide the net is cast, and the environment in which the firm operates.

- The diversity of knowledge inflows—sources, etc.—can have a significant positive impact on performance.

- Firms often permit knowledge outflows as an object of exchange, to gain access to complementary assets, to win a standard, or to expand a downstream market or improve the quality of inputs in their factor markets.

NOTES

1   This introduction is based on the following papers: Afuah, A., & Tucci, C. L. (2012). Crowdsourcing as a solution to distant search. *Academy of Management Review*, 37(3), 355–375. Afuah, A., & Tucci, C. L. (2013). Value capture and crowdsourcing. *Academy of Management Review*, 38(3), 457–460.

2   Tapscott, D., & Williams, A. D. (2006). *Wikinomics: How Mass Collaboration Changes Everything*. New York: Penguin Books.

3   Howe, J. (2006). The rise of crowdsourcing. Retrieved on April 29, 2010, from www.wired.com/wired/archive/14.06/crowds.html. Afuah, A., & Tucci, C. L. (2012). Crowdsourcing as a solution to distant search. *Academy of Management Review*, 37(3), 355–375.

4   Jeppesen, L. B., & Lakhani, K. R. (2010). Marginality and problem solving effectiveness in broadcast search. *Organization Science*, 21(5), 1016–1033 (pp. 1016).

5   *Economist*. (2008, September 4). Following the crowd. *The Economist*, 388 (8596), 10–11.

6   *Economist*. (2008, September 4). Following the crowd. *The Economist*, 388 (8596), 10–11.

7   *Economist*. (2008, September 4). Following the crowd. *The Economist*, 388 (8596), 10–11.

8   von Hippel, E., & von Krogh, G. (2003). Open source software and the "private-collective" innovation model: Issues for Organization Science. *Organization Science*, 14(2), 208–223.

9   Lerner, J., & Tirole, J. (2002). Some simple economics of open source. *Journal of Industrial Economics*, 50(2), 197–234. von Krogh, G., Haefliger, S., Spaeth, S., & Wallin, M. W. (2012). Carrots and rainbows: Motivation and social practice in open source software development. *MIS Quarterly*, 26(2), 649–676.

10 Open-source hardware: Open sesame. (2008). Retrieved June 20, 2013, from www.economist.com/node/11482589

11 Boudreau, K. J., & Lakhani, K. J. (2013). Using the crowd as an innovation partner. *Harvard Business Review*, 91(4), 61–69.

12 Afuah, A., & Tucci, C. L. (2012). Crowdsourcing as a solution to distant search. *Academy of Management Review*, 37(3), 355–375. Afuah, A., & Tucci, C. L. (2013). Value capture and crowdsourcing. *Academy of Management Review*, 38(3), 457–460.

13 For good examples, see Spradlin, D. (2012). The power of defining the problem. Retrieved on August 2, 2013, from http://blogs.hbr.org/cs/2012/09/the_power_of_defining_the_prob.html

14 Afuah, A., & Tucci, C. L. (2012). Crowdsourcing as a solution to distant search. *Academy of Management Review*, 37(3), 355–375. Afuah, A., & Tucci, C. L. (2013). Value capture and crowdsourcing. *Academy of Management Review*, 38(3), 457–460.

15 Katz, R., & Allen, T. J. (1982). Investigating the not invented here (NIH) syndrome: A look at the performance, tenure, and communication patterns of 50 R&D project groups. *R&D Management*, 12(1), 7–19.

16 Lerner, J., & Tirole, J. (2002). Some simple economics of open source. *Journal of Industrial Economics*, 50(2), 197–234. von Krogh, G., Haefliger, S., Spaeth, S., & Wallin, M. W. (2012). Carrots and rainbows: Motivation and social practice in open source software development. *MIS Quarterly*, 26(2), 649–676.

17 Tapscott, D., & Williams, A. D. (2006). *Wikinomics: How Mass Collaboration Changes Everything*. New York: Penguin Books. Marjanovic, S., Fry, C., & Chataway, J. (2012). Crowdsourcing based business models: In search of evidence for innovation 2.0. *Science and Public Policy*, 39(3), 318–332.

18 Lakhani, K. R., Lifshitz - Assaf, H., & Tushman, M. (2013). Open innovation and organizational boundaries: task decomposition, knowledge distribution and the locus of innovation. Chapter 19 in *Handbook of Economic Organization: Integrating Economic and Organization Theory*, edited by Anna Grandori, 355–382. Northampton, MA: Edward Elgar Publishing.

19 Nickerson, J. A., & Zenger, T. R. (2004). A knowledge-based theory of the firm—the problem-solving perspective. *Organization Science*, 15(6), 617–632.

20 Submit a design to Threadless. (2013). Retrieved on July 27, 2013, from www.threadless.com/threadless

21 von Hippel, E. (2005). *Democratizing Innovation*. Cambridge, MA: MIT Press.

22 Afuah, A. N. (2013). The theoretical basis for a framework for assessing the profitability potential of a business model. Working paper, Stephen M. Ross School of Business at the University of Michigan.

23 Afuah, A. N. (1999). Strategies to turn adversity into profits. *Sloan Management Review*, 40(2), 99–109.

24 Teece, D. J. (1986). Profiting from technological innovation: Implications for integration, collaboration, licensing and public policy. *Research Policy*, 15(6), 285–306.

25 Lakhani, K. R., Jeppesen, L. B., Lohse, P. A., & Panetta, J. A. (2007). *The value of openness in scientific problem solving*. Harvard Business School, Working paper, No. 07–050, January 2007.

26 Bayus, B. L. (2013). Crowdsourcing new product ideas over time: An analysis of the dell idea storm community. *Management Science*, 59(1), 226–244.

27   Afuah, A., & Tucci, C. L. (2012). Crowdsourcing as a solution to distant search. *Academy of Management Review*, 37(3), 355–375. Afuah, A., & Tucci, C. L. (2013). Value capture and crowdsourcing. *Academy of Management Review*, 38(3), 457–460.

28   Smith, C. M., & Alexander, P. L. (1988). *Fumbling the Future*. New York: William Morrow and Company. Chesbrough, H. W. (2003). *Open Innovation: The New Imperative for Creating and Profiting from Technology*. Boston, MA: Harvard Business School Press.

29   Page 1 of Chesbrough, H. (2006). Open innovation: A new paradigm for understanding industrial innovation. In Henry Chesbrough, Wim Vanhaverbeke, & Joel West (Eds.), *Open Innovation: Researching a New Paradigm* (1–12). Oxford: Oxford University Press.

30   Allen, T. J., & Cohen, S. I. (1969). Information flow in research and development laboratories. *Administrative Science Quarterly*, 14(1), 12–19. Dahlander, L., & Gann, D. M. (2010). How open is innovation? *Research Policy*, 39(6), 699–709.

31   Laursen, K., & Salter, A. (2006). Open for innovation: The role of openness in explaining innovation performance among U.K. manufacturing firms. *Strategic Management Journal*, 27(2), 131–150.

32   Edmondson, A. C., Bohmer, R. M., & Pisano, G. P. (2001). Disruptive routines: Team learning and new technology implementation in hospitals. *Administrative Science Quarterly*, 46(4), 685–716.

33   Cohen, W. M., & Levinthal, D. A. (1990). Absorptive capacity: a new perspective on learning and innovation. *Administrative Science Quarterly*, 35(1), 128–152.

34   Cohen, W. M., & Levinthal, D. A. (1990). Absorptive capacity: a new perspective on learning and innovation. *Administrative Science Quarterly*, 35(1), 128–152. Zahra, S. A., & George, G. (2002). Absorptive capacity: A review, reconceptualization, and extension. *Academy of Management Review*, 27(2), 185–203.

35   Dane, E. (2010). Reconsidering the trade-off between expertise and flexibility: A cognitive entrenchment perspective. *Academy of Management Review*, 35(4), 579–603. Kaplan, S., & Tripsas, M. (2008). Thinking about technology: Applying a cognitive lens to technical change. *Research Policy*, 37(5), 790-805. Tripsas, M., & Gavetti, G. (2000). Capabilities, cognition, and inertia: Evidence from digital imaging. *Strategic Management Journal*, 21(10–11), 1147–1161.

36   Henderson, R. M., & Clark, K. B. (1990). Architectural innovation: the reconfiguration of existing product technologies and the failure of established firms. *Administrative Science Quarterly*, 35(1), 9–30.

37   Afuah, A. (2000). Do your co-opetitors capabilities matter in the face of a technological change. *Strategic Management Journal*, 21(10–11), 378-404. Afuah, A., & Bahram, N. (1995). The hypercube of innovation. *Research Policy*, 4(1), 51–66.

38   Baldwin, C., & von Hippel, E. (2011). Modeling a paradigm shift: From product innovation to user and open collaborative innovation. *Organization Science*, 22(6), 1399–1417. von Hippel, E. A., de Jong, J., & Flowers, S. (2012). Comparing business and household sector innovation in consumer products: Findings from a representative survey in the United Kingdom. *Management Science*, 58(9), 1669–1681. Bogers, M., Afuah, A., & Bastian, B. (2010). Users as innovators: A review, critique, and future research directions. *Journal of Management*, 36(4), 857–875. von Hippel, E. (2005). *Democratizing Innovation*. Cambridge, MA: MIT Press.

39   Tripsas, M. (2009). Technology, identity, and inertia through the lens of "The Digital Photography Company". *Organization Science*, 20(2), 441–460.

40   Schrader, S. (1991). Information technology transfer between firms: Cooperation through information trading. *Research Policy*, 20(2), 153–170.

41   Alexy, O., George, G., Salter, A. (2012). Cui Bono? The selective revealing of knowledge and its implications for innovative activity. *Academy of Management Review*, 38(2), 270–291.

42   Teece, D. J. (1986). Profiting from technological innovation: Implications for integration, collaboration, licensing and public policy. *Research Policy*, 15(6), 285–306.

5

SOCIAL MEDIA AND BUSINESS MODELS

Reading this chapter should provide you with the conceptual and analytical tools to:

- Question existing definitions of social media.
- Understand the impact of social media on a business model.
- Analyze the business model of a social media firm: Twitter.

INTRODUCTION

In 2013, the phrase "business model"—once an extremely popular phrase—paled in comparison to "social media." An Internet search of "social media" produced more than ten times as many hits as one of "business models." While such growth is interesting, a more important question for managers and anyone else who is interested in the profitability of businesses is: What is the impact of social media on business models? Our goal in this chapter is to explore this question. However, we start with an explanation of those characteristics of social media that are likely to have an impact on a business model.

SOCIAL MEDIA

One way to understand the meaning of social media is first to define the word "social." Three of the definitions of the word "social" in the Merriam-Webster Online Dictionary are: "involving allies or confederates; tending to form cooperative and interdependent relationships with others; of or relating to human society, the interaction of the individual and the group, or the welfare of human beings as members of society."[1] Human beings have always had to balance the need to function as individuals and the need to be social—the need to keep some distance between oneself and others while still forming cooperative and interdependent relationships with others and fostering a sense of community. One solution has been the use of technology. The longer the distance between an individual and "the others" with whom s/he wants to socialize, the more that human beings have had to resort to technology. Hunter-gatherers used smoke signals, drums, and messenger-shouters to convene allies or confederates to fight enemies or hunt for food. Then there was mail—snail mail through the post office—that could be used to build and maintain relationships, effect exchanges, and so on. Then there were books, newspapers, magazines, telex, telephone, radio, and television to cover that distance between an individual and the others with whom s/he wanted to effect information (content) exchanges, collaborate, communicate, etc. These were instruments for enabling individuals to socialize—the *social media* of the time.

The Internet, mobile technologies, and other technological innovations have made dramatic improvements in the *Who?, Where?, When?, What?,* and *How?* of linking the individual to others—of providing a social medium between the individual and others. In the *Who?* and *Where?* domains, the new technologies make it more possible than ever before for anyone anywhere in the world to collaborate, create, share, and exchange content. The *When?* domain is about timing—about how quickly information from an individual can simultaneously reach all others to whom s/he wants to send the information, and how instantaneous interaction between an individual and her/his targets can be. More than ever before, the new technologies greatly increase simultaneity and instantaneity of interaction. The *What?* question deals with, well, *what* the new technologies enable people to do in interacting with each other. Not only can people exchange richer content—photos (images), videos, voice and text—instantaneously, they can also co-create the content using the new technologies.

The *How?* question is, how do the new technologies make it possible for anyone anywhere in the world to collaborate, create, share, and exchange content simultaneously and instantaneously? Answer: by using Internet-based applications offered at different sites. These include blogging, micro-blogging, social bookmarking, social networks, content-sharing communities, Wiki sites, virtual worlds/gaming—collectively called social media.[2] These Internet-based (or mobile-based) applications that enable users to collaborate, create, share, and exchange content are the *social media* of our time.[3] We now explore each application and/or the websites that carry them.

Blogging and Micro-blogging

A blog is a discussion site that consists of date-stamped entries—also called "posts"—that are published. According to the Merriam-Webster Online Dictionary, a blog is "a Web site that contains an online personal journal with reflections, comments, and often hyperlinks provided by the writer."[4] Blogging can be by a person or a business. Blogging firms can even host audio, images, and video rather than linking to them. The contents of such a site are also called a blog and are usually accompanied by comments from readers. Where the amount of content is limited, the site is called a micro-blogger. An example of a microblogger is Twitter, which limits each blog or tweet to no more than 140 characters. Blogging has many advantages for a business over traditional methods such as newsletters that were one-way communications, were sent only to subscribers, could not be searched, and once deleted were gone. Blogging is multidirectional, can be broadcast to anyone, can be searched, and content is difficult to take back once broadcast. Blogging can also be internal—that is, the posts are meant only for employees. In any case, blogging has many of the advantages of a social medium that can have a positive impact on a business model.

Firms Can Establish a Presence on the Web with More Control
Blogging is to today's businesses what Yellow Pages were to businesses in the brick-and-mortar days. It gives a firm a presence on the web. A blog can be searched by anyone from anywhere in the world, giving it the type of presence that Yellow Pages used to give firms in the brick-and-mortar days, but with the large difference that the firm—not a dreaded monopoly phone company—has more control over its own information. More importantly, the firm can modify the blog at any time, and the information can be searched from anywhere. Given the near-infinite capacity of the Internet, past content cannot be deleted by viewers—contrast with throwing away old phone books and yellow pages.

Readers Can Comment on Blogs
For three reasons, the fact that readers can comment on content and the comments can become part of the content, can be critical to value creation and capture. First, a business that establishes a blog can obtain feedback from customers, suppliers, complementors, and anyone else who cares about the subject matter. Where the blogging infrastructure permits, this interaction between the blogging business and readers can mean learning from and by the community. This can enhance a blogger's ability to innovate since the blogger gets faster and more reliable feedback. Second, the firm is indirectly conducting market research, thereby reducing its chances of producing failed products while potentially lowering its costs. Third, the firm can build a community in which readers have a better sense of belonging.

Firms Can Enjoy Network Effects
Since audiences can comment on blogs, some audience members may read the blog not so much because of what they expect to learn from the blogger but because of what they expect from the audience. The larger the audience, the higher would be the likelihood of having audience members who are so good that they attract other audience members.[5] This can have a positive feedback effect in which good audience members attract other good members and so on, resulting in a large audience size that is more difficult for competitors to match or leapfrog. Also, because a blogger is interacting with its audience when it blogs and the audience comments on the blog, the blogger can build relationships with members of its audience. Such ties can prevent a blogger's audience from switching to another blogger—they can amount to switching costs, which can be important to a blogger when it wants to defend its product market position.

Innovation and Brand Building[6]
The fact that a blogger can receive many comments from a diverse audience means the blogger has an opportunity to crowdsource some tasks. A blogger can obtain superior ideas from its audience to complement or replace its own internal ideas, especially during innovation. Bloggers, especially start-ups, can also use blogging to build reputations and brands.[7]

Recruiting Source
The type of comments that audience members make can signal their expertise to the blogger. This improves a blogging firm's ability to locate the job candidates with the expertise that the firm wants.

Real Time Effects

Because social media can be used to send information to anyone anywhere in the world instantaneously and simultaneously, messages or videos from demonstrations or other occasions can provide useful information to outsiders for possible help. This property of social media facilitates crowdsourcing, especially during crisis.

Disadvantages of Blogging for a Business

You and/or your business are not the only ones that know of the advantages of blogging. The first disadvantage of (external) blogging is that there are millions of people and businesses that know about these advantages and would like to profit from them. Since the cost of becoming a blogger is very low, there may be too many bloggers competing for the same audience. Thus, a blogger has to be strategic in its choice of audience, content, and interaction with the audience. Second, any mistakes that a blogger makes are also likely to diffuse virally, just as fast as good messages. Third, detractors can create blogging sites that closely resemble a firm's website and use them to spread unflattering messages about a firm.

Social Bookmarking

Social bookmarking sites let users mark, add, rate, edit, and share bookmarks of other sites. That is, anyone can contribute to helping others know where to look for information, using social bookmarking sites. This can narrow down where to look for information, thereby reducing search costs.

Social Networking

A social network site such as Facebook, MySpace, Forum, and Google+ enables anyone from anywhere in the world to join its network. Within the network, the new member can join the groups that are consistent with their affiliation, background, or interests.[8] The site enables people to build personal profiles, add or delete people from their friends' lists, and so on. The content that can be exchanged can be text, photos, videos, or voice. Businesses can also set up shop in these networks. For example, in 2013, Zynga developed social games that could be played by Facebook members while on the network. Social networking has several benefits.

Network Effects can Be Substantial

The larger a social network, the higher would be the likelihood that a person who joins the network will find a group of people with similar interests, background, and affiliation that s/he can join. Businesses can take advantage of network effects when advertising in a social network. For example, since people are more likely to take advice about purchases from friends than from a seller, advertisers only need to convince one or a few group members who have strong ties (close and frequent relations) with other members. This one person can then spread the message to members of his/her subgroup.

Firms Can Build and/or Exploit Relational Capabilities at Lower Cost

Relational capabilities can be critical to a firm's ability to create and capture value.[9] Because of their lower cost—relative to traditional media—social media can be used to build, maintain, and/or leverage relationships to create and capture value. For example, it only takes a mouse click to send invitations, photos, documents, and so on, to as many people as a firm wants. Compare that to the cost of sending that much content to so many people in a brick-and-mortar world. A member can also leverage his or her ties with friends to obtain information to solve problems. A blogging firm can use a social network to provide the infrastructure to help its employees build social ties within the firm for better integration and value creation.

Source of Information on Others

Social network sites are also a rich source of information for employers, merchants, and the curious. A person's friends, affiliations, and activities can provide a potential employer with a lot of information that is not on a potential employee's CV. What is more, the information costs an employer very little to collect. The information that the owner of a social network site collects on its members is also believed to be a goldmine, but the firm has to be very careful about how it uses the data.

Disadvantages of Social Networking

Social networking also has some disadvantages. Once information is posted on a website for people to see, it can be very difficult to take it back or stop it from spreading. Documents, photos, videos, and voice recordings in a brick-and-mortar world could be destroyed and that would mean the end. Once most information is on the Web, it is difficult to control it. Saboteurs can also cause damage to an individual or business by faking information about the individual or firm.

Wikis

According to the Merriam-Webster Online Dictionary, a wiki is a website "that allows visitors to make changes, contributions, or corrections." Wikipedia is an example of a wiki. The software that underpins a wiki keeps track of all the edits made so that reverting back to any earlier state is easy and accurate. Because anyone, anywhere in the world can bring his or her knowledge to bear on problems, high-value solutions can be obtained at low cost using wikis. Openness also has some disadvantages. For example, people who are not qualified to make contributions can still do so, setting back problem-solving. Because there may be too many people trying to make too many changes, problem-solving can quickly become chaotic. Then there is the occasional opportunist who can take advantage of the openness to sabotage problem-solving. For these reasons, some type of structure has to be put in place to guide the process for public wikis such as Wikipedia. The bad news is that this reduction in openness can shut out innovative solutions.

Firms that have their own internal wikis are in a very good position to provide the structure and rules of the game to exploit the advantages of wikis while alleviating some of its drawbacks. Thus, internal wikis can enable employees to collaborate with other employees who may be located anywhere in the world, decreasing problem-solving times and costs. Wikis can also be used to collaborate with customers, suppliers, and comple-mentors. In particular, wikis can be used to co-create products.[10] Such collaboration can produce higher quality products while also boosting customers' willingness to pay.

Video, Photo, and other Content Sharing

There are also social media sites for sharing content such as videos, images, slides, and books. Examples of these sites are YouTube, Flickr, Slideshare, and BookCrossing. Each of these sites enjoys network effects in that the larger the content in the site, the better will be the chances that a firm will find what it wants in the site. For example, the more videos that there are on YouTube, the better one's chances of finding a video that one wants. A firm can use an external content-sharing site such as YouTube to help it promote its brand, test a new commercial, and so on. Internally, a firm can also use a content-sharing site to locate and share knowledge of old designs, solutions to problems, documents, and so on. However, internal content sharing should be pursued with care because an angry employee can download and send documents to anyone anywhere in the world.

Virtual Worlds and Games

Virtual worlds are three-dimensional virtual environments that try to reproduce the real world in which we live.[11] Individuals appear as avatars that are personalized with the characteristics of their choice and interact with each other as if they were in the real world. This interaction can mean living life the way s/he does in real life, or playing role games.

IMPACT OF SOCIAL MEDIA ON BUSINESS MODELS

With the background information on social media, we now return to the central question of this chapter: What is the impact of social media on a business model? We consider the case in which the business model is that of an organization that uses social media to help it create and capture value. We organize our exploration around the components of a business model that we explored in Chapter 1: Customer value proposition, market segments, revenue model, growth model, and capabilities.

Customer Value Proposition

The customer value proposition component of a business model is about the benefits that a firm and its products offer customers and how much these customers perceive the benefits as valuable to them. So the question is: How do social media impact the benefits that customers perceive as valuable to them? Because social media such as blogs and social networks enable firms to establish a presence with reasonable control on the Web, firms can build and leverage brand equity more effectively, boosting the extent to which customers perceive their products as valuable. Because, as bloggers, firms can get customers, complementors, and suppliers to comment on their value creation activities, these firms can obtain the type of information that can enable them to deliver better products and services to customers. Using wikis, firms can work with their coopetitors to co-create products. Importantly, by adopting the right social media and doing the right things, a firm can contribute to and enjoy network effects, boosting the value that a firm and its customers perceive in a network. All these factors can increase the benefits that a firm offers customers and the value that customers perceive in the benefits.

To concretize some of these ideas, we use the case of Threadless again. Recall that rather than design its own T-shirts, it asks the public to do it—anyone from anywhere in the world can submit T-shirt designs. The winner is chosen by Threadless's community of registered members—1.8 million in 2013—some of whom are T-shirt customers. Many of the T-shirt designers who enter the contests have their own websites where they blog about their designs, and receive comments from their followers, many of whom are members of Threadless's community that will be voting to choose the best T-shirt. Members of the community blog about Threadless' products, post comments about blogs and socialize. All these activities improve the chances that when a T-shirt is produced it will reflect what customers want. Effectively, Threadless uses social media to help it improve its value proposition.

More generally, a focal actor can use blogs, wikis or social networks to interact with coopetitors—customers, suppliers, complementors and other stakeholders—to obtain the knowledge that it needs to develop products that better meet customer needs. Coopetitors can comment on product features as design and development proceed. They can, working with the focal firm, more easily co-develop products that better meet customer needs—customers with a higher willingness to pay. Better still, as in the case of Threadless, a focal firm can crowdsource problem-solving and solution evaluation to members of its network who are connected by a social medium. Of course, a firm can use its presence on social media to build, reinforce, or protect its brand equity—an important factor in the perception of many products.

Market Segments

Recall from Chapter 1 that the market segment component of a business model is about the groups of customers to whom a value proposition is being offered or should be offered, how many customers there are in each group, customers' willingness to pay, and the attractiveness of each market segment. The goal of a firm in pursuing a market segment is to win over as many high-willingness-to-pay customers as possible at low cost while improving the attractiveness of the market. Social media can help a firm's efforts in attaining this goal. How? First, there is the viral (marketing) effect in which information diffuses rapidly from person to person via social media. One of the reasons behind the success of viral marketing via social media is that people are likely to take advice from friends, colleagues, and other people whom they trust and respect than from advertisements. Thus, to get information about a product to members of a network of close friends, a firm only has to reach a few of them and the information will get to the others virally. For example, doctors often depend more on opinion leaders for prescription information than they do on product information from pharmaceutical firms.[12] Thus, in marketing to physicians who are connected by strong ties (frequent and close relationships), one can focus on getting a few opinion leaders convinced. In any case, the right use of blogging, social networking, or any other social medium can facilitate the viral flow of information.

Second, a firm can use social media to build a multisided network with strong ties. An important point to remember here is that there is more to a network than its size.[13] The quality of a network's members can matter a lot more than the size. For example, the quality of comments from an audience is a lot more important than the number of comments. Performing the right activities to attract high quality members can mean not only more customers, but customers with a higher willingness to pay. Finally, a firm can use social media to build its brand and win distribution channels. For example, by using a micro-blogger like Twitter, a firm can increase its following, thereby promoting its brand. Such an improvement in its brand can help a firm differentiate its products, thereby improving its standing vis-à-vis its coopetitors.

Revenue Model

In Chapter 1, we saw that the revenue model component of a business model is about how many customers get to pay how much for what product/service, when and how. It is about getting as many of the customers who like the customer value proposition as possible to pay a price that is close to their maximum willingness to pay without driving them away. How do social media impact revenue models? Take the subscription and freemium revenue models, for example. A subscription model has advantages—e.g. a reduction in cyclicality—over the one-off sales revenue model, but requires more trust between the transacting parties. Customers have to trust that the focal firm will not take subscriptions and run. Social media can enable the focal actor to build this type of trust, enabling the focal actor to pursue a subscription revenue model rather than the traditional one-off model. A social medium can also help reduce the cost of acquiring subscription customers, facilitating the acquisition of more customers. For example, members of a group in a social network who subscribe to a service that they like can spread the word within their group at little or no cost to the producer.

In a freemium revenue model, a firm offers a basic product/service free of charge, but charges money for advanced features or complements. Using a social medium enables a firm to do two things that make a freemium revenue model more viable. First, social media can help reduce the cost of a product enough to make giving it away more practical. For example, having crowds of volunteers design a product using wikis can deliver a product whose cost is low enough for the product to be given away. Second, a focal firm can also use social media—especially blogging, social networking, and wikis—to work with customers to determine and deliver the types of advanced features or complementary products that the firm can sell at higher prices, more than making up for the cost of giveaways.

Also, because social media can enable a firm to know more about its customers, a firm can better partition market segments to facilitate price discrimination. Price discrimination enables a firm to set its prices closer to customers' maximum willingness to pay.

Growth Model

The growth model component of a business model is about growing profitably—about growing revenues while keeping costs low. Recall that growth usually can be achieved by pursuing some combination of three strategies: run, team up, and block.[14]

In a run strategy, a firm constantly innovates so that by the time competitors have copied its innovation, it has moved on to a new one. Since social media can facilitate the process of invention, development, and commercialization, they can facilitate the pursuit of a run strategy. For example, by using wikis to codevelop products with coopetitors, a firm can increase the rate at which it gets out new products. Better still, a firm can use crowdsourcing to solve some of the problems encountered during product development. In 2013, Threadless received over 1, 000 designs each week, from which it selected 10.

In a team-up strategy, a firm partners with coopetitors through strategic alliances, joint ventures, acquisitions, and so on, to better create and/or capture value. To get its job done, partners usually need to collaborate, interact, cocreate, share, and exchange information. Social media are ideal for facilitating these tasks.

In a block strategy, a firm does all it can, including retaliation, to prevent competitors from imitating its business model.[15] A firm can use social media to build rare, difficult-to-imitate relationships with its coopetitors.

A firm can also use social media to reduce both production and transaction costs. For example, by using wikis to design products, as Threadless did, a firm can drastically reduce its production costs. Additionally, social media can drastically reduce the transaction costs associated with searching and acquiring certain types of information. For example, a firm can use blogging and social networks to reduce recruiting costs.

Capabilities

At the core of a business model are capabilities—the resources and activities that a firm needs to offer its customers the right value proposition, target the right market segments, pursue the right revenue model, and chase the right growth model. How do social media impact these capabilities? Social media enable firms to build capabilities in the form of social capital, or leverage existing capabilities (including social capital) to create and capture value. According to Professors Janine Nahapiet and Sumantra Ghoshal, social capital is "the sum of the actual and potential resources embedded within, available through, and derived from the network of relationships possessed by an individual or social unit."[16]

Building Social Capital

Whether it passes through blogging, wikis, social networking, social bookmarking, or content communities, a firm has many opportunities to build social capital.[17] How? A firm can use blogging and comments from its blogging audience to build a large network with members that trust each other, enjoying the size benefits of network effects. It can also join social networks to build strong ties or use wikis to cocreate products. Just as important, a firm can use social bookmarking to locate sites where it can more easily find coopetitors who are trustworthy, and so on.

Leveraging Social Capital

Social media can also help a firm leverage existing social capital to create and capture value. Strong ties (frequent and strong relations) with suppliers, for example, can enable a firm to leverage the skills and innovativeness of suppliers such as the networks of suppliers at Toyota that Professors Dyer and Nobeoka found to be critical to Toyota's innovativeness.[18]

Additionally, if a firm wants to use wikis to cocreate products with its suppliers and customers, prior relations with these coopetitors can help the firm to identify who might be a problem to work with. A pharmaceutical company with prior well-established relationships with medical doctors who have become opinion leaders in a social network of physicians can leverage its relationship with the doctor to introduce a new drug.

SAMPLE BUSINESS MODEL OF A SOCIAL MEDIA FIRM: TWITTER

The second example of a social media business model is that of a firm that provides the social media services that firms can use to improve their business models. We use Twitter (Figure 5.1).

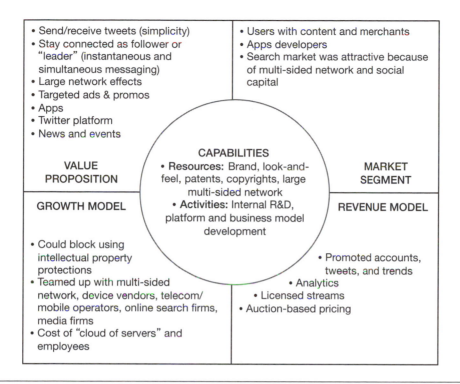

Figure 5.1 Twitter's business model portrait

Customer Value Proposition

Recall that the customer value proposition component of a business model is about the benefits that a firm and its products offer customers and how much these customers perceive the benefits as valuable to them. In 2013, Twitter created value for three sets of customers (clients): (1) users who used Twitter's infrastructure to send, receive, share and discuss content; (2) the merchants who paid for ads or product promotions, and (3) apps developers. Any user from anywhere could send or receive tweets—no more than 140 characters per tweet—from any user. These users could be individuals, businesses or any other organization. Some individuals used the service to listen to friends, politicians, celebrities, brands, experts, and so on. Businesses used it to broadcast messages to their followers, thereby promoting their brands, driving traffic to their sites and so on. Some organizations used it to raise money for good causes.

Several factors were appealing to Twitter's registered members. First, the simplicity of the messages—no more than 140 characters per tweet—meant that one could send messages not only through Twitter's website, Twitter clients, and apps for desktops, but also that one could send messages through smartphones and tablets. Second, Twitter's infrastructure was such that each member could send a message to *all* its followers *simultaneously*. This feature enabled people to report on activities such as political demonstrations real-time—that is, while the events were still unfolding—from their phones.

Third and importantly, Twitter's users enjoyed network effects arising from its large network. To understand the source of these network effects, one can think of a network such as Twitter's as being made up of followers and the celebrities, businesses, brands, and anyone else that they follow. Let's call the latter group leaders. The more leaders that there are in a network, the more valuable that the network is likely to be to followers since they are more likely to find the leaders (celebrities, brands and so on) that they want to follow. Similarly, the more followers that there are in a network, the more valuable that the network is likely to become to leaders since they are more likely to find someone who wants to follow them.[19] Effectively, Twitter's large network—estimated at 517 million in 2012[20]—was more valuable to its members than competitors' smaller networks.

To its merchants, Twitter provided a larger number of users who exchanged or shared content that could reveal information about their preferences, giving merchants information to better target their marketing. The more users that there are in a network, the more valuable that the network is likely to be to advertisers.

Twitter made its applications programming interface (API) open so that anyone from anywhere could develop apps for its platforms. Good applications make a network more valuable. Thus, the more developers that produce apps for a network, the more valuable that the network is likely to be to users since they can find the apps that best meet their needs. Also, the more users that are on a network, the more valuable that the network is likely to be to developers since they are more likely to find someone who will use their apps.

Market Segments

Recall that the *market segment* component is about the groups of customers to whom a value proposition is being offered or should be offered, how many customers there are in each group, their willingness to pay, and the attractiveness of the segments. Since a market can be segmented according to the type of product/service needed, the type of customers and their preferences, geography, and so on, we use the type of customer to segment Twitter's market into three primary categories: users, merchants, and apps developers. (In July 2012, Twitter had 517 million registered accounts, 140 million of them in the United States.[21])

The large number of users and the associated network effects makes each of the market segments attractive. A new user who wants to join a micro-blogging site is likely to be attracted to Twitter's much larger network since it increases the user's likelihood of finding followers or a leader to follow. Existing Twitter registered users are less likely to switch when the network size is large since doing so means abandoning followers and leaders that the user may not be able to find in a smaller network. Merchants with close relationships with users—for example, many users who follow their brands and buy from them—are also not as likely to pick up and leave to try to build the same relationships in smaller networks. Apps developers who have developed apps for Twitter's site and for third-party sites are also not likely to pick up and move to a new site with a smaller network.

Revenue Model

Recall that the revenue model component of a business model is about how many customers get to pay how much for what product/service, when and how. In 2013, Twitter's revenues came from five different sources.[22] First, the company collected fees from licensing full feed of its user's public tweets to search engine firms such as Google,

Microsoft, and Yahoo so that they could use the tweets in their real-time searches. Second, it collected revenues from payments by merchants who promoted their accounts on Twitter. The idea here was that the merchant paid to broadcast messages to followers or people who were seen as being "just like them" and therefore likely to become followers. Third, revenues also came from promoted tweets in which messages were sent to anyone who conducted certain searches. Unlike in promoted accounts where messages were likely to reach followers or people like them, promoted tweets might or might not reach followers.

Fourth, revenues also came from promoted trends. At any point in time, some discussion topics were hotter than others and trends were a reflection of these topics. In 2013, Twitter's trends were displayed next to each user's timeline.[23] Businesses paid for a promoted trend that, for a day, was displayed at the top of the trends list. Users who clicked on the promoted trend were taken to the business's marketing message displayed in the form of a promoted tweet. Fifth, a potential source of revenues was the analytics that Twitter provided to its users. Twitter's analytics software enabled its customers to track their advertising campaigns—impressions, "retweets," clicks, follows, and replies of their promoted tweets—to trend their advertising and promotion activities to obtain insights about customer behavior, and adjust their campaigns accordingly.

As far as pricing was concerned, Twitter charged promoted accounts on a cost-per-follow (CPF) basis—that is, an advertiser was charged when a user became a follower.[24] In 2012, CPFs ran between $1 and $10. Promoted tweets were charged on a cost-per-engagement (CPE) basis—that is, an advertiser was charged only if there was an engagement, where an engagement was defined as a click, favorite, reply of the promoted tweet, or "retweet." The price paid was determined in an earlier auction, enabling Twitter's price to be close to customers' maximum willingness to pay.

From these sources of revenues and pricing strategy, it would appear that Twitter's revenues should be high but they were not in 2013. One reason may be because most of the advertising dollars were still earmarked for desktops rather than mobile devices, and Twitter's presence was a lot stronger on mobile devices. More advertising dollars were expected to be moved to mobile devices, and that might mean more revenues for Twitter.

Growth Model

The growth model component of a business model is about growing profitably—about pursuing some combination of team up, run, and block strategies to keep revenues up and costs down while doing everything else to maintain a low cost structure.[25] The most visible of Twitter's growth strategies was its teaming up. It partnered with apps developers, the search engine owners to whom it licensed feed of public tweets, governments, the worldwide telecommunications operators who allowed their networks to carry tweets from mobile devices, and handheld device owners such as Apple who integrated Twitter into their device operating systems enabling users to tweet directly from the devices. Most important of all, it was building strong relationships with its members and merchants that constituted its large multisided network with its numerous benefits.[26]

The laws of many countries protected Twitter's intellectual property and therefore the firm could use the protection as a basis for a blocking strategy. It was difficult to tell if the firm was pursuing a run strategy even though it was engaged in innovation. In any case, between Q2 and Q4 of 2012, Twitter's number of registered users grew by

288 million.[27] However, its revenues and profits did not keep pace. Because the firm was private in 2013, there was little information on its cost structure.

Capabilities

Twitter's capabilities consisted of resources and the activities that used the resources to create and capture value. Its core resources included its large multisided network of registered members, the look-and-feel of its website, brand, trademarks, platform infrastructure, and the underpinning intellectual property rights such as patents, copyrights, and trade secrets. Its resources also included its applications programming interface (API)—the set of protocols, routines, and tools that developers can use to develop software applications—that provided the building blocks for development of apps for its ecosystem.

Just as critical were its relationships with members of its multisided network, merchants, apps developers, search-engine owners, governments, telecommunications operators, and handheld device owners.

Twitter's activities included developing the software to keep growing and satisfying its large network of registered users, merchants, and apps developers. The activities also included supporting and defending its brand, trademarks and the look-and-feel of its website. Just as important were the activities designed to establish new relationships with members of its ecosystem while maintaining important existing ones.

CONCLUDING REMARKS

Social media—blogging, micro-blogging, social bookmarking, social networks, content-sharing communities, wiki sites, and virtual worlds/gaming—are changing the way that firms conduct business. Firms can use social media not only to build critical capabilities, but also to leverage social capital to create and capture value.

KEY TAKEAWAYS

- There has always been a need for individuals to socialize while living far from each other, and people have always used different media—from smoke signals to television—as instruments for socialization.

- However, Internet-based applications such as blogging, micro-blogging, social bookmarking, social networks, content-sharing communities, wiki sites, virtual worlds/gaming—called social media—enable users to collaborate, create, share and exchange content.

- Blogging and microblogging have the following characteristics that are typical of social media in general:
  - Can enable a firm to establish a presence on the Web with more control than, say, the Yellow Pages of the brick-and-mortar world.
  - Readers can comment on blogs, providing critical feedback.
  - Firms can enjoy network effects with the potential to build social capital.
  - Blogging can be critical to innovation and brand building.
  - Can help firms with recruiting.
  - Has real-time effects benefits.

- Blogging disadvantages include: the fact that many advantages gained by firms using social media may be easy to imitate, any mistakes that firms make can propagate rapidly, and detractors can create sites that satirize firm's blog.

- In addition to having many of blogging's advantages, social networking has more advantages that a firm can exploit:
  - Firm can build and exploit larger network effects.
  - Firm can build and exploit even more social capital at lower cost.
  - Social networks can be the sources of a lot more information on people than blogging.

- Social networking has some of the same disadvantages as blogging.

- Wikis provide the openness that can be critical to value creation. However, value capture can be a problem, if not well managed.

- Content-sharing sites can have large network externalities but their value to firms in creating and capturing value is not as large as that of blogging and social networking.

- The impact of social media on a firm's business model can be huge:
  - Customer value proposition: if social media are used in crowdsourcing, for example, the resulting value proposition can be very high.
  - Market segment: social media can be used to increase customer's willingness to pay, the number of customers, and the attractiveness of the market segment.
  - Revenue model: social media can be used to increase the number of sources of revenues, improve pricing, and increase profitability.
  - Growth model: social media can have an impact on all three growth model strategies: block, run, and team up. They can also have a large impact on cost structure.
  - Capabilities: social media can enable a firm to build and/or leverage social capital.

NOTES

1 Retrieved June 25, 2013, from www.merriam-webster.com/dictionary/social
2 See also, Kaplan, A. M., & Haenlein, M. (2010). Users of the world, unite! The challenges and opportunities of social media. *Business Horizons*, 53(1), 59–68.
3 Kaplan, A. M., & Haenlein, M. (2010). Users of the world, unite! The challenges and opportunities of social media. *Business Horizons*, 53(1), 59–68.
4 Retrieved June 26, 2013, from www.merriam-webster.com/dictionary/blogging
5 Afuah, A. N. (2013). Are network effects all about size? The role of structure and conduct. *Strategic Management Journal*, 34(3), 257–273. Fershman, C., & Gandal, N. (2011). Direct and indirect knowledge spillovers: The "social network" of open-source projects. *Rand Journal of Economics*, 42(1), 70–91. Gandal, N. (1994). Hedonic price indexes for spreadsheets and an empirical test of the network effects hypothesis. *Rand Journal of Economics*, 25(1), 160–170.
6 Poetz, M. K., & Schreier, M. (2012). The value of crowdsourcing: can users really compete with professionals in generating new product ideas? *Journal of Product Innovation Management*, 29(2), 245–256.
7 Afuah, A., & Tucci, C. L. (2012). Crowdsourcing as a solution to distant search. *Academy of Management Review*, 37(3), 355–375.
8 Boyd, D. M., & Ellison, N. B. (2007). Social network sites: Definition, history, and scholarship. *Journal of Computer-Mediated Communication*, 13(1), 210–230.
9 Dyer, J. H., & Singh, H. (1998). The relational view: Cooperative strategy and sources of interorganizational competitive advantage. *Academy of Management Review*, 23(4), 660–679. Dyer, J. H., & Hatch, N. W. (2006).

Relation-specific capabilities and barriers to knowledge transfers: creating advantage through network relationships. *Strategic Management Journal*, 27(8), 701–719.

10 Nambisan, S., & Baron, R. A. (2009). Virtual customer environments: Testing a model of voluntary participation in value co-creation activities. *Journal of Product Innovation Management*, 26(4): 388–406. Nambisan, S., & Baron, R. A. (2010). Different roles, different strokes: Organizing virtual customer environments to promote two types of customer contributions. *Organization Science*, 21(2): 554–572.

11 Kaplan, A. M., & Haenlein, M. (2010). Users of the world, unite! The challenges and opportunities of social media. *Business Horizons*, 53(1), 59–68.

12 Nair, H., Manchanda, P., & Bhatia, T. (2010). Asymmetric social interactions in prescription behavior: the role of opinion leaders. *Journal of Marketing Research*, 47(5), 883–895.

13 Afuah, A. N. (2013). Are network effects all about size? The role of structure and conduct. *Strategic Management Journal*, 34(3), 257–273.

14 Afuah, A. N. (2003). *Innovation Management: Strategies, Implementation, and Profits*. New York: Oxford University Press. Afuah, A. N. (1999). Strategies to turn adversity into profits. *Sloan Management Review*, 40(2), 99–109.

15 Afuah, A. N. (2003). *Innovation Management: Strategies, Implementation, and Profits*. New York: Oxford University Press.

16 Nahapiet, J., & Ghoshal, S. (1998). Social capital, intellectual capital, and the organizational advantage. *Academy of Management Review*, 23(3), 242–266. See also seminal work by Professor Ronald Burt. For example: Burt, R. S. (1997). The contingent value of social capital. *Administrative Sciences Quarterly*, 42(2), 339–365.

17 Reagans, R., & McEvily, B. (2003). Network structure and knowledge transfer: The effects of cohesion and range. *Administrative Science Quarterly*, 48(2), 240–267. Perry-Smith, J. E., & Shalley, C. E. (2003). The social side of creativity: A static and dynamic social network perspective. *Academy of Management Review*, 28(1), 89–106. Adler, P. S., & Kwon, S. W. (2002). Social capital: Prospects for a new concept. *Academy of Management Review*, 27(1), 17–40. Atuahene-Gima, K., & Murray, J. Y. (2007). Exploratory and exploitative learning in new product development: A social capital perspective on new technology ventures in China. *Journal of International Marketing*, 15(2), 1–29. Acquaah, M. (2007). Managerial social capital, strategic orientation, and organizational performance in an emerging economy. *Strategic Management Journal*, 28(2), 1235–1255.

18 Dyer, J. H., & Nobeoka, K. (2000). Creating and managing a high performance knowledge-sharing network: The Toyota case. *Strategic Management Journal*, 21(3), 345–367.

19 Afuah, A. N. (2013). Are network effects all about size? The role of structure and conduct. *Strategic Management Journal*, 34(3), 257–273. Fershman, C., & Gandal, N. (2011). Direct and indirect knowledge spillovers: The "social network" of open-source projects. *Rand Journal of Economics*, 42(1), 70–91.

20 Lundund, I. (2012). Analyst: Twitter passed 500M users in June 2012, 140M of them in US; Jakarta 'Biggest Tweeting' City. Retrieved July 1, 2013, from http://techcrunch.com/2012/07/30/analyst-twitter-passed-500m-users-in-june-2012-140m-of-them-in-us-jakarta-biggest-tweeting-city

21 Lundund, I. (2012). Analyst: Twitter passed 500M users in June 2012, 140M of them in US; Jakarta 'Biggest Tweeting' City. Retrieved July 1, 2013, from http://techcrunch.com/2012/07/30/analyst-twitter-passed-500m-users-in-june-2012-140m-of-them-in-us-jakarta-biggest-tweeting-city

22 Retrieved July 2, 2013, from https://business.twitter.com/products/twitter-ads-self-service

23 Retrieved July 2, 2013, from https://business.twitter.com/products/twitter-ads-self-service

24 Retrieved July 2, 2013, from http://mashable.com/2011/12/06/cost-of-twitter-follower

25 For more information about the run, block, and team up strategies, please see: Afuah, A. N. (1999). Strategies to turn adversity into profits. *Sloan Management Review*, 40(2), 99–109. Afuah, A. N. (2003). *Innovation Management: Strategies, Implementation, and Profits*. New York: Oxford University Press.

26 Parker, G., & Van Alstyne, M. (2005). Two-sided network effects: A theory of information product design. *Management Science*, 51(10), 1494–1504. Brousseau, E., & Penard, T. (2006). The economics of digital business models: A framework for analyzing the economics of platforms. *Review of Network Economics*, 6(2), 81–110. Eisenmann, T. R., Parker, G., & van Alstyne, M. (2006). Strategies for two-sided markets. *Harvard Business Review*, 84(10), 92–101.

27 Retrieved July 2, 2013, from www.globalwebindex.net/twitter-now-the-fastest-growing-social-platform-in-the-world

6

LESS-IS-MORE INNOVATIONS

Reading this chapter should provide you with the conceptual and analytical tools to:

- Define a less-is-more innovation (LIMI).
- Understand the advantages and disadvantage of less-is-more innovations (LIMIs).
- Begin to understand the implications of LIMIs for business model innovations.

INTRODUCTION

In January 2010 when Apple announced its long-anticipated iPad, some product reviewers complained that it had no USB port, no multitasking, no mass storage, no webcam, no flash support, no removable battery, no multiple (OS) support, no CD and DVD support, no RAM upgradability, and other features that users had come to expect in netbooks.[1] In less than two months, after launching the device on April 3, 2010, Apple had sold 2 million iPads, beating all expectations, despite all the missing features—or maybe because of them. Its stock had reached record highs, making it the most valuable high-technology firm, overtaking Microsoft and IBM.

In 2010 Nintendo's Wii outsold game consoles from Microsoft and Sony. This was the fourth consecutive year in which the Wii had outgunned its competitors. What was even more remarkable than the superior sales was the fact that Nintendo actually made money selling consoles while its competitors sold their consoles at a loss, hoping to recoup the losses with game (software) sales. In introducing the Wii back in 2005, Nintendo had decided to *de*-emphasize processor speed and graphical detail by using three-year old microchips that cost very little and delivered images that were less lifelike than avid gamers had come to expect of a new game console. It also stripped off the complex multibutton control that avid gamers had come to expect, replacing it with a wand-type device.

The service offered by McDonald's and Burger King in their early days was a simplified version of traditional restaurant service. They stripped off attributes of formal restaurant dining that traditional diners had come to expect such as sitting customers in nice seats, waiting on them while they were comfortably seated, preparing meals and serving them on plates, and the customer paying for food after eating. Besides, the meal portions in these fast-food restaurants at the time were smaller and the choice more limited than in their traditional counterparts. The two fast-food chains have been very successful.

In what would become known as the Southwest model, Southwest Airlines stripped off some of what major airlines at the time advertised as critical attributes. It offered no meals, no baggage transfer, no assigned sitting, used only one type of airplane—the Boeing 737—and operated primarily out of secondary airports. This model worked so well that for decades, while other US airlines bled and many went out of business, Southwest never lost money (except in 2004). The model would be copied all over the world by other airlines, including Ryanair, Jetair, etc.

Twitter was founded in 2006 and by May 2013, it had amassed over 517 million registered users. While MySpace, Facebook and other social network firms touted the many features that members could use to customize their profiles, Twitter stripped off many of these fancy features. In it, one could not send more than 140 characters.

LESS-IS-MORE INNOVATIONS

In these five examples, winners won by offering customers less of what many of them had come to expect—a simpler or stripped-down product/service.[2] They abandoned the more-is-better ethos that has dominated business thinking for years and embraced a less-is-more approach. They introduced less-is-more innovations (LIMIs). They took advantage of the fact that more is not always good. Less of what some customers perceive as a good thing can actually be good for some customers, and very good for the producer's bottom line. In particular, these firms stripped off or de-emphasized some attributes that customers had come to expect, simplifying the product in the process. In some cases, they combined existing features in innovative ways that simplified the new product. In others, they also added new features that may not have been expected, but making sure that the final product was simplified and cheaper than older ones in the market.

By *not* offering flash support, USB port, multitasking, mass storage, webcam, and so on for its iPad, Apple kept the device simpler, making life a little easier in a world of gadgets that is becoming more and more complicated. Thus, while some customers viewed a lack of these attributes as minuses, others saw it as a positive.[3] Besides, the iPad had additional features such as the onscreen virtual keyboard compared to the competition's physical QWERTY keyboard, and over 140,000 applications available in Apple's iTunes App Store and a lot less for competitors, and so on. The final product was simpler than netbooks.

Nintendo used three-year-old chip technology rather the latest and costly technology that Sony and Microsoft used to achieve the top speeds and graphical detail demanded by avid gamers. It also left out sophisticated DVDs such as Sony's Blue Ray. By de-emphasizing or leaving out these features, Nintendo was able to keep the cost of the Wii so low that it could make money on consoles—a remarkable achievement considering that both Microsoft and Sony lost billions of dollars in console sales, hoping to recoup some of the losses through game sales and online gaming. It also added some new features that avid gamers did not expect, such as the movable wand and games that allowed gamers to exercise their bodies. The result was that Nintendo was able to reach customers for whom graphical detail, fast processors, escapists scenarios, and complicated controls were not a primary attraction. It was also able to reach customers who wanted the physical exercises made possible by the wand.

Many other examples of less-is-more innovations exist. When Netflix entered the US movie-renting business in 2004, Blockbuster had dominated the business for over a decade. However, by 2006, Netflix had Blockbuster on the ropes. It had become very profitable even as Blockbuster was losing a lot of money. In offering its new service, Netflix left out a feature that many movie renters had come to expect: the ability to take home a movie from the store right away. Rather, Netflix's customers had to order the movies that they wanted ahead of time. (Online on-demand movies would later make this point mute.) But these competitors had a much larger selection of movies, and could make better selections with the help of Netflix's community of renters and movie selection algorithms. Besides, everyone in the US with a postal address and access to the Internet, not just those near a movie-rental store, could now rent movies. Another example is Tata Motors whose original Nano had a motorcycle-like engine, a top speed of around 95 kilometers an hour, no radio, no air-conditioner, one rear view mirror, and other de-emphasized or stripped off attributes.[4]

Relationship Between More-is-Better and Less-is-More Innovations

The relationship between more-is-better innovations (MIBIs) and less-is-more innovations (LIMIs) can be explored using the configuration of Figure 6.1. In the figure, the horizontal axis captures the relative cost of an innovation—whether the innovation costs more or less than the products that were in the market before it was introduced. The vertical axis captures the attributes of the new product—whether the new product is a result of (1) improving some attributes of the old product and/or adding new ones, or (2) de-emphasizing or stripping off some of the attributes of the old product and in the process taking away something that some customers have come to expect.

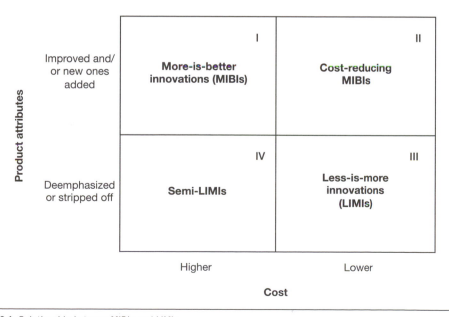

Figure 6.1 Relationship between MIBIs and LIMIs

Products in cell I are what innovations have traditionally been about. The goal of innovators in this cell is to offer their customers products with improved features or with additional ones that they hope customers will like. The more improvements that can be made to existing features, the better the product is thought to be for customers. Additionally, the more new features that are added to what the old product used to have, the better that the new product is perceived to be. The result is usually a new product that is more sophisticated than those in the market. Such new products are so-called more-is-better innovations (MIBIs). Examples of MIBIs abound. Every year, innovations in automobiles, refrigerators, houses, bicycles, computers, tractors, earthmoving equipment, telephones, etc. result in products with improved or added features. This added sophistication results in higher costs that are passed on to customers in the form of higher prices. The improved and/or added features can also result in complexity that some users have difficulties dealing with. A look under the hoods of a 1970s car and a 2010 car underscores the complexity of the latter compared to the former.

Some innovation activities are designed to reduce the cost of products with sophisticated features. Such innovations fall in cell II. The cost of most high-tech products usually starts out high, but as firms go up the learning and experience curves, and take on process or incremental product innovations, costs drop. Many of these cost improvements usually come through so-called process innovations.

The cell of great interest to us in this chapter is cell III. The new products in the cell are the result of performing activities that not only strip off or de-emphasize old products' attributes, but they also lower the cost of the new product. The new product is also simplified relative to existing products. Some attributes that customers may not have expected can also be added, provided the resulting product is still simpler and costs less than the products already in the market. As we will see shortly, a lower-cost product that is simpler to use and that has omitted features that underpin competitors' competitive advantage can have huge strategic significance.

Although not very common, an innovation can result in a simplified product whose cost is higher than that of existing products. Such products would fall in cell IV, what we will call semi-LIMIs. We will be interested in a product in this cell only to the extent that the product's costs can be reduced, moving it into cell III, or that the simplification is so good that customers are willing to pay even more for it.

Effectively, LIMIs have four features (Figure 6.2):

1. Some of their attributes are stripped off or de-emphasized.
2. The resulting product is simpler than previous ones.
3. They have lower costs than predecessor products in the market.
4. They *may* have new unexpected features.

Consequences of a LIMI

When some features are stripped off or de-emphasized, those customers who have come to consider these features as sacred cows are likely to hate the innovation. However, those who—for one reason or the other—did not like the features would be happy to see them go. Besides, in an increasingly complex world in which people are becoming more and more overloaded with information, a simpler product can be welcome news. Importantly, the lower cost that results from stripping off or de-emphasizing features is also welcome news to some customers. Any features that are added, while maintaining

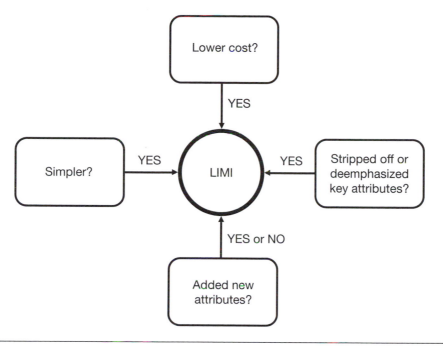

Figure 6.2 Characteristics of LIMIs

simplicity, may also be welcome news to yet other customers. The result is that some customers will gravitate towards the new product while others stay with the old product. That is, there is so-called de facto customer self-selection.[5] Effectively, a LIMI creates an uncontested market space in which the innovator can sell a product that is low cost *and* differentiated.

Strategic Advantages of LIMIs

If introduced carefully into a market, LIMIs can have surprisingly remarkable strategic advantages. We consider nine such advantages here.

Innovation Tasks May be Simpler

Because some attributes have been stripped off or de-emphasized, the task of developing a LIMI may be potentially simpler than that of a more-is-better product. Besides, offering the LIMI may require fewer and less sophisticated resources than its MIBI older sibling.

No Head-to-head Competition

Initially, a LIMI innovator has no head-to-head competition. It is not in a battle to outdo competitors in providing better or more product features. It is in a so-called blue ocean.[6] Having no head-to-head competition in a large market is nirvana for a firm. It can, when legal, exercise market power in the market segment until competition moves in. This can be very profitable if well executed. For example, the innovator can find ways to keep its prices as close to customers' reservation prices as possible without fear of driving customers to competitors since there are none.

Opportunity to Build First-Mover Advantages

Of course, the uncontested market space is not likely to stay uncontested for long. However, by pursuing the right first-mover advantages, the innovator can delay entry into the market space, put itself in a favorable position to fight competitors that venture into the market space, and increase its profits or at least slow their erosion.[7] For example, the innovator can preemptively acquire key complementary assets associated with the new space. Such assets include brand name reputation, distribution channels, relationships with customers, shelf space, and so on. In carrying out its "Southwest model" strategy, Ryanair usually acquired most of the gates and landing slots at the airports that it reinvigorated, preemptively keeping these scarce resources out of the hands of anyone who might like to try to replicate its model on its routes. Of course, there are also first-mover *dis*advantages that a LIMI innovator has to contend with.

Secondary or Disposable Product

Because a LIMI is simpler and cheaper, some customers may decide to own both their MIBI and the LIMI. Many owners of Notebook PCs bought Netbooks for themselves or family members. Many PC owners also bought the iPad. Some owners of Xbox 360s or PS3s bought Nintendo Wiis.

Disabling for Many Incumbents

In the face of an innovation, some of the most formidable competitors can be incumbents who had a competitive advantage in the old game of offering the product that the innovation is supposed to dislodge. Those incumbents who built their competitive advantages around the product features that have been de-emphasized or stripped off can see their former advantages turned into a handicap by smart LIMI innovators. Take the example of video games when Nintendo introduced its LIMI Wii console. For years, game console makers had competed on "the fastest" processor, the most detailed and lifelike graphics, long and complex games, and button-strewn control units—all features that Nintendo de-emphasized or eliminated when it introduced the Wii. How could an incumbent such as Microsoft or Sony now turn around and say that all these features that it had touted for so long as the reason why it had the best product were no longer important? Thus, given the choice of stripping off features that were the basis of the incumbents' competitive advantage and those that were not, a LIMI innovator is better off choosing the former.

Prior Commitments and Fear of Cannibalization Can Handicap Incumbents

An incumbent's prior commitments to coopetitors can also prevent it from pursuing a LIMI. For example, if a firm has a commitment to supply its customers with a product that has certain attributes, building another product that strips off some attributes may not be as profitable for the firm. Some incumbents may also refuse to pursue the LIMI for fear of cannibalizing an existing product.

Resources and System of Activities Underpin Both Low-Cost and Differentiation

In developing and exploiting a LIMI, the system of activities and associated resources/capabilities that an innovator builds are consistent with both differentiation *and* low-cost. This makes it difficult for potential competitors whose activities and resources are rooted in differentiation alone or in low-cost alone to move in and compete in the innovator's as yet uncontested market space. An incumbent differentiator that wants to also become a low-cost producer, is likely to get stuck in the middle—as neither a low-cost producer nor a product differentiator—as it struggles with its established ways of doing things, and the new game that has to be played to offer serious competition for the LIMI.[8]

Counter to Conventional Wisdom

LIMIs are usually counter to conventional wisdom, especially the dominant managerial logic of the industry. To many managers, especially those whose dominant logic is embedded in the industry ethos of *more is better*, LIMIs are a tough sell.[9] That is wonderful news to LIMI innovators since they have enough time to build first-mover advantages and perform other profitable activities before many MIBI managers accept the reality of LIMIs and move into the uncontested space.

Likely to Have Disruptive Component

A LIMI's uncontested market can be the starting point for a LIMI innovator to launch attacks on neighboring markets. LIMIs have some of the characteristics of disruptive technologies. A LIMI is low cost, addresses a new market, and, because its attributes have been stripped off or de-emphasized, may be considered as having inferior performance relative to the old product. If the LIMI's performance improves enough, it may disrupt the established market.

Disadvantages of LIMIs

The biggest disadvantage for LIMIs is that a competitive advantage from them is more difficult to sustain. As explained above, incumbents have three problems that can handicap them when they want to imitate a LIMI innovator: their dominant managerial logic, difficult-to-change prior commitments, and the fear of cannibalizing existing products. However, once they overcome these hurdles, many incumbents can easily strip off product features or de-emphasize them to deliver a LIMI, if and when they decide to do so. More importantly, there is little room for LIMIs to "grow." In traditional more-is-better innovations, many firms grow by improving or adding new product features. LIMIs go in the reverse direction—they strip off or de-emphasize product attributes. Because there is only that much that a firm can strip off or de-emphasize before a product ends up with no desirable attributes, there may not be enough room to grow in the reverse direction. Effectively, it is difficult to grow a LIMI business since growing may mean having to start improving and/or adding product attributes after making a living by de-emphasizing or stripping them off. An alternate growth path is a run strategy in different markets. That is, a firm offers a LIMI in one market, and before competitors have had a chance to imitate it, the firm has moved on to another market and introduced a different LIMI, and so on.

LIMIS AND MORE-IS-BETTER (MIBIS)

As noted earlier, LIMIs are not really new. Witness the founding of the fast-food industry by McDonald's. The question is: Why might one expect LIMIs to be more important now? Before we answer this question, let us first see why more-is-better innovations (MIBIs) have dominated the business landscape for such a long time.

Dominance of the More-is-Better Paradigm

If LIMIs have such profound strategic advantages, why haven't we seen more of them over the years? One reason is that the more-is-better paradigm has also had a lot going for it. When a product is invented, it usually starts out relatively simple. As producers learn more about the technologies that underpin the product, they are able to improve the product's features and, in the case of many high-tech products, reduce the cost. Because it often costs too much to find out the unique needs of each and every customer, and produce a unique product for each customer, firms often resort to developing newer and improved versions of products hoping to meet the needs of some new customers while keeping existing ones happy.

Each new version adds new features to those of the previous version and/or improves existing features. Often, adding features or improving existing ones also adds complexity. The higher prices from the improved or added features of each new version become factored into each firm's expected earnings and stock analysts' expectations. Over time, managers' beliefs about how to make money in the industry become engrained in the more-is-better thinking. Besides, not knowing any better, many customers have gone with the flow, paying more for features that they do not need. How many of the features in the car or software that you use do you really need? How many of the tests that doctors order for their patients are really needed?

Why the Timing is Right for LIMIs

For several reasons, however, the more-is-better ethos may be hitting some turbulence, and providing opportunities for profitable LIMI business models. First, after years of added features or improved attributes, many products have become too complex, and sometimes too costly for the value they deliver. A look under the hoods of a 1970s car and a 2010s car clearly contrasts the complexity of the 2010 car from the simplicity of its predecessor. What is more is that not everyone needs all the features that the complexity under the hood provides. This situation is not limited to cars. The average person uses less than 10 percent of the features provided in software packages such as word processors. Besides, we are constantly bombarded with lots of information. Many of us would prefer not to have to deal with unnecessary complexity from products. Not everyone wants all the perfumes and other additives in detergents or soaps that have little or nothing to do with cleaning.

Second, not only are many products too complex, they often overshoot demand characteristics. For example, many people do not need the maximum speed or rapid acceleration that their cars come with; but these features are bundled with others and the buyer has to pay for all of them, whether s/he likes everything in the bundle or not. Third, technological innovation has enabled firms to introduce new products from Netbook computers that cost less than $300 to Tata Motors' $2,500 car to international phone calls that cost a few cents a minute to free searches on the Internet. As these ultra low-cost and yet valuable products/services proliferate, customers expect and often demand that high-priced products follow suit and offer LIMI-type products.

Fourth, there is the so-called bottom of the pyramid market—the billions of very low-income people whose collective buying power can be significant. Simple low-cost products may be just what these people and their economies need. There are enough such people to offer the type of scale that is needed to keep the cost very low for some products. Fifth, the rich have also gotten so rich and the prices of some LIMIs become so low that some of the rich can afford to add LIMI products to their bag of products even when they already have MIBI products. Many people own a notebook, netbook, iPod, iPad, a cell phone, two desktop PCs, and much more, despite the fact that some of these are LIMIs of others.

Sixth, innovations that start out in developing countries and make their way to developed countries—instead of the other way around—are usually low-cost and are growing in number. (These products have been called reverse innovations.[10]) They introduce low-cost competition and incumbent firms in developed countries have to defend their market positions by developing LIMIs. Seventh, the proliferation of different product platforms sometimes entails taking an existing product and reconfiguring its components and their linkages to better fit the new environment. For example, in porting its Windows operating system to cell phones and netbook PCs, Microsoft had to strip off some of the features of the system so as to fit it on to the new platforms. Other examples include porting products from a developed country to an under-developed one, and from the office or home to "the road" such as handheld devices. Finally, information and communications technologies such as the Internet and cell phones have made it possible for firms to better find out what customers want and therefore give them something closer to what they want, not much more. This makes it more possible to strip off what customers do not want or add just what they need.

LIMIS AND BUSINESS MODELS

Given the advantages of LIMIs and the fact that the environment is becoming more and more conducive for them, the question becomes, how can a firm gain a competitive advantage using LIMIs? That is, how can a firm earn a higher-than-average rate of profitability in the markets in which it chooses to compete with LIMIs? Answer: By exploiting the advantages of LIMIs in its business model. We touch on the influence of some of these LIMI advantages on each component of a business model.

Customer Value Proposition

The customer value proposition from a LIMI is obvious: a simpler product/service with de-emphasized or stripped-off attributes, lower cost, and maybe attributes that customers might not have expected. If the LIMI is a product that exhibits network effects, the many users who buy the simple low-cost product can quickly build a large network that will make the product more valuable to each user. A simplified product can also mean better reliability and ease of repair. In some villages in developing countries, LIMI motorcycles are used as dependable low-cost transportation, and are so simple and easy to repair that most owner-operators can maintain their own motorcycles.

Market Segments

Four types of customers are likely to gravitate towards the LIMI: customers who hated the attributes that have been stripped off or de-emphasized, those who like the lower cost, those who like the simplicity, and those who like any new unexpected attributes that may have been added to the product/service. The LIMI is likely to create a temporary uncontested market—a blue ocean—in which the LIMI innovator can make money until competitors move. How long the innovator's monopoly profits last depends on the competitive environment and whether the innovator is able to build first-mover advantages.

Revenue Model

Recall the Xerox 914 example in which the business model was very profitable because Xerox leased the machines.[11] Each machine was too expensive to be sold outright. As the price of a LIMI drops, there may be less of a need to pursue a lease revenue model since more people can afford to pay for it upfront. More importantly, in developing countries where few or no credit histories exist for citizens, prepaid revenue models make even more sense with LIMIs since their prices are more affordable.

Growth Model

Recall that to grow profitably, firms usually pursue some combination of three strategies: block, run (innovate), and team up, while also keeping an eye out on the cost structure. In a *run* strategy, an innovator stays ahead of competitors by innovating and moving on to another innovation before imitators have had a chance to imitate it.[12] The problem with a LIMI strategy is that it quickly becomes difficult to keep stripping off or de-emphasizing product characteristics to deliver new products, without moving to other industries. Improving product attributes, as most innovators do, means going back to where it all started: complex products with many attributes. Thus, to grow, a LIMI innovator may have to move to different products/services rather than staying with the same product/service and improving its attributes. More importantly, innovation does not have to be only in new products to be profitable. A firm can innovate in any of the other components of its business model.

With LIMIs, an innovator can block by preemptively acquiring first-mover advantages while incumbents are still struggling with the hurdles posed by the LIMIs. These first-mover advantages can constitute barriers-to-entry to keep out imitators from a LIMI innovator's uncontested market space, or delay their entry. In a *team-up* strategy, an innovator welcomes co-opetitors into its market space and cooperates with them to create and capture value. A LIMI innovator can team up with incumbents who often have valuable rare complementary assets to better appropriate the value from the LIMI.

Capabilities

Recall that capabilities are resources and the activities that are used to build resources and/or use them to create and capture value. Also recall that complementary assets/capabilities are often critical to profiting from an innovation. Although stripping off a product's attributes or de-emphasizing them can be more difficult than it appears, LIMIs are ultimately imitable. Therefore, valuable, rare, complementary capabilities can be even more important to profiting from a LIMI than they usually are. Any activities that help a LIMI innovator acquire first-mover advantages can also be critical.

RELATIONSHIP BETWEEN LIMIS AND OTHER RECENT CONCEPTS

Less-is-more innovations (LIMIs) are closely related to four other concepts: blue ocean strategy, disruptive technologies, reverse positioning, and reverse innovations. We now explore the relationship between LIMIs and these other phenomena.

Blue Ocean Strategy

Professors W. Chan Kim and Reneé Mauborgne of INSEAD coined the phrase "blue ocean strategy" to describe a strategy with the following characteristics.[13] First, the system of activities that is performed in the strategy is aligned with and is consistent with both differentiation and low cost. This contrasts with the argument that because of the trade-offs that firms have to make in choosing which activities to perform and which ones not to perform, it is difficult to profitably pursue a system of activities that is consistent with both low cost and differentiation.[14] Trying to pursue a system of activities that supports both low-cost and differentiated products/services, so the argument goes, is likely to result in a situation where the firm is stuck in the middle —the firm ends up being neither a differentiator nor a low-cost firm. Blue ocean strategy is about profitably pursuing low cost and differentiation without being stuck in the middle.

Second, the system of activities of a blue ocean strategy lands a firm in an uncontested market where there is no competition. Thus the firm can collect monopoly rents. Third, the firm is effectively creating demand and is the only one that can supply what is needed to meet demand. The result can be lots of profits. Professors Kim and Mauborgne contrast their blue ocean idea with what they call a red ocean strategy. In a red ocean strategy, a firm's system of activities is aligned with either differentiation or low cost, but not both as in the blue ocean strategy. Moreover, no new demand is created and the firm has to battle with its competitors for a share of the existing demand, thereby making little or no money. Competition is rife.[15]

The system of activities that underpins a blue ocean product is similar to that which underpins a LIMI. In a LIMI, the system of activities is consistent with both differentiation *and* low cost, lands a firm in an uncontested market space where the firm can enjoy monopoly power/rents, creates and captures demand, and so on. The main difference lies in the fact that in LIMIs, the uncontested market is only temporary and the firm must contend with competition sooner or later. The more first-mover advantages that the LIMI innovator can build the better would be its chances of delaying competition. The blue ocean strategy assumes that competitors will not enter the uncontested market, while the LIMI strategy assumes that it is only a question of time before competitors move into the uncontested space.

Disruptive Technologies

Recall that, according to Professor Clayton Christensen, a disruptive technology starts out addressing a new market, is low cost, and its performance is initially inferior to that of the established technology but keeps improving.[16] Eventually, the disruptive technology improves well enough to move from the new market to the established one where it disrupts incumbents' competitive advantages, eventually rendering incumbents' products noncompetitive. LIMIs are also low cost, address a new market, and their performance is usually less than that of the established product since it is obtained by stripping off or de-emphasizing the attributes of the established product. However, there is an important difference: a LIMI does not have to go on and disrupt the established market. Many LIMIs stay in the new market and perform well financially while established firms in the established market do very well too. McDonald's and Burger King did not wipe out traditional dining. Both fast-food chains and traditional dining have been doing very well, despite the fact that the two restaurant chains were very good examples of LIMIs.

Reverse Positioning

The concept of *reverse positioning* strategy was proposed by Professor Youngme Moon of the Harvard Business School as one of three strategies to "break free" from the constraints of a product life cycle.[17] In a breakaway positioning, according to Professor Moon, a firm associates a new product with a radically different product category. For example, when Swatch introduced its watches, it marketed them as fashion accessories and not the jewelry that fine crafted watches had always been associated with. In a stealth positioning strategy, a firm takes a product from a category where customers resist the product to one where it is a less intimidating technology. Finally, in *reverse positioning*, a firm strips off some of a product's attributes that have come to be regarded as sacred cows *and* at the same time, adds new attributes that may not have been expected by customers. Thus, the concept of reverse positioning is very similar to that of LIMIs. The only difference is that a LIMI does not have to have new unexpected attributes but in reverse positioning, the product has to have them.

Reverse Innovations

According to Professors Vijay Govindarajan and Chris Trimble of the Tuck School of Dartmouth College, a reverse innovation is one that starts out in an emerging economy and makes its way to the developed world. These innovations are called reverse because of the direction—they reverse the tradition of innovations being developed in advanced countries and then moving to emerging economies. Defined this way, reverse innovations may be LIMIs but do not have to be. LIMIs can start from anywhere in the world. There is another definition of reverse innovation where "reverse" means going in the reverse direction of technological progress. For example, using old motorcycle technologies to design simple, low-cost motorcycles for Africa.[18] This latter definition of a reverse innovation is more similar to LIMIs than the former.

LIMIs at the Center

As shown in Figure 6.3, LIMIs are the common factor between blue ocean strategies, disruptive technologies, reverse positioning, and reverse innovations.

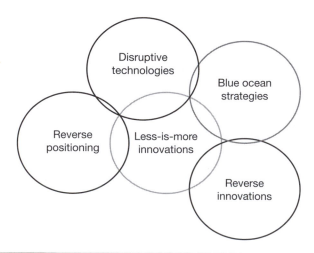

Figure 6.3 Less-is-more innovations (LIMIs) as the common factor

KEY TAKEAWAYS

- Less-is-more innovations (LIMIs) have four distinguishing features:
  - Some of the attributes of an older product are stripped off or de-emphasized to get them.
  - The resulting product is simpler than previous ones.
  - They have lower costs than predecessor products in the market.
  - They *may* have new unexpected features.

- LIMIs have strategic advantages, some of which may not be expected:
  - They can be easier to design and make, and may be more reliable.
  - Initially, they are in an uncontested market space and therefore have no head-to-head competition.
  - Once in the uncontested space, LIMI owners can build first-mover advantages.
  - Because they are lower cost, LIMIs can be seen by some customers as a second product to have (second to the established product).
  - LIMIs can be disabling to incumbents whose competitive advantage rested in the attributes that have been stripped off or deemphasized.
  - The system of activities that a LIMI innovator performs supports both differentiation and low cost, making LIMIs more difficult for incumbents to imitate.
  - Incumbents' prior commitments and fear of cannibalizing existing products can prevent them from entering a LIMI innovator's uncontested market space.
  - The idea of getting a new product by stripping off or de-emphasizing key attributes that customers have come to expect can be counter-intuitive.
  - Some LIMIs end up going on to disrupt the established market.

- LIMIs also have disadvantages. It is difficult to grow a LIMI business since growing may mean having to start improving and/or adding product attributes after making a living by de-emphasizing or stripping them off.

- For years, more-is-better innovations (MIBIs) dominated. However, the fact that products have become too complex and there are many customers who need simpler products and cannot afford the complex ones have increased the opportunities for less-is-more innovations (LIMIs).

- Ultimately, to make money from a LIMI, a firm needs the right business model. A LIMI innovator must have the right customer value proposition, market segments, revenue models, growth model, and capabilities if it is going to make money.

- To sustain profits long-term, a LIMI innovator may have to adopt a run strategy in which it offers LIMIs in different industries and before competitors enter the uncontested market space attained using a LIMI, the innovator has moved on to another market.

- There are some subtle differences between LIMIs and the blue ocean strategy, disruptive technologies, reverse positioning, and reverse innovations. However, the key thing is that LIMIs are the link between these other phenomena.

NOTES

1 Frucci, A. (2010, January 27). 8 Things that suck about the iPad. Retrieved April 3, 2010, from http://gizmodo.com/5458382/8-things-that-suck-about-the-ipad. See also, Stein, S. (2010). 10 things Netbooks still do better than an iPad. Retrieved April 3, 2010, from http://news.cnet.com/8301-17938_105-10443246. Mossberg, W. S. (2010, March 31). Apple iPad Review: Laptop killer? Pretty close. All things digital. Retrieved April 3, 2010, from http://ptech.allthingsd.com/20100331/apple-ipad-review

2 For a similar idea called reverse positioning, see Moon, Y. (2005). Break free from the product life cycle. *Harvard Business Review, 83*(5), 86–94.

3 Pogue, D. (2010, March 31). Reviews: Love it or not? Looking at the iPad from two angles. Retrieved May 9, 2010, from www.nytimes.com/2010/04/01/technology/personaltech/01pogue.html.

4 Naughton, K. (2008, February 25). Small, it's the new big. Retrieved April 3, 2010, from www.newsweek.com/id/112729/page/1

5 Moon, Y. (2005). Break free from the product life cycle. *Harvard Business Review, 83*(5), 86–94.

6 Kim, W. C., & Mauborgne, R. (2005). *Blue Ocean Strategy*. New York: Harvard Business School Press.

7 Lieberman, M. B., & Montgomery, D. B. (1998). First-mover (dis)advantages: Retrospective and link with the resource-based view. *Strategic Management Journal, 19*(12), 1111–1125. Suarez, F., & Lanzolla, G. (2007). The role of environmental dynamics in building a first mover advantage theory. *Academy of Management Review, 32*(2), 377–392.

8 Porter, M. E. (1996). What is strategy? *Harvard Business Review, 74*(6), 61–78.

9 Bettis, R. A., & Prahalad, C. K. (1995). The dominant logic: Retrospective and extension. *Strategic Management Journal, 16*(1), 5–14. Tripsas, M., & Gavetti, G. (2000). Capabilities, cognition, and inertia: Evidence from digital imaging. *Strategic Management Journal, 21*(10–11), 1147–1161.

10 Govindarajan, V., & Timble, C. (2012). *Reverse Innovation: Create Far from Home, Win Everywhere*. Boston, MA: Harvard Business School Press.

11 Chesbrough, H. W., & Rosenbloom, R. S. (2002). The role of the business model in capturing value from innovation: Evidence from Xerox Corporation's technology spinoff companies. *Industrial and Corporate Change, 11*(3), 533–534.

12 Afuah, A. N. (2003). *Innovation Management: Strategies, Implementation, and Profits*. Oxford University Press: New York. Afuah, A. N. (1999). Strategies to turn adversity into profits. *Sloan Management Review, 40*(2), 99–109.

13 Kim, W. C., & Mauborgne, R. (2005). *Blue Ocean Strategy*. New York: Harvard Business School Press.

14 Porter, M. E. (1996). What is Strategy? *Harvard Business Review, 74*(6), 61–78.

15 Wiggins, R. R., & Ruefli, T. W. (2005). Schumpeter's ghost: Is hypercompetition making the best of times shorter? *Strategic Management Journal, 26*(10), 887–911. Chen M-J., Lin, H-C., & Michel, J. G. (2010). Navigating in a hypercompetitive environment: The roles of action aggressiveness and TMT integration. *Strategic Management Journal, 31*(13), 1410–1430. Makadok, R. (1998). Can first-mover and early-mover advantages be sustained in an industry with low barriers to entry/imitation? *Strategic Management Journal, 19*(7), 683-696. Vaaler, P. M. (2008). Are technology-intensive industries more dynamically competitive? No and Yes. *Organization Science, 21*(1), 271–289.

16 Christensen, C. M., & Raynor, M. (2003). *The Innovator's Solution*. Boston, MA: Harvard Business School Press.

17 Moon, Y. (2005). Break free from the product life cycle. *Harvard Business Review, 83*(5), 86–94.

18 Afuah, A. N. (2013). Competitive advantage from reverse innovations. Working paper, Ross School of Business at the University of Michigan.

7

DISRUPTIVE TECHNOLOGIES

Reading this chapter should provide you with the conceptual and analytical tools to:

- Explain what disruptive technologies are all about.
- Understand what makes some technologies more disruptive than others and why that matters.
- Explain how incumbents can tell when to expect new technologies to erode their competitive advantages.
- Explain why incumbents, even very successful ones, often lose out to attackers that use disruptive technologies.
- Begin to appreciate the importance of disruptive technologies to economies.

INTRODUCTION

In 2007, millions of people could make *free* high-quality international phone calls, something that had been unheard of only a decade earlier. One major reason for these free calls was voice-over Internet protocol (VOIP) technology—a technology for routing phone calls over free Internet networks. VOIP threatened the very future of the telephone business as the traditional phone companies had come to know it. To many of these traditional phone companies, VOIP represented a threat. To new start-ups such as Skype, VOIP was a great opportunity. This phenomenon in which existing business models are threatened and often rendered obsolete by a new technology is nothing new. Electric refrigerators replaced kerosene refrigerators, which had replaced hauled ice as a means of keeping foods and medicines cold. PCs replaced mainframe and minicomputers. Internal combustion engine automobiles replaced horse-driven carts. iPods and other MP3 players replaced Walkmans, flat-panel displays displaced cathode ray tube (CRT) displays, and online auctions replaced offline auctions. In some instances, such as the case of contact lenses and eye glasses, the displacements were only partial. As the partial listing of Table 7.1 suggests, the list of such displacements is long.

Table 7.1 The new replacing the old: a partial list

Today's technology	Ancestral technologies
Airplanes	Sail boats, steam boats, trains
Automobiles	Horse-driven carts
Computers	Spike abacus, Slide rules
Contact lenses	Eye glasses
Cotton, silk, polyester, nylon	Grass, bark, animal hides
Digital audio player (MP3)	Record player, eight track, cassette tape, compact disc
Digital photography	Artists, film-based photography
Discount brokers	Traditional brokers
Digital video disk (DVD)	Veneer records, magnetic tapes, compact discs
Electric and gas stoves	Firewood cooking spaces
Electricity	Whale oil (for lighting), wood, coal, gas
Electronic banking	Brick-and-mortar-based banking
Flat-panel displays	Cathode ray tube (CRT) for computer screens, TVs, etc.
Genetically engineered insulin	Pig pancreas-derived insulin
Indoor plumbing	Outdoor services
International ATMs	Traveler's checks
Internet radio TV	Radio, TV
iPod	Walkman
Jet engines	Propeller engine
Mechanical cash registers	Electronic point of sale registers
Money and financial services	Barter system
PCs	Minicomputers
Refrigeration	Hauled ice
Small Japanese cars	Large American cars
Steel	Brick and stone
Telephone	Smoke signals, drums, people, telex
Electronic watches	Mechanical watches

Effectively, almost every product we use today is the result of technological innovation. Additionally, each innovation has created opportunities for some companies and threats for others. One of the first things that business scholars observed about these technological changes in which new technologies displaced established ones was that many incumbents were displaced by new entrants. (Incumbents in the face of a technological change are firms that offered products using the established technology before the new technology was introduced.) For example, the major players in personal computers today were neither major players in mainframes nor in minicomputers. This observation by business scholars raised some interesting questions:

1. How can incumbents tell when to expect innovations that stand to erode their competitive advantages? Knowing when to expect these innovations would help firms to better strategize.
2. Why is it that incumbents (some of them very successful) often lose out during these technological changes? Just what type of changes are these?
3. What can these incumbents do to better profit from such changes?
4. What should new entrants do to be successful? (After all, not all new entrants are successful in exploiting disruptive technologies.)
5. What is the impact of disruptive technologies on economies?

In this chapter, we explore these questions. In particular, we explore Foster's S-curve and Christensen's disruptive technologies models. We then integrate the results from these models with the concepts of business model innovation that we have seen so far to present more complete answers to the five questions raised above. Throughout this chapter, we will use the words "product" and "technology" interchangeably although they are not always the same. For example, we will talk of the PC as being a disruptive technology when we really mean the technologies that go into making a PC.

FOSTER'S S-CURVE

Managers were interested in the first question—how can incumbents tell when to expect innovations that stand to erode their competitive advantages—for obvious reasons. If they could tell, *ex ante*, when to expect these disruptive technologies, managers would be better prepared for them and might even prevent new entrants from eroding their firm's competitive advantages. One of the first business scholars to explore this question was Dr. Richard Foster of McKinsey.[1] He argued that a firm is able to predict when it has reached the limit of its technology life cycle (and therefore can expect a radical technological change) using knowledge of the technology's physical limits.[2] Effectively, by observing the evolution of an established technology, a firm can tell—using the characteristics of the technology—when a new radical technology is around the corner about to displace the established technology.

One way to model this evolution is through what would later be known as Foster's S-curve. In this S-curve, the vertical axis represents the rate of advance of a technology while the horizontal axis captures the amount of effort put into developing the technology (Figure 7.1). Technological progress starts off slowly, then increases very rapidly and then diminishes as the physical limits of the technology are approached. Eventually, diminishing returns set in as the return on efforts becomes extremely small.

A new technology whose underlying physical properties enable it to overcome the physical limit of the established technology must be used if one is to keep meeting the needs of customers. Effectively, when the returns on efforts become very small, that is a signal that a new technology is around the corner. That is especially the case when the rate of progress is not keeping up with demand. Consider, for example, the emission control technology in automobiles. Early in the life of pollution-control technologies, the reductions in emissions were substantial. However, as time went on, the increases in improvement relative to the amount of effort put into development became smaller.

According to Foster's S-curve model of predicting the arrival of new technologies, this low rate of increase in reductions in emission is a signal that other technologies, such as hybrid or electric car technologies, are around the corner as potential replacements for existing internal combustion engine technologies whose physical limits are being reached (Figure 7.1). By the way, a technology S-curve is usually not the same thing as a product S-curve. The vertical axis of the product S-curve is sales while the horizontal axis is time. Moreover, a technology S-curve usually has many product life cycles within it.

As a predictor of when to expect a radical innovation, the S-curve has some limitations. It is difficult to tell exactly when to invest in the new technology and when to drop the established one. It is also difficult to tell just how much better the new technology will be. Moreover, the model does not say much about what managers should do to be able

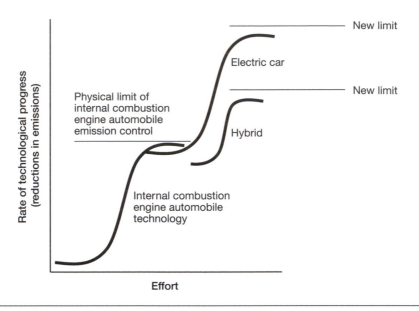

Figure 7.1 S-curves showing physical limits of technologies

to exploit the new technology when they eventually face it. More importantly, the focus of Foster's curve was on "more is better" in which firms pursued technologies to outdo existing product performance characteristics. However, many potentially advantage-eroding technologies are not necessarily those that start out outdoing existing product performance characteristics. The disruptive technologies model and the concepts of this book address these shortcomings.

DISRUPTIVE TECHNOLOGIES: THE PHENOMENOM

The disruptive technologies framework, developed by Professor Clayton Christensen of the Harvard Business School, offered some answers to the first three questions raised earlier: How can incumbents tell when to expect technologies that stand to erode their competitive advantages? Why is it that incumbents often lose out during these technological changes? What can these incumbents do to better profit from such changes?

Characteristics of Disruptive Technologies

Professor Christensen introduced the phrase "disruptive technologies/innovations." These are technologies that exhibit the following three properties.[3]

1. They create new markets by introducing a new kind of product or service. (The dimensions of merit for products in the new market usually are different from those in the established market.)
2. The new product or service costs less than existing products or services, and therefore is priced less.
3. Initially, the new product performs worse than existing products when judged by the performance metrics that mainstream existing customers value. Eventually,

however, the performance catches up and addresses the needs of mainstream customers.

Characteristics of Potentially Displaceable Established Technology

In addition to these characteristics of the disruptive technology, the established technology that potentially could be disrupted also has two important properties:

1. The performance of the established product overshoots demand in the established market. (The product may have too many bells and whistles that customers do not need but are being forced to pay high prices for.)
2. The cost of switching from the old product to the new one is low.

Rationale for Disruption

Why would a technology that exhibits the properties of disruptive technologies outlined above offer an opportunity for new entrants to attack and replace incumbents who have been exploiting an established technology? First, because the technology creates a new market, incumbents who serve the old (mainstream) market are likely to pay attention to meeting the needs of their existing customers (in the old market) and therefore not give the new technology the attention that it deserves. After all, these mainstream customers are the source of the firm's revenues and deserve attention. Moreover, because the performance of products from the new technology is initially inferior to that of existing products and does not meet the needs of customers in the old market, incumbents are even less likely to pay attention to the new technology. And when dimensions of merit in the new market are different from those in the old market, it is even more difficult to give the new technology the attention that it deserves. Sometimes, the "new market" means the least demanding customers of the existing market who are only too happy to use the low-cost product that meets their needs but is perceived as inferior by customers at the high-end of the market. Second, because products from the new technology cost less than established ones and are priced accordingly, incumbents are less likely to pursue the new technology for fear of taking the hit in reduced revenues. It is one thing to cannibalize one's existing products with new ones that bring in about the same revenues, but it is quite another to cannibalize them with products that are priced a lot less. Financial markets do not like drops in revenues.

Third, because the performance of the new products keeps improving, there reaches a time when the new product has improved enough to start meeting the needs of the mainstream customers that incumbents had been serving all along. Some of these customers—especially those who are paying too much for bells and whistles or over-performance that they do not need—switch to the new lower priced products made by the new entrants who have been serving the new market. Many incumbents who now want to start making the new product find out that new entrants are further up the learning curve and perhaps enjoying other first-mover advantages associated with offering the disruptive technology first. Moreover, incumbents' dominant managerial logic in serving the old market, together with the old structures and systems that had been put in place to serve customers in the old market, can become a handicap. These factors increase a new entrant's chances of exploiting the disruptive technology better than an incumbent.

To illustrate these points, consider the invasion of mainframe computers and minicomputers by PCs in the 1980s and 1990s. Mainframes and minicomputers were in the market long before PCs and satisfied the needs of many business customers as far as speed, software and memory capacity were concerned (Figure 7.2). When PCs started out, they were used largely by computer enthusiasts and hobbyists, a new market compared to the business markets served by mainframes and minicomputers. PCs also cost a lot less than mainframes and minicomputers. PCs' performance was also initially inferior to that of mainframes and minicomputers but often more than met the needs of many computer enthusiasts and hobbyists.

As the performance of PCs improved, minicomputer makers kept listening to their customers and offering them the types of minicomputers that they wanted, while not paying enough attention to PCs. Eventually, PC performance improved to a point where it started meeting the needs of some minicomputer customers, and at a much lower price. Understandably, many minicomputer customers switched to PCs. Some minicomputer makers who tried to enter the PC market were handicapped by their dominant managerial logic and the prospects of losing their high-margin, high-revenue minicomputers. Moreover, some PC makers had acquired PC brands and other first-mover advantages and were in a better position to profit from PCs than old minicomputer makers. The result was that, as PCs displaced minicomputers in most applications, new PC makers such as Apple and Dell displaced many of the minicomputer and mainframe makers.

Effectively, according to Professor Christensen, incumbents are usually so busy listening to their customers that they do not pay enough attention to the disruptive technology, which starts out serving the less demanding needs of a new market. Moreover, since the new technology costs less than the established technology, incumbents may be reluctant to suffer the revenue drop that might come with switching to the lower-cost and lower-priced product. Even if incumbents want to switch to the new technology, their established processes, dominant managerial logic, relationships with old mainstream

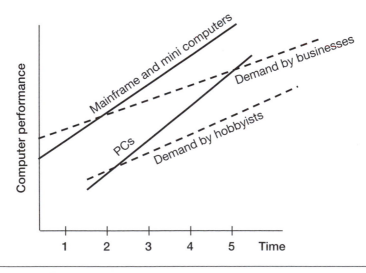

Figure 7.2 PCs versus mainframes and minicomputers

customers and routines may make the transition difficult. Moreover, the new entrants who adopted the technology first may have established first-mover advantages. Table 7.2 provides a list of many technologies that fit the Christensen model of disruptive technologies.

Sustaining Technologies

A *sustaining technology* has the opposite effect on incumbents compared to a disruptive technology in that, rather than displace established products, a sustaining technology is an incremental improvement in established products that helps them get even more entrenched. Sustaining technologies are usually initiated and pursued by incumbents who use them to reinforce their competitive advantages.

Usefulness of Disruptive Technologies Framework for Creating and Appropriating Value

The question is, of what use is the disruptive technologies model in creating and appropriating value? As we pointed out earlier, the model provides answers to three of the questions that we stated at the beginning of this chapter, namely: (1) How can incumbents tell when to expect such innovations that stand to erode their competitive advantages? (2) Why is it that incumbents often lose out during these technological changes? (3) What can these incumbents do to better profit from such changes?

Table 7.2 The disrupted and disruptors?

Disruptor	Disrupted
Compact disc	Cassettes and records
Desktop publishing	Traditional publishing
Digital photography	Chemical film-based photography
Distribution of software by Internet	Distribution through distributors
e-mail	Snail mail
High-speed CMOS video sensors	Photographic film
Hydraulic excavators	Cable-operated excavators
Internet	Electronic data interchange (EDI)
Large-scale Integration (LSI)	Small-scale integration
Minicomputers	Mainframes
Mini-mills for steel	Integrated steel mills
Online auctions	Offline auctions
PCs	Minicomputers
PowerPoint-type software	Drafting software
Small-scale integration	Discrete components
Steam engine, electric motor and internal-combustion engine automobiles	Horse-driven cart
Steamships	Sailing ships
Table-top copiers	Large Xerox-type copiers
Telephone (originally worked for only 3 miles, limited to local phone calls)	Telegraph (Western Union) long distance
Transistor radios	Vacuum tube radio sets
Transistors	Vacuum tubes
Wal-Mart's discount stores in small rural southwestern towns	Discount retailing in cities
Wireless phone service	Fixed-wire phone service

Answering these questions exposes the role of disruptive technologies in creating and appropriating value.

How Can Incumbents Tell When to Expect Such Innovations that Stand to Erode their Competitive Advantages?

The first thing about taking advantage of the opportunities and threats of an environment is to identify them. Because the disruptive technologies model lays out the characteristics of the type of technology that is likely to be disruptive to incumbents down the line and which established technologies risk being displaced, firms can use these characteristics to identify disruptive technologies, *ex ante*. That is, firms can use these characteristics to identify disruptive technologies *before* disruption has taken place. In so doing, incumbents can carefully screen the different innovations that potentially represent a threat or opportunity to their core businesses. New entrants can identify which technologies they can use to invade established or new markets. This can be done by asking the simple questions shown in Table 7.3.

If the answer to all five questions is "Yes," then the technology is potentially disruptive to incumbents of the established market and these incumbents are better off watching out for attackers. For attackers, it means there is a good chance for them not only to dominate the new market but to move into the old market and erode the competitive advantages of incumbents there.

Why is it that Incumbents Often Lose Out in the Face of these Technological Changes?

Professor Christensen argued that two reasons why incumbents often lose out to new entrants in the face of a disruptive technology, are *values* and *processes*. In exploiting an established technology, incumbents usually build resources, processes and values. Processes are "the patterns of interactions, coordination, communication, decision

Table 7.3 To what extent is a technology disruptive to an established technology?

Question	Answer	Example: VOIP vs. old telephone service
Potentially disruptive technology Does the innovation create a new market whose performance requirements are not as demanding as those of the old market?	Yes/No	Yes
Does the innovation cost less than existing products?	Yes/No	Yes
Is the innovation inferior in performance but keeps improving enough to be able to meet performance criteria of the old market?	Yes/No	Yes
Established technology Does the established technology's performance overshoot demand, or are there too many bells and whistles that customers are being forced to pay for?	Yes/No	Yes
Are there little or no switching costs to switching from established technology to disruptive one?	Yes/No	Yes

making employees use to transform resources into products and services of greater worth"[4] while values are "the standards by which employees set priorities that enable them to judge whether an order is attractive or unattractive, whether a customer is more important or less important, whether an idea for a new product is attractive or marginal and so on."[5] Over time, especially if a firm has been successful, these values and processes become embedded in the firm's routines. Managers also develop a dominant logic and cognitive frames.[6] These values, processes, dominant logic, and cognitive frames are strengths when it comes to exploiting established or sustaining technologies, but in the face of some innovations such as disruptive technologies, they can become handicaps.[7]

When a disruptive change or any other innovation comes along and requires different values or processes, the tendency is for the employees to stick with the old routines that have worked before because routines, processes, and values are difficult to change quickly. For example, if employees of an incumbent firm have focused their attention on their existing customers so as to better provide these customers' needs, their values and processes are likely to dictate that they keep their attention on these customers, the sources of their revenues. In so doing, they may miss out on the new market in which the disruptive technology started out. While the technology is gradually getting better, employees in the old market are still paying attention to their dominant customers. By the time that these employees realize that the disruptive technology is now invading their own market, it may be too late to quickly build the new values and processes that are required to exploit the disruptive technology. Effectively, the old values and processes have become handicaps for incumbents. Thus, new entrants, without these old values, processes and dominant managerial logic to handicap them, have a better chance of exploiting the disruptive technology.

What Can these Incumbents Do to Better Profit from Such Changes?

So what should firms do in the face of disruptive innovations? It depends on whether the firm is an incumbent or a new entrant. Professor Christensen suggests several things that incumbents can do to improve their chances.[8]

First, incumbents should convince upper-level management to see the disruptive innovation as a threat to existing core businesses. In so doing, management can commit the types of resources that are needed to tackle the innovation. Since management's instincts are to protect the core businesses that bring in revenues, management is more likely to pay attention to the disruptive innovation when it understands the enormity of the threat that the disruptive innovation possesses to an existing core business.

Second, when funds have been allocated to the innovation and development of products or services is ready to begin, the incumbent should turn over responsibility to an autonomous unit within the firm that can frame the innovation as an opportunity and pursue it as such. By using an autonomous unit, the incumbent can (1) prevent the old processes and values from handicapping the building of the new processes and values that are needed to exploit the innovation, and (2) avoid the dominant managerial logic of the old business, if the autonomous group is staffed with new employees who do not have the old logic. It is also more difficult for political foes from the old business to disrupt the activities of the autonomous unit.

Third, when a product is not yet good enough, the activities to develop the product should be internal and proprietary. When a product becomes good enough and commoditization starts, the incumbent should outsource it. Fourth, firms should organize their business units as a function of the problems that customers want to solve (and associated solutions), rather than by how easy it is to collect data for the company. Paying attention to customers' problems, solutions, and contexts, rather than to the customers themselves, enables a firm to better see other customer's needs and provide them.

The third and fourth items suggested for incumbents also apply to new entrants. In addition, new entrants should go after markets that have been ignored by incumbents first, and then methodically work their way to incumbents' existing markets.

Shortcomings of Disruptive Technologies Model

Like any framework, Christensen's disruptive technologies model has its shortcomings. We explore three of them here: limited coverage, lack of strategy focus, and not enough about profitability.

Limited Coverage

The characteristics of disruptive innovations are important because understanding them enables firms to identify them and pay attention to the threats and opportunities of potential disruptors. However, some innovations that do not meet all three characteristics of disruptive innovations still displace existing products—that is, some innovations that are disruptive in outcome do not meet all the characteristics of disruptive technologies spelled out above. Consider the second property: innovation (new product) costs less than existing ones. Some innovations that start out costing more than existing ones displace the cheaper ones. New pharmaceutical drugs that displace existing ones are a case in point—their initial costs are often higher than those of existing therapies.

Next, consider the third property: innovation starts out with inferior quality (compared to existing products) but keeps improving enough to eventually meet the needs of customers in the old market. Many innovations that start out with superior performance, relative to existing products, still displace the existing products. For example, many medications that start out outperforming existing ones displace their predecessors. Electronic point of sale registers, which displaced mechanical cash registers, were superior in performance to the latter when they started out. Effectively, disruptive innovations, as defined by Christensen's three characteristics, are but only a subset of innovations that can be disruptive. They are an even smaller subset of all innovations. However, the Christensen definition has the advantage that managers can use it, *ex ante*, to tell which innovation will be disruptive and try to do something about it.

Lack of Focus on Strategy: Prescriptions for Managers Are Only About Implementation

The other shortcoming of the disruptive technologies model is that the prescriptions for managers are largely about implementation issues and say very little about the strategy that is being implemented. Recall that, according to Christensen, an incumbent who has a good chance of doing well in the face of a disruptive technology is one who convinces upper-level management to see disruptive technology as a problem, creates an autonomous unit to pursue disruptive technology, develops the product internally when it is still highly differentiated but outsources it when it becomes a commodity, and organizes business units as a function of the problems/solutions that customers want and not as a function of how data is collected. These prescriptions are largely about the organizational structure, systems, and people—the cornerstones of strategy *implemen-*

tation. There is very little about the set of activities of the value chain, value network, or value shop that need to be performed to create and capture value, and when and how these activities should be performed. The prescriptions are also designed largely for incumbent firms, with very little about what a new entrant could do to have a competitive advantage. After all, not all attackers win.

Not Enough about Capturing Value

The primary emphasis of the disruptive technology model is on using the technology to develop products that customers find valuable. Emphasis is on getting the technology right—that is, developing superior products—and very little on capturing value. However, capturing value often takes a lot more than developing superior products. Not only are complementary assets often critical to profiting from a new technology, a firm's position vis-à-vis its coopetitors, its pricing strategy, the extent to which the technology can be imitated, the number and quality of customers, growth strategy, and the sources of revenues can also be critical. In short, the disruptive technologies model is largely about a few components of a business model (customer value proposition and part of capabilities) but leaves out quite a few others (market segments, revenue models, growth model, and a large part of capabilities). These shortcomings can be eliminated by looking at disruptive technologies as part of business model innovations.

THE ROLE OF BUSINESS MODELS IN PROFITING FROM DISRUPTIVE TECHNOLOGIES

What is the role of a business model in profiting from a disruptive technology? To answer this question, we compare incumbent and new entrant business models using the VARIM framework.

Value: Whose business model is more likely to offer benefits that customers perceive as valuable to them?

By definition, a disruptive technology usually starts out serving a new market with an inferior product relative to incumbents' mainstream products. The disruptive product, which keeps improving, costs less than existing products. Thus, for two reasons, an incumbent who has been selling high-performance products at high prices to valued customers may not be able to offer the type of benefits that meet customer needs in the new market. First, firms are usually advised to listen to their customers. Therefore, if a firm's customers want superior products and pay high prices for them, managers are likely to focus on giving these customers what they want. An inferior product is not what the firm's customers want. Therefore, incumbents are less likely to invest in disruptive technologies than new entrants. Second, to profitably sell a product at low prices, a firm needs to have a low-cost structure. Firms that sell differentiated products at high prices usually have high-cost structures and find it difficult to change to low-cost structures overnight because of the trade-offs that they had made in building the capabilities to offer differentiated products.[9] Effectively, relationships with customers that were critical to getting customers what they wanted prior to the disruptive change and a cost structure designed to offer expensive products, can now handicap the incumbent's efforts to listen to and address the needs of the new market. Thus, incumbents are less likely to offer benefits that customers value than new entrants.

Adaptability: Whose business model is more cost-effectively reconfigurable or redeployable to offer benefits that customers perceive as valuable to them?

As we saw earlier, an incumbent's old systems and processes that were fine-tuned to its established technologies can be very effective when the firm faces a sustaining technology. However, when the incumbent faces a disruptive technology, the systems and processes can become a handicap to any efforts to create and capture value using the old system in the face of the disruptive technology. That is, an incumbent's systems and processes can be difficult to cost-effectively reconfigure or redeploy to offer benefits that customers in the markets addressed by disruptive technologies perceive as valuable. New entrants, especially start-ups, do not have these legacy systems and processes to handicap them. Therefore, a new entrant's business model is more likely to be cost-effectively reconfigured or redeployed to offer new value than an incumbent's business model.

Rareness: Which firms are more likely to be the only ones that offer the customer benefits, or the ones that offer superior benefits than the other group?

Since, as listed above, incumbents are less likely to invest in a disruptive technology, are handicapped by their prior systems and processes, and their differentiation-intensive cost structures are more difficult to transform into low-cost structures, incumbents are less likely to be the only ones that offer customer benefits, or the ones that offer better benefits than new entrants. That is, new entrants are likely to be the only ones that offer benefits that customers value, or that offer better value than incumbents.

Inimitability: Whose benefits are more difficult for other firms to imitate, substitute, or leapfrog?

Since new entrants are more likely to be the first to pursue disruptive technologies, they have many opportunities to build first-mover advantages, especially in the new market. For example, new entrants who move first can build customer switching costs, preemptively acquire valuable resources in the new market, build brands and trademarks, and so on. Such first mover advantages can reduce imitation. However, moving first also has disadvantages that followers can exploit. For example, first movers usually bear most of the costs of removing marketing and technological uncertainties. Thus, whether benefits from new entrants or incumbents are more difficult to imitate depends on other factors such as first-mover disadvantages and advantages.

Monetization: Which firm makes or stands to make more money from offering the benefits to customers?

Offering customers benefits that they value is a necessary condition for making money. However, it is not a sufficient condition. Making money depends on a host of other factors beyond offering customers benefits that they value. Profiting from disruptive innovations depends on the complementary assets needed, the pricing strategy pursued, the attractiveness of the market segment being addressed, the sources of revenues, how easy it is to imitate the value, and growth strategy pursued (block, run and/or team-up). For example, empirical evidence suggests that if complementary assets are important but tightly held and the disruptive innovation is easy to imitate, the owners of complementary assets make money.[10] Since incumbents often have the complementary assets, they are likely to be the ones that make money in the face of an innovation.

Effectively, whether incumbents or new entrants make more money in the face of a disruptive technology depends on who has the complementary assets, the inimitability of the innovation, and the firm-specific activities that the new entrant or incumbent pursues in its business model to create and capture value.

HOW GAME CHANGING IS A DISRUPTIVE TECHNOLOGY?

In the disruptive technologies framework that we have explored, there are two types of technologies: disruptive and sustaining. One implicit assumption is that within each of these groups, there is homogeneity—that is, all disruptive technologies have the same level of disruptiveness while all sustainable technologies have the same level of sustainability. However, since not all technologies have the same characteristics, we can expect disruptive technologies to differ in their level of disruptiveness. Thus, an interesting question is, how disruptive is a disruptive technology? That is, how game changing is a disruptive technology? In Chapter 1, we explored the extent to which an innovation is game changing, describing innovations as regular, resource-building, position-building, and revolutionary.[11] We can explore the extent to which a disruptive technology is game changing by using a similar framework (Figure 7.3).

The horizontal axis captures the extent to which the disruptive technology renders existing capabilities for offering the new product obsolete (Figure 7.3). The degree to which a disruptive innovation is game changing increases as one moves from the origin of the matrix to the top right corner, with a regular disruptive technology being the least game changing while the revolutionary disruptive technology is the most disruptive.

In revolutionary disruptive technologies, not only is the degree to which incumbents' existing products are rendered non-competitive high, the degree to which their

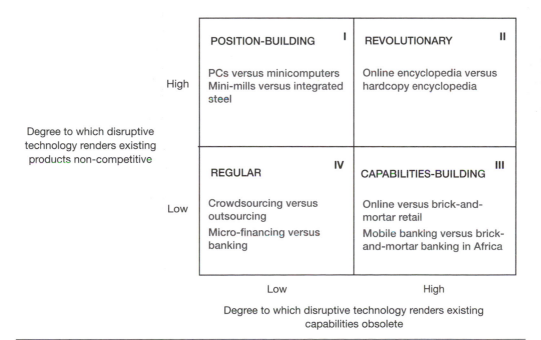

Figure 7.3 Types of disruptive technolgies

capabilities are rendered obsolete is also high. Contrast this with a position-building disruptive technology in which the degree to which incumbents' capabilities are rendered obsolete is low but the degree to which existing products are rendered non-competitive is high. Thus, an incumbent's chances of doing well with position-building disruptive technologies are better than with revolutionary disruptive technologies.

Effectively, such a classification can provide both incumbents and new entrants with useful information as they collect information to decide which disruptive technologies to pursue and which ones not to. The framework can also be used to collect information on competitors and conduct what if analysis during strategic planning.

IMPACT OF DISRUPTIVE TECHNOLOGIES ON ECONOMIES

So far in this chapter, our exploration of disruptive technologies has focused on its impact on firms and their ability to profit from these technologies. However, perhaps the most important thing about disruptive technologies—but the least studied—is its positive impact on economies. For example, a lot has been written about how PCs disrupted minicomputers, how minicomputer makers disappeared, what incumbents can do in the face of disruptive technologies to avoid dying like minicomputer makers, and so on. Little or nothing is said about the positive impact of the PC on world economies. The wealth that PCs have created for users, the productivity increases that stem from the PC, the wealth created for software developers and chip makers, the nonmonetary uses of PCs, and so on, make the loss of a few minicomputer makers trivial.

Disruptive technologies are one of the waves of creative destruction that the economist Joseph Schumpeter preached in his writings.[12] This is *not* to say that focusing research efforts on understanding what incumbents should do to stem erosion of their competitive advantages in the face of disruptive technologies is a bad idea. The point here is that if we understood what the overall impact is on the economy, incumbents might find out that they can create and capture more value somewhere else in the value systems created by disruptive technologies. Some of the best software developers for PCs once worked for minicomputer makers such as Digital Equipment Corporation (DEC) whose demise was spearheaded by the disruptive PC.

It is unfortunate that these technologies are called "disruptive." Perhaps they should be called wealth-creating technologies rather than disruptive technologies.

REVISITING THE QUESTIONS

One way to summarize what we have seen so far is to revisit the questions that were raised at the beginning of this chapter.

How can incumbents tell when to expect innovations that stand to erode their competitive advantages?

As part of monitoring the opportunities and threats of its political, economic, social, technological, and natural (PESTN) environments via, for example, a PESTN analysis, a firm should perform the five-part test of Table 7.3 to determine the extent to which new technologies stand to become disruptive to established technologies. A new technology is potentially disruptive to an established technology if the answers to the questions of Table 7.3 are "Yes." Moreover, by anticipating the likely actions and reactions of coopetitors, a firm may be able to better respond to disruptive technologies since it is monitoring not only the technology but also the actions of firms. A firm is better prepared to cooperate and compete in the face of a disruptive technology if it knows not only about the technology but also about the coopetitors trying to exploit the technology.

Why is it that incumbents (some of them very successful) often lose out in the face of disruptive technologies?

Recall that proponents of the disruptive technologies model argue that incumbents fail because, in trying to get the new technology right, the processes and values that they developed in exploiting the established technology handicap their efforts. The primary goal of actors, according to the model, is in getting the technology right—in developing the type of product that customers, in the new and old markets, want. The business model innovation view maintains that there is more to making money from a new technology than getting the technology right. Thus incumbents can also fail to profit from a disruptive technology if they do not have the right complementary assets, position themselves well vis-à-vis coopetitors, have the wrong pricing strategy, or do not pursue the right sources of revenues in creating and appropriating value. For example, it is widely believed that what killed Kodak was not so much that it did not get out the right digital products, but that it was stuck in its old razor-and-blade revenue model from the chemical/film era—it had the wrong business model.[13] Additionally, a firm may be handicapped by capabilities and product-market-positions that were strengths in the pre-disruptive technology era but that have become handicaps.[14]

What can incumbents do to better profit from disruptive technologies?

The disruptive technologies model argues that an incumbent can improve its performance in exploiting a disruptive technology if it convinces upper-level management to see the technology as a problem, creates an autonomous unit to pursue disruptive technology, develops the product internally when it is still highly differentiated but outsources it when it becomes a commodity, and organizes business units as a function of the problems/solutions that customers want and not as a function of how data are collected. These prescriptions are meant largely to overcome the problems that incumbents face, in trying to develop superior products using the new technology. However, since there is a lot more to profiting from a new technology than getting out the right products, an incumbent not only has to reduce the effects of its handicaps on its ability to get the technology right but also obtain complementary assets, position itself advantageously vis-à-vis its coopetitors, and perform any other activity that will enable it to create and capture value. Note also that incumbents often have at least one advantage over new entrants in the face of a disruptive technology—they usually have complementary assets such as distribution channels, and brands that can be used in exploiting the disruptive technology, especially in the established market. These complementary assets can be used to convince a new entrant, among other things, that has the technology but no complementary assets to team up with the incumbent.

Just as important, incumbents with dynamic capabilities can weather the storm of disruptive technologies much better. For example, according to Dr. Richard Foster of McKinsey and Professor Sarah Kaplan of MIT, the key to the success of incumbents is striking the right balance between knowing what to keep investing in so as to create value, and knowing what to let go, "is the balance they have struck between creativity and destruction—between continuity and change."[15]

What should new entrants do?

Although most research that has explored disruptive technologies has been about their impact on incumbents, most of the value creation and capture activities are among new entrants who enter the new market with inferior low-cost products and work hard to eventually disrupt established markets. The disruptive technology model implies that new entrants should start out by attacking the new market first, reserving entry into the old market for later. New entrants can also exploit the fact that incumbents have handicaps that they do not have. Because many of these start-ups are entrepreneurial organizations, a lot of what we have learnt about entrepreneurship applies to them.[16] For example, entrepreneurs are usually resource strapped but can team up with more established firms with reputations and other resources.[17] Of course, these entrepreneurs have to bring something to the table. Because they are the first to address the needs of the new market in a unique way, entrepreneurs can also build and exploit first-mover advantages. In fact, they can also build and exploit first-mover advantages in the established market since they are the first to offer products at very low prices.

What is the impact of disruptive technologies on economies?

The positive impact of disruptive technologies on wealth creation and overall welfare can be phenomenal. It usually far outstrips the negative impact on the incumbents whose business models are disrupted and go out of business. However, most research has focused on the impact of disruptive technologies on incumbents.

KEY TAKEAWAYS

- Over the years, many new technologies have replaced older ones and in the process, incumbent firms have been replaced. This has raised five questions:
  1. How can incumbents tell when to expect such innovations that stand to erode their competitive advantages?
  2. Why is it that incumbents (some of them very successful) often lose out during these technological innovations?
  3. What can these incumbents do to better profit from such innovations?
  4. What should new entrants do to be successful? After all, not all new entrants do well.
  5. What is the impact of disruptive technologies on economies?

- Foster's S-curve was one of the first models to explore the first question. He argued that a firm can tell that a new technology is about to displace an existing one when the physical limits of the existing technology have been reached— when the returns on efforts become very small.

- According to Professor Christensen, disruptive technologies exhibit the following three characteristics:
  1. They create new markets by introducing a new kind of product or service.
  2. The new product or service costs less than existing products or services, and therefore is priced less.

3. Initially, the new product performs worse than existing products when judged by the performance metrics that mainstream existing customers value. Eventually, however, the performance catches up and addresses the needs of mainstream customers.

- Contrast this with a *sustaining technology* which is an incremental improvement in established products and is often used by incumbents to reinforce their competitive advantages.

- Meanwhile, those established technologies that are prime candidates for disruption usually have products:
  1. Whose performance overshoots demand, with too many bells and whistles that customers are being forced to pay for.
  2. With little or no switching costs for customers.

- The disruptive technologies model was developed by Professor Clayton Christensen and provides some answers to three of the four questions raised:
  1. How can incumbents tell when to expect innovations that stand to erode their competitive advantages? Using the following checklist, a firm can determine, *ex ante*, which technology potentially is likely to disrupt its business models:
     - Does the new technology create a new market whose performance requirements are not as demanding as those of the old market?
     - Does the new technology cost less than existing products?
     - Is the new technology inferior in performance (compared to that of established technology) but keeps improving enough to be able to meet performance criteria of the old market?
     - Does the performance of the established technology overshoot demand?
     - Are the costs of switching from the established technology to the new one low?
  2. Why is it that incumbents (some of them very successful) often lose out in the face of a disruptive technology? Incumbents fail to exploit disruptive technologies because they are handicapped by:
     - Processes developed in exploiting established technology.
     - Values developed in exploiting established technology.
     - Dominant managerial logic and cognitive frames of incumbents.
  3. What can incumbents do to better profit from disruptive technologies? Incumbents can overcome these handicaps by:
     - Convincing upper-level management to see disruptive technology as a problem.
     - Creating autonomous units to pursue disruptive technology.
     - Developing products internally when they are still highly differentiated but outsourcing them when commoditized.
     - Organizing business units as a function of the problems/solutions that customers want.

- Getting the disruptive technology right—that is, developing superior products—does not necessarily mean that a firm will make money from them. Profiting from an innovation requires a business model, of which the product is but a component.

- Some disruptive technologies are more disruptive than others. Therefore, disruptive technologies can be classified as a function of how game changing they are. Doing so provides managers with more strategic information.

- Although research focuses largely on the impact of disruptive technologies on firms and their competitive advantages, their impact on society can be enormous. The welfare gains from disruptive technologies usually far outstrip any loses by incumbents.

KEY TERMS

Disruptive technology	S-curve
Foster's S-curve	Sustaining technology

NOTES

1   Foster, R. (1986). *Innovation: The Attacker's Advantage.* New York: Summit Books.
2   Foster, R. (1986). *Innovation: The Attacker's Advantage.* New York: Summit Books. Utterback, J. M. (1994). *Mastering the Dynamics of Innovation.* Harvard Business School Press, Cambridge, MA. Afuah, A. N., & Utterback, J. M. (1991). The emergence of a new supercomputer architecture. *Technology Forecasting and Social Change,* 40(4), 315–328.
    See also: Constant, E. W. (1980). *The Origins of the Turbojet Revolution.* Baltimore, MD: The Johns Hopkins University Press. Sahal, D. (1985). Technological guideposts and innovation avenues. *Research Policy,* 14(2), 682. Foster, R. N. (1985). *Description of the S-Curve.* Retrieved May 27, 2007, from www.12manage.com/description_s-curve.html
3   Christensen, C. M., & Bower, J. L. (1996). Customer power, strategic investment and failure of leading firms. *Strategic Management Journal,* 17(3), 197–218. Christensen, C. M. (1997). *The Innovator's Dilemma.* Boston, MA: Harvard Business School Press. See also: Christensen, C. M., & Overdorf, M. (2000). Meeting the challenge of disruptive change. *Harvard Business Review,* 78(2), 66–76. Christensen, C. M., & Raynor, M. E. (2003). *The Innovator's Solution.* Boston, MA: Harvard Business School Press. Christensen, C. M., Anthony, S. D., & Roth, E. A. (2004). *Seeing What's Next.* Boston, MA: Harvard Business School Press.
4   Christensen, C. M., & Overdorf, M. (2000). Meeting the challenge of disruptive change. *Harvard Business Review,* 78(2), 68.
5   Christensen, C. M., & Overdorf, M. (2000). Meeting the challenge of disruptive change. *Harvard Business Review,* 78(2), 69.
6   Bettis R. A., & Prahalad, C. K. (1995). The dominant logic: Retrospective and extension. *Strategic Management Journal,* 16(1), 5–14.
7   Tripsas, M. (2009). Technology, identity, and inertia through the lens of "The Digital Photography Company". *Organization Science,* 20(2), 441–460. Tripsas, M., & Gavetti, G. (2000). Capabilities, cognition, and inertia: Evidence from digital imaging. *Strategic Management Journal,* 21(10–11), 1147–1161. Kaplan, S., & Tripsas, M. (2008). Thinking about technology: Applying a cognitive lens to technical change. *Research Policy,* 37(5), 790–805.
8   Christensen, C. M., & Raynor, M. E. (2003). *The Innovator's Solution.* Boston, MA: Harvard Business School Press.
9   Porter, M. E. (1996). What is strategy? *Harvard Business Review.* 74(6), 61–78.
10 Rothaermel, F. T. (2001). Incumbent's advantage through exploiting complementary assets via interfirm cooperation. *Strategic Management Journal,* 22 (6–7), 687–699. Taylor, A., & Helfat, C. E. (2009). Organizational linkages for surviving technological change: Complementary assets, middle management, and ambidexterity. *Organization Science,* 20(4), 718–739. Tripsas, M. (1997). Unraveling the process of creative destruction: complementary assets and incumbent survival in the typesetter industry. *Strategic Management Journal.* 18 (Summer Special Issue), 119–142.

11 Professors Abernathy and Clark's seminal paper also explored a similar classification. However their classification was only about resources—technological and marketing resources—and not about business models as explored in this book. See Abernathy, W. J., & Clark, K. B. (1985). Mapping the winds of creative destruction. *Research Policy*, 14(1), 3–22.

12 Schumpeter J. A. (1950). *Capitalism, Socialism and Democracy* (3rd edn.). Harper: New York. Foster, R. N., & Kaplan, S. (2001). *Creative Destruction: Why Companies that are Built to Last Underperform the Market and How to Successfully Transform Them*. New York: Doubleday/Currency.

13 Tripsas, M. (2009). Technology, identity, and inertia through the lens of "The Digital Photography Company". *Organization Science*, 20(2), 441–460. Tripsas, M., & Gavetti, G. (2000). Capabilities, cognition, and inertia: Evidence from digital imaging. *Strategic Management Journal*, 21(10–11), 1147–1161.

14 Gargiulo, M., & Benassi, M. (2000). Trapped in your own net: Network cohesion, structural holes, and the adaptation of social capital, *Organization Science*, 11(2), 183–196.

15 Foster, R. N., & Kaplan, S. (2001). *Creative Destruction: Why Companies that are Built to Last Underperform the Market and How to Successfully Transform Them*. New York: Doubleday/Currency.

16 Dollinger, M. (2008). *Entrepreneurship: Strategies and Resources* (4th edn.), Lombard, IL: Marsh Publications.

17 Dollinger, M. J., Golden, P. A., & Sazton, P. A. (1997). The effect of reputation on the decision to joint venture. *Strategic Management Journal*, 18(2), 127–140. Stuart T. (2000). Interorganizational alliances and the performance of firms: A study of growth and innovation rates in a high technology industry. *Strategic Management Journal*, 21(8), 791–811.

Part III

Strengths and Weaknesses

8

CAPABILITIES:
THE CORE OF BUSINESS MODELS

Reading this chapter should provide you with the conceptual and analytical tools to:

- Define resources, activities, and capabilities.
- Understand the significance of complementary capabilities in the face of an innovation.
- Understand how to narrow down the list of capabilities.
- Begin to understand the strategic significance of network effects.
- Understand the basic role of resources as a cornerstone of competitive advantage.

INTRODUCTION

In Chapter 1, we established that capabilities—resources and the activities that build and/or transform them into customer benefits and profits—are at the core of a business model. In this chapter, we explore capabilities in more detail. In particular, we explore the critical role that capabilities play in the face of innovations, including business model innovations.

CAPABILITIES: A DEFINITION

Capabilities are the core of value creation and capture. Capabilities are made up of resources and activities. Resources are what a firm *owns* or *has access* to, while activities are what it *does* to build resources or transform them into customer benefits and profits. A pharmaceutical company's capabilities include not only the patents that it owns and the distribution channels that it has access to, but they also include the activities–such as R&D, manufacturing, and marketing—that the firm performs to win more patents and transform knowledge from the patents into medicines that doctors and patients want.

Resources
Resources can be classified as tangible, intangible, or organizational.[1] *Tangible resources* are the resources that are usually identified and accounted for in financial statements

under the category "assets." They can be physical, such as plants and equipment, or financial such as cash. *Intangible resources* are the nonphysical and nonfinancial assets such as patents, copyrights, brand-name reputation, trade secrets, research findings, and relationships that are not accounted for in financial statements and cannot be physically touched.[2] Although intangible resources are usually not identified in financial statements, they can be excellent sources of profits. For example, a patent, copyright, or trade secret that enables a firm to occupy a unique product space and therefore earn monopoly rents is not listed as an asset in financial statements. Important drug discoveries in the pharmaceutical industry, especially in the US where patented drugs enjoy intellectual property protection, often earn companies billions of dollars. Intangible resources are also referred to as *intangible assets* or just *intangibles. Organizational* resources consist of the know-how and knowledge embodied in employees as well as the routines, processes, and culture that are embedded in the organization.

Resources can be critical to creating and capturing value, especially in the face of an innovation. For example, to build and profit from its A380—the world's largest airplane—Airbus needed sophisticated computer-aided tools, skilled engineers, huge assembly plants, logistics systems, relationships with coopetitors, and financing. Behind Google's financial success were skills and know-how in software and computer engineering, patents, trademarks, trade secrets, banks of servers, the Google brand, equipment, and other resources without which the relevant searches and the firm's ability to monetize the searches would not be possible. To make its cola drinks readily available to customers whenever they wanted them, Coca-Cola needed shelf space at its distributors and contracts with its bottlers.

Activities

Although resources are critical to value creation and capture (appropriation), resources in and of themselves are not enough to make money. A firm also needs to perform the activities to build and/or transform resources into customer benefits and profits.[3] Customers are not likely to scramble to a firm's doors because the firm has modern plants, geniuses, and patents. The firm has to use the plants, geniuses and the knowledge and protections embodied in the patents to offer customers benefits that they value. Patients do not buy patents or skilled scientists from pharmaceutical companies; they buy medicines that have been developed, manufactured, approved, and marketed. Patents help give firms monopoly power over the patent life of the drug so that the firm can make larger profits to recoup its R&D costs. To be successful with the A380, Airbus had to finance and perform the complex R&D needed to produce a safe and profitable airplane. It also had to manufacture and market the plane. Effectively, a firm must perform a series of activities to build and/or transform resources into benefits that customers want and capture the value created.

The degree to which a firm is successful in building new resources and/or creating and capturing value is a function of *which* activities it performs, *when* it performs them, *where* it performs them, and *how* it performs them.[4] The choice of *which* activities to perform and the associated trade-offs is critical.[5] For example, by leasing rather than selling its innovative Xerox 914 copiers, Xerox was able to make a lot of money on a copier that some of the best minds in consulting at the time had predicted was doomed to failure.[6] On the *when* side, in the face of technological innovation, not going first— that is, being a follower—has the advantage that many marketing and technological uncertainties are resolved before followers move in. However, being a follower also has the disadvantage that first-movers can preemptively acquire critical resources. More recent research suggests that crowdsourcing some problems might be the best way to solve them, a reminder about the importance of *where* activities are performed.

Relational Capabilities

The capabilities that a firm uses to create and capture value do not have to be limited to the resources that it owns and/or the activities that it performs. A firm can also count on its relational capabilities.[7] These are capabilities to which a firm has access by virtue of its relationships to its coopetitors. For example, when Apple introduced the iPod, it obtained access to a huge library of songs from record labels by teaming up with them. Coke and Pepsi have access to distribution channels and shelf space by virtue of agreements or contracts with bottlers and distributors. Many pharmaceutical start-ups obtain access to financing, clinical testing, brand name reputations, and distribution by teaming up with established pharmaceutical companies that have these capabilities but need access to the startups' technology. The network effects that a firm enjoys by virtue of being a member of a large network are also relational capabilities. Relational capabilities have also been called social capital. Recall that social capital can be defined as "the sum of the actual and potential resources embedded within, available through, and derived from the network of relationships possessed by an individual or social unit."[8]

CAPABILITIES IN THE FACE OF INNOVATION

Having defined capabilities, we now turn to a central question of this chapter: What is the role of capabilities during value creation and capture (appropriation) in the face of an innovation? Innovation is about doing things differently. More specifically, innovation is about performing new value chain activities, or performing existing value chain activities differently—it is about problem-solving. We can group the capabilities that a firm needs to profit from an innovation into two categories: invention capabilities and complementary capabilities. *Invention capabilities* are those that directly underpin the innovation or new way of doing things. Apple's invention capabilities in its iPad innovation included its design skills, ability to integrate software and hardware, and the intellectual property that underpinned the look-and-feel of its products. *Complementary capabilities*—also called *complementary assets*—are all the other capabilities, beyond invention capabilities, that a firm needs to create and capture value in the face of an innovation. Apple's complementary capabilities for its iPad innovation included its brand, its retail stores, marketing, apps developers, loyal customers, and app store. Effectively, both invention capabilities and complementary capabilities play important roles in a firm's ability to profit from an invention.

Complementary Capabilities

Professor David Teece of the University of California at Berkeley was one of the first business scholars to explore the role of complementary capabilities—which he called complementary assets—in profiting from inventions or discoveries.[9] He was puzzled by why EMI invented the CAT scan—an invention that was so important that Sir Godfrey Hounsfield won the 1979 Nobel Prize in Medicine for its invention—and yet, GE and Siemens, not EMI the inventor, made most of the profits from the invention. He was also puzzled by why RC Cola had invented diet and caffeine-free colas, and yet Coke and Pepsi made most of the profits from the two inventions. Professor Teece argued that to make money from an invention or discovery, two factors are important: complementary capabilities and imitability.

Complementary capabilities, as defined above, are all the other resources, beyond those that underpin the invention or discovery that a firm needs to create and capture value in the face of an innovation. For example, in pursuing its direct-sales and build-to-order innovation activities, Dell needed manufacturing processes that would enable it to manufacture a customer's computer in less than two hours once the order had been received. It also needed good relationships with suppliers who supplied components just-on-time, for example, delivering monitors directly to customers. Later, Dell also needed a brand.

In pursuing direct-to-consumer marketing for its Lipitor, Pfizer also needed a sales force to call on doctors, and manufacturing to produce the drug once doctors started prescribing it. Dell's manufacturing processes, brand, and its supplier relationships were complementary capabilities. So were Pfizer's manufacturing capabilities and sales force.

Imitability

Imitability comes into the profitability picture for the following reason. If an invention or discovery can be imitated, customers may go to competitors rather than the firm, thereby reducing the ability of the firm to capture the value that it created. These two variables—complementary capabilities and imitability—form the basis for the Teece Model, which we now explore.

The Teece Model: The Role of Complementary Capabilities and Imitability[10]

The elements of the Teece Model are shown in Figure 8.1. The vertical axis captures the extent to which an invention or discovery can be imitated, while the horizontal axis captures the extent to which complementary capabilities are scarce and important. When imitability of an invention or discovery is high and complementary capabilities are easily available or unimportant, it is difficult for the inventor (first mover) to make money for a long time (cell I in Figure 8.1). That is, because any potential competitors that want to offer the same customer benefits that the firm offers can easily imitate the invention and find the complementary capabilities needed. A new style of jeans for sale on the Internet is a good example. It is easy to imitate new jeans styles and selling them on the Internet is not unique or distinctive to any one firm. Thus, it is difficult to make money for a long time selling a particular style of jeans on the Internet. Effectively, it is difficult to make money in situations such as cell I.

If, as in cell II, the invention is easy to imitate but complementary capabilities are scarce and important, the owner of the complementary capabilities makes money. That is, because even though competitors can imitate the invention, they cannot easily replicate the complementary capabilities. More importantly, the owner of the important complementary capabilities can easily imitate the invention but its complementary capabilities are difficult to imitate. The invention of CAT scans by EMI falls in this category. The invention was easy to imitate but complementary capabilities such as relationships with hospitals, sales forces, brands, and manufacturing were scarce and important to selling the machines to hospitals. The inventions of diet and caffeine-free

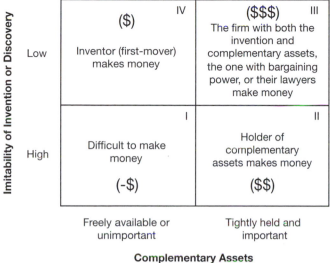

Figure 8.1 The role of complementary capabilities

colas by RC Cola also fall in this category. Both inventions required brand-name reputations, shelf space, marketing, and distribution channels which are important to making money from soft drinks but are tightly held by Coca-Cola and Pepsi. Thus, Coke and Pepsi profited the most from diet and caffeine-free colas. Light beer offers another good example. The Miller Brewing Company and Budweiser did not invent light beer even though they make the most money from it. Light beer was invented by Dr. Joseph Owades at Rheingold Breweries. However, because Miller and Budweiser had the complementary capabilities, they ended up making more money from it than Rheingold.

If imitability of an invention is low and complementary capabilities are important and scarce, one of two things could happen (cell III). If the inventor also has the complementary capabilities, then it stands to make lots of money from its invention. Patented pharmaceutical products in the US are a good example because their intellectual property protection keeps imitability low, and good sales forces, the ability to run clinical tests, and other complementary capabilities that are important to delivering value to customers are scarce. If the firm that has the scarce complementary capabilities is different from the inventor, both firms will make money if they cooperate. If they do not cooperate, their lawyers could make all the money.

Finally, as in cell IV, if imitability of the invention is low but complementary capabilities are freely available or unimportant, the inventor stands to make money (cell IV). Popular copyrighted software that is offered over the Internet would fall in this category since its copyright protects it from imitation and the Internet, as a distribution channel for software, is readily available to software developers and other complementary capabilities are either not scarce or unimportant.

Effectively, firms with scarce and important complementary capabilities are often the ones that profit the most from innovation activities, whether they moved first in performing the innovation activities or were followers. Having important scarce complementary capabilities is one of the hallmarks of exploiters. Microsoft did not invent word processing, spreadsheets, presentation software, windowing operating systems, etc., even though it makes a lot of money from them. Its complementary capabilities—especially its installed base of compatible software and relationships—have been primary drivers of its success.

Strategic Consequences

An important strategy question is: What should a firm do if it found itself in one of the situations depicted in Figure 8.1? For example, what should RC Cola have done to better profit from its invention of Diet Coke, given that the invention was easy to imitate and complementary capabilities were scarce and important? In that case (Figure 8.2, quadrant II), the firm may have been better off teaming up with a partner that had the complementary capabilities. *Teaming up* can be through a joint venture, strategic alliance or a merger through acquisition. If an inventor decides to team up, it may want to do so early before the potential partner with complementary capabilities has had a chance to imitate the invention or come up with something even better. The question is, why would a firm with scarce, valuable complementary capabilities want to team up with an inventor if it knows that it can imitate the invention later? The inventor has to show the owner of the complementary capabilities why it is in their joint interest to team up. For example, RC Cola could have gone to Pepsi and explained that teaming up with it (RC Cola) would allow Pepsi to have a first-mover advantage in diet drinks before Coke and therefore give Pepsi a chance at beating Coke.

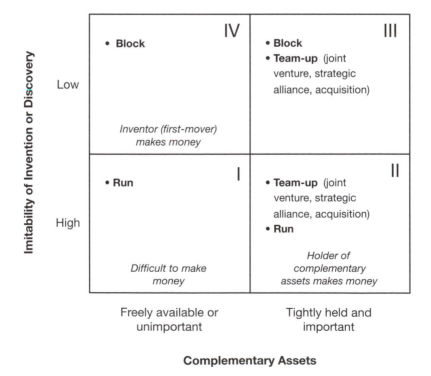

Figure 8.2 Strategies for exploiting complementary capabilities

Effectively, in cell II where an invention is easy to imitate and complementary capabilities are important and scarce, the inventor is better off teaming up with the owner of complementary capabilities through strategic alliances, joint ventures, acquisitions, or other teaming up mechanisms (Figure 8.2).

If an invention is difficult to imitate and complementary capabilities are scarce but important (cell III), the inventor can pursue one of two strategies: block or team up. If the inventor also owns the scarce complementary capabilities, it can block rivals and potential new entrants from having access to either. In a *block* strategy, a firm defends its turf by taking actions to preserve the inimitability of its invention or valuable resources. If another firm (other than the inventor) has the complementary capabilities, both firms can team up using strategic alliances, joint ventures, acquisitions, or other teaming-up mechanisms. In the pharmaceutical industry, for example, many biotechnology start-ups usually develop new drugs whose patents limit imitation. However, many of these start-ups do not have complementary capabilities such as sales/marketing, and the resources needed to carry out the clinical testing that is critical to getting a new drug approved for marketing in the US. Consequently, there is a considerable amount of teaming up between biotech start-ups and the established large pharmaceutical firms that have the complementary capabilities. Many start-ups offer themselves to be bought. If the inventor of a difficult-to-imitate invention and the owner of scarce and important complementary capabilities decide not to cooperate and instead fight, there is a good chance that they will make their lawyers rich—they dissipate rather than create value.

If an invention is difficult to imitate but complementary capabilities are abundant or unimportant (cell IV), a firm may be better off pursuing a block strategy in which it tries to prevent potential competitors from imitating its invention or strategy. If the invention is easy to imitate and complementary capabilities are abundant or unimportant (cell 1), a firm can pursue a so-called run strategy. In a *run* strategy, the inventor or first mover constantly innovates and moves on to the next innovation before competitors imitate its existing innovation activity.

Dynamics

There are two things to note about the strategies of Figure 8.2. First, in practice, many firms pursue at least two of these strategies at any one time. For example, many firms pursue both *block* and *run* strategies at any one time—they defend their intellectual property for an existing product while forging ahead with the next invention to replace the existing product being protected. Second, a firm can sometimes go contrary to what Figure 8.2 suggests so as to lay a foundation for future gains. For example, an inventor may decide to team up in cell IV, rather than block as suggested by the framework, so as to win a standard and block after winning the standard. Intel's case offers a good example of both instances. In the late 1970s and early 1980s, it encouraged other microprocessor makers to copy its microprocessor architecture. When its architecture emerged as the standard for Wintel PCs, Intel started blocking—it decided not to let anyone imitate its technology again and sued anyone who tried to.[11] It also practiced the run strategy by introducing a new microprocessor generation before unit sales of an existing generation peaked. Effectively, Intel teamed up early in the life of its microprocessor to win a standard. After winning the standard, it started blocking and running.

Limitations of the Teece Model

It is important to note that although the complementary capabilities/imitability model can be very useful, it has limitations. Like any model, it makes some simplifying assumptions that may not apply to all contexts all the time. For example, it assumes that the only two variables that underpin profitability are complementary capabilities and imitability. It leaves out the other determinants of appropriability such as a firm's position vis-à-vis coopetitors in an attractive market, pricing strategy, sources of revenues, and the activities that increase the number of customers that buy a particular product. It is true that an inimitable product and scarce important complementary capabilities can give their owner some bargaining power over customers. However, they may not give the firm bargaining power over suppliers, complementors, or customers with monopoly power in their industry. Moreover, even where a firm has unchallenged power over its coopetitors, it may still leave money on the table if it has the wrong pricing strategy.

ASSESSING THE PROFITABILITY POTENTIAL OF A TEAM

Suppose a firm decides to team up to obtain complementary capabilities or an invention, and there are many potential candidates with complementary assets. How could the firm narrow down the list of potential teammates to only a few that potentially would make the best teammates? One answer is to use the VARIM framework to assess the profitability potential of the combined capabilities from the team and each potential teammate. A ranking of the potential profitability of the teams can help the firm make a more informed choice of a teammate. Table 8.1 shows the competitive consequences of using capabilities from each team to create and capture value. The capabilities from Team 1 are valuable, adaptable, rare, inimitable, and the team makes money from them. Therefore the capabilities give Team 1 a sustainable competitive advantage. As shown in Table 8.1, the answers to the VARIM questions are all "Yes."

Team 2's capabilities are valuable, rare, inimitable, generate money, but are not adaptable—that is, they are not cost-effectively reconfigurable or redeployable to offer customers benefits that they consider valuable. Therefore, in the face of a radical technological innovation or any other major change, the team's competitive advantage is likely to be eroded. Thus, the team's competitive advantage is only temporary. Team 3's capabilities also give it a temporary competitive advantage since they can be imitated. In an age of rapid technological change and globalization, temporary competitive advantages are more common than sustainable ones.

Team 4's capabilities are valuable and adaptable. However, because they are not rare, anyone can have them, making it difficult for anyone to have a competitive advantage. Instead, there is so-called competitive parity among the firms that use these capabilities to create and capture value. Team 5 also has competitive parity with the many other firms that choose to be in the market until change wipes them out since their capabilities are not adaptable. Team 6 is the worst case since its capabilities score "No" in all questions—it has a competitive *dis*advantage.

PRE-INNOVATION CAPABILITIES: ASSET OR HANDICAP

Every firm brings to an innovation some capabilities—invention or complementary—from prior innovations. These can be deep knowledge of an older technology, close

Table 8.1 Rank ordering capabilities from different teams

VARIM component	Team 1	Team 2	Team 3	Team 4	Team 5	Team 6
Value: *Does the team offer benefits that customers perceive as valuable to them?*	Yes	Yes	Yes	Yes	Yes	No
Adaptability: *Is the team—or core parts of it—cost-effectively reconfigurable or redeployable to offer benefits that customers perceive as valuable to them?*	Yes	No	Yes	Yes	No	No
Rareness: *Is the team the only one that offers the customer benefits? If not, is the team's level of the benefits higher than that of competitors?*	Yes	Yes	Yes	No	No	No
Inimitability: *Are the benefits difficult for other firms to imitate, substitute, or leapfrog?*	Yes	Yes	No	No	No	No
Monetization: *Does the team make, or stand to make, money from offering the benefits to customers?*	Yes	Yes	Yes	No	No	No
Competitive consequence	Sustainable advantage	Temporary advantage	Temporary advantage	Parity	Parity	Disadvantage
Strategic action	What can firms do to reinforce the Yes answers, and reverse or dampen the effect of the No replies?					

relationships with coopetitors, distribution channels, reputations, contracts with employees or governments, and so on. As a function of their usefulness in creating and capturing value, these capabilities fall into three categories: (1) those that are useful in the face of the innovation, (2) those that are useless, and (3) those that become a handicap, preventing its owner from creating and capturing value. Since the third category is more difficult to detect and has received less attention in the literature than the first two, we focus on it here. Identifying which capabilities might become handicaps can, depending on the type of innovation, be critical to winning.[12]

There are two ways in which a capability can become a handicap in the face of an innovation: (a) The firm can be prevented by its capability from engaging in the innovation, and (b) the firm engages in the innovation but fails because of the capabilities.

Prevented by Capability from Engaging in the Innovation

Capabilities such as contracts, agreements, emotional attachments, and other prior commitments can prevent a firm from engaging an innovation.[13] This is best illustrated with some examples. A noncompete clause in an important employee's contract with a previous employer may prevent a firm from using the employee on some projects for the duration time stipulated in the contract with the previous employer. That can be very limiting in pursuing some innovations. As we saw earlier in this book, when Dell became very successful using its direct sales and build-to-order business model, bypassing distributors, Compaq wanted to switch from its build-to-stock model and imitate Dell's build-to-order direct model. However, Compaq could not get out of the agreements with distributors. The agreements with distributors effectively became a handicap to the firm's efforts to follow Dell and sell directly to end-customers.

Another example is that of the French wine industry that dominated the world market for centuries with wines that were made using no new technologies and no sugar, and that were classified and named by French locations such as Bordeaux, Champagne, Côtes du Rhone, etc.[14] New wine-makers from South Africa, Australia, and the US entered some wine markets with wines that were made using new technologies such as drip irrigation, reverse osmosis, computerized aging, steel tanks, and oak-chip flavoring, and classified their wines using grape type such as merlot or chardonnay rather than location, as in France. Many French wine-makers considered it an abomination to break their traditional ways of making wine and therefore did not adopt the new world ways of making wine.

Firm Engages in the Innovation but Fails Because of Pre-innovation Capabilities

When a firm engages in an innovation, its pre-innovation capabilities can still hurt it if the capabilities are the wrong ones, or the firm does not know how to use them in the new context. Blockbuster's case serves as a good example. Before Netflix entered the movie rental business in the United States, Blockbuster's many rental brick-and-mortar stores in good locations gave it a competitive advantage. When Netflix introduced movie rental via the Internet, all it needed was a few distribution centers located in remote low-cost areas, not the thousands of brick-and-mortar rental stores that would be needed to serve the same customers. Blockbuster entered the online business but retained the rental stores so that some online customers could return rented movies to the stores. The rental stores were too costly and Blockbuster had to declare bankruptcy. Commenting on Blockbuster's behavior, Forbes said:

> It always appears logical to leverage what you have. But the quick path isn't always the best path. Incumbents fighting back against attackers with different business models have to be willing to "forget" critical pieces of their core business. If not, they'll end up with a quick but ultimately unsatisfying response.[15]

Finally, another way to consider how prior capabilities can handicap a firm during innovation is to think of personal relationships. When a person moves from an important relationship to another, there may be things about the old relationship that he or she would rather leave behind but, often, these things would not go away. That might not help the new relationship.

NETWORK EFFECTS

With the growing importance of technologies such as the Internet, computers, cell phones, video games, social networks, and so on, the role of network effects cannot be neglected when exploring business models. In this section, we define network effects and explore the phenomenon's role in creating and capturing value.[16]

Definition and Role of Size

The value of a product to customers usually depends on the attributes of the product in question.[17] However, for some products, customer value depends not only on product attributes but also on the network of consumers that use the product or a compatible one. In particular, a technology or product exhibits *network effects* if the more people that use it, the more valuable it becomes to each user.[18] Telephones exhibit network effects since their value to each user increases with the number of people that are on the network. Applications software products such as Adobe's Acrobat (for creating and reading pdf files) exhibit network effects because the more people who own the software that can read pdf files, the more useful each user's software for creating and mailing pdf files is likely to be. In an auction network, the more sellers who are in the network, the more valuable that the network is likely to be to each buyer. Such network effects are called *direct* effects because the benefits that each user of a product/technology derives from the network of other users come from interacting—economically or socially—directly with other actors within the network.

Products that need complements can also exhibit network effects. Take computers, for example. The more people who own computers of a particular standard such as the Wintel standard, the more software that is likely to be developed for them since developers want to sell to the large number of users. Additionally, the more software that is available for a computer standard, the more valuable the computers are likely to become to users since software is critical to computers. Such effects are called *indirect* effects because the increased value experienced by each user is indirect, through the increased availability of complements.

How valuable is size to a network? One estimate suggests that the value of a network is proportional to the square of the size of the network—that is, if the size of a network is N, the value of the network is N^2. This relationship is what has been called Metcalfe's law.[19] Some theoretical estimates put the value of a network as high as N^N when network members not only can communicate but can also co-create value in the network.[20] This has been called Reed's law.

However, more recently research suggests that the value of a network depends on other factors beyond size—the structure and nature of a network may be just as important as its size.[21]

Structure

The *structure* of a network is the pattern of relationships between the players in the network. For example, social network websites such as Facebook enable members to have their own subnetworks within the larger network. Each subnetwork can be made up of college friends, members of the same religious affiliation, people living in the same area, graduates of the same university, and so on. Once a subnetwork is formed, additional members to the larger network do not necessarily increase the value of the network to every subnetwork member. For example, a new member who joins the network because of religious interests may not necessarily add value to members whose primary affiliation is the college they attended. Effectively, the internal structure of a network, like the conduct of the people within the network, also impacts the value of the network.

In a consumer-to-consumer (C2C) auction network, any consumer can be a seller or buyer. This structure contrasts with that of a business-to-consumer (B2C) online retail network in which one vendor sells to many buyers. Thus, while both types of networks are valuable to customers, the C2C network is more valuable to each buyer than the B2C one since buyers in the latter network only have one seller to buy from while those in the former have many sellers to choose from. A network with both sellers and buyers belongs to a group of networks called two-sided networks. A *two-sided network* has two distinct user groups that provide each other with benefits.[22] There are numerous other examples of two-sided networks. A credit card network has two groups: cardholders and merchants. A video game network has two groups: gamers and game developers. Users of pdf files consist of creators of pdf files and readers of pdf files. In a *single-sided network*, there is only one type of user. Examples include telephone networks, e-mail, and faxes.

Nature of Network

Other factors beyond structure also impact the value of a network to its members and owner. The value of a network depends on the conduct of the players within the network. For example, although the size of eBay's network is large, one reason why some customers may find the network more valuable than another network of equal size is its reputation for safety and its brand as an auction venue. The company built its reputation partly by rating sellers and buyers, a practice that may have selectively kept out some opportunistic potential members and discouraged some members from behaving opportunistically. In fact, a large network that is full of opportunistic members is likely to be less valuable than a smaller one.

Exploiting Network Effects

So what if a technology or product exhibits network effects? Although the value of a network to users increases with the number of other users, it is usually the owner of the network or prominent member that makes most of the money from the network. In a credit card network, it is the credit company that makes most of the money, not the cardholders or merchants. So, the question is: What can the owner of a network do to increase its chances of profiting from the network? Firms can (1) exploit *direct* network effects by building an early lead in network size and reputation, (2) price strategically, and (3) take advantage of *indirect* network effects by boosting complements.

Exploit Direct Network Effects by Building an Early Lead in Size and Reputation
The idea here is simple. Since an early lead in a network market share can escalate into a dominant market position, a firm may want to pursue the kinds of actions that would give its products/service a critical market share or installed base lead. One such action is to team up with other firms to flood the market with one's version of the product/technology. An example is Google, which used the Open Handset Alliance (OHA) to make its Android handset operating system open and freely available to anyone who wanted to use it to build smartphones, while competitors Apple and Microsoft kept their handset operating-system technologies proprietary. The idea was to flood the market with Android handsets, tipping the scales away from Apple, Microsoft, and the other proprietary technology owners, giving Android an advantage. Decades earlier, IBM had made its PC architecture open and it quickly became the standard.

Another action that can improve a firm's chances of winning a standard is to use technological innovation.[23] Although a superior technology does not always win the standard in the face of a technological innovation, any firm that hopes to win the standard has to at least adopt the technological innovation to have a chance.

Price Strategically

A firm's pricing strategy can also play an important role in increasing the size of its network. In one-sided networks, an owner of a network can pursue penetration pricing—also known as a bait-and-hook pricing model—in which it initially sells its network product at very low prices and makes money by raising prices later or offering related products for which customers have a higher willingness to pay.[24] In two-sided networks, the platform provider can set the price of the service/product low for the group with a lower willingness-to-pay but with the potential to increase the number of users on the other side. It can then charge the side with a higher willingness to pay.[25] For example, surfers who conduct Web searches on Google have a lower willingness-to-pay for the searches than advertisers' willingness-to-pay for searchers' "eye balls." Thus, searches on Google are free but advertisers are charged. Adobe gave away its reader software to anyone who wanted to be able to read pdf files, but charged anyone who wanted to create pdf files.

Exploit Indirect Network Effects by Boosting Complements

Since, early in the life of a network technology, there potentially exists a chicken-and-egg cycle in which complementors prefer to develop complements for the product with many users, and users want the product with many complements, the cycle can be jump-started by boosting the number of complements. Thus, for example, a supplier of the network product might produce some of the complements itself, help the complementor distribute complements, codevelop complements with complementors, or finance the activities of start-up complementors.

Numerical Example: Leveraging Effect of Intangible Resources

We explore one way of indirectly valuing intangible resources by considering a numerical example from personal computers.

Example 3.1: At an estimated development cost of $1 billion, Microsoft's Windows XP operating system was released on October 25, 2001 and earned Microsoft an estimated $55 to $60 per copy sold.[26] An operating system is a computer software program that manages the activities of different components (software and hardware) of a computer. From 1996 to 2001, Apple's market share dropped from 5.2 to 3.0 percent.[27] In 2001, 133.5 million desktops, notebooks and PC-based servers were shipped worldwide.[28] One estimate in 2007 had Apple's installed base of Macs at 4.5 percent of total personal computer-installed base.[29] For many businesses, the active PC life cycle was three years. Given this information, what is the value of installed base to Microsoft and Apple? (Installed base is an intangible resource.)

Answer: One way to get a feel for the value of an installed base for each firm is to perform a breakeven analysis. Let's start by making the calculations for Microsoft.

Microsoft

Contribution margin per unit = P–Vc = ($57.5–0) (average of $55 and $60)

$$\text{Break-even quantity} = \frac{\text{Fixed Cost}}{\text{Contribution Margin}} = \frac{\$1B}{\$57.5} = 17.39\text{m units} \qquad (1)$$

Of the 133.5 million personal computers that were sold in 2001, 3 percent or 4 million were Apple machines. The remaining 97 percent, or 129.5 million (10.8 million per month) were Windows machines that used the Microsoft operating system. That is, 10.8 million units of Microsoft's operating system were sold each month for the remaining two months of 2001 and beyond if we assume that sales of PCs remain at about their 2001 levels for the coming years. Since Microsoft needs to sell 17.39 million units of the operating system to break even, and it sells 10.8 million units a month, it would have taken the company

$$\frac{17.39\ M}{10.8\ M}\ \text{months} = 1.6\ \text{months}$$

to break even. That is, it would have taken Microsoft 1.6 months to recover the $1 billion that it spent on R&D to develop the operating system. After the 1.6 months, the money coming in is largely profits. Note that equation 2 could have been used to calculate the breakeven time where breakeven quantity is 17.39 million, while the sales rate is 10.8 million per month.

$$\text{Break-even time} = \frac{\text{Breakeven Quantity}}{\text{Sales Rate}} \qquad (2)$$

Apple

Now, suppose that Apple developed an operating system at the same cost as Microsoft and sold it at the same price. It too (Apple) would need to sell 17.39 million units to breakeven. However, because Apple sells only 4 million units a year or 0.333 million per month, its breakeven time would be

$$\frac{17.39\ M}{0.333\ M}\ \text{months} = 52.22\ \text{months}$$

If Apple wanted to break even in the same 1.6 months as Microsoft, it would have to sell each copy of its operating system at $1,856.76 or

$$\frac{52.22}{1.6}\ (\$57.25)$$

The Microsoft advantage is largely because of its installed base—that is, the millions of Windows PCs and their owners (businesses and consumers) who have learned how to use the Microsoft operating system, bought software that runs on it, are comfortable with the operating system and applications, and prefer to stay with the Windows PCs rather than change to Apple. For similar reasons, many Apple users do not want to switch from Apple to the Windows camp either. Thus, after the PC active life of three years, many customers who had Windows PCs buy new Windows PCs, while many customers who had Apple machines buy new Apple machines. Each new Windows machine means a sale of a Windows-operating system for Microsoft. Effectively, the installed base of Windows machines is an intangible asset for Microsoft that is a key driver of how many copies of its operating system that it can sell, while the installed base of Apple machines is an asset for Apple, and a major driver of how many Macs Apple can sell.

The other Microsoft intangible asset was the relationships that it had with PC makers. PC makers loaded Microsoft's operating system onto each PC that they shipped and paid Microsoft a royalty.

The importance of intangibles is also seen in Apple's iTunes for iPod. Apple launched a Windows version of its iTunes in October 2003. In just three and a half days, over one million copies of the iTunes software for Windows had been downloaded, and over one million songs purchased using the software.[30] A few months earlier, in April 2003, it had taken seven days for Apple to sell one million songs when it launched iTunes on Apple machines. Effectively, even Apple stood to benefit from the Windows installed base.

KEY TAKEAWAYS

- A firm's *capabilities*—made up of *resources* and *activities*—are what enable it to create and capture value. Resources are what a firm *owns* or *has access* to, while activities are what it *does* to build resources and/or transform them into customer benefits and profits.

- Resources play a critical role in the creation and appropriation of value. There are three types of resources: tangible, intangible, and human. *Tangible resources* are the resources that are usually identified and accounted for in financial statements under the category "assets." *Intangible resources* are the nonphysical and nonfinancial assets such as patents, copyrights, brand-name reputation, trade secrets, research findings, relationships with customers, shelf space, and relationships with vendors that cannot be touched and are usually not accounted for in financial statements. *Organizational resources* consist of the know-how and knowledge embodied in employees as well as the routines, processes, and culture that are embedded in the organization. A firm's capabilities are its ability to turn resources into customer benefits and profits.

- Activities are central to building and/or using resources to create and capture value. The degree to which a firm is successful in building new resources and/or creating and capturing value is a function of *which* activities it performs, *when* it performs them, *where* it performs them, and *how* it performs them.

- To understand the role of capabilities during innovation, capabilities can be divided into invention and complementary. *Invention capabilities* are those that directly underpin the innovation or new way of doing things. *Complementary capabilities*— also called *complementary assets*—are all the other capabilities, beyond invention capabilities, that a firm needs to create and capture value in the face of an innovation.

- The Teece Model helps us better understand why many inventors do not profit from their inventions. In the model, capturing value from an invention depends on (1) the extent to which the value can be imitated, and (2) the extent to which complementary capabilities are important and scarce. Inventors whose inventions are easy to imitate and require important and scarce complementary capabilities do not make money from the inventions. Rather, the owners of the complementary capabilities make the money. Depending on the level of imitability and the need for and importance of complementary capabilities, a firm can use a *run*, *block*, and *team-up* strategy to help its efforts to profit from an innovation. This model, while very useful, has some limitations. For example, it leaves out the other factors that impact appropriability: position vis-à-vis coopetitors, pricing strategy, number of customers, etc.

- If a firm decides to team up to acquire capabilities, it may have many potential partners. A VARIM analysis can be used to assess the profitability potential of the possible teams that the firm can form with each potential teammate. This can help the firm choose a partner—one with whom the firm can form the team with the most potential for having a sustainable competitive advantage.

- The capabilities that a firm had prior to an innovation can either prevent it from engaging in the innovation or handicap it during value creation and capture with the innovation.

- A technology or product exhibits *network effects* if the more people that use it, the more valuable it becomes to each user. Network effects can be direct or indirect.

- Although the size of a network is important, size is not everything. The structure of a network and the conduct of members within the network also contribute to the value that each user, or owner of the network, enjoys in a network.

- Intangible resources are usually not quantified in financial statements. One way to get a feel for the value of a firm's intangible resources is to zoom down on intangible resources that can be measured and try to estimate their significance to a firm.

KEY TERMS

Activities	Profitability potential of resources/capabilities	Structure of a network
Capabilities		Tangible resources/ capabilities
Complementary capabilities	Relational capital	Teece Model
Core competences	Resource-based view (RBV) of the firm	Two-sided networks
Intangible resources/ capabilities	Resources	Valuing intangible resources
Network effects	Single-sided networks	
	Social capital	

NOTES

1   Grant, R. M. (2002). *Contemporary Strategy Analysis: Concepts, Techniques, Applications.* Oxford, UK: Blackwell.

2   Given the critical role that intangible resources play in market value, many firms are taking another look at their financial statement reporting. See, for example, Stewart, T.A. (1997). *Intellectual Capital: The New Wealth of Organizations.* New York: Currency/Doubleday.

3   Porter, M. E. (1996). What is strategy? *Harvard Business Review,* 74(6), 61–78. Stabell, C. B., & Fjeldstad, O. D. (1998). Configuring value for competitive advantage: On chains, shops, and networks. *Strategic Management Journal,* 19(5), 413–437.

4   Afuah, A. (2004). *Business Models: A Strategic Management Approach.* New York: Irwin/McGraw-Hill.

5   Porter, M. E. (1996). What is strategy? *Harvard Business Review,* 74(6), 61–78.

6   Chesbrough, H. W., & Rosenbloom, R. S. (2002). The role of the business model in capturing value from innovation: Evidence from Xerox Corporation's technology spinoff companies. *Industrial and Corporate Change,* 11(3), 533–534.

7   Dyer, J. H., & Singh, H. (1998). The relational view: Cooperative strategy and sources of interorganizational competitive advantage. *Academy of Management Review,* 23(4), 660–679. Dyer, J. H., & Hatch, N. W. (2006). Relation-specific capabilities and barriers to knowledge transfers: creating advantage through network relationships. *Strategic Management Journal,* 27(8), 701–719.

8   Nahapiet, J., & Ghoshal, S. (1998). Social capital, intellectual capital, and the organizational advantage. *Academy of Management Review,* 23(3), 242–266. See also seminal work by Professor Ronald Burt. For example, Burt, R. S. (1997). The contingent value of social capital. *Administrative Sciences Quarterly,* 42(2), 339–365.

9   Teece, D. J. (1986). Profiting from technological innovation: Implications for integration, collaboration, licensing and public policy. *Research Policy,* 15(6), 285–306.

10 This model is derived from Professor David Teece's seminal paper: Teece, D. J. (1986). Profiting from technological innovation: Implications for integration, collaboration, licensing and public policy. *Research Policy,* 15(6), 285–306.

11 Afuah, A. N. (2003). *Innovation Management: Strategies, Implementation and Profits.* New York: Oxford University Press.

12 Leonard-Barton, D. (1992). Core capabilities and core rigidities: a paradox in managing new product development. *Strategic Management Journal,* 13 (Summer Special Issue), 111–125. Gargiulo, M., & Benassi, M. (2000). Trapped in your own net: Network cohesion, structural holes, and the adaptation of social capital. *Organization Science,* 11(2), 183–196. Uzzi, B. (1997). Social structure and competition in interfirm networks: The paradox of embeddedness. *Administrative Science Quarterly,* 42(1), 35–67. Atuahene-Gima, K. (2005). Resolving the capability-rigidity paradox in new product innovation. *Journal of Marketing,* 69(4), 61–83.

13 Argyres, N. S., & Liebeskind, J. P. (1999). Contractual commitments, bargaining power, and governance inseparability: Incorporating history into transaction cost theory. *Academy of Management Review,* 24(1), 49–63.

14 Bartlett, C. A., Cornebise, J., & McLean, A. N. (2002). Global wine wars: New world challenges old. *Harvard Business School Press,* Case # 9-303-056

15 Anthony, S. D. (2008, May 3). Is Blockbuster back? Retrieved July 6, 2013, from www.forbes.com/2008/05/03/blockbuster-netflix-walmart_leadership_clayton_in_sa_0503claytonchristensen_inl.html.

16 Afuah, A. N. (2013). Are network effects all about size? The role of structure and conduct, *Strategic Management Journal,* 34(3), 257–273. Fershman, C., & Gandal, N. (2011). Direct and indirect knowledge spillovers: The "social network" of open-source projects. *Rand Journal of Economics,* 42(1), 70–91. Gandal, N. (1994). Hedonic price indexes for spreadsheets and an empirical test of the network effects hypothesis. *Rand Journal of Economics,* 25(1), 160–170.

17 Katz, M. L., & Shapiro, C. (1992). Product introduction with network externalities. *Journal of Industrial Economics,* 40(1), 55–84. Farrell, J., & Saloner, G. (1986). Installed base and compatibility: Innovation, product preannouncements, and predation. *American Economic Review,* 76(5), 940–955.

18 Katz, M. L., & Shapiro, C. (1985). Technology adoption in the presence of network externalities. *Journal of Political Economy,* 94(4), 822–841. Sheremata, W. A. (2004). Competing through innovation in network markets: Strategies for challengers. *Academy of Management Review,* 29(3), 359–377. Schilling, M. A. (2002). Technology success and failure in winner-take-all markets: The impact of learning orientation, timing, and network effects. *Academy of Management Journal,* 45(2), 387–398.

19 Briscoe, B., Odlyzko, A., & Tilly, B. (2006). Metcalfe's law is wrong-communications networks increase in value as they add members-but by how much? *IEEE Spectrum,* 43(7), 34–39.

20 Reed, D. P. (2001). The law of the pack. *Harvard Business Review,* 79(2), 23–24.

21 Afuah, A. N. (2012). Are network externalities all about size? The role of structure and conduct. *Strategic Management Journal*, 34(3), 257–273. Fershman, C., and Gandal, N. (2011). Direct and indirect knowledge spillovers: The "social network" of open-source projects. *Rand Journal of Economics*, 42(1), 70–91.

22 Parker, G., & Van Alstyne, M. (2005). Two-sided network effects: A theory of information product design. *Management Science*, 51(10), 1494–1504. Rochet, J., & Tirole, J. (2003). Platform competition in two-sided markets. *Journal of the European Economic Association*, 1(4), 990–1029. Brousseau, E., & Penard, T. (2006). The economics of digital business models: A framework for analyzing the economics of platforms. *Review of Network Economics*, 6(2), 81–110. Eisenmann, T. R., Parker, G., & van Alstyne, M. (2006). Strategies for two-sided markets. *Harvard Business Review*, 84(10), 92–101.

23 Sheremata, W. A. (2004). Competing through innovation in network markets: Strategies for challengers. *Academy of Management Review*, 29(3), 359–377. Schilling, M. A. (2002). Technology success and failure in winner-take-all markets: The impact of learning orientation, timing, and network effects. *Academy of Management Journal*, 45(2), 387–398. Gawer, A., & Cusumano, M. A. (2008). How companies become platform leaders. *MIT Sloan Management Review*, 49(2), 28–35.

24 Conner, K. (1995). Obtaining strategic advantage from being imitated: When can encouraging "clones" pay? *Management Science*, 41(2), 209–215.

25 Parker, G., & Van Alstyne, M. (2005). Two-sided network effects: A theory of information product design. *Management Science*, 51(10), 1494–1504. Conner, K. (1995). Obtaining strategic advantage from being imitated: When can encouraging "clones" pay? *Management Science*, 41(2), 209–215.

26 Yoffie, D. B., & Wang, Y. (2002). Apple Computer. *Harvard Business School Press*, Case # 9-702-469.

27 Quittner, J. (2002). Apple's latest fruit: Exclusive: How Steve Jobs made a sleek machine that could be the home-digital hub of the future. Retrieved August 23, 2007, from www.time.com/time/covers/1101020114/cover2.html

28 Kanellos, M. (2002, June 11). IDC ups 2001 PC-shipment estimate. Retrieved July 16, 2008, from http://news.cnet.com/IDC-ups-2001-PC-shipment-estimate/2100-1001_3-935176.html

29 Market Share vs Installed Base: iPod vs Zune, Mac vs PC. (2007, March 18). Retrieved August 23, 2007, from www.roughlydrafted.com/RD/RDM.Tech.Q1.07/9E601E8E-2ACC-4866-A91B-3371D1688E00.html

30 One million copies of iTunes for windows software downloaded in three and a half days. (20 October 2003). Retrieved September 15, 2007, from www.apple.com/pr/library/2003/oct/20itunes.html

9

VALUE CREATION AND CAPTURE DURING INNOVATION

Reading this chapter should provide you with the conceptual and analytical tools to:

- Understand what value creation and capture mean.
- Increase your understanding of the determinants of value creation and capture.
- Analyze how much value each member of a value system captures and why.
- Strengthen your ability to think strategically.

INTRODUCTION

Do you own a PC, iPhone, car, airplane, shoes, or a tablet PC? How much of what you value in each of these products do you think was created by the "maker" of the product? How much of the value does the "maker" capture (appropriate)? What is the firm's business model? How many countries contribute to the benefits that you value in the product? Consider one of these products, the iPhone: each owner of an iPhone perceives value in the device when he or she navigates through the device by touching the screen, makes or receives phone calls, uses an app, surfs the Web, sends or receives e-mail, takes or views pictures, and so on. Apple conceived of and designed the iPhone but did not manufacture the product when it introduced it in 2007. The hundreds of components that went into the product came from numerous suppliers from the US, Europe and Asia, and were shipped to an Asian manufacturer who assembled and shipped them to the US for distribution. Many of the critical components, especially the microchips, were themselves systems that were designed and either manufactured by the suppliers, or manufactured by their subcontractors before being shipped to Apple's own subcontractors for assembly. (Microchips, with their rapidly increasing functionality but dropping prices, are what have made innovations such as the iPhone possible.) Infenion AG, a German company, supplied the digital baseband, radio-frequency transceiver, and power-management devices.[1] Samsung, a South Korean company, made the video processor chip, while Sharp and Sanyo, Japanese firms, supplied the LCD display. The touch-sensitive modules that were overlaid on to the phone's LCD screen to make the multi-touch control possible were designed by Balda AG, a German company and produced in its factories in China. Marvel Semiconductor of the US provided the WiFi chips. The camera lens was supplied by Largan Precision of Taiwan, while the camera module was supplied by three Taiwanese companies: Altus-Tech, Primax, and Lite-On. Delta Electronics supplied the battery charger. Various other firms supplied other components. Apple also supplied the operating system and other software that manage the device.

The question is, how much value does Apple create and capture in offering the iPhone? How much value is created and/or captured by each supplier? How much value is created by which country? We will return to these questions later in this chapter. We start the chapter with a very important discussion of what creating and appropriating value is all about. We then explore the impact of innovative activities on the creation and capture of value. We conclude with the reminder that value creation can be as important as value capture and focusing only on one and not the other can make for bad strategy. One need only recall the example of musicians, who create lots of value but often do not capture all of it, to be reminded of the significance of value capture (value appropriation).

CREATING AND CAPTURING VALUE

The concepts of creating and capturing value are central to business models and one way to understand them is through the illustration as shown in Figure 9.1. Recall that business models are about making money and that revenues come from customers who buy products or services from firms. A customer buys a product from a firm because it perceives the product as providing it (the customer) with benefits, B. However, to provide the benefits, B, a firm has to perform value-adding activities such as R&D, purchasing of equipment and materials, transformation of these materials into products or services, marketing these products and services to customers, and distributing the products to customers.

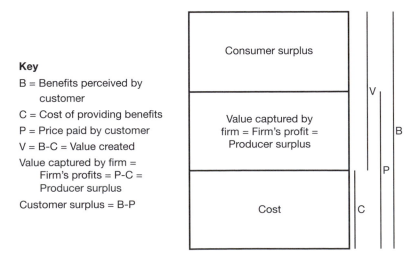

Figure 9.1 Value creation and capture

These activities cost C. The economic *value created*, V, by the firm is the difference between the benefits, B, that a customer perceives in the product and how much it costs the firm to provide the benefits.[2] That is, $V = B-C$. The customer pays a price P for the benefits that it receives. This gives the firm a profit of P–C, and the customer gets to keep B–P. That is, the *value captured* by the firm is the profit, P–C, from the value created. This profit is sometimes called the producer's surplus, while what the customer gets to keep, B–P, is called the consumer's surplus. As an example, consider the value created when a firm builds and sells a car. Suppose a carmaker develops and markets a new car that customers love so much that they would be willing to pay $30,000 for the benefits that they perceive in owning the car. Also suppose that it costs the firm $15,000 to produce the car (including R&D, marketing, and manufacturing costs) whose price the firm sets at $20,000. From Figure 9.1, the value created is $15,000 (30,000–15,000), the carmaker's profit is $5,000 (20,000–15,000). The customer's consumer surplus is $10,000 (30,000–20,000).

Note that although the value created by the firm is B–C, the firm only captures a fraction of it in the form of profits (P–C). Customers capture some of it in the form of consumer surplus. Effectively, making money involves both creating value and capturing the value created. Next, we discuss value creation and capture in more detail.

Value Creation

Recall that the value created is the difference between the benefits that customers perceive and the cost of providing the benefits. Value creation is about performing value chain activities so as to offer customers something that they perceive as beneficial to them, and insuring that the cost of offering the benefits does not exceed the benefits—it is about benefits and costs. The benefits that customers derive from a product can be from the product's features (performance, quality, aesthetics, durability, ease of use), the product's or firm's brand, the location of the product, the network effects associated with the product, or the service that comes with the product. Thus, designing a product, manufacturing, and testing it all add value since they all contribute to the product's features. Advertising a product also adds value when it improves customers' perception of the product. Distributing a product adds value when it brings the product closer to customers who would otherwise not have access to it. For products that exhibit network effects, performing activities that add more customers constitutes value creation because the more people that use the product, the more valuable that it becomes to each user.

There are numerous things that a firm can do to keep its costs down while creating benefits for customers. It can innovate by using new knowledge or combination of existing knowledge to drastically improve existing ways of performing activities, thereby drastically lowering its costs. It can take advantage of economies of scale, if its products are such that the higher its output, the lower the per unit costs of its products. It can take advantage of economies of scope, if the different products that it sells are such that the costs per unit of producing these products together is less than the costs per unit of producing each product alone. The firm can lower its costs by taking advantage of what it has learnt from its experiences in moving up different learning curves. It can also take advantage of any unique location that it may have, such as being close to a cheap source of labor or resource. A firm can also take advantage of industry or macro-related strategic factors. For example, if a firm has bargaining power over its suppliers, it can negotiate to pay lower prices for its inputs, thereby keeping its costs lower. It can also use that power to work more closely with suppliers to keep component costs lower so that the supplier can pass on some of the costs savings to the firm in the form of lower input costs. Finally, a firm can keep its costs low by putting in place the right incentives and monitoring systems to reduce agency costs. Agency costs are the costs that firms incur because employees or other agents are not doing what they are supposed to be doing—for example, surfing the Internet instead of working. Effectively, firms can create value by offering more benefits and keeping down the costs of providing the benefits.

Coopetition and Value Creation

Since value created is the difference between the benefits that a customer perceives and the costs to a firm of providing these benefits, value creation can be as much a function of what the firm does as it is a function of what its coopetitors–the customers, complementors, rivals, suppliers, and other institutions or organizations with which a firm cooperates to create value and competes to capture it—do.[3] The quality of the inputs from a firm's suppliers impacts the quality of the benefits that the firm can offer customers. For example, the benefits that a customer enjoys in a PC are as much a function of how the PC maker designs, manufactures, and markets the product as they are a function of the quality of the microprocessor (from suppliers of microchips), and of the software from complementors (Microsoft and others) as well as of how the customer uses the PC. The cost to a firm of providing benefits to its customers is also a function of its suppliers and the relationship between the firm and these suppliers.

Additionally, the extent to which a customer perceives a product as meeting his or her needs is a function of the customer's unique characteristics, including the customer's need for the product. Moreover, the price that a customer gets to pay a firm is a function of the relationship between the customer and the firm. In fact, value is often created by coopetitors who cooperate through alliances, informal understandings, joint ventures, venture capital investments, and so on. Effectively, *a firm usually has to cooperate to create value and compete to capture the value.* In a perfect (competition) world, each firm would capture value equivalent to how much it created. (Your slice of the pie would be equivalent to your contribution to making it.) In practice, most firms do not live in a perfect world. Many organizations, individuals, nations, and institutions capture more value than they create. Therefore, understanding how to capture value is critical to business model and strategy formulation/execution.

Value Capture During Innovation

Value capture is about who gets to profit from the value created. It is about what slice of the pie one gets to keep. Referring again to the producer, the firm only keeps a fraction of the value created (firm's profit), while customers and suppliers keep the rest. The question is: Why might an innovator not be able to capture all the value that it creates? Since business models are about value creation and capture, one way to answer this question is to turn to the components of a business model to see what else—apart from value creation—it takes to capture value from an innovation. Doing so suggests that there are five reasons why a firm that innovates may not be able to capture all of the value that it creates:

1. The *value proposition* (from the value created) may not be compelling enough to attract many high willingness-to-pay customers.

2. The firm may not be well-positioned vis-à-vis its coopetitors in an attractive *market segment.*
3. The firm may have the wrong *revenue model.*
4. The firm may have the wrong *growth model.*
5. The firm may not have the technology and complementary *capabilities* needed to profit from the innovation.

Value Proposition May Not Be Compelling Enough

To make money from the value that it has created, a firm has also to get enough customers to want the benefits that it offers and pay a high enough price for them. That would be the case if, for example, the value proposition that the firm offers is compelling enough to attract many high willingness-to-pay customers. If customers' willingness to pay is low, they may pay prices that are too low for the firm to make money.

May Not Be Well-Positioned in an Attractive Market Segment

Another reason why a firm that creates value may not be able to capture all of it is because the party with the most bargaining power is not always the one that created the value or that makes the largest contribution towards value co-creation. In the coopetition between Intel, Microsoft, and PC makers that delivers value to PC users, Microsoft is the most profitable, but it is doubtful that it creates the most value in that value system. (Creating value is synonymous with working together to make a pie, while capturing value is equivalent to dividing the pie.) Each party's position vis-à-vis its coopetitors determines the share of the pie that it gets.

If a firm's suppliers or buyers have bargaining power over the firm, it may have difficulties capturing the value that it has created. For example, if a firm has only one supplier of a critical component, the supplier can charge so much for the component that the firm's profit margins will be reduced to zero—the supplier effectively captures most of the value that the firm has created. Buyers with power can also extract low prices out of the firm, reducing the amount of value that it can capture. Thus, pursuing activities that increase a firm's bargaining power can better position the firm to capture the value created. A classic example is that of Dell, which we saw in Chapter 8. By bypassing distributors to sell directly to businesses and consumers, it was moving away from having to confront the more concentrated and powerful distributors to dealing directly with the more fragmented end-customers who had less power than distributors.

Good relationships with coopetitors can also help a firm better capture value. For example, if a firm works more closely with its customers to help them discover their latent needs for its products, the willingness-to-pay of these customers may go up, thereby increasing the firm's chances of appropriating more of the value it creates.

Wrong Revenue Model

Having the wrong revenue model is the third reason why a firm that creates new value may not be able to capture all of it. If a phone company in a developing country offers very good service but insists on a subscription revenue model rather than a prepaid model, it is not likely to make money. Why? Most developing countries do not have credit histories, making a subscription model difficult to implement. Besides, many people in these developing countries simply do not earn enough money each month to make regular monthly payments.

The other factor that impacts value capture is the pricing strategy. The closer that a firm sets its price to each customer's reservation price, the more of the value created that the firm gets to keep, if the higher price does not drive customers away. Recall that a customer's reservation price for a product is the maximum price that it is willing to pay for the product. The higher a customer's reservation price, the higher the chances that the price demanded will fall enough below the customer's reservation price to leave it some consumer surplus. Also, the higher a customer's reservation price, the better the chances that the price demanded by the firm will not drive the customer away. The price demanded, in turn, is a function of the relationship between the firm and the customer, especially the bargaining power of one over the other, and the firm's pricing strategy. The higher a firm's bargaining power over its customer, the more that it can extract higher prices from the customer, thereby raising the fraction of the value that it keeps (profits). Also, a firm that has good relationships with its customers can better work with such customers to discover and meet their needs, thereby increasing the customer's reservation price and lowering costs, all of which increase the value created and captured.

Effectively, if a customer has a high reservation price but a firm sets its price below the reservation price, the customer keeps the difference and walks away with a higher consumer surplus while the firm leaves with a lower profit. Pricing above customers' reservation prices drives them away. Thus, a firm is better off pursuing a pricing strategy that gets it as close as possible to a customer's reservation price, without driving customers to competitors or out of the market. A firm's *sources of revenues* also determine the amount of revenues that it collects and, in a way, the value that it captures. Innovative activities that create new sources of revenues can increase the total value that a firm can capture. Take the case of Ryanair in 2013. In addition to the revenues that it collected from airline tickets, it also earned revenues from advertising, sales of snacks and duty-free goods, and commissions on hotel accommodation and car rental reservations made through its website. Effectively, the primary value that Ryanair offered its passengers was flying them from one place to another. However, while getting passengers to their destinations, Ryanair was able to extract more value from them using other instruments.

Firm May Have the Wrong Growth Model

Recall from Chapter 1 that to grow profitably, a firm may need to pursue a subset of three strategies—*block, run,* or *team up*—while keeping costs low. One advantage of pursuing these strategies is to reduce the threat of imitation and substitutability so as to keep revenues up and costs down. If competitors are able to imitate the value that a firm creates, its prices and the quantity that it sells are likely to drop. If other firms can offer viable substitutes, customers can switch to these substitutes if a firm's prices are higher than they would like. This reduces the value that the firm can capture. The right combination of block, run, and team up reduces the effect of imitation and substitutes.

Firm May Not Have the Right Capabilities

As we saw in Chapter 8, if an innovation requires scarce and important capabilities—both technology and complementary ones—to profit from it, the owner of the complementary capabilities may be the one that captures the value and not the firm that created the value. This is particularly true for products that are easy to imitate. Recall that complementary capabilities are all the other capabilities—beyond those that underpin an innovation—that a firm needs to create and capture value. They include brands, distribution channels, shelf space, manufacturing, relationships with coopetitors, complementary technologies, access to complementary products, installed base, relationships with governments, and so on. Therefore, a firm that innovates may need to establish prior positions in complementary capabilities so as to profit from the innovation. In the music industry case, recording companies and agents have complementary capabilities such as contacts, brands, and distribution channels, and that may be one reason why they capture most of the value created by musicians.

Of course, a firm may fail to profit from an innovation because it does not have the capabilities that it takes to pull off the innovation. Many firms fail in the face of an innovation because they do not have what it takes to offer a product that is compelling enough to customers.

THE WHO CAPTURES HOW MUCH VALUE QUESTION

At the very beginning of this chapter, we raised an important question: Who creates and/or captures how much value in a value system? We then postponed the question so as to explain the concepts needed to better explore the question. Now, we are ready. We explore the question using two examples.

Example 9.1: Who Captures What in a Book Value System

In 2000, it was estimated that for each dollar a customer paid for a book, the author received 10 cents, the publisher of the book got 32 cents, the printer received 8 cents, while the distributor and retailer obtained 20 cents and 30 cents respectively.[4] Profit margins for authors, publishers, printers, distributors and retailers were −3.2 percent, 13.1 percent, 6.0 percent, 6.8 percent, and 17.3 percent.[5] How much value did each player in the value chain capture? Are the players who capture the most value really the ones that create the most value?

Solution to Example 9.1

We start to answer the question by considering publishers. They received 32 cents of each dollar of sales and had profit margins of 13.1 percent. The value captured by publishers is the profit that they make from the value created.

$$\text{Therefore, Profit Margin} = \frac{Profit}{Sales} = \frac{Profit}{\$0.32} = 0.131 = 13.1\%$$

Thus, Profit = $0.32 × 0.131 = $0.042. This is the value captured by publishers. Publishers' costs are $0.32 − $0.042 = $0.278.

Similarly, we can calculate the amounts captured by each player and its cost. These numbers are shown in Figure 9.2. Also shown in the figure is percentage of value that each player captured. Retailers captured 47.6 percent of the value created, the most of any player. Why did retailers capture so much value compared to other players? For one thing, retailers controlled the shelf space in the *offline world* and therefore had bargaining power over their suppliers and buyers. They typically paid publishers only 50 percent of the suggested retail price.[6] At some locations, such as universities and retail malls, book retailers constituted local monopolies. Effectively, retailers have complementary

	Author	Publisher	Printer	Distributor	Retailer	Total
Revenues	$0.100	$0.320	$0.080	$0.200	$0.300	$1.000
Profit margins	-3.2%	13.1%	6.0%	6.8%	17.3%	10.9%
Costs	$0.103	$0.278	$0.075	$0.186	$0.248	$0.891
Value captured	-$0.003	$0.042	$0.005	$0.014	$0.052	$0.109
% Value captured	-2.9%	38.5%	4.4%	12.5%	47.6%	100%

Figure 9.2 A book value chain

capabilities and power over coopetitors, and good locations differentiate them from rivals. For the others, many retailers could resale old books, making good profits without lifting a finger. Publishers captured 38.5 percent of the value created, second only to retailers. They had lots of power over the average author, although famous authors commanded a lot of power over publishers because of the pull that famous-author names establish at consumers.

Distributors (which include wholesalers) were next with 12.5 percent of the value captured. They transported the books and often stored them in warehouses until retailers needed them. The least value was captured by printers and authors with 4.4 percent and –2.9 percent respectively. Printers were highly fragmented with little or no power over their suppliers or buyers. Authors were also highly fragmented and therefore had little power over publishers (except famous authors). Although famous authors commanded lots of money, the average author lost money. He or she captured no value; rather, he or she had to "pay" other members of the value system to take the book from him or her. He or she "paid" the equivalent of 2.9 percent of the price of a book. Effectively, the average author makes little or no money directly from books. Since most people who buy books buy them for their content, it is doubtful that 47.6 percent of what readers get out of a book comes from retailers. Effectively, some players captured more value than they created.

Example 9.2: Who Creates and Captures What Value in an iPhone?

In 2007, when Apple shipped the first iPhones, some financial analysts estimated that the cost of the components and final manufacturing for the phone were $234.83 and $258.83 for the 4GB and 8GB versions, respectively (Table 9.1).[7] The recommended retail prices for both versions (4GB and 8GB) were $499 and $599. The wholesale discount for electronic products was estimated to be 25 percent. The question is, how much of the value that customers saw in the iPhone did Apple and each of its suppliers capture? How much value was created by each actor? How much of it was created in the US?

Table 9.1 Estimated costs for the iPhone in 2007

Component	Supplier	Cost for 4GB iPhone (US $)		Cost for 8GB iPhone (US $)	
		US$	%	US$	%
ARM RISC application processor	Samsung, Korea	14.25	6.07	14.25	5.51
NAND flash memory	Samsung, Korea	24	10.22	48	18.54
SDRAM (1Gig)	Samsung, Korea	14	5.96	14	5.41
3 chips: digital base band LSI, transceiver LSI, and power management unit	Infineon Technologies AG, Germany	15.25	6.49	15.25	5.89
Touch screen module	Balda AG, Germany, and Tpk Solutions, Taiwan	27	11.50	27	10.43
LCD module	Epson Imaging Devices Corp., Sharp Corp. and Toshiba Matsushita Display Technology Co.	24.5	10.43	24.5	9.47
Bluetooth chip	CSR plc of the UK	1.9	0.81	1.9	0.73
Wi-Fi base band chip	Marvel Semiconductor Inc., USA	6	2.56	6	2.32
802.11b/q		15.35	6.54	15.35	5.93
Accessories/packaging etc.		8.5	3.62	8.5	3.28
Final manufacturing	Various contractors	15.5	6.60	15.5	5.99
Royalties for EDGE		4.61	1.96	4.61	1.78
Operating system (OS X)	Apple	7	2.98	7	2.70
Voice processing software		3	1.28	3	1.16
Camera module	Altus-Tech, Primax, and Lite-On	11	4.68	11	4.25
Battery		5.2	2.21	5.2	2.01
Mechanical components/enclosure		12	5.11	12	4.64
Other hardware/ software components		25.77	10.97	25.77	9.96
Total cost of inputs		234.83	100.00	258.83	100.00

Source: iSuppli Corporation: Applied Market Intelligence. Author's estimates.

Solution to Example 9.2

We start with the *value captured*:

> Recall that value captured = price – cost of providing benefits. The retail price for the 4GB iPhone was $499. Therefore, wholesale price = $(1 - .25) \times \$499 = \$374.25$. (Distributors and retailers received $124.75 of the $499—i.e. 25 percent of the retail price.)

The cost of inputs for the 4GB is $234.83 (from Table 9.1). Therefore, estimated value captured by Apple = Price – Cost = $374.25–$234.83 = $139.42.

How much value was captured by Apple's suppliers? Consider Samsung, which supplied at least three components. The problem here is that although we know the prices of each component, we do not know Samsung's cost for each component. Firms do not release details of individual product costs. However, they provide gross profit margins in their financial statements, which we will use for our estimates. Samsung's gross profit margin in 2006 was 18.6 percent. That is:

$$\frac{P - C}{P} = 18.6\%$$

Therefore, $P - C = P \times 0.186$ = value added

For NAND Flash memory (Table 9.1), value captured by Samsung = $24 \times 0.186 =$ $4.46

If the LCD module is provided by Sharp, we can also calculate the value captured by Sharp using its 2006 gross profit margin of 22.6 percent. This value is $24.5 \times 0.226 =$ $5.54. If we assume that the firms that perform final manufacturing (assembly) for Apple have profit margins of 15 percent, then each gets $15.5 \times 0.15 =$ $2.33 for every 4GB iPhone that it manufactures.

Effectively, for each $499 that a customer pays for a 4GB iPhone, retailers and distributors take $124.75, Apple captures $139.42, Samsung captures $4.6 for the NAND flash memory alone, Sharp captures $5.54 for the LCD module when it is bought from Sharp, each final "manufacturer" (assembler) gets $2.33, and so on. The value captured by any of the other suppliers can be similarly calculated. (This calculation also tells us why the Apple retail stores in the United States can be so profitable: Apple gets to keep another 25 percent of its products instead of paying them out to retailers.)

We now turn to the *value created*. Recall that:

Value created = benefits perceived by customers – cost of providing the benefits.

> = Customer's willingness-to-pay – cost of providing the benefits
> = Customer's reservation price – cost of providing the benefits

One problem here is that it is not always easy to determine a customer's reservation price or willingness to pay. In the case of Apple, for example, we know that many of the customers who bought the iPhone—especially the diehard Apple fans—could have paid a lot more than the listed retail price. That is, their reservation prices for the product were higher than the retail prices. However, we do not know exactly how much more each customer would have paid. What we can say is that the average reservation price of customers was higher than the retail price that they ended up paying. We do not know what Apple's reservation prices for each of the components was either. The important thing for a strategist to remember is always to look for ways to get as close as possible to each customer's reservation price so as to extract as much of the value created as possible, without driving the customer to competitors or away from the market. At the same time, a firm also tries to do the best to extract a price from its suppliers that is below its reservation price, without adversely affecting the ability of the supplier to keep supplying high quality components.

International Component to Value Creation and Appropriation

One interesting thing to observe in the example above is that although each contract manufacturer that assembled the iPhone for Apple only captured $2.33 of every $499 that each customer paid for a 4GB iPhone, the manufacturer's home country was credited with exports of $234.83, the factor cost of the product assembled in the country. This is unfortunate because, even though the manufacturing country captures very little value, it is still seen as the largest benefactor of the exports.

Consider the opposite example, where a large US exporter may be getting more credit for exports than the value-added approach would suggest. In the 1980s, 1990s and 2000s, Boeing Corporation was one of America's largest exporters. So how much of the value that airlines saw in a Boeing 787 in 2013, for example, was created in the United States? Boeing designed the aircraft and performed the R&D and rigorous testing that are critical to aircraft success. The aircraft was being assembled in Everett, Washington, USA. However, almost all of the major components (subassemblies) that were put together in Everett— all of them systems in themselves—were manufactured and tested in other countries before being shipped to Everett for assembly.[8] For example, the wings, center wing box, main landing-gear wheel well, and forward fuselage were manufactured by Mitsubishi and Kawasaki Heavy Industries in Nagoya, Japan. The other forward fuselage was produced in the US by Vought in South Carolina, the center fuselage in Italy by Alenia, while the aft fuselage was produced in Wichita, Kansas, USA, by Spirit AeroSystems.[9] The horizontal stabilizers were manufactured in Italy by Alenia Aeronautica. Passenger doors were made in France by Latecoerc, while the cargo doors, access doors, and crew escape door were made in Sweden by Saab. The ailerons and flaps were manufactured in Australia by Boeing Australia, while the fairings were produced in Canada by Boeing Canada Technology. Finally, the 787 would be powered by the General Electric (USA) GEnx and Rolls-Royce (UK) Trent 1000 engines.

Thus, although Boeing added value to the 787 by conceiving of and designing the plane, integrating all the components, coordinating all the suppliers, and assembling the subassemblies, the critical components of the airplane—such as the engines, fuselage, landing-gear systems, wings, tail, etc.—were designed, developed, tested, and assembled by its suppliers. These firms added a huge amount of value that airlines and passengers saw in a 787. Moreover, in designing the plane, Boeing also worked very closely with its customers—the airlines that would buy the planes. Also, many of these coopetitors were outside the United States. However, if a Japanese airline were to buy a 787, the full cost of the plane would be credited to US exports to Japan. We get a better picture of what is going on when we think in terms of value created and captured rather than products exported or imported.

Shifts in the Location of Value Creation and Appropriation During Innovation

So far, we have focused on how and why value is created and captured in the face of an innovation. However, innovation can also shift the locus of value creation and appropriation along a value system. For example, in the mainframe and minicomputer era, most of the value in the computer industry was created and captured by vertically integrated computer companies that produced the microchips and software that were critical to their products. In the advent of the PC, a lot of the value in the industry was captured by Microsoft, a complementor and supplier, and Intel, a supplier. Of course, customers also benefited tremendously since prices dropped, performance went up, and hundreds of millions of people could use them at work and at home. Effectively, value creation and appropriation shifted from computer makers to their customers, suppliers, and complementors.

One of the more interesting examples of a shift in value creation and capture in the face of an innovation is that of Botox. Before Botox, cosmetic surgery was performed by surgeons who charged high specialist fees for the procedure, and their suppliers obtained little or nothing per procedure. The procedure could last hours and patients were put under anesthesia and, after surgery, it took weeks for a patient to fully recover. After the FDA approval of Botox in 2002, any doctor could use Botox to perform cosmetic procedures. A vial of Botox cost its maker, Allergan, $40 and it sold it to doctors for $400, who marked it up to about $2,800 per procedure.[10] Each vial could be used to treat 3–4 patients. The Botox procedure lasted a few minutes and the patient could return to work or other normal activity the same day. Effectively, the introduction of Botox substituted some of a cosmetic surgeon's skills with a product and shifted some of the value creation and appropriation from cosmetic surgeons to Allergan, their supplier, as well as general practitioners, and of course, patients.

LATENT LINK BETWEEN COOPERATION AND COMPETITION

On one hand, most strategy frameworks are either all about competition or all about cooperation. Porter's Five Forces, for example, is all about competitive forces impinging on industry firms. Even the versions of the Five Forces that incorporate complementors say little or nothing about the cooperation that may exist between industry firms and suppliers, buyers, rivals and potential new entrants. On the other hand, models of cooperation between firms say very little or nothing about the underlying implicit competition that exists between the cooperating firms. However, as we argued earlier, where there is cooperation there is likely to be competition. And where there is competition, there are probably opportunities for cooperation.

For two reasons, these two statements are even more apropos in the face of innovative activities. First, innovative activities, especially those that underpin revolutionary business models, usually have more uncertainties to be resolved than non-innovative activities. Such uncertainties, especially when they are technological, are best resolved through some sort of cooperation.[11] Thus, for example, a firm that is developing a new product whose components are also innovations is better off cooperating with suppliers of such components to resolve product development uncertainties that they face rather than seeing each supplier only as an adversary over whom the firm wants to have bargaining power.[12] Moreover, competitors in a relatively young market have an incentive to cooperate to grow the market. Second, as we saw earlier in this chapter, profiting from innovative activities often requires complementary capabilities, many of which are often obtained through cooperation. And where there is cooperation to create value, there is also competition, even if only implicit, to share costs and the value created.

The Missed Opportunities During Cooperation and Competition

Effectively, then, each time that firms miss out on an opportunity to cooperate during competition, they may be missing out on making a larger pie. For example, rather than use its bargaining power over suppliers and force them to take low prices, a firm can work with the suppliers to reduce their costs and improve the functionality and quality of the components. In so doing, the firm may end up with better components that cost less than the previous inferior ones and a supplier that is even more profitable and happier than before. Of course, each time a firm forgets about the implicit competition that is taking place during cooperation, it may be reducing its share of the pie.

The Whole Grape or a Slice of the Watermelon

One mistake that is easy for coopetitors to make in the face of the competition that often takes place during cooperation is to forget to think of one's alternatives. In particular, before dumping your partner because your percentage of the pie is small relative to your partner's share and your contribution, think very carefully about who else is out there that you can create a pie with. Will the value that you create with this new partner be as large as the one that you can create with your existing partner? In leaving your existing partner for an outsider, you may be leaving 10 percent of a watermelon for 90 percent of a grape.[13]

TYPES OF PLAYERS

Not all the firms that pursue an innovation in any particular market move at the same time. Nor do all players pursue the right innovation strategies. Thus, we can categorize players as a function of when they pursue an innovation and the extent to which they pursue the right strategies. Such a classification can help a firm to understand where it stands strategically, relative to its competitors in the face of an innovation, as a first step towards understanding what it needs to do next. The classification can help an entrepreneur understand what strategic spaces might be good ones to pursue. The classification results in four types of players: explorers, superstars, exploiters, and me-toos (Figure 9.3).

Explorers

An *explorer* is a firm that moves first in pursuing an innovation but does so largely for the fun of it. Its activities are driven, not so much by a clear strategy for creating and capturing value, but by what it just happens to find itself doing or enjoys doing. Explorers may pursue the activities more to make a difference in the world or their community than to make money. They may also pursue the activity for knowledge's own sake. They often create value or establish a foundation for creating value but do not capture it. They help reduce technological and market uncertainty and pave the way for exploiters (see below) to come in and take advantage of the foundation for value creation and make money. Many inventors (firms and individuals) fall into this category. AT&T, which

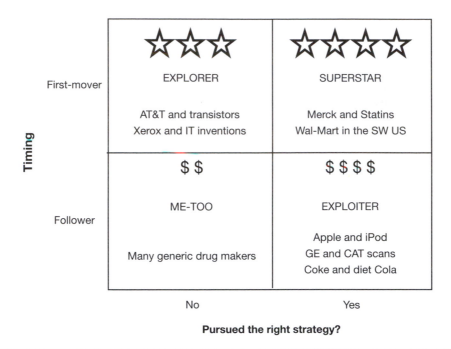

Figure 9.3 Types of players

invented the transistor, and inventors such as Tesla are good examples. Another example is Xerox, through its Xerox Palo Alto Research Center (PARC) which invented, among other things, laser printing, Ethernet, the personal computer graphical user interface (GUI) paradigm (or Windows), and object-oriented programming, but never made much money from them. This is not to say that some explorers do not appropriate the value that they create. Some do make money but the money does not come through a deliberate attempt to create and capture value.

Superstars

A *superstar* is a firm that moves first in pursuing an innovation and diligently performs those activities that substantially improve its chances of building and exploiting first-mover advantages, countering first-mover disadvantages, and taking advantage of competitors' handicaps. Usually, a superstar has a clear strategy for how to create and appropriate value when it moves first. Like explorers, a superstar is interested in exploring new ways of creating value. However, unlike explorers, superstars are also genuinely and purposefully interested in exploitation—in making money. A superstar works hard at performing innovative activities and capturing the resulting value. It does the right things and does them right. With some luck, such a firm not only can gain a competitive advantage, it can also change the structure of its industry to its advantage. It can become the superstar of its industry. Largely because the superstar has built the right first-mover advantages and is taking advantage of them, followers usually have a difficult time catching up with or leapfrogging the superstar.

Moreover, a superstar may also have countered potential first-mover disadvantages, and taken advantage of potential competitors' handicaps. This does not mean that a superstar's competitive advantage is forever. Merck was a superstar when it performed the relevant R&D to discover and exploit Mevacor, the first cholesterol drug from the group of cholesterol drugs called statins that would revolutionize cholesterol therapy. Wal-Mart was a superstar when it established its discount retailing operations in rural southwestern United States. Superstars usually make money, but not necessarily all the time. Their deliberate pursuit of value creation and appropriation increases their chances compared to those of an explorer. However, because superstars often face the huge technological and marketing uncertainties associated with moving first, they are not always likely to appropriate most of the value that they have created.

Exploiters

An *exploiter* is a follower that waits for explorers and superstars to move first and reduce technological and market uncertainty, and then enters. An exploiter usually has or can quickly develop the ability to take advantage of first-mover disadvantages to better create and/or capture value than first movers. Exploiters usually do not invent or discover anything but can make most of the money from inventions or discoveries. They usually have complementary assets—all the other assets, apart from those that underpin the innovation that firms need to create and appropriate value. There are many examples of exploiters in many industries. General Electric and Siemens did not invent CAT scans but made most of the money from the innovation. Coke and Pepsi did not invent diet or caffeine-free colas but made most of the money from them. Microsoft did not invent many of the products from which it makes money. The iPod was not the first MP3 player but dominated the market in 2007. Like superstars, exploiters have clear strategies for creating and appropriating value. In doing so, however, they take advantage of their complementary assets and ability to exploit first-mover *dis*advantages. They usually know when to enter and what to do when they enter. Some entrepreneurs see exploiters as an important part of their exit strategies since they can sell themselves (and their technologies and ideas) to the exploiters for good money. Some explorers see exploiters more as piranha.

Me-too

Me-too players are followers who have no clear strategy for taking advantage of first-mover *dis*advantages to better create and capture value than first-movers. Many of them are incumbents who are forced to defend their competitive advantages from attacking first-movers or exploiters but do not quite know how. Some are firms that take advantage of first-mover disadvantages to create or enter niche markets. In that case, they may have clear strategies for attacking the niche in question but not for toppling first-movers or exploiters. Many suppliers of generic pharmaceuticals are me-too players.

Competition and Coopetition

It is important to note that the success of each player type depends on the competition that it faces. Superstars are less likely to shine brightly if they start executing their strategies at about the same time that other firms with more valuable and scarce complementary assets enter the market. They are also less likely to do well if exploiters enter the market before the superstars have had a chance to build first-mover advantages. If explorers are never challenged by exploiters or superstars, they may make money simply because they do not have strong competitors. Exploiters are less likely to make money if they enter the market at about the same time that other exploiters enter or enter after superstars have had a chance to build first-mover advantages. Me-toos can do well if they enter niche markets and neither superstars nor exploiters bother to challenge them. Effectively, the competition that a player faces plays an important role in the extent to which the player can make money.

A player's performance may also depend on the extent to which it is better able to cooperate with other players in creating and capturing value. An explorer that is more capable of invention may team up with an exploiter that has complementary assets to form a team that has a better chance of winning than either player alone. Exploiters and superstars can also team up to exploit their complementary assets, especially if each player comes from a different country that has something unique to offer.

Applications of the Player-Type Framework

Although the player-type framework is very simple, it has some potentially powerful applications. It is versatile, and can be used to provide an elementary but useful look at a firm's innovation strategies (1) for different products, (2) in different countries, and (3) over a time period.

Explore Different Product Innovation Strategies

It is not unusual that, at any one time, one firm can be an exploiter for one product, an explorer for another product, and a superstar or me-too for yet another. Managers can use the player-type framework to explore the different strategies that underpin each of these products and make some decisions on what to improve. Figure 9.4 offers an example of how the framework can be applied to a computer maker. In the year 2000, the company offered three products: laptops, servers, and MP3 players. The area of each circle in Figure 9.4 is proportional to sales revenues or profits at 2000 prices. The earlier a firm introduced a product before its next major competitor, the higher the circle. The more that the firm was seen as having gotten the innovation strategy for the product right, the more the circle would lie to the right. Thus, in both 2000 and 2007, the firm was an explorer when it came to strategies for its laptops. However, in 2007, it behaved a little more like a superstar since the laptop circle moved to the right (the firm was still an explorer).

The strategy also appears to have paid off since its 2007 revenues were higher than its 2000 revenues. As far as servers were concerned, the firm behaved as a superstar. Its revenues increased from 2000 to 2007 as the firm appeared to have fine-tuned its strategy. Finally, the firm appeared to have improved its strategy for MP3s from 2000 to 2007 as an exploiter but its revenues dropped. Why the drop? It is possible that competition increased even as the firm improved its strategy. While very simple, this analysis is still a good starting point for a management discussion about whether to continue offering all three products, focus on one or two, and if so, whether to still do so as a superstar, exploiter, or explorer, or may be even as a me-too.

Performance of Different Product Innovation Strategies in Different Markets

The framework can also be used to examine a multiproduct/service firm's strategies in different countries or regions. Consider a firm that pursues different strategies in the European Union, China, and the USA (Figure 9.5). Again, the area of the circle is proportional to the revenues or profits that the firm earns in each region in the period

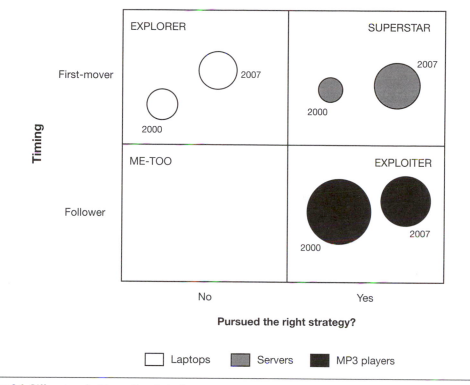

Figure 9.4 Different product innovation strategies

being explored. In the European Union, the firm does well as an explorer and an exploiter, somewhat well as a me-too but not so well as a superstar. Such a firm could be a fast-food company such as McDonald's or Kentucky Fried Chicken that operates as an explorer in some countries where it is usually the first fast-food company in each of the locations where it opens its stores, an exploiter in others, and so on.

In China, the company acts as a superstar, exploiter, and me-too. It is more successful as an exploiter and me-too than as a superstar (each has a larger circle area than the me-too). The firm could also be a fast-food company or a retailer that has different strategies for different regions of China. In the US, the firm offers four different products, with each one reflecting a different player type. The firm is most successful as a superstar, followed by being an exploiter and then an explorer. Being me-too works the least. Such an analysis can be a good starting point for whether to continue trying to be all things to markets or focus on only being a superstar, explorer, exploiter, or me-too in each market.

History of a Firm's Innovative Strategies

In the third example, a firm can use the framework to explore where it has been and how well it has performed as a superstar, explorer, exploiter and me-too (Figure 9.6). Such a firm could be a pharmaceutical company that introduced different drugs using different strategies. In the example, the firm started out in the 1980s as an explorer and offered two products that did relatively well. However, the product for which the firm

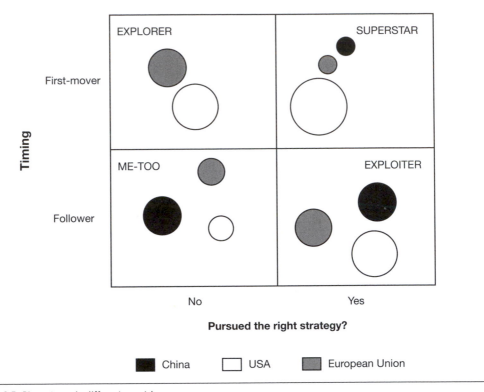

Figure 9.5 Player types in different countries

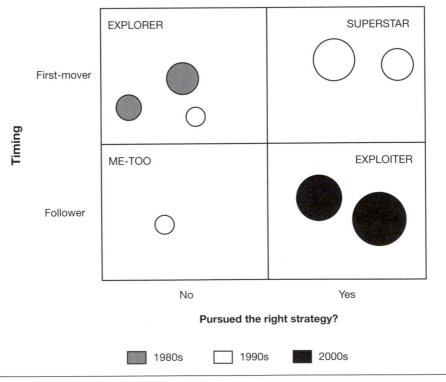

Figure 9.6 A firm's evolution as explorer, superstar, me-too, and exploiter

had more of a strategy than the other (the one to the right in the explorer quadrant) had more revenues. In the 1990s, the firm decided to try being a superstar and me-too in addition to being an explorer. Its revenues as a superstar were much higher than those as an explorer and me-too. In the 2000s, the firm had become an exploiter and was doing very well. This analysis is also a good starting point for managers to discuss what next for the company. It suggests, for example, that the firm might want to continue being an exploiter, assuming that everything else—e.g. competition or technological innovation—remains the same. One other thing that the results suggest is that the firm may have been riding a technology lifecycle. At the onset of such a cycle, the environment is usually more conducive to explorers and superstars. As uncertainty unravels, exploiters and me-toos move in.

KEY TAKEAWAYS

- Business models are about creating and capturing (appropriating) value.

- A firm creates value when it offers customers something that they perceive as valuable (beneficial) to them and the cost of offering the benefits does not exceed them. The value captured (appropriated) is the profit that a firm receives from the value it created.

- Value creation is often undertaken by coopetitors, not one firm or individual. Thus, firms often have to cooperate to create value and compete to capture it. Where there is cooperation, there is likely to be competition. And where there is competition, there are opportunities to cooperate.

- As the case of many authors and musicians suggests, many firms or individuals that create lots of value get to capture only a small fraction of it. A firm may not be able to capture all the value that it creates because:
  - (a) The *value proposition* (from the value created) may not be compelling enough to attract many high willingness-to-pay customers.
  - (b) The firm may not be well-positioned vis-à-vis its coopetitors in an attractive *market segment.*
  - (c) The firm may have the wrong *revenue model.*
  - (d) The firm may have the wrong *growth model.*
  - (e) The firm may not have the complementary and technology *capabilities* needed to profit from the innovation.

- The value added by many exporting countries is often a lot less or more than the export value attributed to them.

- In the face of innovative activities, there are likely to be opportunities for cooperation during competition. And during cooperation, there is always implied competition.

- Innovation can shift value creation and capture along a value system.

- In the competition to capture value that takes place during cooperation, it is important not to forget to think of what one's alternatives are. That is, before dumping your partner because your percentage of the pie is small, think very carefully about who else is out there that you can create a pie with. How much more pie will cooperation with your new partner create and how much of it will you get? In leaving your existing partner for an outsider, you may be leaving 10 percent of a watermelon for 90 percent of a grape.

- Firms can be grouped as a function of when they pursue an innovation and whether they pursue the right strategy or not:
  - Explorers: move first but have no clear strategy for creating and capturing value, for building and taking advantage of first-mover advantages and disadvantages, and for exploiting competitor's handicaps.
  - Superstars: move first and have a clear strategy for creating and appropriating value, for building and taking advantage of first-mover advantages and dis- advantages, and for exploiting competitor's handicaps.
  - Exploiters: followers that use their complementary assets and other capabilities to take advantage of first-mover's disadvantages and other opportunities to better create and appropriate value than first- movers.
  - Me-toos: followers that, unlike exploiters, have no clear strategy for beating first- movers at their game. Me-toos are sometimes niche players.

KEY TERMS

Coopetition	Explorers	Value captured
Coopetitors	Me-toos	Value chain factors
Exploiters	Superstars	Value created

QUESTION

1. Table 9.2 below shows the eight most expensive components/inputs of the 30-GB Video iPod that Apple introduced in October 2005. According to Portelligent Inc., the product had 451 components, with a total cost of $144.40.[14] The iPod retailed for $299. Assuming a wholesale discount of 25 percent, what is the value captured by Apple and each of the suppliers. How much value is captured by each country? How much of that value is added by each actor?

NOTES

1 Apple iPhone to generate 50 percent margin, according to iSuppli's preliminary analysis. (2007, January 18). Retrieved July 9, 2007 from www.isuppli.com/news/default.asp?id=7308

2 See similar definitions in Besanko, D., Dranove, D., & Shanley, M. (2000). *Economics of Strategy*. (2nd edn.). New York: John Wiley & Sons. Ghemawat, P. (1991). *Commitment: The Dynamics of Strategy*. New York: Free Press. Saloner, G., Shepard, A., & Podolny, J. (2001). *Strategic Management*. New York: John Wiley. Lepak, D. P., Smith, K. G., & Taylor, M. S. (2007). Value creation and value capture: A multilevel perspective. *Academy of Management Review*, 32(1), 180–194.

3 Brandenburger, A. M., & Stuart, H. W. (2007). Biform games. *Management Science, 53*(4), 537–549. MacDonald, G., & Ryall, M. (2004). How do value creation and competition determine whether a firm captures value? *Management Science, 50*(10), 1319–1333. Lipman, S., & Rumelt, R. (2003). A bargaining

Table 9.2 Top eight most expensive components/inputs of a 30GB iPod (October, 2005)

Component/input	Supplier	Firm's country HQ	Manufacturing location	Price (US$)
Hard drive	Toshiba	Japan	China	73.39
Display module	Toshiba-Matsushita	Japan	Japan	20.39
Video/multimedia processor	Broadcom	US	Taiwan or Singapore	8.36
Portal player CPU	PortalPlayer	US	US or Taiwan	4.94
Insertion, test and assembly	Inventec	Taiwan	China	3.70
Battery pack	Unknown			2.89
Display driver	Renesas	Japan	Japan	2.88
Mobile SDRAM 32MB memory	Samsung	Korea	Korea	2.37

Source: Linden, G., Kraemer, K.L., & Dedrick, J. (2007). Who captures value in a global innovation system? The case of Apple's iPod. Retrieved July 10, 2007, from www.teardown.com/AllReports/product.aspx?reportid=8

perspective on resource advantage. *Strategic Management Journal*, 24(11), 1069–1086. Afuah, A. N. (2000). How much do your co-opetitors' capabilities matter in the face of technological change? *Strategic Management Journal*, 21(3), 387–404.

4 Laseter, T. M., Houston, P. W., Wright, J. L., & Park, J. Y. (2000). Amazon your industry: extracting value from the value chain. *Strategy & Business*, 18(1), 94–105. Digman, L. A. (2006). *Strategic Management: Competing in the Global Information Age*. New York: Thomson.

5 Laseter, T. M., Houston, P. W., Wright, J. L., & Park, J. Y. (2000). Amazon your industry: Extracting value from the value chain. *Strategy & Business*, 18(1), 94–105. Digman, L. A. (2006). *Strategic Management: Competing in the Global Information Age*. New York: Thomson.

6 Laseter, T. M., Houston, P. W., Wright, J. L., & Park, J. Y. (2000). Amazon your industry: Extracting value from the value chain. *Strategy & Business*, 18(1), 94–105.

7 Apple iPhone to generate 50 percent margin, according to iSuppli's preliminary analysis. (2007, January 18). Retrieved July 9, 2007 from http://www.isuppli.com/news/default.asp?id=7308
Kanoh, Y. (2007, July 6). Samsung Electronics Supplies Largest Share of iPhone Components: iSuppli. Retrieved July 9, 2007, from http://techon.nikkeibp.co.jp/english/NEWS_EN/20070706/135572/.

8 Wallace, J. (2006, June 27). Boeing Dreamliner 'coming to life.' Retrieved July 8, 2007, from http://seattlepi.nwsource.com/business/275465_japan27.html

9 Gates, D. (2005, September 11). Boeing 787: Parts from around world will be swiftly integrated. *The Seattle Times*.

10 Creager, E. (2002). Move over, Tupperware: Botox injections are the latest thing at home parties. Retrieved September 14, 2007, from www.woai.com/guides/beauty/story.aspx?content_id=16358daf-d7db-4ade-a757-9e8d7cf30212

11 Dyer, J. H., & Singh, H. (1998). The relational view: Cooperative strategy and sources of interorganizational competitive advantage. *Academy of Management Review*, 23(4), 660–679.

12 Afuah, A. N. (2000). How much do your co-opetitors' capabilities matter in the face of technological change? *Strategic Management Journal*, 21(3), 387–404. Dyer, J. H., & Singh, H. (1998). The relational view: Cooperative strategy and sources of interorganizational competitive advantage. *Academy of Management Review*, 23(4), 660–679.

13 My thanks to Scott Peterson from whom I obtained the "grape versus watermelon" comparison in the STRAT 675 MBA class that I teach at the Stephen M. Ross School of Business at the University of Michigan in the Fall of 2007.

14 Linden, G., Kraemer, K. L., & Dedrick, J. (2007). Who captures value in a global innovation system? The case of Apple's iPod. Retrieved July 10, 2007, from www.teardown.com/AllReports/product.aspx?reportid=

10

FIRST-MOVER ADVANTAGES/DISADVANTAGES
AND STRATEGIC CONSEQUENCES

Reading this chapter should provide you with the information to:

- Explain the advantages and disadvantages of moving first.
- Understand that first-mover advantages are usually not endowed on everyone who moves first; rather, they have to be earned.
- Understand why first-movers sometimes win and sometimes followers win.
- Understand the roles played by explorers, superstars, exploiters, and me-toos in the face of an innovation.

INTRODUCTION

Consider the following: eBay was the first online auction firm and went on to dominate its industry. However, Google was not the first search engine company but went on to also dominate its own industry. Coca-Cola invented the classic coke and went on to dominate the market for colas, with some help and challenges from Pepsi. However, neither Coke nor Pepsi invented diet cola even though they dominate that market. Apple did not invent the MP3 player and yet its iPod went on to dominate the market for MP3 players. The question is, why is it that sometimes first-movers go on to dominate their markets, but at other times followers (second-movers) are the ones that go on to dominate their markets? In this chapter, we look deeper into the advantages and disadvantages of moving first. We start the chapter by exploring what first-mover advantages are all about. Next, we explore first-mover *dis*advantage—also known as followers' or second-mover advantages. In doing so, we are reminded that first-mover advantages and disadvantages are not automatically bestowed on any first mover. Rather, first-mover advantages have to be earned and disadvantages can be minimized. We conclude the chapter by exploring why it is that sometimes first movers win and sometimes followers win.

FIRST-MOVER ADVANTAGES

A *first-mover advantage* is a capability, or product-market-position that (1) a firm acquires by being the first to carry out an activity, and (2) gives the firm an advantage in creating and appropriating value. A firm has an opportunity to acquire first-mover advantages when it is the first to introduce a new product in an existing market, create a new market, invest in an activity first, or perform any other value chain, value network or value shop activity first such as bypassing distributors and selling directly to end-customers.[1] First-mover advantages fall into six categories (Table 10.1):

1. Total available market preemption.
2. Lead in technology, innovation, and business processes.
3. Preemption of scarce resources.
4. First-to-customer.
5. First to establish a system of activities.

Total Available Market Preemption

If, in moving first, a firm introduces a new product, it has a chance to do the right things and capture as much of the total available market as possible before followers start moving in. Since such a firm is the only one in the market, it has a 100 percent share of the new product no matter how many units it sells. Thus, the emphasis here is in capturing as much of the *total available* market as possible and selling as many units as possible before followers move in—that is, emphasis is on preemption of total available market. Having captured as much of the total available market as possible, the firm potentially enjoys five advantages: scale economies, size effects (beyond economies of scale), economic rents and equity, network effects, and relations with coopetitors.

Table 10.1 First-mover advantages (FMAs)

Source of first-mover advantage	FMA mechanism
Total available market preemption	Economies of scale Size (beyond economies of scale) Economic rents and equity Network externalities Relationships with coopetitors
Lead in technology, innovation, and business processes	Intellectual property (patents, copyrights, trade secrets) Learning Organizational culture
Preemption of scarce resources	Complementary assets Location Input factors Plant and equipment
First-to-customers	Buyer switching cost Buyer choice under uncertainty Brand (preemption of consumer perceptual space or mindshare)
First to establish system of activities	Difficult-to-imitate system of activities
First to make irreversible commitments	Reputation and signals

Scale Economies

There are *economies of scale* in production if the more of a product that is produced, the lower the *per unit* cost of production. There can be economies of scale in R&D, advertising, distribution, marketing, sales, and service if the more units that are sold, the less the *per unit* cost of each activity. The scale advantage derives largely from the fact that the (total) fixed cost of each activity can be spread over the larger number of units. For example, an ad slot on TV costs the same for Coca-Cola's diet cola as it does for Shasta's diet cola. Since Coca-Cola sells hundreds of millions of cans of its diet cola compared to a few million cans for Shasta, Coke has lower per unit advertising costs compared to Shatsta. If a firm moves first and performs the right activities, it can pre-preemptively capture as much of the total available market as possible. Additionally, if the firm's industry and market are such that there are economies of scale, its per unit cost of R&D, advertising, distribution, marketing, sales, service, etc. can be lower. This lower per unit cost from economies of scale has several implications for the different components of its ability to create and appropriate value.

If a firm that moved first has captured as much of the total available market as possible and enjoys scale economies, rational potential new entrants know that if they were to enter the market to compete head-on with the first-mover, they would have to capture the same market share (as the first-mover) so as to attain the same per unit costs as the first-mover. However, doing so would mean bringing in the same capacity as the first-mover to the same market, thereby doubling the capacity. This might result in a price war that lowers profits for the new entrant. Thus, rational potential new entrants might refrain from entering. Effectively, if a first-mover can capture as much of the total available market as possible, it can attain scale economies, thereby creating barriers to entry for some potential followers. These barriers to entry are more difficult to surmount if the minimum efficient scale is large relative to the total available market and if the first-mover has a system of activities or distinctive resources and capabilities that are difficult to imitate. When we say that a first-mover's preemption of total available market raises barriers to entry, we do not mean that it is impossible for new entrants to enter. New entrants do enter sometimes but pursue niche markets. However, they would have a much more difficult time competing head-on with a first-mover that has captured most of the total available market where economies of scale exist. Another exception is when a firm pursues a revolutionary strategy and takes advantage of a technological innovation to move in, leapfrogging the first-mover.

Size Effects Beyond Economies of Scale

A first-mover that pursues the right strategies and captures as much of the total available market as possible has another advantage beyond economies of scale—size. A large firm buys more from its suppliers than its competitors and, in some cases, can command considerable bargaining power over its suppliers. For example, Wal-Mart's size gave it a tremendous amount of power over its suppliers in the mid-2000s.[2] Power play or none, it is also easier for suppliers to cooperate with larger firms. For example, to have suppliers locate near a firm, the firm needs to buy large enough output from the supplier to make it worth the supplier's investment in plants, equipment and people to serve a customer at a particular location. A large firm can also afford to undertake more innovation projects since it can spread its risk over more stable and less risky projects.

Economic Rents and Equity

Before competitors move in, a first-mover is effectively a monopolist and can collect economic rents if it formulates and executes a profitable business model. If it captures most of the total available market and keeps growing fast, that first-mover's market valuation (capitalization) may go up as investors anticipate positive future cash flows from economic rents. Such money can serve the first-mover well, especially in cases where capital markets are not very efficient and therefore financing is not readily available to anyone who needs it. The first-mover can use the money to buy fledgling new entrants, make venture capital investments, invest in more R&D, or acquire important complementary assets. If a first-mover accumulates cash, a small new entrant is less likely to be tempted to start a price war since the first-mover has more cash to sustain losses.

The other side to a first-mover earning economic rents is that these rents are likely to attract potential new entrants who want a share of these profits. If the first-mover has accumulated enough cash or has enough equity, it can establish a reputation for fighting or take other measures such as forming alliances, joint ventures, and so on, to fend off attacks.

Network Externalities

As we saw in Chapter 8, a product (or technology) exhibits network externalities if the more people that use the product or compatible one, the more useful the product becomes to users. An example is an auction network such as eBay's. The more registered users that eBay has in its community of registered users, the more valuable that the network becomes to each user. That is because, for example, the larger the network, the more that a potential buyer of an antique is likely to find the antique in the network, and the more that the seller of an antique is likely to find a buyer in the network. More people would therefore tend to gravitate towards larger networks rather than smaller ones.

Therefore, if a first-mover has preemptively captured a lot of the available market for a product or technology that exhibits network externalities, customers are likely to gravitate towards its network or products, further increasing the number of users of its network or products. Thus, a first-mover that has an initial lead can see that lead balloon to an even larger lead. Products that require complements such as computers also exhibit network externalities effects. That is because the more users that own a particular computer or compatible one, the more software that will be developed for it. And the more software that there is for the particular computer or compatible one, the more users that want the computer. Thus, a first-mover that has a large installed base of products that require complements is likely to see more users gravitate towards its products, further increasing its installed base and attracting yet more customers.

A large network size or installed base has several implications for the different components of a firm's business model. First, since the larger a network, the more valuable it is to customers, a large proprietary network can be a differentiating factor for first-movers. Second, rational potential new entrants know that if they were to enter, they would need a network as large as the first-mover if they wanted to offer the same value to customers as the first-mover. However, new customers tend to gravitate towards the larger network. Thus, a large proprietary network acts as a barrier to entry for some potential new entrants. Again, this does not mean that no firms enter the industry. Some usually enter but compete in niche markets or use technological changes and innovation to compete against the first-mover with the large network.[3]

Also, a large network acts as a barrier to entry only when it is proprietary. If it is open, as was the case with the Wintel PC, barriers to entry are lower. Third, since, all else equal, customers would prefer a large network over a smaller one, customers within a first-mover's network would prefer to stay within the larger network than move. Effectively, a large network constitutes switching costs for customers. Thus, a first-mover can dampen customer bargaining power by building in switching costs at customers in the form of a large proprietary network. Fourth, a large proprietary network also reduces rivalry between the owner of the network and those of smaller networks. That is because the firm's larger network differentiates it from its smaller rivals. As we saw earlier in Chapter 8, other factors beyond size sometimes also impact the value that customers perceive in a network.

Relationships with Coopetitors

In our discussion about first-mover advantages so far, we have treated suppliers, customers, buyers, rivals, and potential new entrants as competitors whose goal is to sap profits out of the first-mover. Often, as we saw in Chapter 9, these actors are more than just competitors. They are coopetitors—the firms with which one has to cooperate to create value and compete to appropriate it—and relationships with them can be critical. A first-mover has an opportunity to build relationships not only with coopetitors, but also with institutions such as government agencies or universities. Such relations can, among other things, help the collaborators to win a standard or dominant design.

Lead in Technology, Innovation and Business Processes

A first-mover often has an opportunity to establish leadership positions in business processes, technology, and organizational innovation. These leadership positions can be manifested in the quality and levels of intellectual property, learning, and culture that they can integrate into their business models.

Intellectual Property

Innovations in business processes, technology, and organizational processes can be a source of advantage to firms and consequently, some firms try to protect them using patents, copyrights, trademarks, or trade secrets. For many products, patents do not offer their owners enough protection from imitation since they can be circumvented. Copyrights and trademarks are not protected by the laws of many countries and when they are protected by law, there is often little monitoring and enforcement of the laws. Trade secrets often are revealed through employees who move to other firms or through reverse engineering of products.

Despite these often-cited shortcomings of intellectual property protection, intellectual property often serves a useful purpose in the profitability of a first-mover's business model. First, in some industries and countries, patents and copyrights give their owners reasonable protection for a period of time during which they can collect monopoly rents from their invention or discovery. For example, one reason why many so-called blockbuster pharmaceutical drugs such as Lipitor bring in such high amounts of revenues is because they enjoy patent protection during their patent lives. Once a drug's patent protection runs out and generics can be introduced, revenues from such drugs can drop by as much as 86 per cent.

Second, although many patents, copyrights, trademarks, and trade secrets may not prevent entry, they can slow it down. Circumventing a patent, though less costly than developing an original patent, can still be costly to get it right, if one ever does. Third, even when intellectual property protection does not prevent entry or slow it down, it can still be the source of revenues and profits. The case of Google and Overture is very illustrative of how intellectual property can be used. Google developed a search engine that, using its PageRank algorithm, delivered some of the most relevant search results. To more optimally make money from its search capabilities, the company needed a better advertising revenue model than pop-up ads. Overture, formerly known as Goto.com, had invented and, in July 2001, received a patent for a bid-for-placement mechanism— an ad-placement mechanism that allowed advertisers to bid for the placement of ads next to or above search results.[4] In August 2004, Google and Yahoo (which had bought Overture in July 2003) settled the lawsuit for 2.7 million shares of Google class A common shares.[5] On June 28, 2006 the 2.7 million shares were worth just over one billion dollars.

Qualcomm's case offers another example. In 2010, most of the company's profits came from the royalties on its patents. Effectively, first-movers can make money from their intellectual properties even when followers enter their market spaces. Third, a first-mover can use its intellectual property as bargaining chips for other important resources that it may need to profit from its inventions or discoveries. For example, a start-up that invents a new product needs marketing, manufacturing, distribution, shelf space, and other complementary assets so as to profit from the invention. It can use its intellectual property as a bargaining chip to gain access to such complementary assets. That is just what many biotech firms do when they team up with established pharmaceuticals.

Learning

In performing R&D, manufacturing, marketing and other value-adding activities, a first-mover accumulates know-how and other knowledge. Although some of this knowledge can spill over to potential competitors through employee mobility, informal know-how trading, reverse engineering, plant tours, and research publications, first-movers still do benefit from their accumulated learning in several ways. First, as suggested by the standard learning or experience curve model, a firm's production cost for a particular product drops as a function of the cumulative number of units that the firm has produced since it started producing the product. Thus, to the extent that the knowledge is difficult to diffuse or the firm can keep it proprietary, the firm can have a cost advantage over followers. This can reduce potential new entry since any new entrant would have to accumulate as much knowledge in order to bring its costs down to those of the first-mover. A firm can also use its accumulated knowledge as a bargaining chip for complementary assets. The case of Pixar and Disney illustrates this. Pixar was the first to move into the digital animation movie technology and used its know-how to gain access to Disney's brand-name reputation in animation, storytelling, merchandising might, and its distribution channels through an alliance that was beneficial to both firms.

Organizational Culture

An organization's culture is the set of values, beliefs, and norms that are shared by employees.[6] Since a culture is embedded in a firm's routines, actions, and history, it is often difficult to imitate and takes time to cultivate. Moving first can give a firm the valuable time that it needs to build the culture. Where culture is valuable, difficult-to-imitate and rare, it can be a source of competitive advantage.[7] It can lower costs or allow a firm to be more innovative than its competitors, thereby differentiating its products. Southwest Airlines' culture was often associated with it being the most profitable airline in the United States from the 1970s well into the 2000s. The company's employees cared about each other, were flexible in the types of jobs that they were willing to perform, and were happy to work harder for longer hours than employees at competing airlines.

Preemption of Scarce Resources

A first-mover often has the opportunity to acquire important scarce resources, thereby preempting rivals.

Complementary Assets

For many firms, moving first usually means inventing a new product or introducing a new technology. To profit from such an invention or new technology, a firm needs complementary capabilities (complementary assets)—capabilities beyond those that underpin the invention or the new technology. A firm that moves first has the opportunity to preempt rivals and acquire complementary assets. Once such critical resources are gone, there is not much that potential new entrants can do. For example, first movers Coke and Pepsi preempted most potential new entrants in the soda business by taking up most of the shelf space in stores for sodas. Preemption of complementary assets can constitute an important barrier to entry. Rational potential new entrants who know that they cannot obtain the necessary complementary assets are less likely to enter, or when they enter, they are likely to seek alliances with those that have the assets. Complementary assets such as brands can also differentiate a first-mover's products from those of followers.

Location

In many arenas, there is only so much room for so many competitors. Thus, a first-mover that pursues the right strategies can preempt rivals by leaving little room for followers. Take geographic space, for example. At airports, there is usually a limited number of gates and landing slots. An airline that moves into an airport early and introduces many flights can take up most of the gates and landing slots, leaving followers to the airport with few gates and landing slots. When Wal-Mart entered the retail market in the Southwestern United States, it saturated contiguous towns with stores, thereby erecting a barrier to entry since any potential new entrant who expected to enjoy the same costs benefits from economies of scale as Wal-Mart would have to build as many stores and distribution centers as Wal-Mart. However, doing so would result in over-capacity and the threat of a price war. Such a potential threat of price wars would prevent some rational potential new entrants from entering.

Establishing positions in geographic space does not have to be through saturation of contiguous locations as Wal-Mart did. The first-mover can establish the positions in such a way that occupying the interstices will be unprofitable for a follower.[8] For example, good market research might allow the first-mover to pick out the more lucrative locations to occupy, leaving out the less profitable ones for followers.

Location preemption can also take place in product space. First-movers can introduce many products with enough variation in attributes to cover the potentially profitable product-attribute spaces, leaving very little or no so-called "white space"—potentially lucrative product space that others can occupy. Such a lack of white space can deter entry.

Input Factors

In some industries, first-movers may be able to attract talented employees and, with the right incentives, retain them when followers enter. In some situations, moving first and performing the right research can provide superior information about resource needs and availability. Such information can enable a first-mover to purchase assets at market prices below those that will prevail as followers move in. (Note that the first-mover can also profit from such superior information by buying options for the assets where such markets for options exist.) For example, a mineral or oil company that goes to a developing country and explores for mineral or oil deposits has superior information about the potential of the country, compared to local officials or competitors that have not yet ventured into the country. Such a firm can secure access to such deposits by signing contracts with local officials. Access to superior information can also help firms in structuring contracts with employees.

Plant and Equipment

If a firm builds a plant to produce a particular product and the plant cannot be profitably used for any other purpose, the firm is said to have made an *irreversible investment* in the plant. First-movers who make irreversible investments in equipment, plants, or any other major asset, signal to potential followers that they are committed to maintaining higher output levels following entry by followers. That is because their plants and equipment cannot be profitably used elsewhere and therefore managers are likely to keep producing so long as the prices that they charge are high enough to cover their variable costs. If followers were to enter, such first-movers could engage in price wars so long as their prices are high enough to cover their variable costs. Effectively, irreversible investments in plants and equipment can deter entry and can be a first-mover advantage.

First-at-customers

Customers play a critical role in the profitability of a business model and being the first to reach customers can give a firm an opportunity to attain first-mover advantages. We explore three such potential advantages.

Switching Costs

A buyer's *switching costs* are the costs that it incurs when it switches from one supplier (firm) to another. These include the costs of training employees to deal with the new supplier; the time and resources for locating, screening, and qualifying new suppliers; and the cost of new equipment such as software to comply with the supplier. Switching costs can also arise from incompatibility of a buyer's assets with the new supplier. For example, frequent flyer miles accumulated on one airline may not work on some other airlines. If buyers' switching costs for a firm's products are high, the buyers are less likely to switch to another firm's products. Potential new entrants who know that buyers will not switch are less likely to try to enter. Rivals who know that buyers are less likely to switch are less likely to try to win customers using lower prices. Thus, if a first-mover can build switching costs at buyers before followers move in, it can have an advantage.

It is important to note that while switching costs can prevent existing customers from switching to new firms, they usually have little effect on new customers who have no switching costs to worry about. Thus, in a growing market, followers can focus on new customers to increase their market share.

Buyer Choice Under Uncertainty

The information that customers have about the benefits from some products is imperfect. Buyers of such products may therefore stay with the first brand that meets their needs satisfactorily.[9] This is particularly true for *experience goods*—products or services whose characteristics are ascertained only after consumption since it is difficult to observe their characteristics in advance. For example, because a drug's efficacy and side-effects can vary from patient to patient and cannot be determined in advance, doctors tend to stick with the first drug that works for their patients and are not likely to switch to a follower's drugs unless there are compelling reasons. Such *brand loyalty* can be particularly strong for low-cost convenience goods where the search costs of finding another product that meets a customer's taste often exceed the benefits of changing brands. (Convenience goods are products such as soaps and pasta that one purchases frequently and with minimum effort.) The effect is less strong for *search goods*—products or services such as airplanes whose characteristics are easy to evaluate objectively before purchase.

Brand Mindshare: Preemption of Consumer Perceptual Space

Also, research suggests that pioneering brands can have a strong influence on consumer preferences.[10] In some cases, the first product introduced may actually receive disproportionate attention in the press and in consumer's minds. A case in question is Viagra, which received lots of free press from unlikely sources such as TV comedians. A follower must have a superior product or have to spend a lot more on building its brand to dislodge the first product.

First To Establish a System of Activities

One of the more durable first-mover advantages that a firm can have is a difficult-to-replicate system of activities.[11] Why is a system of activities difficult to imitate? Although imitating some individual activities in such a system of activities may be easy, imitating a whole system can be difficult since it entails imitating not only the components of the system but the interactions between the components. The extent to which it can be difficult to imitate a system of activities is illustrated by the now familiar Dell example. Dell was the first major PC maker to pursue direct sales and build-to-order. It established a system of activities to support this strategy that followers found difficult to imitate.

First to Make Irreversible Commitments

First-mover advantages can not only change the likely expectations of followers, but they can also change their behavior. One goal of making irreversible investments is to deter or slow down followers. However, to have such an effect, there must be something about the first-mover that suggests that it is committed to that particular first-mover advantage. For example, a first-mover can establish a reputation for retaliating against any firm that infringes on its intellectual property by suing anyone who attempts to violate its patents or copyrights. For a commitment to be effective in deterring or slowing down competitors, it must be credible, visible to competitors and understandable.[12]

A commitment is *credible* if there is something about it that makes competitors believe in it and the options that it creates or limits. The primary drivers of credibility are reputation and irreversibility of the commitment. If a firm has a reputation for fighting the first set of followers that venture into its product market space, it is likely to do so with the next set. Such a reputation for retaliation can deter likely entrants. A commitment is *irreversible* if it is costly or difficult to walk away from or undo. As we saw earlier, that would be the case, for example, if the assets that underpin the commitment cannot be profitably redeployed elsewhere. The idea here is that if a first-mover's commitment is irreversible, it is more likely to stay and fight followers rather than accommodate them or exit. Commitments such as physical plants are visible to many people but others such as commitments to a culture are more difficult to observe. When commitments are not very visible, signals can be used to indicate their presence. Signals can also be used to help competitors understand the nature of a firm's commitments. Effectively, a firm that moves first has the opportunity to make commitments that are credible, visible, and understandable. Doing so can deter or slow down followers.

FIRST MOVER *DISADVANTAGES*

There are also *dis*advantages to moving first. These first-mover *dis*advantages are also called follower advantages.[13] Followers sometimes stand to benefit from freeriding on the spillovers from first-movers' investments, resolution of technological and marketing uncertainty, changes in technology or customer needs, and first-mover inertia.

Free-Riding on First-Mover's Investments

First-movers, especially those that pioneer new products, sometimes have to invest heavily in R&D to develop the new product, in training employees for whom the technology and market are new, in helping suppliers better understand what they should be supplying, in developing distribution channels, and in working with customers to help them discover their latent needs. Followers can take advantage of the now available knowledge from first movers' R&D, hire away some of the employees that the first-mover trained, buy from suppliers who have a better idea about what it is that they should be supplying, use proven distribution channels and go after customers who may be willing to switch or new ones who are waiting for a different version of the pioneer's product. Effectively, a follower's costs can be considerably lower than those of the first-mover on whose investments the follower free rides. The fact that these free-riding opportunities exist does not mean that every follower can take advantage of them. Whether a follower is able to take advantage of these opportunities is a function of the imitability of the first-mover's product and the extent to which the follower has the complementary assets for the product.[14] It is also a function of the business models that the first-mover and follower pursue.

Resolution of Technological and Marketing Uncertainty

In some cases, first-movers face lots of technological and marketing uncertainty that must be resolved. This uncertainty is gradually resolved as the first mover works with suppliers, customers, and complementors to better deliver what customers want. For example, the emergence of a standard or dominant design can drastically reduce the amount of uncertainty since firms do not have to make major costly design changes and suppliers know better what to supply.[15] Followers who enter after the emergence of a standard or dominant design, for example, do not have to worry as much about what design to pursue or whether a market exists or not, as did the pioneer. Whether followers can erode a first-mover's competitive advantage depends on what the pioneer did when it moved first. A first-mover that pursues the right strategies can win the standard or dominant design, and therefore have a say as to the extent to which followers can profit from the standard or dominant design.

Changes in Technology or Customer Needs and First-Mover Inertia

Technological change or a shift in customer needs that requires a first-mover to change can give a follower an opening if the first-mover's inertia prevents it from changing. For example, if a technological change makes it possible to introduce a new product that potentially replaces a first-mover's product, the first-mover is not likely to be in a rush to introduce the new product for fear of cannibalizing its existing product.

COMPETITORS' HANDICAPS

When a firm moves *first* and enjoys first-mover advantages, it is because its competitors (present and potential) decided not to move first or to follow immediately. The question is, what is it about some firms that would make them not move first or not move at all despite the potential first-mover advantages? Put differently, if there are so many advantages to moving first, what is it about a first-mover's competitors that prevents them from moving first? We explore five factors that can prevent competitors from moving first or following: competitors' dominant logic, lack of strategic fit, prior commitments, a lack of the capabilities required to move, and the fear of cannibalization.

Dominant Logic

Every manager has a set of beliefs, biases, and assumptions about the structure and conduct of the industry in which his or her firm operates, what markets her firm should focus on, what the firm's business model should be, who to hire, who the firm's competitors are, what technologies are best for the firm, and so on.[16] This set of beliefs, biases, and assumptions is a manager's *managerial logic* and defines the frame within which a manager is likely to approach management decisions.[17] Managerial logic is at the core of a manager's ability to search, filter, collect, evaluate, assimilate new information, and take decisions using the newly acquired information.[18]

Depending on organizational values, norms, culture, structure, systems, processes, business model, environment (industry and macro), and how successful the firm has been, there usually emerges a *dominant managerial logic*—a common way of viewing how best to do business in the firm. Also called mental map, managerial frame, genetic code, corporate genetics, and corporate mindset, dominant logic is very good for a firm that has been performing well so long as there are no major changes. That is, dominant managerial logic is usually a strength. In the face of some innovations, a firm is likely to pass over some opportunities if they lie outside its managers' dominant logic—outside manager's beliefs, biases and assumptions about how best to do business. Thus, competitors' dominant logic may be one reason why a first-mover is the one that moves first and not its competitors.

Strategic Fit

Competitors' dominant logic may be such that they can understand the benefits of moving first but management might still decide not to move first. That would be the case, for example, if moving first does not fit the firm's strategy. Exploiters with valuable scarce complementary assets often pursue a so-called *follower strategy* and wait for others to introduce a new product first. They then quickly imitate the product and use their scarce complementary assets to overcome the first-mover and profit from the first-mover's inventions. IBM pursued such a follower strategy in the 1970s, 1980, and 1990s. It did not invent the personal computer but used its brand-name reputation, installed base of customers, and software developers to temporary gain about 60 percent of the PC market share before seeing that share drop dramatically and eventually getting out of the market. It also waited until Apollo Computers and Sun Microsystems had developed the computer workstation business before it entered and used its installed base of customers and brand to quickly attain an important market share. As we saw in Chapter 8, EMI, the British music record company, invented CAT scans but GE and Siemens used their complementary assets to make most of the profits from the invention.

Prior Commitments

Even if it is in the interest of a competitor to move first or follow a first-mover, the competitor may still be prevented from taking action because of prior commitments that it made in its earlier activities. We examine two types of commitments: relationship-related and sunk cost-related.

Relationship-Related Commitments

Relationship-related commitments are commitments such as contracts, network relationships, alliances, joint ventures, agreements, understandings within political coalitions, and venture capital investments that involve more than one party. Sometimes, pursuing an innovation requires a firm to get out of or modify the terms of prior relationship-related commitments. If a change is not in the interest of the other party, the party might refuse to cooperate. A popular example, which we saw earlier in this book, is that of Compaq, the PC maker, which was prevented from changing its strategy by its relationships with distributors of PCs.

Sunk Cost-Related Commitments

In sunk cost-related commitments, a firm makes irreversible investments in plants, equipment, capacity or other resources, sometimes to signal its commitment to stay in a market. If pursuing an innovation requires resources that are different from a firm's irreversible investments but its existing product-market-positions (PMP) remain competitive, staying with one's irreversible investments rather than investing in the innovation may appear to be the profitable thing to do. Why? For the incumbent, investing in the innovation requires new investments and this money must come from somewhere else since the firm's existing investments are sunk and therefore their costs cannot be recovered and reinvested in the innovation. Thus, if the firm pursues the innovation, it must incur all the new costs. If it stays with its existing activities, it does not have to spend any new money since its products from the sunk investments are still competitive. If products from the innovation improve at a faster rate than those from existing activities, there may come a time when customers start migrating to the innovation and the firm that stuck with the sunk investments will see its market share eroded.

Do Not Have Scarce Capabilities

In some industries, pursuing an innovation requires distinctive capabilities that competitors may not have. Developing a new microprocessor or operating system can require billions of dollars and many very skilled engineers. These are scarce capabilities that few firms have. Thus, competitors may not be able to compete with a first-mover because they do not have the scarce capabilities needed to compete. For example, many countries cannot afford a car industry because they do not have what it takes to build and run one profitably. This is the old barriers to entry story.

Fear of Cannibalization

Firms are not likely to pursue an innovation if doing so cannibalizes their existing products, especially if the new products have to be priced less than the old ones. For a while in the 1990s, Sun Microsystems was not eager to introduce Linux Intel-based servers since the latter cost less to buy, use, and service than Sun's UNIX-based servers. Intel-based servers eventually won the battle.

FIRST-MOVERS VERSUS FOLLOWERS: SOME CONCLUSIONS

To make more connections between the different concepts that have been explored in this chapter so far, we return to the question that was posed at the beginning of the chapter: Why is it that first movers sometimes go on to dominate their markets and, at other times, followers are the ones that go on to dominate their markets? The answer to this question is a combination of the following five reasons:

1. First-mover advantages have to be earned and exploited diligently.
2. The owner of scarce important complementary assets usually has an edge.
3. First-mover *dis*advantages can be minimized.
4. Competitive, macro, and global environments matter.
5. Type of player and its business strategy also matter.

First-Mover Advantages Have to Be Earned and Exploited Diligently

As we saw earlier, first-mover advantages are not automatically bestowed on whoever moves first. They have to be built and exploited by pursuing the right activities. If first-movers do not diligently pursue and exploit first-mover advantages, they leave room for followers, especially exploiters, to come in and possibly dominate. For example, if a pharmaceutical company wants the benefits of patent protection, it has to pursue the type of activities that will not only allow it to discover something worth patenting but also to apply for, obtain, and defend the patent in the right countries. Moreover, the firm also has to turn its patents into medicine that patients can use since patents do not cure illnesses. Perhaps more importantly, performing these activities effectively and efficiently often requires distinctive capabilities that not all first-movers have. For example, not all pharmaceutical companies have the R&D skills, knowledge base, and know-how to discover the types of compounds that can be patentable.

Effectively, if a first-mover cannot earn and exploit first-mover advantages—either because it did not know which activities to pursue or did not have or could not build the necessary distinctive capabilities—there is room for followers to come in and do well, especially followers that already have the right complementary assets or can build them quickly.

Owner of Scarce Important Complementary Assets Has an Edge

To profit from an innovation, a firm usually needs complementary assets. Thus, if a firm moves first to invent or discover something, other firms that enter the market later can make most of the profits from the invention or discovery if they have scarce important complementary capabilities that the first-mover does not have. Effectively, whoever has scarce important complementary capabilities, be it a first-mover or follower, has a better chance of being the one to profit from an innovation.

Can Minimize or Exploit First-Mover Disadvantages

If a first-mover is able to minimize the effects of first-mover *dis*advantages, it has a better chance of doing well. Take, for example, the fact that followers often can free ride on the first-mover's investments by taking advantage of the R&D knowledge generated by the first-mover, hiring from the first-mover, going after its customers, and so. A first-mover can reduce these negative effects by better protecting its intellectual property or entering into the right agreements with employees or customers. Such measures, coupled with first-mover advantages may be able to give the first-mover a better chance. If this is not possible, a follower can take advantage of first-mover disadvantages. A follower not only can free ride on first movers' R&D, it can also take advantage of the reduced technological and marketing uncertainty as well as any changes in technological change or customer needs that may have occurred since the first-mover made commitments as to which activities to perform.

The Competitive, Macro, and Global Environments

Whether the firm that goes on to dominate a market is a first-mover or follower is also a function of its competitive environment—of its rivals, suppliers, customers, potential new entrants, and substitutes. For example, if the first-mover is a new entrant that uses a disruptive technology to attack incumbents, there is a good chance that it will defeat the incumbents. If the industry has plenty of white space in the market, first-movers have more opportunities to create unique value for customers and build first-mover advantages than if they were in a more crowded market space. A dominant buyer can force a firm to find second sources for the products that the buyer buys, effectively neutralizing some of the firm's first-mover advantages. For example, in the 1970s and 1980s, IBM usually required that chipmakers that supplied it with chips had to cooperate with at least one other chipmaker to help it also supply the same chips to IBM, or transfer the know-how to IBM so that it could make the same chips if it had to.

The extent to which a firm can earn first-mover advantages is also a function of the macro environment—a function of the political, economic, technological, social, and natural environments. For example, if the political/legal environment in a country is such that there is no respect for intellectual property protections, a first-mover cannot rely on patents or copyrights as a first-mover advantage. This increases the chances that a follower can free ride on first-movers' investments in R&D, manufacturing, and marketing. If the rate of technological change is high, first-movers' commitments are more likely to make it difficult for them to adjust to technological changes, allowing followers to have a better chance. In some countries, there are restrictions on how many firms can enter some industries. First-movers in such industries are therefore more likely to do better than late followers.

Type of Player and Business Strategy

Whether a first-mover or follower wins in the face of an innovation is also a function of whether the firm is pursuing the innovation as an explorer, superstar, exploiter, or me-too. Many exploiters prefer to wait until some other firms have moved first, and both technological and marketing uncertainties have been drastically reduced before they enter. Even if exploiters accidentally discover or invent something, they usually still wait until someone else has developed the invention further and tried to commercialize it, thereby proving that there is a market for it. IBM and Microsoft are good examples. Such firms usually have the right distinctive difficult-to-imitate complementary assets. They usually also develop the skills and know-how to quickly develop and commercialize a product once they decide that technological and market uncertainty have dropped enough for them to enter. After pursuing such strategies for a long time, they may develop competences in excelling as followers. Thus, when exploiters face *explorers,* especially in the face of changing technologies or changing consumer tastes, followers are more likely to win than first-movers.

Similarly, *superstars* are usually at the forefront of inventions and pursuing the right strategies to enable them to create and capture value. They usually develop competences for moving first and pursuing the types of strategies that give them a good chance of doing well. Intel was a superstar when it invented the microprocessor, the EPROM memory device, and advanced its microprocessor technology at a pioneering rate by introducing a newer generation of its microprocessors before unit sales of an older one had peaked. Superstars are particularly likely to do well if they face only explorers or me-toos.

Effectively, if a firm's strategy is predicated on it moving first and it has developed the underpinning capabilities to back the strategy, it is likely to move first and go on to do well in its market. If its strategy is to be a follower and it has the capabilities to back it, it is likely to do well as a follower.

Numerical Example: The Value of Efficient Exploitation of First-Mover Advantages

In 1997, the cholesterol drug Lipitor was granted FDA approval. This was one year earlier than expected, because of several measures that Warner-Lambert, its inventor, had taken. Table 10.2 shows a forecast of sales up to the expiration of the patent life of the

Table 10.2 Lipitor's projected sales

Year	1997	1998	1999	2000	2001	2002	2003	2004	2005	2006	2007	2008	2009	2010
Revenues ($B) (1997 FDA)	0.9	2.2	3.4	4.6	5.6	6.7	7.7	8.7	9.7	10.7	11.7	12.7	13.7	2.06 (14.7)

Source: ING Baring Furman Selz, LLC, April 12, 1999

drug in 2011. When a drug's patent expires, the price of the drug can drop by as much as 86 percent as a result of the introduction of generic versions. The number in parenthesis in 2010 is the projected sales if the patent did not expire. How much money did the firm save by obtaining FDA approval one year earlier?

Solution to Example

When a US firm obtains a patent for a drug, it is gaining a first-mover advantage since the patent gives it intellectual property protection. However, the clock for the patent life starts running from the time the firm files for the patent. Thus, if a firm does not pursue the right activities for turning the discovery (for which the patent is granted) into an approved drug that customers want, the patent life could expire without it making money. The faster a firm can get the drug approved and to doctors and patients, the more time that it has to exercise its monopoly power before the patent life expires and generics move in. This example illustrates how much money can be at stake. In Table 10.3, two sets of sales numbers have been shown: sales generated when FDA approval was granted in 1997 and those generated if FDA approval had been one year later in 1998.

The NPV of revenues in 1997, given that FDA approval was in 1997 is $44.5 billion (Table 10.3). The NPV of revenues in 1997 dollars if the drug had been approved one year later is $36.86 (Table 10.3). Therefore, extra revenues earned as a result of getting FDA approval one year earlier (in 1997 dollars) are $44.50–$36.86 billion = $7.64 billion. Thus, by performing the type of activities that allowed Lipitor to be approved one year earlier, Warner-Lambert stood to make an extra $7.64 billion, in 1997 dollars, over the life of its patent. Effectively, Warner-Lambert was better able to exploit its first-mover advantages as far as Lipitor is concerned.

Table 10.3 NPVs for the different revenue flows

Year	1997	1998	1999	2000	2001	2002	2003	2004	2005	2006	2007	2008	2009	2010
Revenues (1997 FDA)	0.9	2.2	3.4	4.6	5.6	6.7	7.7	8.7	9.7	10.7	11.7	12.7	13.7	2.06 (14.7)
Revenues (1998 FDA)	0.9	2.2	3.4	4.6	5.6	6.7	7.7	8.7	9.7	10.7	11.7	12.7	1.92	(13.7)

NPV Revenues (1997 FDA) = $44.5 billion
NPV Revenues (1998 FDA) = $36.86 billion

KEY TAKEAWAYS

- A *first-mover advantage* is a resource, capability, or product-market-position that (1) a firm acquires by being the first to carry out an activity, and (2) gives the firm an advantage in creating and capturing value. In moving first to pursue an innovation, a firm usually has an opportunity to build and exploit first-mover advantages.

- First mover advantages include:
  - Total available market preemption:
    - economies of scale;

- size (beyond economies of scale) advantages;
- economic rents and equity;
- network externalities (installed base);
- relationships with coopetitors.
  - Lead in technology and innovation:
    - intellectual property (patents, copyrights, trade secrets);
    - learning;
    - organizational culture.
  - Preemption of scarce resources:
    - complementary assets;
    - location;
    - input factors;
    - plant and equipment.
  - First-at-buyers:
    - buyer switching costs;
    - buyer choice under uncertainty;
    - brand (preemption of consumer perceptual space).
  - First to establish system of activities:
    - difficult-to-imitate or substitute system of activities.
  - First-to make irreversible commitments.

- First-mover *dis*advantages include:
  - Followers can free ride on first-mover's investments.
  - Followers enter a market when technological and marketing uncertainties have been considerably resolved.
  - Followers can also take advantage of changes in technology or customer needs that have occurred since first-movers moved. First-movers may also be handicapped by inertia.

- Competitor's handicaps include:
  - Competitors may have developed dominant managerial logics prior to the innovation.
  - The innovation may not fit a competitor's strategy.
  - It may be difficult for competitors to get away from pre-innovation prior commitments.
  - Competitors may not have the type of resources that are needed to pursue the innovation.
  - The fear of cannibalizing their existing products may prevent some firms from moving first or following a first-mover.

- From the preceding, one can argue that first-movers win sometimes and followers win at other times because of one or more of the following reasons:
  - First-mover advantages have to be earned and exploited well. Thus, when first-movers do not perform the type of activities that will enable them to earn and exploit first-mover advantages, followers have a chance to move in and do well.
  - Followers may have critical complementary assets that first-movers do not.

- First-mover *dis*advantages can be minimized. Therefore, when first-movers do not minimize first-mover *dis*advantages, followers have a chance to exploit them.
- Industry factors, such as the number of competitors in a market, may favor one type of firm over another. Whoever is favored—first-mover or follower—is likely to win.
- Macro-environmental and global factors such as government regulations may favor first-movers over followers, or followers over first-movers.
- The type of player and business strategy of the player can also determine whether a first-mover or follower wins. In industries with very good exploiters, first-movers' chances are usually considerably reduced.

KEY TERMS

Competitors' handicaps	First-mover	Preemption of resources
Dominant logic	disadvantages	Second-mover
First-mover	Follower's advantages	advantages
advantages	Irreversible commitments	Switching costs

NOTES

1 Many of the first-mover advantages and disadvantages outlined here were laid out by an award-winning paper by Professor Lieberman of UCLA and Professor Montgomery of Northwestern University. Please see: Lieberman, M. B., & Montgomery, D. B. (1988). First-mover advantages. *Strategic Management Journal, 9,* 41–58. Lieberman, M. B., & Montgomery, D. B. (1988). First-mover (dis)advantages: Retrospective and link with the resource-based view. *Strategic Management Journal,* 19(12), 1111–1125. See also: Suarez, F., & Lanzolla, G. (2007). The role of environmental dynamics in building a first mover advantage theory. *Academy of Management Review,* 32(2), 377–392.

2 See, for example, Fishman, C. (2006). The Wal-Mart effect and a decent society: Who knew shopping was so important? *Academy of Management Perspectives,* 20(3), 6–25.

3 Sheremata, W.A. (2004). Competing through innovation in network markets: Strategies for challengers. *Academy of Management Review,* 29(3), 359–377.

4 Latif, U. (2005, May 31). Google's Bid-for-placement Patent Settlement Cover-up. Retrieved July 16, 2008, from www.techuser.net/gcoverup.html. Olsen, S. (2003, July 18). Overture to a patent war? Retrieved July 16, 2008, from http://news.com.com/Overture+to+a+patent+war/2100-1024_3-1027084.html

5 The settlement included another charge against Google that Yahoo had made in connection with a warrant that Yahoo held in connection with a June 2000 services agreement between the two firms.

6 Besanko, D., Dranove, D., & Shanley, M. (2000). *Economics of Strategy.* New York: John Wiley.

7 Barney, J. (1986). Organizational culture: Can it be a source of sustained competitive advantage? *Academy of Management Review,* 11(3), 656–665.

8 Schmalensee, R. (1978). Entry deterrence in the ready-to-eat breakfast cereal industry. *Bell Journal of Economics,* 9(2), 305–327.

9 Schmalensee, R. (1982). Product differentiation advantages of pioneering brands. *American Economic Review,* 72(3), 349–365.

10 Carpenter, G. S., & Nakamoto, K. (1989). Consumer preference formation and pioneering advantage. *Journal of Marketing Research,* 26(3), 285–298.

11 Porter, M. E. (1996). What is strategy? *Harvard Business Review.* 74(6), 61–78. Rivkin, J. W. 2000. Imitation of complex strategies. *Management Science,* 46(6), 824–844.

12 Ghemawat, P. (1991). *Commitment: The Dynamics of Strategy.* New York: Free Press.

13 Lieberman, M. B., & Montgomery, D. B. (1988). First-mover advantages. *Strategic Management Journal*, 9, 41–58. Lieberman, M. B., & Montgomery, D. B. (1988). First-mover (dis)advantages: Retrospective and link with the resource-based view. *Strategic Management Journal*, 19(12), 1111–1125.

14 Teece, D. J. (1986). Profiting from technological innovation: Implications for integration, collaboration, licensing and public policy. *Research Policy*, 15(6), 285–306.

15 Suarez, F. F., and J. M. Utterback. (1993). Dominant designs and the survival of firms. *Strategic Management Journal*, 22(1): 1–21, 1993.

16 Hamel, G. M., & Prahalad, C. K. (1994: 49). *Competing for the Future*. Boston, MA: Harvard Business School Press. p. 49.

17 Tripsas, M., & Gavetti. G. (2000). Capabilities, cognition, and inertia: Evidence from digital imaging. *Strategic Management Journal*, 21(10–11), 1147–1161. Kaplan, S., & Tripsas, M. (2008). Thinking about technology: Applying a cognitive lens to technical change. *Research Policy*, 37, 790–805.

18 Bettis, R. A., & Prahalad, C. K. (1995). The dominant logic: Retrospective and extension. *Strategic Management Journal*, 16(1), 5–14.

11

IMPLEMENTING BUSINESS MODEL
INNOVATIONS

Reading this chapter should provide you with the conceptual and analytical tools to:

- Understand the significance of business model innovation implementation.
- Get introduced to the relationship between business model, structure, systems, people, and environment (BS²PE).
- Understand some of the roles that individuals can play during innovation.
- Recall the definitions of functional, matrix, M-Form, network-assisted, and networked organizational structures.
- Explore what structure, systems, and people a firm may need in the face of a regular, position-building, capabilities-building, or revolutionary innovation.

INTRODUCTION

Every business model innovation has to be executed well if its full potential is to be realized. Executing a business model innovation involves organizing people to carry out the set of innovation activities that are required to create and capture value—it is about who carries out which activities, who works for whom, how to measure and reward performance, how information should flow in the organization, who to hire, what culture one would like to see develop, and so on. For example, to perform all the activities that enabled it to provide relevant searches, and monetize them using a paid-listing revenue model, Google used an organizational structure that fit its informal tech culture, developed its own incentive systems, and hired the right type of technical and nontechnical personnel. When IBM decided that services were going to be just as important as products to its business model, it had to restructure its organization to fit the new model, put in the right systems to measure and reward performance, hire the right people, and try to build the right culture. Effectively, to successfully execute a business model innovation, a firm needs an organizational structure, systems, and people that reflect not only the business model but also the environment in which it is being pursued. Business model implementation is about the relationships among the model, the structure of the organization that must execute the model, the systems and processes that complement the structure, and the people that must carry out the tasks in the given environment. We explore some of these relationships using a business model, structure, systems, people, and environment (BS²PE) framework (Figure 11.1).[1]

THE BS²PE FRAMEWORK

The idea behind the BS²PE framework is simple. Business models are conceived of and executed by people who often differ considerably. Moreover, the tasks that people must perform to execute a business model vary from model to model. Therefore, not only do individuals need to perform different roles in the face of a business model innovation, what motivates them to perform a task differs from task to task, individual to individual, industry to industry, and country to country. Therefore, the type of people that a firm hires, who reports to whom, how performance is measured and rewarded, and the type of information systems that are needed depend on the type of business model innovation and the environment in which the firm operates.[2] Effectively, some organizational structures, systems/processes, and people would be more suitable for some business models than others, given the environments in which the business models must be executed.[3] The objective, in executing a business model innovation in a given environment, is therefore to find those structures, systems, and people that best fit the set of activities that a firm chooses to perform, *how, where* and *when* it performs them.

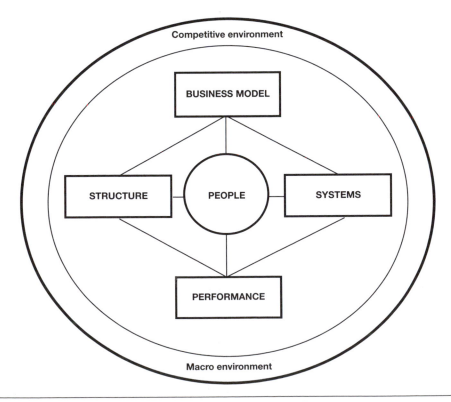

Figure 11.1 Business model, structure, systems, people, and environment (BS²PE)

We quickly explore each component of the BS²PE framework before turning to the impact of innovation on them.

Business Model

Recall that a firm's business model is its framework for creating and capturing value. A firm's structure, systems, and people usually depend on its business model, although there may be cases where structure, systems, and people drive a business model.

Structure

While a firm's business model is about the set of activities that the firm performs to create and capture value, a firm's structure tells us who reports to whom and who is responsible for which activities.[4] An organizational structure has three primary goals. First, the structure of an organization should facilitate timely information flows to the right people for decision-making while preventing the wrong people from getting the information. Second, an effective structure requires the ability to be able to juggle differentiation (in the organizational structure sense) and integration. A firm's manufacturing and marketing units are maintained as separate functions because each one necessarily has to specialize in what it does in order to be both efficient and effective in carrying out its activities. Giving each unit the opportunity to specialize in what it does so as to be the best at it, is what *differentiation* in the organizational sense is about. However, to efficiently and effectively develop and offer customers unique benefits, a firm's different functions often have to interact with each other. That is, the value creation and capture activities that a firm's different areas perform must be *integrated*.[5] Third, a final goal of an organizational structure is to coordinate interactions between units to effect integration. A new product launch would be more effective if the product development and marketing groups *coordinated* their activities—telling each other what they are doing and when, using information from each other as inputs.

Firms use variants of the following five organizational structures to effect differentiation, integration, and coordination: functional, multidivisional (M-form), matrix, social network-assisted and networked.

Functional Structure

In a *functional* structure, employees are organized by the functions that they perform in the organization. Marketing employees report to marketing supervisors, sales employees report to a sales supervisor, engineering employees report to engineering managers, and so on. Formal reporting and communications is primarily within each functional unit, usually up and down the organizational hierarchy. Each functional unit gets its directions from corporate headquarters via the functional head. The functional organization has several advantages. First, since employees are organized by function, there is de facto division of labor that enables employees to acquire in-depth function-specific knowledge, skills, and know-how—to specialize in the functional tasks that differentiate each functional unit from others. Second, since each functional unit has people with similar knowledge and know-how that are grouped together and may be located in the same physical location, they can communicate more often and are therefore more likely to develop in-depth knowledge of their functional area.

The functional structure also has some disadvantages. First, when tasks entail considerable coordination with other functional units, a functional unit is likely to have subpar performance because of its limited knowledge and lack of direct communication lines with other units. Second, the more specialized each functional unit gets, the more difficult it becomes for headquarter's management to know what is going on within each function. This is compounded by the fact that the different functional units do not communicate directly with each other. Third, because of the differences in their skills, experiences, and capabilities, functional departments may have goals that are not consistent with cooperating with other functional units.

M-Form or Multidivisional Structure

In an *M-form* or *multidivisional* structure, employees are organized by divisions or business units rather than by functional units, as is the case with the functional structure.[6] Divisions can be organized by the type of product that each division offers (product line), by the type of customer, by the geographic scope that the firm covers, or by the brand name that the firm offers. Authority in the M-form structure is decentralized to the divisions in contrast to the functional structure where authority is centralized at corporate headquarters. Each unit usually has profit-and-loss responsibility. The multi-divisional structure has two major advantages. First, since each division has profit-and-loss responsibility, there is better accountability for the firm's performance. Second, since management responsibility is not as centralized as in the functional structure, managers in the M-form only need focus their attention on their division. This is a more manageable task since each manager is more likely to have the type of in-depth knowledge of his/her product line, brand, customer, or geographic scope that they need to better manage the business. The major disadvantage of the divisional structure is that firms may not be able to build as much in-depth knowledge of functional areas such as R&D as they would in a functional structure.

Matrix Structure

The goal of a *matrix structure* is to capture some of the benefits of both the functional and divisional structure. It is a hybrid structure between functional and divisional, and therefore comes in many different forms. In one form, individuals from different functional areas are assigned to a project, but rather than report only to a project or functional manager, each employee reports to both a functional *and* a project manager. The idea behind the matrix organization is to (1) have cross-functional coordination that is needed to carry out projects that require skills and knowledge from different functional areas, (2) maintain some performance accountability at the project level, and (3) allow project members to keep in close touch with their functional areas so as to benefit from intrafunctional learning, especially in industries where deep functional knowledge is important. In another form of the matrix structure, people from different functions, divisions, or geographic areas work on projects and report not only to their project managers, but also report to their functional, geographic, and divisional managers.

The matrix structure has three major advantages. First, the structure captures some of the benefits of both the functional and divisional structures. Second, since employees have one foot in their functional areas and the other in their project group, they can bring the latest thinking from their functional areas to the project and vice versa. Third, since the rate of change of technological or market knowledge is likely to vary from one function to another, employees can spend time on project management commensurate with the rate of change of the knowledge in their functional area. This can lead to more efficient use of personnel. Fourth, some employees may be able to work on more than one project, thereby helping cross-pollinate not only functional knowledge but also project knowledge.

The matrix structure has several disadvantages. First, since physical co-location with fellow project members can be critical to project performance, and physical co-location with functional colleagues can also be critical to functional learning, employees in a matrix structure may have to physically co-locate in both their project and functional areas. This can be costly and inefficient since an employee cannot be physically present in two different places at the same time. Second, since project members in the matrix organization have to report to both a functional and project manager, they may have to manage two bosses at the same time. When there is a conflict, employees may have difficulties deciding where their allegiance falls—whether to the project manager or functional manager. Third, the matrix structure can be more costly than the functional one since the structure requires some duplication of effort. For example, having both a functional and a project manager means one too many managers. Finally, the matrix structure still has much less accountability than the divisional organization.

Social Network-Assisted Hybrid Structure

The social network-assisted hybrid organization arises from the realization that the primary problem with the matrix structure is not so much that it tries to coordinate activities across geography, functions, and divisions.[7] The problem is that the matrix organization formalizes this coordination. For these complex organizations that span functions, geographies, and product divisions, such coordination is absolutely critical. In *social network-assisted* structures, firms are organized by geography, function, and product division, but rather than use the formal relationships of a matrix structure to coordinate activities, these organizations use incentives and other systems to encourage employees to seek informal relationships—social networks—between functions, divisions, and geography. These social networks can be through bricks-and-mortar or through electronic social media such as blogging, online social networks, wikis, and so on. Procter and Gamble used such an organizational structure to improve its ability to innovate in the 2000s.[8]

Network or Virtual Structure

In the *network* or *virtual* structure, firms outsource all the major value-adding activities of their value chains and coordinate the activities of their outsourcees.[9] The emergence of this organizational form has been facilitated by advances in technological innovation such as the Internet. In such a structure, the coordinating firm contracts a market research firm to perform market research for a particular product or idea, finds a design firm to design the product, buys the components from suppliers, and finds another firm to manufacture the product. The network structure has several advantages. First, a firm can avoid making major investments in assets since it outsources all the major value-adding activities of its value chain. Second, in industries with a high rate of technological change that often renders existing capabilities obsolete, having a virtual structure means that a firm does not have to worry about important assets being rendered obsolete since it has not invested in any.[10] Such a firm has the flexibility to switch suppliers, manufacturers, or distributors whenever it finds one that can do the job better. The network structure has two major disadvantages. First, it is difficult to have a competitive advantage when one does not perform major value-adding activities. However, whether this is a disadvantage depends on the firm's core competence. If a firm has a strong brand or architectural capabilities—capabilities that enable a firm to coordinate other capabilities—that are valuable, scarce and difficult to imitate, the firm may still be able to make money since it can offer customers something that competitors cannot.[11] Second, contracting out all major activities deprives a firm of the ability to learn more about creating value along the value chain.

Systems

Organizational structures are about who reports to whom and what activities they perform, but say very little about how to keep employees motivated as they carry out their assigned tasks and responsibilities in executing a business model.[12] *Systems* are about the incentives, performance requirements and measures, and information flow and accountability mechanisms that facilitate the efficient and effective execution of business models. We can group systems into two: organizational systems/processes and information systems.

Organizational Systems/Processes

Organizational systems are about how the performance of individuals, groups, functional units, divisions, and organizations is sought, monitored, measured, and compensated. They include financial measures such as profits, market share, cash flows, gross profit margins, stock market price, return on investment, earnings per share, return on equity, and economic value added (EVA). Organizational systems also include reward systems such as pay scales, profit-sharing, employee stock option plans (ESOPs), bonuses, and non-financial rewards such as recognition with certificates or having one's name engraved somewhere on a product that one helped develop. Systems also include so-called processes.

A firm's *processes* are the "patterns of interaction, coordination, communication, and decision making [that] employees use to transform capabilities into products and services of greater worth."[13] These patterns are a function of the type of business model, organizational structure, and incentive system in place. For example, in a process it called "chemicalization", Sharp Corporation compulsorily transferred the top 3 percent of the scientists from each of its divisional R&D groups between laboratories every three years. This process forced top scientists to interact with scientists in other laboratories, exchanging knowledge that may not be easily transferred through memos or scientific publications. Being transferred at Sharp was also a signal that a scientist was good—an important reward for scientists. Moreover, visiting other laboratories gave Sharp scientists an opportunity to cultivate relationships that could come in handy later when they returned to their home divisions or functions. Another example is "Google's 20 percent rule"—the fact that at Google, employees were encouraged to spend 20 percent of their time on innovative projects that had very little or nothing to do with their officially assigned projects. Benchmarking, total quality management (TQM), re-engineering, and X-engineering are also processes that firms have used to more effectively and efficiently execute business model innovations.

Information Systems

Although a good organizational structure, coupled with the right organizational systems, can result in a reasonable amount of internal information flow, information systems can also be used to facilitate the efficient flow of information to the right targets at the right times for decision-making. For discussion purposes, we can group information flow systems into two: (1) the information and communication technologies that allow electronic information to be exchanged and (2) the physical building layouts that facilitate in-person, sometimes unplanned, interaction. Digital networks such as the Internet make it possible for anyone anywhere in an organization anywhere in the world to have access to information anywhere within the organization.[14] For example, during product development, information on the status of products, ideas for better products and so on, are available to anyone anywhere in the world with permission and access to the company's intranet. Information systems can be used to supplement or complement information flows that take place by virtue of the structure of the organization.

Although lots of information can be exchanged electronically over the Internet, some types of information still need in-person, face-to-face interaction. For example, it is difficult to feel the aura and smell of a new car or painting via the Internet. Moreover, chanced physical encounters can lead to ideas that planned electronic encounters might not. Research by Professor Tom Allen of MIT suggests that the physical layout of buildings can play a significant role in the amount of communications between engineers/scientists, and therefore can have a significant impact on innovation.[15] Buildings that are designed to facilitate physical in-person interaction can facilitate the flow of new ideas. If different organizational units of a firm—e.g. marketing, R&D, and operations—are located in the same physical space, eat in the same cafeteria, share the same bathrooms, and bump into each other often, they are more likely to exchange new ideas than if they were located in different buildings or regions.

People

People are central to any business model since they conceive of, formulate, and execute business models. The extent to which a firm's employees can thrive within its organizational structure, are motivated by the performance and reward systems that it has put in place, or can effectively use the information systems that it established, is a function of the firm's organizational culture, capabilities, and the type of employees.

Culture

What is culture? Uttal and Fierman defined organizational culture as:

> a system of shared values (what is important) and beliefs (how things work) that interact with the organization's people, organizational structures, and systems to produce behavioral norms (the way we do things around here).[16]

Professor Schein of MIT also defined culture as:

> the pattern of basic assumptions that a given group has invented, discovered, or developed in learning to cope with its problems of external adaptation and internal integration, and that have worked well enough to be considered valid, and, therefore, to be taught to new members as the correct way to perceive, think, and feel in relation to these problems.[17]

A firm's culture is critical to its ability to create and capture value.[18] Basically, people within an organization develop shared values (what is important) and beliefs (how things work). These shared values and beliefs then influence who else is hired or stays in the organization, how it is reorganized and how the systems change or do not change. The results of these interactions are behavioral norms (the way we do things), which then determine how well a business model is executed or formulated. If the structure, systems, and people are just right, the norms can lead to a system of activities that is difficult to imitate. One reason why Southwest Airlines's employees have been more productive than employees at other airlines may be its culture. The wrong culture can be a competitive *dis*advantage.

Type of People

Quite simply, not everyone is meant for every job. Nor is every reward system going to motivate every employee. Thus, in executing a business model, it is important to get the right people to perform the right tasks. In the mid-2000s, Google's advertisements for new hires reflected its overt focus on hiring largely the mathematically and intellectually gifted.[19] However, when Southwest Airlines hired people, it was more interested in their attitude than in their skills.

Roles People Play During Innovation

Since people are central to executing any business model, it is important also to understand the roles that people play during innovation.

Top Management Team and Dominant Managerial Logic

As we saw in Chapter 10, each manager brings to every innovation a set of beliefs, biases, and assumptions about the innovation, the market that his/her firm serves, who to hire, what technologies the innovation needs, who the other players in the innovation are, and what it takes to create and appropriate value in the innovation.[20] These beliefs, assumptions, and biases are a manager's managerial logic. They define the mental frame or model within which a manager is likely to approach decision-making.[21] Depending on the innovation, a firm's business model, structure, systems, processes, values, norms, and how successful it has been, there usually emerges a dominant managerial logic, a common way of viewing how best to create and appropriate value in the firm.[22] Dominant managerial logic is usually good for a firm that has the right business model and has taken the right measures to implement it. However, during innovation in which a new business model, structure, systems, processes, values, or norms are needed, pre-innovation dominant managerial logic that had worked so well before can become a handicap. Managers may be stuck in the old values (what was important), old beliefs (how things worked), and old behavioral norms (the way we did things around here). Doing so can impede their understanding and acceptance of the new values (what is important in the innovation), new beliefs (how things should work in the innovation), and new behavioral norms (the way we should be doing things around here now). This can be problematic since top management is often responsible for allocating the resources that are critical for innovation.

Champions

Formulating and implementing a business model innovation to win usually requires a champion. A *champion* for a business model innovation is someone who articulates a vision of what the business model is all about, and what's in it for the firm and employees who are engaged in formulating and implementing the business model.[23] By evangelically articulating a captivating vision of the potential of the business model to the right players, a champion can help other employees understand the rationale behind the business model, especially how value will be created and appropriated, thereby motivating and inspiring the employees who are at the core of business model implementation. A firm often has to also champion the business model to its coopetitors—the other players in its innovation ecosystem. In fact, in many revolutionary and position-building innovations, a firm has to articulate a vision of a new product to customers and help them discover their latent need for the product. Steve Jobs was a great champion for Apple's products.

Sponsors

A *sponsor* of a business model innovation is a senior-level manager who provides behind-the-scenes support for the innovation.[24] This senior-level manager is like the godfather who protects the innovation from political enemies. By acting as a sponsor, the top manager is also sending a signal to political foes of the innovation that they would face the wrath of a senior manager and sponsor. In so doing, a sponsor is also assuring the champion and other key individuals who are working on the business model that they have the support of a senior manager. In some cases, the champion is also the sponsor. Steve Jobs played both roles for key products at Apple.

Gatekeeper and Boundary Spanners

In many firms, especially those with functional organizational structures, each employee is likely to have deep knowledge of his/her unit and little or no knowledge of the other units. Moreover, each unit may have its own culture, language, needs, and history that have an effect on the information that the unit can or cannot share. For example, an R&D department may have its own acronyms, scientific jargon, and culture that marketing and manufacturing do not understand. Marketing and manufacturing may see R&D scientists as snobs who live in an ivory tower. *Boundary spanners* are individuals that span the "hole" between two units within a firm, acting as a transducer for information between units. They take information from one department and translate it into what people in another department can understand.[25] They understand the idiosyncrasies of their units and those of other units and can take unit-specific questions, translate them into a language that other departments can understand, obtain answers, and translate them into something that their home units can understand. *Gatekeepers* play a similar role between different organizations.

Project Manager

If a business model innovation entails developing a new product, project managers can play important roles. Project managers are responsible for plotting out who should do what and when so as to complete a project that meets or exceeds requirements. A project manager is to meeting schedules what a champion is to articulating a vision of the potential of a business model. He or she is the central nervous system of the project—relaying information to the right people at the right time. Project managers have been classified as heavyweight or lightweight based on the managers' span of control.[26] A *heavyweight project manager* is one with extensive authority and responsibility for the project from concept creation through design to manufacturing, to marketing and making money, including the project's budget.[27] A lightweight project manager's authority and responsibilities are not as extensive as those of the heavyweight project manager—his or her authority is usually limited largely to engineering functions with no authority or responsibility over concept creation and other market-related aspects of the product such as budgeting.

External Environment

For two reasons, a firm's structure, systems, and people (S^2P) are also a function of its competitive and macro environments. First, as we have seen on several occasions, a firm's business model is a function of the competitive forces that impinge on it as well as of the macro environment in which it creates and appropriates value. To the extent that structure, systems, and people (S^2P) depend on the business model, it must be the case that a firm's S^2P also depend on its competitive and macro environments. Second, each of structure, systems, and people depends on the environment in its own right. For example, in fast-paced industries where technologies and markets change rapidly, a firm needs to be able to maintain deep knowledge of the technologies that underpin its products and of the markets that it must serve. One good choice of structure in such fast-paced environments is a matrix structure since it allows employees who are working on a project to have one foot in the project group and another in their functional groups. In countries where people's identities are closely tied to the firms that employ them, employees may be more willing to do whatever it takes for their company to win. Countries with well-educated workforces offer firms more opportunities to hire the types of employees that they need for high value-adding jobs.

IMPLEMENTING A BUSINESS MODEL INNOVATION

How much do structure, systems, people, and environment matter when a firm is executing a business model innovation? It depends on the type of business model innovation—on whether the innovation is regular, position-building, capabilities-building, or revolutionary (Figure 11.2).

Regular Innovation

In a regular business model innovation, old products remain competitive and old capabilities can be used to pursue the business model innovation. Therefore, any changes that incumbents have to make to their pre-innovation capabilities and positions in a regular innovation are incremental. That means any changes that need to be made to an incumbent's structure, systems, and people (S^2P) are also incremental. Take culture, for example. Those incumbent values (what is important) and beliefs (how things work) and behavioral norms (the way we do things around here) that worked prior to a regular innovation still work during the innovation. Incumbents' processes or "patterns of interaction, coordination, communication, and decision making"[28] are likely to still work. The introduction of diet cola was a regular innovation and both Coke's and Pepsi's S^2P did not change when they introduced the product.

Revolutionary Innovation

In a revolutionary business model innovation pre-innovation products cannot compete with products from the innovation, and the capabilities needed by the new business model

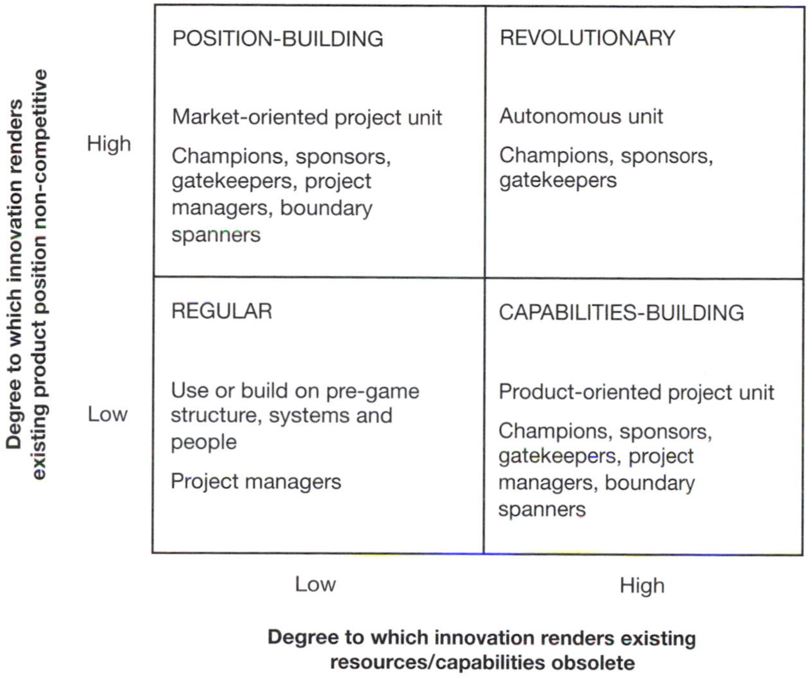

		POSITION-BUILDING	REVOLUTIONARY
	High	Market-oriented project unit Champions, sponsors, gatekeepers, project managers, boundary spanners	Autonomous unit Champions, sponsors, gatekeepers
	Low	REGULAR Use or build on pre-game structure, systems and people Project managers	CAPABILITIES-BUILDING Product-oriented project unit Champions, sponsors, gatekeepers, project managers, boundary spanners
		Low	High

Degree to which innovation renders existing product position non-competitive

Degree to which innovation renders existing resources/capabilities obsolete

Figure 11.2 Impact of innovation on S^{2}P

are so different that pre-innovation capabilities are useless. Incumbent values (what is important), beliefs (how things work), and behavioral norms (the way we do things around here) that worked prior to the innovation are obsolete in the face of a revolutionary innovation. In fact, these values, beliefs, and norms may become handicaps. Pre-innovation processes—"patterns of interaction, coordination, communication, and decision making"[29]—are also likely to be rendered useless and may become handicaps too.

If an innovation is revolutionary, an incumbent may want to use an autonomous unit that has its own structure, systems, and people. Why an autonomous unit? Since the values, beliefs, and behavioral norms that are needed are radically different from pre-innovation ones and it takes time to change pre-innovation values, maintaining the same pre-innovation structure, systems, and people is not likely to help. An autonomous unit with its own structure, systems, and people can more quickly build the types of values, beliefs, norms, and innovation processes that are needed to successfully create and appropriate value in the face of a revolutionary innovation.

In addition to creating an autonomous unit, a firm that is executing a revolutionary business model innovation may also want to use champions, sponsors, and gatekeepers. The existence of a sponsor reminds upper-level management that the autonomous unit is important and no one should think of messing with it. Since things are usually in a state of flux early in the life of a revolutionary innovation, a champion can help articulate a vision of what the outcome of innovation is likely to be and what needs to be done to achieve that outcome. Gatekeepers act as transducers between the autonomous unit and the rest of the firm as well as coopetitors.

Position-Building Innovation

In a position-building innovation, the new product renders existing products noncompetitive but pre-innovation capabilities are still important in executing the innovation. If the market addressed by the innovation is the same as the pre-innovation market, an incumbent's S^2P may not have to change that much. For example, when Intel introduced the Pentium that replaced the 486, it did not have to restructure its organization to better address the PC market in which the Pentium was replacing the 486s. However, if the market is different, some important elements of S^2P may have to change. The PC used the same technology as minicomputers but in addition to addressing the minicomputer market, it also addressed the home computer market. The market for consumers was very different from the business market that minicomputers had addressed before the PC. Clearly, selling to this new market required something different from incumbents' sales norms.

Effectively, if a business model innovation is a position-building, a firm can use a market-targeting project unit whose primary responsibility is to make sure that the needs of the market are incorporated into the new product on time. Such a focus on the market is particularly important if the market for the product is new. Why not use an autonomous unit? Since the product from the innovation must still be built using pre-innovation technological capabilities, using an autonomous unit would mean moving the capabilities to the new unit or duplicating them, either one of which can be very costly. In other words, in the face of a position-building innovation, capabilities-related S^2Ps are strengths that could be useful in the innovation and foregoing such strengths can be costly. The case of IBM and the PC illustrates this. When IBM decided to enter the PC market, it formed an autonomous group to design, manufacture, and market the product. Because the PC group was autonomous, it decided to use an Intel microprocessor and a Microsoft operating system when other units at IBM could have used their existing computer capabilities to quickly build the two components. Effectively, IBM missed out on the two components of the Wintel world that appropriate the most value created. However, by not using an autonomous unit, a firm runs the risk of being handicapped by old market-targeting values, beliefs and norms. These handicaps can be identified and avoided. To complement the project unit, a firm also needs sponsors, champions, and boundary spanners. A sponsor would signal to all units that the program is important and therefore the project unit should get the support that it needs. A champion would articulate the benefits of the project for the different units that must corporate with the project group. Boundary spanners would span the hole between the project unit and other units, facilitating knowledge transfers.

Capabilities-Building Innovation

In a capabilities-building innovation, the capabilities that a player needs to pursue the innovation are radically different from pre-innovation capabilities but existing products can still compete in the innovation. Thus, as far as the activities for building products are concerned, S^2P requirements should be similar to those for revolutionary innovations—they are likely to require changes in structure, systems and people. Take the example of an electric razor that requires a radically different technology from that for mechanical razors. A firm that has been supplying mechanical razors but wants to enter the electric razor market may need a unit or units that reflect the fact that the design, development, and manufacturing for electric razors are very different from those for their mechanical counterparts.

If the innovation is a capabilities-building innovation, a firm can use a product-targeting project unit whose activities are geared towards building the new capabilities and using them to build the new product. As is the case with position-building innovations, there are advantages and disadvantages to using a project unit rather than an autonomous unit. By using a project unit, a firm can more easily take advantage of marketing and other buyer-focused capabilities than using an autonomous unit since in a capabilities-building innovation, the product-market-position (PMP) does not change much. At the same time, by not using an autonomous unit, a firm risks being handicapped by the values, beliefs, and norms from the capabilities that are being displaced. These handicaps can also be identified and corrected.

KEY TAKEAWAYS

- A business model innovation is not likely to attain its full potential unless it is well implemented. Implementing a business model innovation is about getting right the relationships among business model, structure, systems, people, and environment. That is, to successfully execute its business model innovation, a firm needs an organizational structure, systems, and people (S^2P) that reflect not only the business model but also the environment in which the business model is being pursued.

- An organizational structure is about who reports to whom and performs what activities when. It has three primary goals:
    - An organizational structure should facilitate timely information flows to the right people for decision-making while preventing the wrong people from getting the information.
    - An effective structure requires the ability to be able to juggle differentiation (in the organizational structure sense) and integration.
    - An effective organization should help coordinate interactions between units to effect integration.

- Firms use variants of the following five organizational structures to effect differentiation, integration, and coordination: functional, multidivisional (M-form), matrix, social network-assisted, and networked structures.

- Systems are about the incentives, performance requirements and measures, and information flow and accountability mechanisms that facilitate the efficient and effective execution of business models. They are about what it takes to motivate employees.

- The extent to which a firm's employees thrive within its organizational structure, are motivated by the performance and reward systems that it has put in place, or effectively use the information systems that it established, is a function of the firm's organizational culture, and the type of employees.

- Culture is "a system of shared values (what is important) and beliefs (how things work) that interact with the organization's people, organizational structures, and systems to produce behavioral norms (the way we do things around here)." [30]

- Since structure, systems, and people depend on the business model, and a business model is a function of the environment, it must be the case that structure, systems, and people are a function of the environment.

- During innovation, people play different important roles:
    - Top management plays the leadership role but the dominant management logic that is a strength when there is no major change can become a handicap in the face of revolutionary, position-building, or capabilities-building innovation.
    - A champion for a business model innovation is someone who articulates a vision of what the innovation is all about, what's in it for the firm and the employees who are engaged in formulating and implementing the business model.
    - A sponsor of a business model innovation is a senior level manager or godfather who provides behind-the-scenes support for it.
    - Boundary spanners are individuals who span the "hole" between two units within a firm, acting as a transducer for information between units.
    - Gatekeepers span the holes between different companies.
    - Project managers are responsible for plotting out who should do what and when so as to complete a project that meets or exceeds requirements.

- What a firm does in the face of an innovation as far as its structure, systems, and people (S^2P) are concerned depends on the type of innovation being pursued:
    - In the face of a regular innovation, an incumbent is better off keeping its pre-innovation S^2P.
    - In the face of a revolutionary innovation, a firm may be better off creating an autonomous unit to be used to pursue the innovation.
    - If an innovation is position-building, a firm may want to create a market-targeting project unit.
    - If an innovation is capabilities-building, the firm may be better off creating a product-targeting project unit.

KEY TERMS

Champions	Dominant managerial	Network structure
Coordination	logic	Processes
Culture	Functional structure	Project managers
Differentiation in the	Matrix structure	S3PE framework
organizational structure	M-form structure	Sponsors
sense	Multidivisional structure	Systems (organizational)

NOTES

1   This section draws on Chapter 5 of Afuah, A. N. (2003). *Innovation Management: Strategies, Implementation, and Profits*. New York: Oxford University Press.
2   Galbraith, J. R. (1982). Designing the innovating organization. *Organizational Dynamics*, 10(3), 5–25.

3   Argyres, N. S., & Silverman, B. S. (2004). R&D, organization structure, and the development of corporate technological knowledge. *Strategic Management Journal*, 25(8–9), 929–958.
4   This section draws heavily on Afuah, A. N. (2003). *Business Models: A Strategic Management Approach*. New York: McGraw-Hill/Irvin.
5   Lawrence, P. R., & Lorsch, J. W. (1967). *Organization and Environments: Managing Differentiation and Integration*. Homewood, IL: Irwin.
6   Chandler, A. D. (1962). *Strategy and Structure: Chapters in the History of the Industrial Enterprise*. Cambridge, MA: MIT Press.
7   Grant, R. M. (1998). *Contemporary Strategy Analysis: Concepts, Techniques, Applications*. Oxford: Blackwell.
8   Lafley, A. G., & Charan, R. (2008). P&G's innovation culture: How we built a world-class organic growth engine by investing in people. *Strategy + Business*, 52(4), 1–10.
9   Miles, R. E., Snow, C. C., Mathews, J. A., Miles, G., & Coleman, H. J., Jr. (1997). Organizing the knowledge age: Anticipating the cellular form. *Academy of Management Executive*, 11(4), 7–24. Byrne, J. A., & Brandt, R. (1993, February 8). The virtual corporation. *Business Week*, 3304(2), 98–102. Davidow, W. H., & Malone, M. S. (1992). *The Virtual Corporation*. New York: HarperCollins.
10 Afuah, A. N. (2001). Dynamic boundaries of the firm: Are firms better off being vertically integrated in the face of a technological change? *Academy of Management Journal*, 44(6), 1211–1228.
11 Henderson, R., & Cockburn, I. (1994). Measuring competence? Exploring firm effects in pharmaceutical research. *Strategic Management Journal*, 15(8), 63–84.
12 Hill, C. W. L., & Jones, G. R. (1995). *Strategic Management: An Integrated Approach*. Boston, MA: Houghton Mifflin.
13 Christensen, C. M., & Overdorf, M. (2000). Meeting the challenge of disruptive change. *Harvard Business Review*, 78(2), 66–77.
14 Afuah, A. N., & Tucci, C. L. (2003). *Internet Business Models and Strategies: Text and Cases*. New York: McGraw-Hill. Afuah, A. N. (2003). Redefining firm boundaries in the face of the Internet: Are firms really shrinking? *Academy of Management Review*, 28(1), 34–53.
15 Allen, T. (1984). *Managing the Flow of Technology*. Cambridge, MA: MIT Press.
16 Uttal, B., & Fierman, J. (1983, October 17). The corporate culture vultures. *Fortune*, 108(8), 66–73.
17 Schein, E. (1985). *Organizational Culture and Leadership*. San Francisco, CA: Jossey-Bass.
18 Barney, J. (1986). Organizational culture: Can it be a source of sustained competitive advantage? *Academy of Management Review*, 11(3), 656–665.
19 Fuzzy maths: In a few short years, Google has turned from a simple and popular company into a complicated and controversial one. (2006, May 11). *The Economist*. Retrieved August 3, 2013, from www.economist.com/node/6911096.
20 Bettis, R. A., & Prahalad, C. K. (1995). The dominant logic: Retrospective and extension. *Strategic Management Journal*, 16(1), 5–14. Tripsas, M., & Gavetti, G. (2000). Capabilities, cognition, and inertia: Evidence from digital imaging. *Strategic Management Journal*, 21(10–11), 1147–1161. Kaplan, S., & Tripsas, M. (2008). Thinking About Technology: Applying a Cognitive Lens to Technical Change. *Research Policy*, 37(5), 790–805.
21 Walsh, J. P. (1995). Managerial and organizational cognition: Notes from a trip down memory lane. *Organizational Science*, 6(3), 280–321.
22 Hamel, G. M., & Prahalad, C. K. (1994). *Competing for the Future*. Boston, MA: Harvard Business School Press.
23 The concept of champions was first developed by Schön in his seminal article: Schön, D. A. (1963). Champions for radical new inventions. *Harvard Business Review*, 41(2), 77–86. Also see: Howell, J. M., & Higgins, C. A. (1990). Champions of technological innovation. *Administrative Sciences Quarterly*, 35(2), 317–341.
24 Roberts, E. B., & Fusfeld, A. R. (1981). Staffing the innovative technology-based organization. *Sloan Management Review*, 22(3), 19–34.
25 Allen, T. (1984). *Managing the Flow of technology*. Cambridge, MA: MIT Press.
26 Clark, K. B., & Fujumoto, T. (1991). *Product Development Performance: Strategy, Organization, and Management in the World Automobile Industry*. Boston, MA: Harvard Business School Press.
27 Clark, K. B., & Fujumoto, T. (1991). *Product Development Performance: Strategy, Organization, and Management in the World Automobile Industry*. Boston, MA: Harvard Business School Press.
28 Christensen, C. M., & Overdorf, M. (2000). Meeting the challenge of disruptive change. *Harvard Business Review*, 78(2), 66–77.
29 Christensen, C. M., & Overdorf, M. (2000). Meeting the challenge of disruptive change. *Harvard Business Review*, 78(2), 66–77.
30 Uttal, B., & Fierman, J. (1983, October 17). The corporate culture vultures. *Fortune*, 108(8), 66–73.

Part IV
Applications

12

GLOBALIZATION AND
BUSINESS MODEL INNOVATION

Reading this chapter should provide you with the conceptual and analytical tools to:

- Define globalization, and the different strategies that firms can pursue in going international.
- Get introduced to the strategies that firms pursue when going global.
- Understand the drivers of globalization and why firms go international.
- Analyze who appropriates how much value from products that are developed and sold globally.
- Start to understand the critical role that governments can play in value appropriation.

INTRODUCTION

Oil is arguably the most global of all global products. It is explored and extracted from countries in all six continents, by people and equipment from all over the world. It is refined, transported, sold, and used in all corners of the earth. All countries need it and depend on each other for it, and for the technologies that go into finding, transporting, and processing it. The list of products that are produced using oil is endless. Towards the middle of 2008, the price of a liter of gasoline at the pump reached record highs in many countries even as the price of oil futures flirted with the $150 per barrel record price. Oil companies recorded very high profits and some analysts wondered what the high prices would do to the world economy.[1] Some consumers wondered if the oil companies deserved the high profits. Using our terminology, people wondered if the oil companies created all the value that they were appropriating. If that were not the case, who was creating the value that the oil companies were capturing? If they deserved the high profits, who was capturing most of the value perceived by customers? How about the oil-exporting or importing countries? How much of what consumers paid for oil from each of these countries actually went to the countries? We will explore these questions in this chapter. We start the chapter with an example on how to calculate the value that is appropriated by different players along an international oil value chain. We then briefly discuss globalization and its drivers. This is followed by a discussion of innovative strategies that firms use when they go global.

INTRODUCTORY EXAMPLE: CAPTURING VALUE IN GLOBALIZATION

Suppose a firm pursues the right global innovation strategy (given its strengths and handicaps) to create value, how much of the value can it appropriate? It depends on how much of the value created the other players, especially governments appropriate. Governments have infinite power and can use it to appropriate most of the value created in a value chain, leaving the creators of such value with very little to show for their efforts. To illustrate what can happen in a value chain, let us explore a very short mini-case. We use the oil industry because it is one of the most global industries in the world. Directly or indirectly, oil touches almost every life on earth. Firms and governments benefit from oil.

Example Mini-Case: Who Creates and Who Appropriates Value in the Oil Industry?
In the 2000s, Nigeria was Africa's largest exporter of oil and exported some of its oil to many countries including the United States, India, France, Italy, Spain, Canada, and the Netherlands.[2] Finding costs for Africa had jumped from $7.55 per barrel in 2002–2003 to $15.25 in 2003–2005.[3] In 2003, lifting costs and production taxes were $3.57 and $1.00 per barrel respectively. On July 3, 2008, the price of a barrel of oil was $142 on electronic trading. Table 12.1 shows the June 2007 gasoline prices, taxes, cost per barrel of oil, and currency exchange rates for the Organization for Economic Cooperation and Development (OECD) countries as reported by the International Energy Agency (L'Agence internationale de l'énergie), an OECD agency.[4] There are 158.98 liters to the barrel. The joint ventures that produced oil in Nigeria are shown in Table 12.2.[5] The price that consumers paid for gasoline reflected the cost of crude oil to refiners, refinery processing costs, marketing and distribution costs, the retail station costs, and taxes. Crude oil costs, in turn, included the cost of exploring and finding oil, drilling for it, pumping it out, transporting it to refiners, and export taxes paid to the exporting country.

Table 12.1 OECD gasoline prices and taxes (June, 2007)

Country	Price (in country's currency)	Tax (in country's currency)	Exchange rate for a dollar	Price (US$)	Tax (US$)	April crude oil prices (US$/barrel)
France (Euro)	1.316	0.818	0.743	1.771	1.101	65.72
Germany (Euro)	1.393	0.877	0.743	1.875	1.18	65.67
Italy (Euro)	1.348	0.789	0.743	1.815	1.063	64.51
Spain (Euro)	1.079	0.545	0.743	1.452	0.733	63.73
UK (Pound)	0.966	0.628	0.504	1.917	1.246	67.73
Japan (Yen)	139	60.4	121.61	1.143	0.497	62.38
Canada (C$)	1.066	0.312	1.061	1.005	0.294	65.96
USA (US$)	0.808	0.105	1	0.808	0.105	59.64

International Energy Agency (L'Agence internationale de l'énergie). OECD/IEA. (2007). End-user petroleum product prices and average crude oil import costs. Retrieved August 9, 2007, from www.iea.org/Textbase/stats/surveys/mps.pdf

Table 12.2 Oil joint ventures in Nigeria

Joint venture operated by	Estimated production in 2003 (barrels per day)	% of Nigerian production in 2003	Partners in joint venture (share in partnership) %
Shell Petroleum Development Company of Nigeria Limited (SPDC), operated by Royal Dutch Shell a British/Dutch company	950,000	42.51	NNPC (55) Shell (30) TotalFinaElf (10) Agip (5)
Chevron/Texaco Nigeria Limited (CNL), operated by Chevron/ Texaco of USA	485,000	21.70	NNPC (60) Chevron (40)
Mobil Producing Nigeria Unlimited (MPNU), operated by Exon-Mobil of USA	500,000	22.37	NNPC (60) Exxon-Mobil (40)
Nigerian Agip Oil Company Limited (NAOC), operated by AGIP of Italy	150,000	6.71	NNPC (60) Agip (20) ConocoPhillips (20%)
Total Petroleum Nigeria Limited (TPNL), operated by Total of France	150,000	6.71	NNPC (60) Elf (now Total) (40)

Source: Energy Information Administration of the US Department of Energy (2003). *Nigeria.* Retrieved July 30, 2007, from www.eia.doe.gov/emeu/cabs/ngia_jv.html

Question 1 How much of the value in a liter of gasoline that used crude oil from Nigeria was captured by (1) each OECD country, (2) by the oil companies, and (3) by Nigeria? How much of the value was created by governments?

Question 2 Can you explain the difference between the amount appropriated by Nigeria and that appropriated by each OECD country?

Answer We perform the calculations for France first, and simply state the results for the other countries. All calculations are in US dollars and liters.

Of the $1.771 paid by customers in France for a liter of gasoline (Table 12.1), France captured $1.101 (62.17 percent). Therefore, the amount left to be shared by other players in the value chain is $0.670 ($1.771–$1.101). That is, $0.670 of the $1.771 has to be shared by (a) the oil companies that explore for crude oil, drill, pump, and transport it to refineries; (b) the refiners (often oil companies) who refine, market, and transport to gas stations for sale to customers, and the gas station's take; and (c) the exporting country, Nigeria in our case.

We are told that the average crude price in France in April was $65.72/barrel =

$$\frac{\$65.72}{158.98} \text{ per liter} = \$0.4134/\text{liter}.$$

Therefore, distribution and marketing, and refining and profits account for $0.2566 ($0.670-$0.4134) or 14.49 percent of the $1.771. The crude price of $0.4134/liter includes finding costs, lifting costs, production taxes, "profits" for exporting country, and oil company partners.

The question now is, what fraction of the $0.4134/liter goes to Nigeria? To estimate Nigeria's share, we first estimate the finding and lifting costs, and production taxes as follows:

Cost of oil extraction is $19.83 ($15.25 finding costs + $3.57 lifting costs + $1.00 production taxes) per barrel =

$$\frac{\$19.83}{158.97} \text{ per liter} = \$0.1247 \text{ per liter.}$$

Thus, finding costs, lifting costs, and production taxes account for $0.1247 or 7.04 percent of the $1.771 price per liter. Therefore, Nigeria and its venture partners (Shell, Chevron/Texaco, Agip, Total, Mobil) are left with $0.2887 ($0.4134-$0.1247) to share.

To estimate Nigeria's share of the oil ventures, we first estimate what share of the oil shipped belongs to it. The weighted average of Nigeria's share is 57.87 percent (from Table 12.2, sum of Nigeria's percent ownership in each venture multiplied by the number of barrels produced per day by the venture, all divided by the total number of barrels per day from all ventures).

Therefore, of the $0.2887 amount, Nigeria appropriates $0.1671 (0.5787 × 0.2887) or 9.43 percent of the $1.771 that the customer pays per liter, while its partners appropriate the remaining $0.1216 ($0.2887–$0.1671), or 6.87 percent of the $1.771. The results are summarized in Table 12.3.

This calculation can be repeated for each OECD country. The results from these calculations are summarized in Table 12.4, and displayed in Figure 12.1. France appropriates more than six times the value that Nigeria appropriates from Nigerian oil and more than eight times the value that oil companies appropriate. By oil companies, we mean the companies that explore for and find oil, drill for it, lift it (pump it into tankers), transport it to refineries, refine it, distribute it and sell it—the companies that create most of the value that customers pay for. Germany appropriates a little more than France while Italy and Spain appropriate slightly less than France but still a lot more than Nigeria, the oil-exporting country.

Table 12.3 What each player gets

Player(s)	Amount appropriated per liter	Percentage appropriated %	Comment
The French Government	$1.101	62.17	
Distribution and marketing, and refining and profits	$0.2566	14.49	
Crude oil:			
• Finding costs, lifting costs, and production taxes	$0.1247	7.04	
• Nigeria	$0.1671	9.43	$0.4134 (23.34%)
• Venture partners (Shell, Chevron/ Texaco, etc.) combined	$0.1216	6.87	
Total (per liter France price)	$1.771	100	

Table 12.4 How much does each OECD member capture from a gallon of gasoline?

Country	Value appropriated by country		Distribution, marketing, refining and profits		Finding costs, lifting costs, production taxes		Value appropriated by Nigeria		Value appropriated by venture partners	
	US$	%	US$	%	US$	%	US $	%	US $	%
France	1.101	62.2	0.2566	14.5	0.1247	7.0	0.1671	9.4	0.1216	6.9
Germany	1.18	62.9	0.2819	15.0	0.1247	6.7	0.1669	8.9	0.1215	6.5
Italy	1.063	58.6	0.3462	19.1	0.1247	6.9	0.1627	9.0	0.1184	6.5
Spain	0.733	50.5	0.3181	21.9	0.1247	8.6	0.1598	11.0	0.1164	8.0
UK (Pound)	1.246	65.0	0.2449	12.8	0.1247	6.5	0.1744	9.1	0.1270	6.6
Japan (yen)	0.497	43.5	0.2536	22.2	0.1247	10.9	0.1549	13.6	0.1128	9.9
Canada (C$)	0.294	29.3	0.2961	29.5	0.1247	12.4	0.1680	16.7	0.1223	12.2
USA (US$)	0.105	13.0	0.3278	40.6	0.1247	15.4	0.1449	17.9	0.1055	13.1

Implications of Government's Insertion into a Value Chain

By imposing a tax on an import or a subsidy on an export, a government is inserting itself into the product's international value chain and influencing the way value is created and appropriated by each player. This can have huge consequences on globalization. We consider the effects of taxes and subsidies, separately.

Effect of Import Duties and Taxes

By appropriating 2 per cent of the value in a liter of gasoline, the French government is extracting some consumer surplus from customers as well as some supplier surplus from the oil companies and exporting countries such as Nigeria. How much of the value extracted is supplier surplus and how much is consumer surplus depends on the price elasticity of the demand for oil. The *price elasticity of demand* of a product is the change in quantity demanded that results from a change in the product's price. The more elastic the demand, the more that the oil suppliers and exporters suffer, since the large taxes reduce the quantity that customers buy. The more inelastic the demand, the more customers suffer since they still buy a lot of the product, despite higher prices from the high taxes. To illustrate the effect of taxes and value appropriation along an international value chain, let us use the simple but informative illustration of Figure 12.2.[6] If there were no taxes, suppliers would supply the equilibrium quantity Q_E at the equilibrium price P_E. With a tax T, not only does the quantity that is demanded fall from Q_E to Q_T, the price that these suppliers get also drops from P_E to P_S. This double whammy of a drop in quantity and price results in a drop in revenues from $OP_E RQ_E$ to $OP_S MQ_T$. The more elastic the price elasticity of demand, the larger would be the drop in revenues. The drop also means that firms that would have been profitable at prices between P_E and P_S are no longer profitable and likely to go out of business. On their part, the customers who can still afford the high prices get to pay P_C rather than P_E, foregoing $P_E P_C NR$ in consumer surplus that they could have pocketed. Whether the overall effect of taxes on consumers is good or not, depends on what the government does with the money. The effect on suppliers and the supplying country is not good.

The demand for the product in Figure 12.2 is elastic since, for example, the ratio $Q_T Q_E / P_C P_E$ is greater than one. If the demand were inelastic, the drop in suppliers'

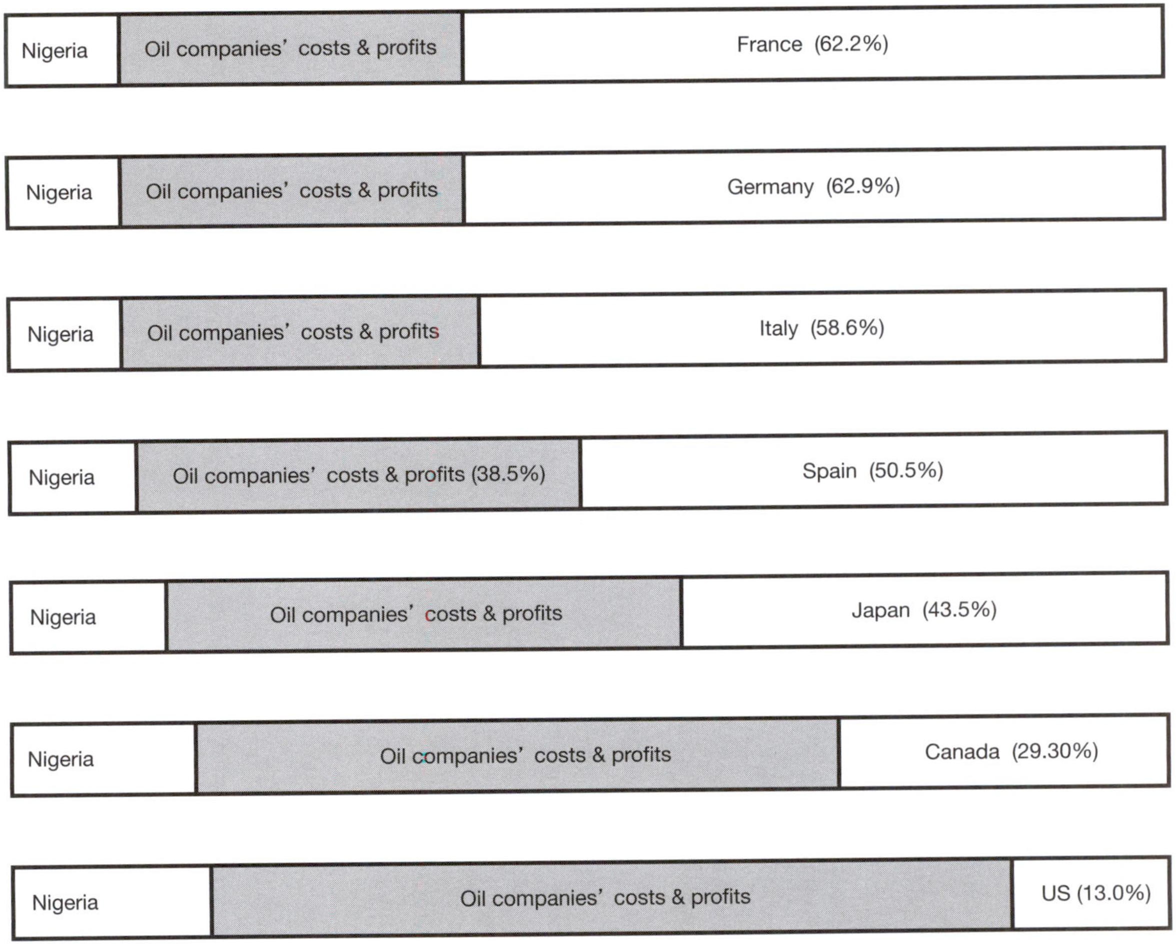

Figure 12.1 Who appropriates how much from Nigerian oil?

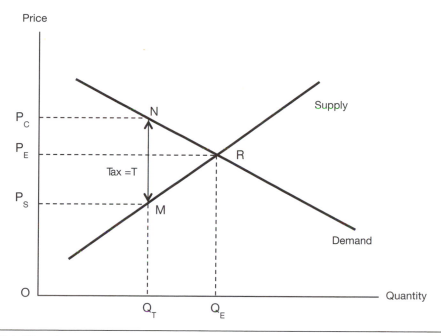

Figure 12.2 Effect of taxes on value capture

revenues and resulting negative effect on the exporting country would still be there but not as high, while the overall effect on consumers would be worse. Returning to the petroleum example, there is some evidence that demand for oil is inelastic in the short run but elastic in the long run. In other words, if the price of gasoline went up today, most people would not, for example, go out and buy a new fuel-efficient car right away, unless they had been planning to buy a car. Rather, they are more likely to keep driving their existing cars but when it is time to buy the next car, they may buy one that is more fuel-efficient. It is also true that some people would forego that family vacation because of the cost of gas.

Effect of Export Subsidies

A government can also influence globalization activities in an industry by subsidizing exports. An export *subsidy* is an amount that each supplier (exporter) is paid for a certain quantity that it exports. The subsidy can be in the form of a cash payment, a tax break, or the free use of government assets such as land. Subsidies are usually good for the exporters but not for the competitors that the subsidized firms face in the market. To understand what the impact of export subsidies can be on competitors and the importing country, consider Figure 12.3.[7] Without subsidies, all exporters can sell a quantity Q_E at a price P_E. Now, suppose a government decides to subsidize its exporters with a subsidy d. With the subsidy, suppliers who would have exported their products at a loss because of their high cost structures can remain in the market because they are now, given the subsidies, getting an effective price of P_S instead of P_E.

Additionally, because of the subsidy, the price that subsidized exporters charge customers is actually P_C. The overall effect is that more of the product is sold at lower prices than before the subsidy. Customers get lower prices, thanks to the subsidies.

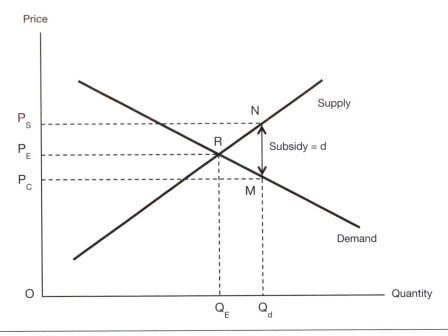

Figure 12.3 Effect of subsidies on value capture

However, for suppliers that do not have the subsidies and their costs are higher than the new subsidized price, subsidies can spell disaster. An example that has been used to illustrate the bad effects of subsidies is that of cotton farmers in Niger and Mali[8]. Many farmers in these countries, most of whom live on less than a dollar a day, took loans from the World Bank to grow cotton. Because US cotton farmers obtained subsidies from the US government, they were able to sell cotton in the world market at prices that were well below what the farmers in Niger and Mali could afford without subsidies. The result was that these farmers from Niger and Mali lost everything.

Classifying Value Creators and Appropriators

We can classify members of a value chain as a function of whether they capture more value than they create or create more value than they capture. This classification is shown in Figure 12.4. The vertical axis of the figure captures the extent to which a firm's contribution to value creation is high or low, while the horizontal axis captures the extent to which a firm's value appropriation is low or high. We use animals and insects to represent the different types of players.

Bees

In every value chain, there usually are some firms or individuals who create lots of value but do not get to appropriate a lot of the value. Like bees, these firms or individuals work very hard all the time to create value but other players capture more of the value than they deserve, leaving these bees with less than they created (other players take away their honey). From our example above, oil companies would fall in this category. They capture value all right, but not as much as they create compared to the exporting and

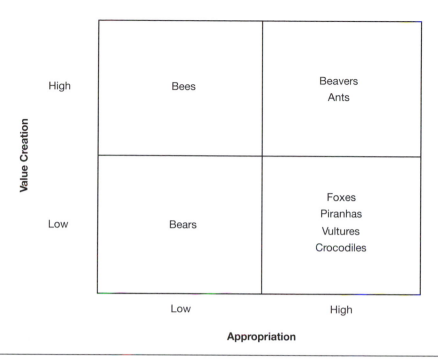

Figure 12.4 Who appropriates more value than it creates?

importing governments. As we saw in Chapter 10, there are several reasons why a firm may not be able to capture all the value that it creates. One of these reasons is that the player with more power may capture more value than it creates. In the oil industry case, governments have more power than the oil companies and can therefore appropriate more value than the creators of the value. In countries where governments regulate drug prices, it is possible that pharmaceutical companies appropriate less value than they create when they sell drugs at lower prices than patients, or insurance companies and governments may be willing to pay. Where drug prices are not regulated, it is also possible that firms extract more from desperate patients than the drugs are worth. It is possible that coffee growers capture very little of the value that coffee drinkers perceive in a cup of coffee. It is also possible that cocoa growers capture only a very small fraction of the value that chocolate lovers perceive in a bar of chocolate.

Beavers (Ants)

In some value chains, the firms that work hard to create value get to appropriate all of it. We call such firms "beavers," who work very hard to create value and often derive lots of benefits from their hard work.

Foxes (Piranhas, Vultures, Crocodiles)

As we saw in the oil industry example, some firms or governments appropriate a lot more value than they create. In some cases, they do not even create value but get to appropriate a lot of it. They reap a lot more than they sow. Such players are more like foxes since they do very little but capture a lot of value.

Bears

In their value chains, some firms play niche roles in which they do not care much about having a competitive advantage. They do enough to just get by. They are the opposite of beavers who work all the time. They are more like bears. They create very little value and do not appropriate much of it either. They have been called piranhas, vultures, and crocodiles.

GLOBALIZATION

Globalization is the interdependence and integration of people, firms, and governments to produce and exchange products and services.[9] It creates opportunities for new jobs, learning, new and improved products/services, increased trade, financial flows, and enhanced standards of living. However, globalization also poses a threat to some businesses, jobs, and ways of living. That is particularly true when globalization is not pursued correctly. If pursued well, globalization can result in improvements in the standard of living of participants—it can be a positive-sum game. That is, if globalization is pursued well, everyone should be better off. If not pursued well, it becomes a zero-sum or even a negative-sum game. That may be one reason why to some people, globalization means the dominance of the rest of the world by a few countries and powerful firms at the expense of local jobs and cultures. And to others, it means exploitation of the poor in developing countries, the destruction of the environment, and the violation of human rights. To advocates of globalization, however, it is a powerful tool for reducing poverty as the world's economies and societies get more and more integrated. Each player has a better chance of creating or adding value to something that someone somewhere in the world values. Each player also has a better chance of finding something that he or she likes.

For a firm, globalization is about asking and answering questions such as: What is the right product space and system of activities—what set of activities meets the need for local responsiveness and exploits the benefits of global integration? How does a firm build the right capabilities from the right countries? How does a firm deal with each country's macro-environment, especially with the different governments? For an oil firm, for example, deciding which country to explore for oil, working with government officials of the country, investing in the oil fields, locating the right people and equipment, finding the oil, pumping it out, transporting it, dealing with governments of importing countries, and refining and distributing the oil are all globalization issues that it has to deal with.

The Multinational Corporation

A major player in globalization is the multinational corporation. A *multinational corporation* (MNC) is a firm that has market positions and/or capabilities in at least two countries. (From now on, we will use the word "products" when we really mean "products and services.") MNCs increasingly depend on sales and capabilities from outside their home countries. They can be grouped as a function of where they choose to sell their products, and of the capabilities that they need. This classification is shown in Figure 12.5. In the figure, the vertical axis captures the effect of a firm's market-position. In particular, it captures whether a firm's products and services are sold domestically only or in other countries as well. The horizontal axis captures the extent to which the valuable capabilities that a firm needs to make (conceive, design, develop,

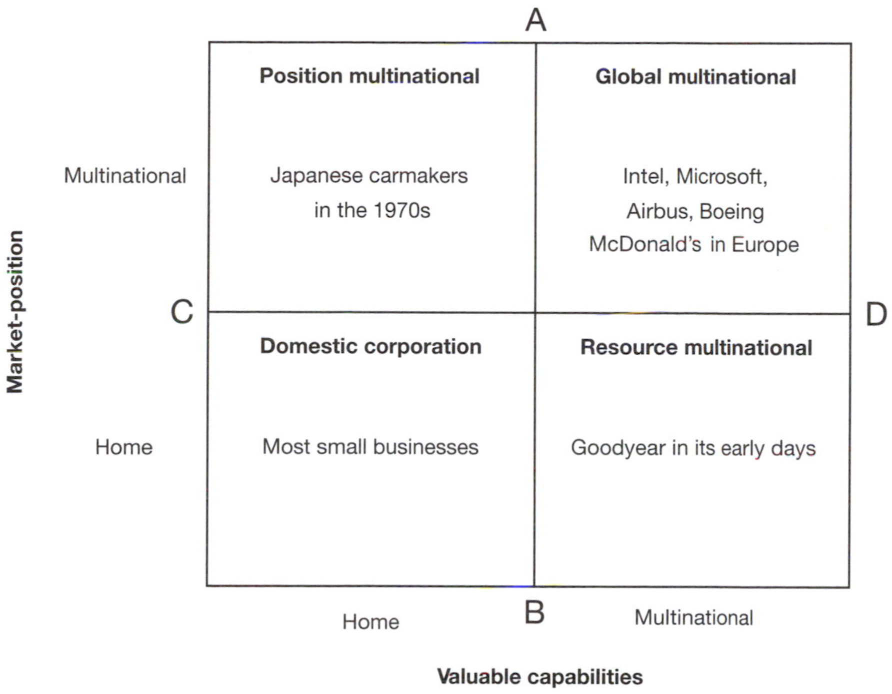

Figure 12.5 Types of multinationals

and manufacture) the product are domestic only or are also foreign. If the capabilities that a firm needs to make its products are all from its home country and the firm sells all its products within its home country, we call it a *domestic corporation* (Figure 12.5). Many small businesses fall in this category. If a firm designs, develops and produces its products at home, but sells them in two or more countries, we say the firm is a *position multinational* since it has product-market-positions in countries other than its home country. Japanese car companies in the 1960s and 1970s were largely position multinationals. All their cars were designed, developed, and manufactured in Japan and shipped to the US and other countries for sale. When a firm's design, development, and production of a product is done in many countries but the product is sold in only one country, the firm is said to be a *resource multinational* since it depends on more than the home country for its capabilities. Early in the life of US tire companies, they established rubber plantations in different developing countries and shipped the rubber to the US to be used to make tires that were sold only to domestic car companies. If a firm sells its products in two or more countries and the capabilities that it needs come from two or more countries, the firm is classified as a *global multinational*. Most of today's major companies fall into this category. Intel's microprocessors are sold all over the world and the company has design centers and microchip fabrication and assembly plants in many countries.

Drivers of Globalization

What makes globalization more likely to take place than not? That is, what drives more cross-border utilization of labor and know-how, exchange of knowledge, movement of capital, trade, human migration, and integration of financial markets and other activities? Four factors influence the process of globalization: technological innovation, consumer tastes, government policies, and firms' strategies.

Technological Innovation

One of the largest drivers of globalization has been technological innovation. First, technological innovation has made it possible to develop products that more and more people all over the world like, thereby facilitating trade in these products and the integration of the activities that underpin the products. For example, the cell phone—a technological innovation that is itself a product of many technological innovations—is a product that most people in the world want. The microchips, LCD screen, battery, and many components that go into a cell phone are complex systems that require different skills and know-how that many different countries posses. Designing, developing, marketing, selling, and delivering this global product requires the integration of ideas, skills, products, and people from different countries. The same can be said of jet engines, the Internet, computers, drugs such as Viagra, Prozac, Lipitor, and so on.

Second, technological innovation has facilitated communications, capital flows, exchange of know-how, interaction between people and firms, and reduced transportation time and costs. Because of the Internet, designers for a major company in Japan can work on a design, hand it over to fellow designers in Europe before leaving for the day. Before the engineers in Europe go home for the day, they can also hand over the design to engineers in California, who hand over to their Japanese counterparts before going home for the day. The engineers in each of these countries can be nationals of different nationalities but just happen to want to live in the countries. Financial institutions use the Internet and other communications and computer systems to route funds all over the world. These funds can finance international projects from major chip fabrication plants in Silicon Valley or Asia to micro-projects in southern Africa. Availability of the Internet also means that people can compare prices of products and labor from all over the world, often instantaneously. Worldwide telecommunications systems also mean that firms can better advertise and try to harmonize consumer tastes. Lower communications and transportation costs mean that consumers are more exposed to lower cost products that they may like.

Some of the first innovations to have a huge impact on globalization were in transportation. Motorized ships that ran across the Atlantic Ocean played a major role in the transatlantic migration and trade that were critical to building the American economy. Later, the jet airplane would change world travel not only by transporting people worldwide but also in transporting important business documents in much shorter times. More importantly, ocean transportation has become so cost-effective that steel, as heavy as it is, can be made in Korea and still be cost-competitive in California. Effectively, technological progress moves the vertical line AB in Figure 12.5 leftwards, increasing the zone in which global and resource multinational activities can take place. It also moves the line CD downwards, thereby increasing the zone in which position and global multinational activities can take place.

Consumer Tastes and Needs

Consumer tastes and needs have always been a major driver of globalization. Europeans' taste for spices, for example, was an important reason for their trading with India and why Columbus ended up in the Americas. Diseases in many countries can be cured by medications developed in others. Some of these tastes or needs are dormant until they are woken by firms through advertising or the introduction of the new product. Very few people in the world knew that they needed the Internet or cell phones until the products were introduced. Lower communications and transportation costs often mean more availability of low-cost products that can influence consumers' taste. Consumers' tastes can also be influenced by the experiences that they had as a result of innovations in communications and transportation that made it possible for them to travel to other lands, or find out about them via, for example, the Internet.

Government Policies

Government policies play one of the most significant roles of all the drivers of globalization. Governments can use quotas, tariffs, taxes, subsidies, and import duties to stifle or greatly facilitate imports or production. In addition to having an influence on what gets imported, governments can have great influence over what is produced and exported. In some sectors such as healthcare, some governments control prices, and what can or cannot be sold. Governments also influence the other drivers of globalization such as technological innovations in transportation and communications. A country can decide to enforce or not enforce intellectual property protection laws. Governments control the flow of currency and therefore investment capital. A country's ability to protect foreign investments from vandalism or nationalistic activities also plays a role in who invests in the country.

Firms' Strategies

Globalization is also driven by the extent to which firms want to take advantage of the other drivers of globalization to create and appropriate value. For example, if a firm's strategy rests on extending its existing core competences to many markets, using worldwide labor, taking advantage of economies of scale, or learning from abroad, the firm may decide to push for globalization. As part of its strategy, a firm may advertise to influence consumer tastes in different countries, or work with policy makers in different countries to obtain legislation that favors globalization. Many multinational corporations have larger budgets than most poor countries and can be very influential when it comes to globalization legislation. They can also innovate to offer the kinds of products that will help consumers discover their latent needs. They can influence not only the flow of capital to their worldwide investment sites but also help bring down trade barriers by influencing policy makers.

Why Firms Go International (Global)

The question is, why would any firm want to enter global markets rather than focus on its home market? That is, why would any domestic company want to become a multinational? There are several reasons for going global: to search for growth, stabilize earnings, pursue an offensive move, take advantage of factors of production abroad, follow a buyer, pursue economies of scale, take advantage of easier regulations, participate in a larger market, and learn from abroad.

In Search of Growth

If a firm's domestic market is stagnant, declining, too competitive, mature, or not growing fast enough, the firm may see foreign markets as places where it could find the growth that it does not have at home. This is particularly true if the firm's market valuation has factored in growth and capital markets expect the firm to continue to grow at a rate that the home market cannot support. One of many alternatives is for the firm to diversify into other markets within its home country, unless there are other compelling reasons to go global.

Opportunity to Stabilize Earnings

Since a firm's profits often depend on domestic economic factors, its profits are likely to rise and fall with domestic economic cycles. By going international, a firm may be able to reduce this cyclicality if it can successfully enter a country with the right cyclicality.

High Cost of Production at Home

One of the most common reasons for firms to go international is the high domestic cost of factors of production. For example, the cost of labor for low-tech manufacturing in many Western countries and Japan has become so high that many firms in the West move some of their manufacturing activities to China, Taiwan, Korea, or India.

Firm May Be Following Buyer

Very often, a firm goes international because its key buyer is going international. Some Japanese auto suppliers moved with the automobile makers when the latter decided to start assembling cars in the US. When McDonald's entered the Russian market, the J.R. Simplot Company went along to produce potatoes for McDonald's french fries.

Offensive Move

A firm can also start operating in a foreign country to preempt competitors that it believes are likely to enter the foreign country. This is particularly true if there are first-mover advantages to be had in the foreign country.

Economies of Scale and Extension of Capabilities

When a firm offers a product with very high fixed (upfront) costs and very little or no variable costs, every unit sold after breakeven volume is profit. Going global increases a firm's chances of selling even more units and making even more money. This is particularly true for products such as software that do not need major modifications to suit local tastes and therefore can be sold anywhere in the world at little extra cost. This is also particularly true if the home market is very small relative to the minimum efficient scale of the firm's technology. One reason why many Swiss firms such as Nestlé went international very early was because their home market was too small for the kinds of volumes that they needed to compete with foreign firms that had larger home markets.

Regulations Overseas May Be Easier than at Home

It is not unusual for developing economies to have little or no regulations on safety, environmental pollution, and no anti-competitiveness laws. Some firms may move to these countries to take advantage of these laws.

Larger Market and Free Market Principles

Some markets are simply larger and more free-market than others. Thus, firms may enter such markets to take advantage of the large size and free-market atmosphere. The US is one such country.

Learn from Abroad (Market Idea, Acquire New Skills, etc.)

Although it has traditionally been thought that knowledge flow is one way—from the home country to the host country that the firm is moving into—there is growing recognition that firms can also learn from their host countries and take the knowledge home or to other markets.

GLOBALIZATION FOR A COMPETITIVE ADVANTAGE

Suppose a firm wants to sell its products to a foreign country or take advantage of the capabilities in the foreign country to produce new products. Is there anything that it can do to increase its chances of having a competitive advantage as a result of the move? A framework for exploring this question is shown in Figure 12.6. As we saw in Chapter 1, a firm's profitability in a market is a function of its product-market-position (PMP) and the capabilities that underpin the position. Recall that a firm's product-market-position consists of the benefits (low-cost or differentiated products) that the firm offers and the associated system of activities that it performs to offer the product. To occupy such a position and perform the relevant activities, a firm needs capabilities. Thus, we can explore the profitability of a firm's entry into a foreign country as a function of its PMP in the new country and the capabilities that it uses to create and/or appropriate value in the country (Figure 12.6).

Figure 12.6 Different global strategies

Unique Product-Market-Position (PMP)

The vertical axis captures the product-market-position that the firm occupies—whether the position is unique (white space, sweet spot) or a battlefield. Occupying a *unique* product-market-position means that a firm (1) offers a product/service with benefits that no one else in the market segment or country does, and/or (2) performs a distinctive system of activities that underpins the benefits. The benefits can be product features, location, lower cost, or better bang for the buck. The product-market-position can be unique because of the perceived uniqueness of the product/service features. It can also be unique because of the location or region of the country that the firm serves. The unique position can be in one country or in many countries. Since the benefits that the firm offers its customers are unique, the effect of rivalry on the firm is low, the threat of substitutes is low, and the firm has more power over buyers than it would have if it were in a battlefield. The fact that a firm moves into a unique position does not tell us much about barriers to entry or its position vis-à-vis suppliers but there are things that the firm can do to raise barriers to entry into its unique space and increase its power over coopetitors. For example, it can pursue first-mover advantages such as building switching costs at customers. Building a brand that is associated with the unique space can also raise barriers to entry.

A *battlefield* is a product-market space that already has players. Such players usually have been in the market long enough to have developed rivalries, understandings, cooperative relationships, and other capabilities to create and appropriate value in the market. Why would anyone enter a battlefield? Although battlefields can be rife with competition, they have some advantages. Technological and marketing uncertainties are usually reduced and a new entrant with important complementary assets may be able to do well. A firm may also enter because it has distinctive capabilities that it uses to give it an advantage in the foreign country. Many firms do enter battlefields. Some do so because they believe that there is something distinctive about them that will allow them to win when they come in. Others do so because of other strategic reasons. In any case, a firm is usually better off pursuing a unique PMP.

Valuable Global Capabilities

The horizontal axis of Figure 12.6 captures the type of major global capabilities that a firm utilizes to conceive of, design, manufacture, market the product and position itself to make money—whether the capabilities are scarce and important, or easily available or unimportant. Capabilities are *scarce and important* if they are difficult to imitate or substitute, and make a significant contribution towards value creation or appropriation. These capabilities can be in a firm's home country, in the foreign country that the firm is entering, or worldwide. Examples of scarce and important capabilities include exclusive rights to explore oil in oil-producing countries, relationships with government officials in foreign countries, patents in pharmaceuticals, shelf space in offline stores, some major brands, a large network in an industry that exhibits network externalities, etc. Such capabilities therefore stand to give a firm a competitive advantage. If the capabilities are important but easy to imitate, their owners quickly lose any advantage that they may have had as competitors swoop in, making it difficult to appropriate any value that a firm may have created using the important capabilities. An example of capabilities that are important but easy to imitate is low-tech manufacturing capabilities. They are important but because they are usually easy to imitate and therefore easily available, we classify them as "easily available or unimportant" in Figure 12.6.

Global Strategy Types

Depending on whether a firm decides to pursue a unique product-market-position or enter a battlefield, has scarce difficult-to-imitate capabilities or can build them, a firm's strategy falls in one of the following four categories: global adventurer, global star, global heavyweight, and global generic (Figure 12.6).

Global Adventurer

In a *global adventurer* strategy, a firm enters a country or countries by occupying a unique product-market-position, but the major capabilities that it uses to create and appropriate value are easily available or unimportant. The product/service that embodies the unique value can target one country or many countries. The product can be made in the foreign country or in the home country and exported to the foreign country. Many exports that target an unmet need in a country fall in this category. Japanese automobile makers were utilizing a global adventurer strategy when they exported fuel-efficient dependable cars to the US during the 1970s when US automakers GM, Ford, American Motors, and Chrysler focused on making larger and less fuel-efficient cars. All the major capabilities for the cars were Japanese and although it may not feel that way today, selling small Japanese cars in the US in the late 1960s through the 1970s was an adventure.

A retailer that builds the first retail store in a region of a foreign country is pursuing an adventurer strategy. Whether the global adventurer strategy works for a firm is a function of the drivers of globalization—a function of technological developments, consumer tastes, government policies, firm's corporate strategy, and the type of products in question. Take the example of Japanese cars in the US in the 1970s. Shipping technology had improved to a point where cars could be shipped cost-efficiently from Japan to California, 5,500 miles away. Because of the oil crises in the US in the 1970s, some consumers were interested in looking at fuel-efficient dependable cars. US government policies were less protective at the time, compared to those of the governments of other rich countries. That is, until the US government imposed a quota on Japanese cars. There had also been attempts by Japan's powerful Ministry of International Trade and Industry (MITI) to prevent Honda from entering the car production business at home. An important part of Honda's strategy was to expand abroad and the large US market, where it had been selling motorcycles, presented some good opportunities. Its chances of growing profitably were better in the US than in Japan.

A unique product-market-position gives a global adventurer some opportunities to take advantage of the innovativeness of the position, including first-mover advantages. Honda went on to build a brand that associated the company with zippy engines, and dependable reliable low-cost cars. It then, together with Toyota and Nissan, introduced luxury cars to compete with BMW, Mercedes, and other luxury imports to the US. Honda introduced the Acura, Nissan the Infiniti, and Toyota introduced the Lexus.

The primary advantage to the global adventurer strategy is the fact that it identifies and focuses on a unique product-market-position with its associated benefits and shortcomings. There is one major drawback to the strategy. Since the capabilities that a global adventurer uses are easily available or unimportant, the unique product-market-position can be easily imitated unless the firm takes steps to build first-mover advantages that raise barriers to entry.

Global Star

In a *global star* strategy, a firm enters a country or countries by occupying a unique product-market space, and the global capabilities that it uses to create and appropriate value are scarce and important. Thus, pursuing a star strategy gives a firm both the advantages of having a unique product-market-position and scarce important capabilities. Ikea's strategy for entering the US market in the 2000s is an example. It occupied a unique position, relative to its competitors (fun shopping experience, low-cost but fashionable furniture, no delivery, little in-store service, and furniture that was not guaranteed to last forever), and had a scarce important worldwide network of experienced designers, and an ability to coordinate and integrate the activities of its suppliers of materials and manufacturers worldwide.[10] Strategies for both the Airbus A380 and the Boeing 787 also fall in this category. Each occupies a unique spot on the product-market-position maps for airplanes and the capabilities needed to offer the plans are scarce and important. Often, one of the important capabilities of a global star is its ability to coordinate and integrate capabilities and know-how from different countries and differing cultures. Making both the A380 and Boeing 787 required coordination of many different capabilities and capabilities from different countries. This coordination and integration is facilitated by technological innovation.

Global Heavyweight

In a *global heavyweight* strategy, a firm enters a country or countries by confronting existing competitors, but has scarce and important capabilities that it uses to create and appropriate value. The capabilities can be from one country or many countries. Such a firm is effectively in a battlefield where it confronts existing industry firms in creating and appropriating value, using its scarce capabilities. When an oil company goes into a country where other companies are already exploiting for oil and obtains exploration rights to find and sell oil to the world, it is employing a global heavyweight strategy. Airbus pursued a global heavyweight strategy when it introduced its A320 airplanes. The plane was designed to compete directly with the Boeing 737 and the McDonnell Douglas DC 9 and MD-80. While some of the technological know-how to build the plane may have been easily available, the A320 fly-by-wire technology was the first for a large plane. Moreover, coordinating the activities of the makers of major airplane components from French, German, and British companies was no easy task. Many of the ideas utilized in McDonald's restaurants in each European country came not only from the country and the US, but also from other European countries.[11]

Global Generic

In a *global generic* strategy, a firm enters a country or countries by confronting existing competitors, and the major capabilities that it uses are easily available or unimportant. Firms that produce commodity products in low-cost labor nations and export them to other countries to compete with other commodity products from other countries are pursuing this strategy. Many producers of generic drugs for export usually have generic strategies. So do makers of textiles. Many products are usually introduced to a foreign country through exports that were designed, developed, and produced at the home country and exported to the foreign country. As the product gains acceptance, local capabilities are built to better respond to local differences.

Competitive Consequence and Implications

Pursuing any of the four strategies—global star, global adventurer, global heavyweight or global generic—has a strategic consequence. A global adventurer usually enjoys a so-called PMP-based competitive advantage. A firm has a *PMP-based competitive advantage* if its position in a market is such that the threat of any firm replicating its position is low (barriers to entry are high), the effect of rivalry on it is low, buyers and suppliers have little power over it, and the threat of substitutes is low. This usually comes from a system of activities that the firm performs. Because a global adventurer chooses a unique product-market-position when it enters a foreign country but the capabilities that it uses are easily available or unimportant, any advantage that it has comes from the unique position—the advantage is PMP-based. A firm's PMP-based advantage is eroded when competitors find ways to overcome barriers to entry, rivals find ways to increase rivalry, or buyers and suppliers increase their power over the firm. Thus, one way for a firm with a PMP advantage to maintain the advantage is to find ways to reinforce friendly competitive forces such as raising barriers to entry.

A global heavyweight usually enjoys a resource-based competitive advantage. A firm has a *resource-based competitive advantage* if its important scarce capabilities are difficult to imitate or substitute. Because a global heavyweight chooses to use its scarce, important, and difficult-to-imitate capabilities to confront existing competitors in their PMPs in the foreign country that it is entering, any advantage it has in going international is largely from its capabilities. A resource-based advantage is eroded when competitors find a way to replicate or substitute the resource, or develop another resource that can enable them to leapfrog the value offered by the firm.

Since a global star enters a foreign market by choosing a unique PMP and uses scarce, important, and difficult-to-imitate capabilities, it stands to enjoy both the PMP-based advantages of a global adventurer, and the resource-based advantages of a global heavyweight. Thus, its chances of having a sustainable competitive advantage are higher than those of either a global adventurer or heavyweight. Because a firm that pursues a global generic strategy, in entering a foreign country, chooses to confront incumbents in their PMPs in the country, and does so using generic capabilities that are easy to imitate, such a firm has neither a PMP-based advantage nor a resource-based advantage. Effectively, of the four strategies, the global star strategy offers a firm the best chance of attaining and sustaining a competitive advantage. The global adventurer and heavyweight have the next best chance, while the generic has the least chance.

USING INNOVATION TO GAIN A GLOBAL COMPETITIVE ADVANTAGE

If a firm's chances of having a sustainable competitive advantage are best when it pursues a global star strategy rather than the other three strategies, why can't all firms that pursue the same global star strategy do well? One reason is that not every firm is going to pursue the right business model innovation. One way to test if a firm is pursuing the right business model innovation is to use a VARIM framework:

1. **Value**: Does the business model offer benefits that customers perceive as valuable to them?
2. **Adaptability**: Is the business model—or core parts of it—cost-effectively reconfigurable or redeployable to offer benefits that customers perceive as valuable to them?
3. **Rareness**: Is the firm the only one that offers the customer benefits? If not, is the firm's level of the benefits higher than that of competitors?
4. **Inimitability**: Are the benefits difficult for other firms to imitate, substitute, or leapfrog?
5. **Monetization**: Does the firm make or stand to make money from offering the benefits to customers?

A VARIM analysis follows the examples that we explored in Chapter 2. However, it is important to note the following that can be useful in profiting from international businesses. First, when going international, it is best to avoid head-on competition. A firm can enter an uncontested market through innovation, teaming up, or looking for market spaces that it can fill with its existing capabilities. For example, Apple's iPhone was welcome by customers in most developed countries. However, innovation can also be stealth—as in disruptive technologies. One of the best examples of entering through stealth innovation is that of Japanese automobile makers who enter the US market. These companies started by exporting small low-cost cars to the United States at a time when gas was cheap and US automakers sold large gas-guzzling cars at high margins. The Japanese companies kept improving the quality and reliability of their cars and US automakers did not view them as a threat at all. Eventually, the quality of Japanese cars rose to a point where they started taking market share from the higher ends of the automobile industry, including luxury cars.

Second, when going international, leveraging one's capabilities can be critical in capturing value. A firm can leverage its capabilities not only to offer foreign customers what they want, it can also use the capabilities as bargaining chips to team up and acquire complementary capabilities.

KEY TAKEAWAYS

• At the international level, governments can capture a lot of the value that firms create.

• Actors (firms and governments) can be classified as a function of whether they create the value that they capture: bees create lots of value but others capture most of what they create. Beavers create lots of value and capture most of it. Foxes create little or no value but capture a lot of the value created by others. Bears create little value and capture little too.

• Government-imposed taxes and subsidies can result in value destruction.

• **Globalization** is the interdependence and integration of people, firms, and governments to produce and exchange products and services.

• A key character in globalization is the multinational corporation (MNC). This is a firm that has established product-market-positions and/or capabilities in at least two countries. A firm is a *position multinational* if it designs, develops, and produces its products at home, but sells them in two or more countries. If a firm's design, development, and production of a product are done in many countries but the product is sold in only one country, the firm is said to be a *capabilities multinational*. If a firm has market positions in two or more countries and the capabilities that it needs come from two or more countries, the firm is classified as a *global multinational*.

- The extent to which globalization takes place in an industry is a function of:
  - technological innovation;
  - consumer tastes and needs;
  - government policies;
  - multinationals' strategies.

- Some reasons for firms becoming multinationals include:
  - the search for growth;
  - opportunity to stabilize earnings;
  - high cost of production at home;
  - following a buyer;
  - offensive move;
  - opportunity to take advantage of scale economies;
  - easier regulations overseas;
  - larger market abroad;
  - chance to learn from abroad.

- In using innovation to go international, a firm can locate in a unique product-market space where it offers unique value to customers and has few competitors, or enter a battlefield where there are competitors already. The capabilities that a firm uses to create and appropriate value in a unique product space or battlefield can either be scarce and important capabilities, or easily available or unimportant. In going international, four strategies are possible:
  - In a *global adventurer* strategy, a firm enters a country or countries by occupying a unique product-market space, but the major capabilities that it uses to create and capture value are easily available or unimportant.
  - In a *global star* strategy, a firm enters a country or countries by occupying a unique product-market space, and the global capabilities that it uses to create and appropriate value are scarce and important.
  - In a *global heavyweight* strategy, a firm enters a country or countries by confronting existing competitors, and has scarce and important capabilities that it uses to create and appropriate value.
  - In a *global generic* strategy, a firm enters a country or countries by confronting existing competitors, and the major capabilities that it uses are easily available or unimportant.

- Which strategy a firm pursues has competitive consequences. A global adventurer strategy is likely to give a firm a product-market-position (PMP) advantage—an advantage based on the product space it occupies in the market. A global heavyweight strategy is likely to give a firm a capabilities-based competitive advantage, while a global star strategy is likely to give a firm both a PMP and capabilities-based advantage. A global star strategy is the most likely to give a firm a sustainable competitive advantage while a global generic strategy is the least likely to give a firm a competitive advantage.

- If a firm's chances of having a sustainable competitive advantage are best when it pursues a global star strategy rather than the other three strategies, why is it that not all firms who pursue a global star strategy do well? One way to answer this question is to use VARIM analysis.

KEY TERMS

Bears	Foxes	Global star
Beavers	Global adventurer	Multinational
Bees	Global generic	Position multinational
Capabilities multinational	Global heavyweight	
Drivers of globalization	Global multinational	

NOTES

1   Nigerian Bonny Light (Bonny Lt crude oil spot prices in Europe went as high as $80 in July. In France there was a tax of 0.5892 euro per liter of unleaded and a TVA of 19.6 percent.)
2   Energy Information Administration of the US Department of Energy. (2007). *Nigeria: Oil.* Retrieved July 16, 2008, from www.eia.doe.gov/emeu/cabs/Nigeria/Oil.html
3   Energy Information Administration of the US Department of Energy. (2006). Performance profiles of major energy producers 2006 (Form EIA-28). Retrieved July 31, 2007, from www.eia.doe.gov/emeu/perfpro/tab12.htm
4   International Energy Agency (L'Agence internationale de l'énergie). OECD/IEA. (2007). End-user petroleum product prices and average crude oil import costs. Retrieved August 9, 2007, from www.iea.org/Textbase/stats/surveys/mps.pdf
5   Energy Information Administration of the US Department of Energy. (2003). Nigeria. Retrieved July 30, 2007, from www.eia.doe.gov/emeu/cabs/ngia_jv.html. Vernon, C. (2006). *UK Petrol Prices.* Retrieved July 30, 2007, from http://europe.theoildrum.com/story/2006/5/3/17236/14255
6   Pindyck, R.S., & Rubinfeld, D.L. (1992). *Microeconomics* (4th edn.). Upper Saddle River, NY: Prentice Hall.
7   Pindyck, R.S., & Rubinfeld, D.L. (1992). *Microeconomics* (4th edn.). Upper Saddle River, NY: Prentice Hall.
8   Baxter, J. (2003, May 19). Cotton subsidies squeeze Mali. Retrieved September 10, 2007, from http://news.bbc.co.uk/1/hi/world/africa/3027079.stm
9   This definition is closest to the one offered by *Economics A–Z.* (n.d.). Retrieved July 26, 2007, from http://economist.com/research/Economics/alphabetic.cfm?letter=G#globalisation
10 *IKEA.* (2007). Retrieved August 10, 2007, from http://en.wikipedia.org/wiki/Ikea
11 Happy meal: How a Frenchman is reviving McDonald's in Europe. (2007, January 25). *The Economist.*

Part V
Cases

Case 1

SQUARE*

INTRODUCTION

Jack Dorsey was still recovering from what he described as being "punched in the stomach" after being ousted from Twitter, the company he helped create.[1] While contemplating his next move, he spoke with his friend, Jim McKelvey. McKelvey casually commented on the fact that he had recently lost a large sale of blown-glass bathroom taps because he was unable to take his customer's credit card payment. The two were both talking on iPhones and, realizing the immense processing power those devices held, they wondered why those devices couldn't process credit card payments.[2] Shortly after this conversation Dorsey would go on to change the way that payments were made and give people the ability to use credit cards to make payments virtually anywhere, for a small fee. It changed the way that small businesses operated and provided the majority of users (groups like cab drivers, farmers markets, babysitters, Girl Scouts, and many others) the ability to accept card payments for the first time.

JACK DORSEY

Jack Dorsey was no stranger to the entrepreneurial world. As a child he was always fascinated with computer programming and enriching people's lives with technology. At the age of 15, he programmed dispatch software to help cab drivers and police officers coordinate locations. Among his many jobs during his youth, he also interned for McKelvey, a relationship that provided the inspiration for Square. Dorsey dropped out of New York University to pursue his dream in Silicon Valley, where he utilized his programming skills to create a small company known as Twitter. Starting with the debut tweet by Jack in March 2006, Twitter catapulted into a communication and marketing

---

* This case was written by Erin Braddock, Preeti Gupta, Molly Mehaffey, Susan Merrill, Allison Myers, and Allison Rosen under the supervision of Professor Allan Afuah as a basis for class discussion and is not intended to illustrate either effective or ineffective handling of a business situation.

tool used by top celebrities and even US presidential candidates Barack Obama and John McCain while campaigning for the 2008 election. Twitter has been credited for helping organize the demonstration during 2009's political unrest in Iran.[3]

Despite success at Twitter, Dorsey was forced out of the CEO position in 2008, which gave him time to work on his new product, Square. He documented his learnings from leading Twitter and applied them to his management of Square's culture and idea creation process.[4] Dorsey was asked to come back to Twitter in March 2011 as executive chairman and gradually decreased his responsibilities there to focus on Square. Dorsey found successfully leading two companies understandably difficult, and he thus employed a unique management approach involving a weekly cadence,[5] where every day of the week was dedicated to focusing on a different business area. Any meetings involving more than two people required meeting minutes, which were then distributed to the entire company. Dorsey himself spent most of the day working from stand-up tables, frequently walking around the office to foster an environment of open communication and transparency. A believer in the "power of threes," he has stated he would conceptually love the idea of a third company.

INCEPTION OF SQUARE

Shortly after Dorsey's infamous conversation with McKelvey, they went to dinner together along with McKelvey's wife, Anna. They spent dinner discussing whether or not they should start a company that would make it easier to make payments and ultimately decided to go ahead with the idea. On the way home from dinner, while waiting for McKelvey to get some water, Dorsey and Anna observed a squirrel running across the street. Dorsey began thinking how squirrels run around and collect acorns, like currency. He thought about how people "squirrel" away their treasures and about complementary acorn-shaped hardware.[6] He moved ahead and developed a prototype of a mobile credit-card processing device a short ten days later, which even made a sound similar to the squeak of a squirrel when a card was swiped. With those simple conversations and thoughts, Dorsey revolutionized the way credit card payments are processed. He developed hardware that connected to most smart devices such as iPhones, iPads and Android to enable the user to swipe credit card payments virtually anywhere, eliminating the need for a traditional register system. The name of the application was eventually changed to Square Register after learning that there was already a payment system called Squirrel. The hardware also changed to a square shape. Associations such as "a square deal is a fair one" and two parties "squaring up" enhanced the product name's relevance.

Having one's credit card swiped through a plastic reader attached to a merchant's personal mobile device often elicited questions and puzzled looks from consumers not used to this payment system. However, the option to pay by credit card (including all four of the major US players: Visa, MasterCard, American Express and Discover) where merchants previously only accepted cash outweighed the potential initial confusion. Square did not provide physical receipts for customers, and merchants agreed to provide handwritten receipts to customers for transactions over $15 as part of the terms of agreement to use Square. Customers could also forego the receipt altogether, or opt to have a receipt sent via either SMS messaging or email in addition to the handwritten receipt.[7]

Square generated revenue through transaction fees paid by merchants in exchange for use of the service. Square offered two pricing options: a 2.75 percent fee for every transaction, or a $275 monthly fee for unlimited transactions. Although the majority of transaction fees were paid to credit card companies, Square's ability to run a low-cost operation enabled the firm to both exist and not price gouge their end-users. Employee count was small and there was no dedicated sales force, which did not hamper Square's facility in increasing the number of merchants who use its service. The growth was largely due to Square's ability to offer credit card services to small businesses which did not have the infrastructure, history, or transaction volume to tap into the banking system on their own. The flat fee option made the service available to a wider set of merchants, and extra services (such as loyalty programs and data analytics for purchase) helped Square remain a competitive player.

Development of Square

In 2012, Fast Company magazine named Square 5th Most Innovative Company, and it has come a long way since its inception.[8] Early challenges involved navigating the complicated financial transactions market. The major stakeholders included:[9]

1. Cardholders—individuals and businesses that obtained and utilized credit and debit cards.
2. Merchants—entities that accepted different cards as a form of payment from their customers; merchants paid interchange fees to card associations to use the service.
3. Issuers (member banks)—banks that issued credit cards branded with card associations and essentially underwrote the transactions via credit card; authorized transactions at point of sale; extended credit, or collected, assessed and set cardholder fees or interest charges.
4. Acquiring (merchant) banks—banks that managed relationships with merchants and obtained the funds from the issuer for the sale.
5. Card associations—these organizations helped facilitate the transaction process between the member banks and acquiring banks; Visa and MasterCard were major players.

Card associations earned revenue from transaction/interchange fees, international fees, and data-processing services offered to members, financial institutions, and the public sector. Since per-transaction revenue was small, Square relied on high transaction volumes to increase revenue. Traditionally, consumers and merchants did not have the power to control the fees charged by banks and card associations, but the broader adoption of Square made the possibility that the power balance could change, as Dorsey wanted to make financial transactions better and more consumer-focused.

Developing a system that utilized the traditional automated clearing houses (ACH) to move money between banks was required for Square to become functional. While some stakeholders felt threatened by Square and its progressive vision of credit card usage, Visa and other credit associations were excited, as Square's adoption allowed more transactions to occur since more businesses accepted credit cards. Early strategic partnerships occurred with Visa and Starbucks.

Square's initial idea (Card Case) involved setting up individual credit cards for each business a consumer interacted with via an app on their mobile device. An Apple iPhone product manager, Shuvo Chatterjee, commented in an interview that this did not streamline the process, and subsequently he was brought in to manage Card Case, leading to the more current interface of the application.[10]

As more imitators entered the space, Square evolved and developed a swipeless method for conducting transactions called Square Wallet that relied on phone GPS to track when a Square customer entered a participating vendor. This "digital wallet" did not require the Square Register attachment for merchants, but did require consumers have a smartphone. It quickly proved itself to be more imitable than Register by the number of competitors in the digital wallet space. Many compared Dorsey to the late Steve Jobs of Apple, Inc., and no one knew what this innovative leader would end up creating next.

Competition for Square

As the number of retailers and restaurants handling payments via mobile devices increased, so too did the number of solutions on the market.[11] Google Wallet, PayPal Here, and GrouponPayments were a few of the many examples jumping on the bandwagon. Retail giants including Wal-Mart and Target announced a joint venture, Merchant Customer Exchange, to develop their own mobile payment offering. Banks, such as Bank of America, also tried to capture a piece of this pie with offerings of their own. Square faced powerful challengers in the digital wallet race but as of December 2013, it was definitely "hip" to be Square.

GOOGLE WALLET[12]

Google Inc. offered Google Wallet, which let consumers pay by tapping an Android phone against a terminal. Google Wallet used near-field communications (NFC) chips, which were built into certain phones that ran the company's Android operating system. The chips communicated on contact with the credit card terminals at many retail stores. When setting up an account, consumers entered their credit card information into their Google Wallet. Then they could use that card by entering a PIN and tapping the phone against the terminal. However, only a few of the latest 2012 Android phones were compatible, and only one of the nation's four biggest cell phone carriers—Sprint Nextel Corp.—allowed its Android phones to interact with Google Wallet. Additionally, customers faced challenges in getting the service to work at retail stores.

PAYPAL HERE[13]

One of Square's biggest rivals was PayPal, which released its "PayPal Here" card reader in March 2012. PayPal's per-transaction fee was 0.05 percent lower than Square's (2.7 vs. 2.75 percent), and accepted payments at more than 7,000 physical locations in the United States. PayPal, which was developed ten years earlier when it established itself as a popular method of paying online, was already hooked into bank accounts for its 117 million active users, said Hill Ferguson, a PayPal vice president. To move into the digital wallet space, PayPal simply needed to prod those users to use PayPal at physical store locations as well, he commented. "We have a really good head start," Ferguson said. "PayPal essentially created this category." PayPal had also rolled out its product outside of North America to the Asia-Pacific region (Japan, Hong Kong, and Australia) as well as the UK.[14] Square's only expansion outside the US was to Canada in October 2012, but its hire of former US Trade Negotiator Demetrios Marantis to head up its international expansion office in May 2013 seemed a promising step in the right, global direction.[15]

GROUPONPAYMENTS[16]

Groupon Inc., the world's largest online daily deals provider, launched a payment business in September 2012, GrouponPayments, which allowed local businesses to run credit cards using an iPhone or iPod Touch. Any merchant that ran a daily deal with Groupon in the United States could sign up for the payments service, the company added. Groupon touted its device as the "lowest cost option," saying businesses would pay 1.8 percent per credit card swipe, plus a 15-cent fee. (The charge jumped to 3 percent for American Express purchases.) The device was tied into Groupon Merchants, so retailers that were Groupon members and those that ran deals with Groupon could use the device for that rate. Others would be charged about 2.2 percent per transaction.

MERCHANT CUSTOMER EXCHANGE (MCX)

MCX was a company created by a collaboration of some of the leading US retail companies. The joint venture was announced on August 15, 2012 with the desired purpose of offering a new platform for smartphone-based transactions.[17] After almost a year post-announcement, the company's website stated, "Development of the mobile application is underway, with an initial focus on a flexible solution that will offer merchants a customizable platform with the features and functionality needed to best meet consumers' needs."[18] MCX intended to make their application available on all major smartphone platforms. The company was led by merchants, including 7-Eleven, Inc., Alon Brands, Best Buy Co., Inc., CVS/pharmacy, Darden Restaurants, HMSHost, Hy-Vee, Inc., Lowe's, Michaels Stores, Inc., Publix Super Markets, Inc., Sears Holdings, Shell Oil Products US, Sunoco, Inc., Target Corp., and Wal-Mart Stores, Inc. The initial retailers accounted for about $1 trillion in annual sales. Combined, these participating member merchants served nearly every smartphone-enabled American on a weekly basis, thus creating a competitor with a major convenience value-add for consumers once the platform was realized.[19]

BANK OF AMERICA[20]

Bank of America released its own mobile credit card reader, entering the mobile payments market and raising the stakes in the intense competition for small business accounts. "We saw this whole space maturing," said Tom Bell, chief executive of BofA merchant services. "We started studying our business model, we started studying their business model, and we realized there's a way for us to do this safely and profitably." The move was aimed at keeping up with a technology it saw gaining traction among the millions of small businesses that had never before accepted credit cards. However, it was also defensive, as BofA noticed that some of its established customers were walking away from their traditional cash registers and card swipe systems to experiment with an iPad-based mobile system such as Square. Now, using technology and a "secret sauce" underwriting model, BofA has struck at Square's strongest competitive point by offering a lower fee of 2.7 percent.

As competition heated up, industry experts wondered how Square, which had yet to hire a substantial sales force, would make its pitch to millions of small and medium-sized businesses. "Small business owners are tough to reach because they're working in their stores all day, every day," said Logan LaHive, the founder of Belly, a digital loyalty card service who took the sales approach of flooding the streets of US cities with sales people.

For small business owners, at least, the slickness of Square's software design proved to be alluring and helped to keep Square's customers from trying out other new products. In Houston, Matt Jeffryes, who started Crescent Moon Coffee with his mother, said salesmen from other card processors had pitched him with better rates after he converted to Square, and he seriously considered switching to PayPal. However, he stuck with Square because he found its software interface to be useful and intuitive, and his customers paid him occasional compliments on the payment method. "If you look purely at the cost factor, they weren't very competitive," Jeffryes said. "But having that whole package was more important than saving a fraction of a cent in a transaction."[21]

Square not only had to keep ahead of the myriad companies entering the market, but also the disruptive technology game changers that were omnipresent yet unknown threats. Many smartphone makers, including Research In Motion Ltd., were moving to include near-field communications (NFC) chips in their devices, which enabled users to pay for items simply by holding their smartphone near a digital reader. Square made clear its wait-and-see stance on NFC. Chief Operating Officer Keith Rabois told Gigaom.com in 2011 that "I've never met a single merchant in the US who says I want this NFC thing," and added that the company would consider NFC later if it turns out to be popular.[22]

WHAT'S NEXT?

Shift from Card Readers to Software

Due to the highly competitive electronic payments business, Square's business focus had shifted subtly, from card readers to nifty software.[23] Square started providing free software and easily generated spreadsheets that tracked customer preferences. Merchants utilized data captured from Square to gain insight into their customers: "I don't have to go to the store to look at the register, I just have to go to the app," Pham said. "It will show me sales of the last hour, 10 hours and month. All that data can be tracked."[24]

Expansion of Customer Base

Square hoped that as more shoppers downloaded its consumer-facing Square Wallet app they would begin using it not only as their main means of paying for goods, but also as a tool for finding nearby businesses and special deals, eventually leading to the elimination of physical credit cards altogether. In the case of the Starbucks partnership, Square was registered as the "agent of record" that processed Starbucks' credit and debit card transactions, but the nuts-and-bolts of fetching and depositing money in every sale were actually handled by its partner, Chase Paymentech. For Square, the Starbucks partnership was really about encouraging new consumers to download its app, which let users order and pay for drinks on their smartphone.

Capturing Big Businesses

Square was a competitive option for food trucks and taxi drivers, but needed to convince large brick-and-mortar businesses and chain stores, too, to survive long term. COO

Rabois said: "Our path is to have every single business in the U.S. use Square . . . It won't happen tomorrow, but it will happen."[25] But going after bigger businesses presented a different set of challenges. Large retailers often negotiated their own credit-card processing fees, and paid much less than 2.75 percent. Plus, they already had sophisticated sales-tracking software and loyalty programs. Furthermore, as previously mentioned, several of these large retailers were teaming up to develop a competing product.

NOTES

1   Kirkpatrick, David. Jack Dorsey tells David Kirkpatrick how it felt to be ousted from Twitter and discusses his big new idea: Square. *Vanity Fair.* March 3, 2011. Downloaded from: www.vanityfair.com/online/daily/2011/03/jack-dorsey. Accessed December 4, 2012.

2   Levy, Steven. Jack Dorsey created Twitter, now he's taking on the banks with Square. Wired.co.uk. July 5, 2012. Downloaded from: www.wired.co.uk/magazine/archive/2012/08/features/jack-dorsey?page=all. Accessed December 15, 2012.

3   The Biography Channel Website. Jack Dorsey – Biography. The Biography Channel Website. www.biography.com/people/jack-dorsey-578280?page=2. Accessed December 4, 2012.

4   Levy, 2012.

5   Savitz, Eric. Jack Dorsey: Leadership secrets of Twitter and Square. www.forbes.com/sites/ericsavitz/2012/10/17/jack-dorsey-the-leadership-secrets-of-twitter-and-square/3. Accessed December 4, 2012.

6   Levy, 2012.

7   Square: Merchant user agreement. https://squareup.com/legal/ua. Accessed December 15, 2012.

8   McGirt, Ellen. The world's 50 most innovative companies. Fast Company. www.fastcompany.com/most-innovative-companies/2012/square. Accessed December 14, 2012.

9   MasterCard. 10-K Annual Report. http://biz.yahoo.com/e/120216/ma10-k.html. 2011.

10 Levy, 2012.

11 Cashill, Margaret. Mobile payment services proliferate, business owners save. *Tampa Bay Business Journal.* American City Business Journals, Inc. November 30, 2012.

12 Bray, Hiawatha. Smartphones become the new credit cards; Tech Lab. *The Boston Globe.* July 26, 2012.

13 Shih, Gerry and Sarah McBride. Jonathan Weber, Editor. Burnished by Starbucks, upstart Square battles payment giants. November 15, 2012. *Reuters News.* www.reuters.com/article/2012/11/13/us-square-payments-idUSBRE8AC06L20121113. Accessed December 13, 2012.

14 Rao, Leena. Focusing on international expansion, Square hires former US trade negotiator Demetrios Marantis to head policy efforts. *Tech Crunch.* http://techcrunch.com/2013/05/08/focusing-on-international-expansion-square-hires-former-us-trade-negotiator-demetrios-marantis-to-head-policy-efforts. Accessed May 8, 2013.

15 Rao, 2013.

16 Shalvey, Kevin. Groupon shares pop 8% as it takes on PayPal, Square. *Investor's Business Daily.* September 19, 2012.

17 Leading retailers form merchant customer exchange to deliver mobile wallet. August 15, 2012. www.businesswire.com/news/home/20120815005172/en/Leading-Retailers-Form-Merchant-Customer-Exchange-Deliver. Accessed December 13, 2012.

18 MCX Website. www.mcx.com. Accessed July 8, 2013.

19 Sidel, Robin. Payments network takes on Google. *The Wall Street Journal.* Pages C1, C2. August 15, 2012. http://online.wsj.com/article_email/SB10000872396390444042704577589523094336872-lMyQjAxMTAyMDEwNTAxODU3Wj.html. Accessed December 13, 2012.

20 Dembosky, April. BofA takes on the mobile payments start-ups. *Financial Times.* November 13, 2012. www.ft.com/cms/s/0/c11c81ec-2af0-11e2-a048-00144feabdc0.html#axzz2Ex8vCkS1. Accessed December 13, 2012.

21 Shih, 2012.

22 Ho, Victoria. Local mobile payments firm goes up against the big boys. *Business Times Singapore.* November 5, 2012. www.btinvest.com.sg/personal_finance/credit-card/local-mobile-payments-firm-goes-against-big-boys-20121105. Accessed December 13, 2012.

23 Shih, *et al.*, 2012.

24 Cashill, 2012.

25 Shih, 2012.

Case 2

VITAMINWATER: IS ITS FUTURE AS HEALTHY AS ITS PAST?*

Patrick Samkarrich[1], a new Coca-Cola brand manager just assigned to the VitaminWater product line, stared at the bright-colored, fully stocked bottled beverage display at his local upscale supermarket. He slowly scanned over the different products: "Activate," "Ooba," "Sparkling Ice," and others—the brand names all familiar, but still mysterious-sounding, to him. Despite it being a Sunday afternoon, Patrick's mind quickly turned from food shopping to his job. He reached for his phone and reopened the emails that he had first read earlier. Sure enough, this week would be his first chance to discuss the functional beverage competitive landscape with the senior manager of the entire Glaceau brand. Patrick asked himself, "Why has VitaminWater been so successful?" He then followed up the question with another question: "Can any of these new functional beverages replicate the success of VitaminWater?"

EARLY HISTORY OF ENERGY BRANDS

In 1996, J. Darius Bikoff felt a cold coming on so he reached for a few vitamin C pills and washed them down with mineral water. As he did, he asked himself why water and vitamins were not combined so that consumers could get the best of both—the health benefits of water versus alternative options and the added boost of nutrient-rich vitamins.[2] Within a few months, Bikoff ran with his idea and formed Energy Brands, focusing on making nutrient-based drinks without the excess sugar and artificial ingredients that dominated the water-alternative market.

Energy Brands' first drink was Glacéau Smartwater (all Energy Brands' products carried the name Glacéau rather than Energy Brands). Energy Brands marketed Smartwater as bottled vapor distilled water—meaning that it replicated the natural precipitation process of water originating from clouds. As opposed to most bottled waters

---

* Steve Harutunian, Patrick Hopkins, Apoorva Kelkar, Matthew Richter, and Jeffrey Samotny wrote this case under the supervision of Professor Allan Afuah as a basis for class discussion and is not intended to illustrate either effective or ineffective handling of a business situation.

that promoted natural spring or lake sources, Glaceau promoted that Smartwater mimicked the earth's natural process but in a cleaner, more scientifically advanced way and also included electrolytes.[3]

Bikoff launched Smartwater by personally promoting and selling it to independent, natural food stores throughout New York. After some early success with Smartwater, Bikoff developed a product called Fruitwater in 1998. Like Smartwater, Fruitwater boasted distilled water but also added flavorful fruit tastes. Fruitwater served as the precursor to Bikoff's next product—the product would cement Energy Brands as a growing player in the beverage industry: VitaminWater.[4]

After two years of success with Fruitwater, Bikoff developed VitaminWater in 2000. Building on the success of vapor distilled water and then fruit-flavored enhanced water, Bikoff next added a boost of vitamins to the mix. The idea was simple: continue to add new enhancements to a familiar product, so long as all the enhancements only added nutritional benefit and did not take away from the taste.

UNITED STATES NON-ALCOHOLIC BEVERAGE INDUSTRY

The $48.3 billion (2012 estimated revenue) United States non-alcoholic beverage industry consisted of juices, carbonated soft drinks (CSDs), and bottled water. Juices carried 57 percent ($27.3 billion)[5] of this market, while CSDs carried 34 percent (16.2 billion)[6] and bottled water carried 10 percent ($4.8 billion). However, these market shares had changed significantly over recent years, as the non-alcoholic beverage industry had been impacted significantly by macroeconomic factors and changes in consumer preferences. Specifically, throughout the early and mid-2000s, increasingly health-conscious consumers had shifted their preferences from sugary juices and CSDs to bottled water. By 2007, bottled water comprised approximately 31 percent of non-alcohol beverage consumption by volume. However, in 2008, during the global recession, consumers significantly decreased their bottled-water consumption, as water by nature was a beverage that they could obtain at virtually no cost from their homes.

Overall, the non-alcoholic beverage industry was dominated by three large players: PepsiCo, Coca-Cola, and Nestlé. Each company achieved substantial economies of scale and scope given their ample manufacturing, distribution, and marketing capabilities, along with post-acquisition integration experience. Competition among brands was fierce, and anticipating rapidly shifting customer demand preferences is critical to the success of products. These companies acquired niche players frequently, given their significant financial resources, and thus significant new players rarely emerged.

Early Demands for Healthy Beverages
Sports Drinks
During the early1990s, US consumers began to realize the health and athletic performance benefits of hydration. This new demand for hydration was addressed by Gatorade, a product invented in 1965 at the University of Florida (UF) for the UF football team, and that had been sold by Quaker Oats in a limited manner to other sports teams since then.[7] Quaker Oats's 1991 $13 million *Like Mike* Gatorade marketing campaign, featuring the iconic Michael Jordan,[8] made the electrolyte-loaded product the world's preeminent response to consumers' desires for hydration.

At the same time, Coca-Cola was bringing its sports drink, Powerade, to the market. Initially rolled out through fountain drinks, consumer demand drove Coca-Cola to make Powerade available through numerous mediums including supermarkets, general merchandisers, food services, and vending machines in 1992.[9] Throughout the rest of the 1990s, Gatorade continued to use top athletes, including Peyton Manning and Derek Jeter to market itself. Coca-Cola, meanwhile, utilized non-traditional marketing, including using lesser known athletes and promoting it as a drink for more than just consumption during athletic play, to try to differentiate Powerade from Gatorade.

In 2001, with Gatorade controlling nearly 70 percent of the global sports drink market, PepsiCo acquired Quaker Oats for $13.4 billion in stock.[10] PepsiCo's robust marketing and distribution channels facilitated further growth of Gatorade's brand worldwide.

Bottled Water

Given consumers' increasing desire for hydration beverages, the 1990s and early 2000s saw a significant rise in the popularity of bottled water. During the 1990s, bottled-water consumption in the US tripled. Nestlé was clearly the US market leader, having brought its products sold in the more mature Europe bottled-water market to America. In 1994 and 1999 PepsiCo and Coca-Cola, respectively, entered the market.[11]

A NEW TYPE OF BEVERAGE

In 2000, Bikoff developed VitaminWater and introduced it to the market as an alternative to the sugary alternatives of CSDs and sodium-containing options of sports drinks. Around the same time, a somewhat comparable product—Propel Fitness Water—was launched by Pepsi. However, Propel Fitness Water tasted like water with a slight hint of fruit flavor while VitaminWater tasted like a strong sports or fruit drink. Additionally, Propel Fitness Water was clear (like water), while VitaminWater was brightly colored like a fruit drink. The products differed in terms of vitamin content as well.

A single 8-ounce serving of VitaminWater usually included 100 percent of the daily recommended dosage of vitamin C and 40 percent of generally four types of vitamin B. (Vitamin C is a natural antihistamine found in many fruits and vegetables and was believed by some to reduce the duration of the common cold. B vitamins are usually found in unprocessed foods and play a role in cell metabolism.) Some VitaminWater flavors also included vitamin A, vitamin E, calcium, and other vitamins. Propel Fitness Water only included about 25 percent of the daily recommended dosage of three types of vitamin B, and only 10 percent of the daily recommended dosage of vitamin C. Finally, Propel Fitness Water contained sodium, whereas VitaminWater was sodium-free.[12,13]

New Marketing Methods

VitaminWater's added vitamins, as well as its low sugar content (compared to CSDs) and lack of sodium enabled the product initially to be placed onto a limited number of store shelves. However, Glacéau's marketing of VitaminWater cemented the product as a game-changer in the beverage industry.

In 2001, Rohan Oza (Ross MBA '97) left his marketing position at Coca-Cola and joined the quickly growing Energy Brands. Energy Brands did not have the billion-dollar budgets of the big beverage companies, but it had cache and appeal to a young audience and those who already felt in-the-know about the various Glacéau offerings. Building on this, Oza developed a hyper-local, highly visible marketing strategy that placed ten VitaminWater wrapped vehicles in major cities with VitaminWater "hydrologists" sharing free VitaminWater and the high energy of the brand.[14] While Oza was building the brand from the bottom-up and using "hydrologists" to acquire customers one beverage at a time, he knew that he also needed a wider reaching, larger statement to give VitaminWater mass appeal. Propel Fitness Water was beginning to catch on with consumers on a mass level (the product had sales of over $250 million in 2004[15]), and Glacéau recognized that VitaminWater could achieve similar—or better—success if it was marketed appropriately.

50 Cent

While watching television, Oza saw a Reebok sneaker commercial in which rap artist 50 Cent (birth name Curtis Jackson) was drinking a VitaminWater—even though VitaminWater had not been informed and had not paid to be part of the advertisement.[16] At the time, in 2004, 50 Cent was one of the most popular rappers, producing chart-topping songs, selling millions of albums and alluring fans who were fascinated by his tough-upbringing backstory: 50 Cent had survived being shot nine times earlier in his life. However, in addition to being tough and on top of the rap scene, 50 Cent was incredibly health-conscious and a great athlete who worked out multiple hours a day. Oza viewed him—the new guy who was making headlines and moving fast, but also knew the importance of health, fitness, hydration, and vitamins—as the perfect association with VitaminWater.

Energy Brands and 50 Cent hammered out a deal that gave the rapper a certain amount of equity in the company. Though the equity amount was never disclosed, it was widely rumored to be nearly 10 percent of the company.[17]

After setting the ownership stakes, Glacéau and 50 Cent turned to choosing the flavor for a developed but not yet marketed VitaminWater beverage very coincidentally named "Formula50" because it contained at least 50 percent of the recommended daily allowance of seven vitamins. The result was VitaminWater's first grape-flavored drink. The idea behind the grape flavor was that while new fruity flavors such as strawberry and kiwi were gaining popularity in other beverage categories, those flavors were not popular with the crowd 50 Cent knew most about—the young, aspirational black market purchasing at neighborhood convenience stores.[18]

Soon, Glacéau launched a nationwide marketing campaign featuring 50 Cent. Although beverage brands had used musical artists in their advertisements, never before had a beverage brand so closely associated an artist with a beverage. By 2005, VitaminWater found itself established in the beverage industry.

In the late 2000s, Glacéau expanded its strategy of closely associating celebrities with VitaminWater. National Football League player Brian Urlacher and National Basketball Association superstar LeBron James became endorsers of the product, helping advance VitaminWater's status as a beverage for the physically fit. American idols Kelly Clarkson and Carrie Underwood lent their star-power to VitaminWater (specifically the "Focus" and "Energy" flavors), helping associate the product with attractive, lively people. Comedian and talk-show host Ellen DeGeneres became an advocate of the drink, furthering its status as a beverage for fun, modern people. DeGeneres was the face of Vitamin Water Zero—VitaminWater's brand extension that featured a zero-calorie beverage.[19]

Product Labeling and Coloring

Glacéau also applied innovative marketing techniques in regards to the appearance of the VitaminWater product. The assortment of VitaminWater offerings spanned the color spectrum. This variety of colors, when contrasted with the bottles' white labeling, made for an eye-catching display in stores. Furthermore, each flavor had a unique purpose: focus, energy, defense, power, etc., and each flavor had a cleverly written story on its bottle that spoke directly to the drinker in a unique, generation Y-type tone. For example, in 2013, the Revive fruit punch-flavored drink read:

> If you woke up tired, you probably need more sleep. If you woke up drooling at your desk, you probably need a new job. If you woke up with a headache, on a ferris wheel, wearing a toga, you probably need answers. Not to mention this product. It's got B and C vitamins to help you recover and feel refreshed—kinda like in those old Norsca© soap commercials. And if you're like our boss, Mike, and woke up married to an Elvis impersonator, you probably need a lawyer.

NEW ENTRANTS TO THE MARKET

As VitaminWater boomed during the mid-2000s, the enhanced water product category also grew as a whole (Exhibit 2.1). VitaminWater was the clear driver of such growth, as the large beverage companies attempted to launch competing products but failed. By 2005, PepsiCo had launched Aquafina Essentials and Coca-Cola had launched NutriWater, both of which contained vitamins. However, these products fared poorly and the companies discontinued these products soon after launching them. (Coca-Cola's product did not last even a year.)

In 2006, PepsiCo's SoBe brand launched LifeWater, a group of colored, vitamin-enhanced drinks that was the most similar product to VitaminWater launched as of that time. Pepsi's SoBe name derived from the South Beach area of Miami, an area that boasted a fun culture, lively nightclub scene, and attractive populace, in an attempt to give a playful, live-free association to the brand.[20]

In 2007, PepsiCo again tried launching a vitamin-enhanced water under the Aquafina brand. Again, the product (Aquafina Alive) did not do well and PepsiCo discontinued the product shortly after launching it.

Coca-Cola Acquisition

On May 25, 2007, Coca-Cola announced that it had reached an agreement to acquire Energy Brands for $4.1 billion in cash. At the time, Energy Brands was generating annual revenue of approximately $350 million.[21] The acquisition provided Coca-Cola with a strong platform for marketing active lifestyle beverages. "It's a perfect match connecting the hottest active lifestyle brand with the full resources of the world's best beverage company," claimed Bikoff at the time of the deal.[22] E. Neville Isdell, the then chief executive officer of Coke stated "Glaceau has built a great business with high-quality growth . . . We envision even faster growth for Glaceau as part of Coca-Cola's enhanced range of brands for North American customers and consumers."[23] By acquiring the

Glacéau brands, Coca-Cola expanded its ability to provide beverages to the entire spectrum of beverage consumers—from health-conscious ones to less health-conscious ones. By being acquired by Coca-Cola, Energy Brands became capable of selling its products to international markets and in larger quantities to distributors.[24]

The purchase agreement provided for Glacéau operating as a separate business unit within Coca-Cola North America (CCNA). This structure was intended to allow Glacéau to continue to win in the marketplace by maximizing its focus, speed, sales, and execution capabilities, while leveraging the scale of CCNA's resources in supply chain, marketing, and consumer insights, large customer management and food service. During the acquisition negotiations, Glacéau's top three executives (Bikoff, co-founder Mike Repole, and Mike Venuti) stated their intent to lead the business for a minimum of three years, and for other key managers to remain in the business.[25] CCNA president Sandy Douglas put it more directly: "The number one error we could make is that we think we could drive the business better than the team does today."[26]

MORE MARKETING INNOVATION

After applying his creative marketing techniques for a number of years, Oza turned to VitaminWater consumers to help source a new drink in 2009. Glacéau developed a Facebook application, called "flavorcreator," through which fans could submit designs for their own desired flavors, name the flavors, and write the descriptions (catchy blurbs) associated with the flavors.[27] Glacéau offered $5,000 to the creator of the best submission as judged by VitaminWater management—and 50 Cent and Underwood. For VitaminWater, the tool provided access to exactly what customers wanted in 2009. And for the winning creator, it provided money and a feeling of personal accomplishment.

Effect on Marketing Strategies of Competitors

As VitaminWater rose to popularity, Pepsi adjusted its marketing strategies for Propel and LifeWater to reflect those of Glacéau for VitaminWater.

In 2009, Pepsi made its first major changes to the Propel brand. First, it removed the words "Fitness Water" from the beverage's packaging. This change signaled the brand's attempt to distance itself from Gatorade products and the product's association with athletics. In 2011, Pepsi discontinued its production of Propel altogether and began to produce and market only Propel Zero, a version of the product made without sucrose and artificial sweeteners.[28] Additionally, seemingly in a page taken out of Glacéau's book, Pepsi signed legendary supermodel Cindy Crawford as a spokeswoman for Propel Zero. These moves signified that Pepsi was attempting to tie Propel Zero to the masses, just as VitaminWater had done. Esperanza Teasdale, director of marketing for Propel stated:

> We were the original enhanced water, positioned toward a competitive athlete in an intense sport. However, as the category evolved, so did our consumers. They're using us way more than just in the gym. We're trying to show consumers that we hear them.[29]

Pepsi's efforts had a marginal positive effect on Propel Zero's sales; they helped increase the product up to a $300 million product by 2011 (Exhibit 2.2).[30]

Pepsi upped its marketing game for SoBe Lifewater as well. First, it overhauled the LifeWater bottle. The new LifeWater packaging, a rigid, curved shaped bottle with an artistically designed lizard (the brand's mascot) wrapped around it, appeared more associated with the fun "SoBe" lifestyle. Then, in 2008, Pepsi advertised the product during the National Football League Super Bowl, arguably the largest televised advertising event each year. Shortly after, the company signed supermodel Naomi Campbell for a series of commercials for the product.[31] These marketing moves helped LifeWater generate an estimated $250 million of sales in 2011.[32]

By the turn of the decade, small companies had entered the marketplace with products very similar to VitaminWater. Color and creative packaging drove the marketing for these products, just as such factors had played a role in VitaminWater marketing. Furthermore, the companies promoted a better taste of the products (than Vitamin-Water), and in some cases, lower sugar content. In 2012, Talking Rain Beverage Company's Sparkling Ice emerged as the leader of these smaller brands, garnering sales of nearly $200 million.

Challenges in 2013

In 2012, VitaminWater generated revenues of approximately $900 million and was the enhanced beverage market leader.[33] Leveraging Coca-Cola's existing distribution system had been a main driver in the brand's growth. However, VitaminWater's future faced significant challenges to its success.

Health Benefit or Detractor?

In 2009, the Center for Science in the Public Interest (CSPI) filed a class-action lawsuit against Coca-Cola in the Northern District of California Court. The suit claimed that the marketing of the drink as a healthy-choice alternative to carbonated beverages was deceiving and in violation of Food and Drug Administration guidelines. The consumer group stated that "according to CSPI nutritionists, the 33 grams of sugar in each bottle of VitaminWater do more to promote obesity, diabetes and other health problems than the vitamins in the drinks do to perform the advertised benefits listed on the bottles."[34] Coca-Cola dismissed the suit as "ridiculous," on the basis that it had included all legally required nutrition on the bottle and that consumers should not assume that VitaminWater is a healthy beverage. However, some opponents considered the product name "VitaminWater" still to be misleading, considering that the public associates the word "vitamin" with health. Four years later, in 2013, the situation continued to be a point of contention in the beverage market.

Exhibit 2.1 US liquid refreshment beverage market

Segments	% Change 2007/2008	% Change 2011/2012
Energy drinks	9.0	14.3
Ready-to-drink coffee	1.6	9.5
Bottled water	−1.0	5.8
Ready-to-drink teas	−1.8	4.9
Sports drinks	−3.1	2.3
Value-added water	8.3	−1.5
Carbonated soft drinks	−3.1	−1.8
Fruit beverages	−2.0	−4.1
Total	**0.9**	**1.0**

Source: Beverage Marketing Corporation (news release, March 30, 2009 and March 25, 2013)

Glacéau Brand Image

Might Glacéau's maintenance of a hip image throughout the 2010s have been their most difficult challenge? The brand had initially boasted the advantage of coming into the market with a new product concept. In addition, it had used innovative marketing to get such a new product out into the hands of the masses. But perhaps the enhanced water concept was becoming less of an exciting one as many companies had begun producing the products. Or perhaps the Glacéau brand was to become "uncool" as new brands had emerged. Overall, was VitaminWater going to be soon in need of a bottle of its own Revive?

Exhibit 2.2 Liquid refreshment beverage market share by volume, 2007

	2007 Gallons (M)	Mkt share %
Carbonated soft drinks	14,688	48
Bottled water	8,757	29
Fruit beverages	4,009	13
Sports drinks	1,361	4
Ready-to-drink tea	875	3
Value-added water	506	2
Energy drinks	335	1
Ready-to-drink coffee	47	0

Source: Beverage Marketing Corporation (March 2008)

NOTES

1   Fictional character.
2   Davidson, Andrew. Coke's water man J. Darius Bikoff gushes forth. *Times Online.* 28 May, 2008.
3   Smartwater. Glacéau website. Drinkbetterwater.com. Retrieved December 4, 2012.
4   Dillon, Nancy. High-energy formula for successful biz. *Daily News.* April 23, 2001.
5   IBISWorld Industry Report 31211c Juice Production in the US.
6   IBISWorld Industry Report 31211a Soda Production in the US.
7   www.gatorade.com/history
8   http://authorviews.com/authors/rovell/rovell-obd.htm
9   www.nhra.net/2001/news/December/120302.html
10   http://archives.cnn.com/2000/fyi/news/12/04/pepsi.purchase/index.html
11   Gimeno, Javier. The evolution of the bottled water industry. INSEAD. 2012.
12   http://productnutrition.thecoca-colacompany.com/products/
13   Williams, Yona. Powerade option versus Gatorade Propel. Yahoo! Voices. August 29, 2006.
14   Charnas, Dan. How 50 Cent scored a half-billion. *Washington Post.* December 19, 2010.
15   Moskin, Julia. Must be something in the water. *New York Times.* February 15, 2006.
16   Ibid.
17   Ibid.
18   Ibid.
19   Celebrities for bottled water. *The Filtered Files.* Filtersfast.com, June 4, 2010.
20   Lifewater. SoBe website. Retrieved December 6, 2012.
21   Sorkin, Andrew Ross and Martin, Andrew. Coca-Cola agrees to buy VitaminWater. *New York Times.* May 26, 2007.
22   O'Brian, Chris. Coca-Cola to spend a healthy $4.1 billion on VitaminWater. *NewHope 360.* April 24, 2008.
23   Sorkin, Andrew Ross and Martin, Andrew. Coca-Cola agrees to buy VitaminWater. *New York Times.* May 26, 2007.
24   Berk, Christina Cheddar. Coca-Cola to buy VitaminWater maker Glaceau for $4.1 Billion. www.cnbc.com. May 25, 2007.

25 Coca-Cola buys VitaminWater. *QSR*. May 26, 2007.

26 Company Filings, 10k for the fiscal year ended December 30, 2007.

27 Eldon, Eric. VitaminWater to crowdsource new flavor through Facebook app. *Inside Facebook*. September 8, 2009.

28 Gatorade brands. PepsiCo website. Retrieved December 6, 2012.

29 Zmuda, Natalie. Propel cuts the calories, boosts spending for ad push. *AdvertisingAge*. March 17, 2011.

30 Cuneo, Alice. PepsiCo moves Propel Water brand to Goodby. *AdAge* Agency News, February 11, 2008.

31 Zmuda, Natalie. PepsiCo's SoBe Life Water: A marketing 50 case study. *AdvertisingAge*. November 17, 2008.

32 Stanford, Duane. How PepsiCo refreshed its Sobe water brand. *Bloomberg Businessweek*. June 24, 2010.

33 2012 state of the industry: Bottled water. *Beverage Industry*. July 18, 2012.

34 Gregory, Sean. Is VitaminWater really a healthy drink? *Time*. July 30, 2010.

Case 3

NETFLIX:
CHANGING THE RULES OF THE GAME*

In June 2013, Reed Hastings reflected on Netflix's last decade as he drove through Los Gatos, CA on his way to the company's headquarters. Ten years earlier, Netflix was trying to steal market share in the DVD rental market from a $6 billion publicly traded company with stores visited by movie watchers across America. Now, with that competitor a mere fraction of its former self and Internet streaming the method of choice for millions of movie and TV watchers, Netflix was sitting at a very large table of movie and TV streaming competition, one that included companies from across the entertainment and electronics industries and some of the largest firms in the world. Reed had seen his company's stock price skyrocket, plummet, and skyrocket again over the past three and a half years. He wanted Netflix to have more stable success in the coming years. With the entertainment industry continuing to change around him, he had several ideas for strategic moves, but which of these would be most likely to hold off the competition and continue the success of the company that he founded?

MOVIE RENTAL BEFORE NETFLIX

In 1977, the first brick-and-mortar video rental store opened in a 600-square foot storefront on Wilshire Boulevard in Los Angeles.[1] At that time, only 50 video titles from 20th Century Fox were available on Betamax and VHS for consumers to rent. However, business was strong enough for the business owner, George Atkinson, to add 42 affiliated stores within 20 months. The business was renamed *The Video Station*, and Atkinson announced he would start franchising the stores. The Video Station paved the way for thousands of other video rental stores, including Blockbuster Video, which opened its first store in Dallas, Texas in 1985. Within three years, Blockbuster Video captured the

* This case was written by Christian Chock, Tania Ganguly, Chad Greeno, Steven Harutunian, Julie Knakal, and Tony Knakal under the supervision of Professor Afuah as a basis for class discussion and is not intended to illustrate either effective or ineffective handling of a business situation.

top video retailer spot in the United States with more than 500 stores and revenues exceeding $200 million.[2]

Video rental stores quickly discovered that rental revenues roughly followed Pareto's rule where 80 percent of the revenues were driven from 20 percent of the video titles. Therefore, for the 4,000–5,000 titles in stock at a typical store, most shelf space was dedicated to displaying multiple copies of new release, "hit" movies.[3]

The dynamics of the industry shifted significantly in the spring of 1997 with the introduction of the DVD-video format. The DVD player passed the 10 percent adoption rate milestone by late 2000, making it one of the most rapidly adopted consumer electronics products in history. By 2005, the DVD format would dominate the global recorded video sales and rental market with 91.8 percent market share.[4]

In 1999, while Netflix and movie rental through the Internet and snail mail were still new, Blockbuster held a 24 percent market share in this $18.5 billion industry.[5] Blockbuster continued to lead the industry in market share in 2006 with approximately 35 percent of the market.[6]

NETFLIX'S ENTRY INTO ONLINE DVD RENTALS

The size and weight of the physical DVD facilitated shipping videos directly to customers' homes, and a new branch of the video retailing industry began with the founding of Netflix. Founded in 1997 by Marc Randolph and Reed Hastings, Netflix began offering DVD rentals requested over the Internet and delivered through the mail in 1998. The initial business model charged a fee per rental, as was typical of brick-and-mortar stores at the time. By late 1999, Netflix had changed to a subscription fee that allowed subscribers to rent as many videos as they wanted on a monthly basis.[7] It made various subscription plans available to subscribers that allowed customers to determine how many movies they wanted to have at their home at a time. This allowed Netflix to differentiate customers by how often they watched rented movies. The subscription model eliminated aggravation related to due dates and late fees. Indeed, Reed Hastings cited the unlimited-use-for-one-fee model used by his health club as one of the inspirations for Netflix's subscription model.[8] In February 2003, Netflix surpassed the 1 million subscriber mark landing it firmly at the top of the online DVD rental industry.

Through Netflix's website, subscribers could create a queue of movies that they wanted to rent. These movies could be prioritized to reflect when the subscriber wanted to receive each film. Whenever a subscriber returned a movie via a pre-paid mailer, the next movie in the queue was sent out. Users could create a large rental queue and not be required to visit the website while they viewed movies sent from their queue, or they could update their queue every time a movie was returned.

The Netflix subscription-based service offered several advantages over the brick-and-mortar rental store model that had been prevalent in the industry. By having a few centralized shipping centers, rather than a large number of storefronts, Netflix was able to pool resources and offer a wider range of titles than possible at a single rental store. Operating a few centralized shipping centers also offered several cost advantages over operating stores in every neighborhood. Netflix was aggressive in recruiting new customers. It increased its marketing expenses every year and its number of customers increased every year.

Cinematch Recommendations System

To help customers identify which titles might interest them, Netflix used a recommendation engine called Cinematch. Cinematch used customer movie ratings to predict what other movies customers might be interested in. About 60 percent of movies requested through Netflix were identified through this recommendation system.[9] The combination of a large movie selection and a recommendation system to help customers find movies they might like appeared to increase the number of movie titles that customers rent. In June 2006, Netflix had an inventory of 60,000 titles and on any given day 35,000–40,000 of these titles were rented by at least one Netflix customer.[10]

Netflix even released some independent films that were not popular enough for a traditional distribution contract through its Red Envelope Entertainment division. When video stores only stocked 4,000–5,000 titles, these movies would not have been popular enough to justify the required shelf space. With Netflix distribution centers that served a larger number of customers and a recommendation system to help those customers find titles that might interest them, a market for these movies was created.[11]

Netflix also rolled out a Netflix *Friends* feature that let users see what their friends were renting and how they rated different movies. This feature enabled users to create communities of movie watchers through the Netflix webpage. The friends feature utilized past user ratings of users on Netflix, taking advantage of its longer history in the online rental business.

DVD Subscription Plans

In 2007, Netflix offered a range of subscription choices, each allowing the customer a different number of movies that could be simultaneously rented. These ranged from a basic plan allowing up to two rentals per month, rented one at a time, to a plan allowing four rentals out at one time with unlimited total monthly rentals. Each plan also included a varying amount of instant viewing hours that could be used to have movies streamed directly to the customer's computer.

COMPETITION WITH NETFLIX'S ONLINE DVD RENTAL BUSINESS

Wal-Mart

The world's largest retailer, Wal-Mart, entered the online DVD rental market in 2002, with a catalog of over 12,000 titles from which customers could choose. The system was essentially the same as that offered by Netflix, with customers creating a list of titles they wanted to see, and then ordering them online, with shipping by mail. Its subscription rates undercut Netflix by about $1, with a three movies rented at any one time DVD package costing $18.86.[12] Executives at Netflix predicted that Wal-Mart could only guarantee overnight delivery within a limited radius of its Georgia distribution center, and would have to settle for a three- to five-day delivery for the rest of the country.[13] In June 2004, Wal-Mart opened three new distribution centers to support the online DVD rental business. Additionally, it expanded its rental catalog to 15,000 titles (at the time, Netflix offered about 22,000 titles for rent. By mid-2005, however, Wal-Mart had given up on the online DVD rental business. In leaving, Wal-Mart directed its customers to Netflix, and established a deal whereby former Wal-Mart customers could get a discounted two DVD rental plan if they signed up for a one year Netflix subscription (regularly priced at $14.99, and discounted to $12.97).[14] The reason for Wal-Mart's exit was thought to be a lack of sufficient subscriber sign-up, an important figure in the online rental business.

BLOCKBUSTER

Blockbuster Online

On August 11, 2004, Blockbuster announced its entry into the US online movie rental business with the creation of Blockbuster Online, a move they had been discussing since that spring.[15] Like Netflix and Wal-Mart, it had a tiered monthly fee system based on the number of movies the consumer wanted to have at a time. Initial pricing was positioned between Netflix and their low price rival, Wal-Mart. Blockbuster subscribers chose from a catalog of 25,000 titles, compared with 30,000 titles available from Netflix at that time. Part of Blockbuster's strategy was for the online service to encourage foot traffic in its physical stores, with two coupons for free rentals at the stores being sent to each online customer once a month.

Relying on its strong brand recognition among consumers and physical presence with over 5,600 company-owned and franchised brick-and-mortar stores at the time of the launch, Blockbuster hoped to reach many of the over 4 million estimated online renters that made up the market at the time of the launch.[16] The market for online rentals was estimated at $8 million at the time, and Blockbuster saw it as a growing area within the overall rental business. While only 8 percent of industry revenue came from online rentals in 2005, growth was strong, increasing from 5 percent in 2003, according to Adams Media Research.[17]

To accommodate the new online service, Blockbuster established a new distribution system, separate from its existing network that handled its brick-and-mortar stores. To handle the mailing of DVDs, Blockbuster had to establish a set of distribution centers, similar to Netflix's, from which it could mail the rented DVDs. The separate distribution was also put in place to accommodate the different rental preferences of online subscribers as compared to in-store patrons.[18]

The launch of Blockbuster Online was at an estimated initial cost of $50 million, with additional losses in operating revenues for several quarters after launch. These figures, combined with the loss of revenue from late fees (usually a good source of income for Blockbuster that previously made up 13 percent of revenue), contributed to a difficult financial situation. Subscriber growth was thought to be a key statistic, and subscriber acquisition was expensive. By the fourth quarter of 2005, Blockbuster Online had about 1 million subscribers, versus 4 million subscribers for Netflix. This was after a 39 percent increase in advertising for the first three quarters of 2005.[19]

In 2005, Blockbuster's stock had dropped 50 percent from its 52-week high. To stem the bleeding, it announced a cost-cutting program that included advertising reductions. These cuts were to take effect from the second quarter of 2005 through the second quarter of 2006. After the poor subscriber acquisition results, Blockbuster announced that it would increase advertising for its online service, despite the cost-cutting initiative.[20]

By 2005, price wars between the major online renters had broken out. Blockbuster dropped its three-out DVD rental monthly subscription by $3 to undercut Netflix. Also, it rolled out a trial program in Seattle where online customers had the option of returning DVDs to their local Blockbuster store,[21] foreshadowing the 2006 launch of Blockbuster Total Access.

Blockbuster Total Access

In November 2006, Blockbuster launched an updated version of Blockbuster Online, called Blockbuster Total Access. In addition to offering movie rentals requested over the Internet and delivered through the mail, as Netflix and the original Blockbuster Online had, Total Access sought to utilize Blockbuster's stores to offer additional benefits. Blockbuster Total Access' customers could return their movies rented through the mail through the mail service and have their next title shipped to them. Alternatively, customers could return movies to any Blockbuster location. When returning an online rental at a store, customers received a free in-store rental in addition to having their next online rental shipped.[22] Blockbuster promoted this advantage and the instant gratification it provided using slogans such as "Never be without a movie." Blockbuster Total Access subscriptions also gave customers a coupon for one free in-store rental each month. The coupon could be used for a movie or video game rental.[23]

On June 12, 2007 Blockbuster added Blockbuster by Mail as an option for its online service. Customers choosing this option would be permitted to return movies to Blockbuster stores, but they would not receive a free rental in exchange. The return of their movie to the store would electronically stimulate the next movie in their queue to be sent from the Blockbuster distribution center. These users also would not receive a free rental coupon each month. In return for giving up these privileges, subscription fees were $1 less per month than the full Blockbuster Total Access plan. The addition of Blockbuster by Mail provided a more direct comparison with Netflix subscription plans and drew attention to the added benefit of in-store rentals. Blockbuster promoted its plan as a way to save money for customers who did not live near a Blockbuster location.[24]

Other Competitors

Many other smaller competitors sprang up once the DVD format had taken hold. Some were forced to exit the market but a few remained, existing on the fringe, trailing far behind giants Netflix and Blockbuster. These included Intelliflix, DVD Overnight, DVD Barn, Rent My DVD, DVD Whiz, and Qwikfliks.

DOWNLOADABLE VIDEO

In September 2006, Apple (through its iTunes store) and Amazon (through its Unbox store) began allowing users to use the Internet to download TV shows and movies for a set price per video (generally $8–16 per movie) and then watch them on their computers as many times as they liked without an Internet connection. In other words, the companies allowed users to purchase the videos, and thus this new technology did not directly affect the DVD rental industry. However, Amazon's Unbox store also gave users the option of renting the videos for $1.99–$2.99 per movie by making the videos viewable for only a certain period of time after purchase. This option, though not yet overwhelmingly popular with consumers, marked a challenge to Netflix's DVD rental business.[25]

"Watch Now" Streaming Feature

In 2007, Netflix began offering subscribers the option to stream TV shows and movies over the Internet. Although streaming required a fast Internet connection, the rise of broadband and DSL connections made it possible for some subscribers to take advantage of this feature. Hastings spoke of the streaming service launch, "While mainstream consumer adoption of online movie watching will take a number of years due to content and technology hurdles, the time is right for Netflix to take the first step. Over the coming years we'll expand our selection of films, and we'll work to get to every Internet-connected screen, from cell phones to PCs to plasma screens."[26]

Netflix had to enter agreements with media companies in order to stream their content. Streaming movies was essentially similar to renting DVDs of movies in that viewers selected a full-length commercial-free movie, often also available in the same form on DVD, and watched it. As a result, Netflix's streaming negotiations with the movie studios were similar in many respects to those between the companies for DVD rentals. However, streaming TV shows presented a new situation in that viewers selected a single commercial-free episode—not available on DVD except perhaps in a "full season" DVD—and watched it. Therefore, Netflix's streaming negotiations with the television studios were rather complex.

DVD + Streaming Plans

Netflix's first streaming plans, launched in early 2007, allotted subscribers a certain number of streaming hours (between 5 and 24 hours) in addition to their DVD rentals. In August 2007, Netflix decreased the prices of three of the plans by $1. January 2008 brought the first indications of competition in the video on-demand space. Apple began offering movie rentals[27] (in a way similar to that of Amazon) and released a software upgrade to its Apple TV device which gave users the ability to purchase or rent and watch movies directly from the TV, as opposed to from a computer.[28] Likely in response to this move, Netflix changed its limited streaming and DVD rental plans to unlimited streaming and DVD rental plans.

Project Griffin and Roku

Unknown to the public at the time, Netflix had been working on "Project Griffin." Project Griffin was a set-top box that would allow users to stream Netflix movies directly to their TV sets. This was a significant research and development effort because TV sets generally had much larger screens, sharper sound, and better resolution than computer screens and thus allowed for better viewing experiences. By December 2007, Netflix had nearly completed Project Griffin. However, instead of having Netflix launch the product and thus directly entering competition with Apple, Hastings decided to spin the device and its developers into a stand-alone hardware company, Roku, and have Roku launch the device.[29] In June 2008, Roku launched the device.[30] The public did not know of Netflix's role in the Roku device product development until the next year.[31]

EARLY COMPETITION WITH WATCH NOW

Soon after Netflix launched its unlimited streaming plus DVD rental plans, other companies began to enter the streaming space.

Hulu

In 2007, NBC Universal and News Corp, two of the four largest media companies at the time, joined efforts to create a company that would provide streaming of TV shows and movies. After much discussion about the name of the company, they decided on Hulu. In late 2007, Hulu released a beta version of its website.[32] In March 2008, Hulu launched its website to the public. Hulu offered free streaming of a limited number of recent episodes of NBC and Fox TV shows.[33] (News Corp owned Fox.) In April 2009, Disney, owner of ABC, another of the four largest media companies, invested in and began contributing content to Hulu.

Pay TV providers

Around the same time, the major cable, satellite TV, and telephone companies developed "on-demand" services of their own and rolled them out with traditional cable TV packages. Comcast, the largest pay TV provider in the United States, led the charge in this movement, but all companies eventually added the services. Initially, the companies charged a fee for the on-demand capabilities, as well as a set price per show or movie. However, as the services gained popularity, the companies began to offer many shows and movies at no cost.

Apple

In January 2008 (in connection with the Apple TV software upgrade), Apple began allowing users to rent TV shows and movies by downloading videos that could only be watched for a certain time period. At this point, Apple became a direct competitor of Netflix.

NETFLIX PRIZE

In 2009, Netflix awarded a $1 million prize to a team for devising the best way to improve the company's movie recommendation engine by 10 percent. Netflix considered movie recommendation feature a key to its success, and stated that "winning a 10 percent improvement on its recommendation algorithm for $1 million would be a tremendous bargain."[34] Netflix had announced the contest in 2006 and received 50,000 submissions by the 2009 deadline. Interestingly enough, the winning team, "BellKor's Pragmatic Chaos", earned the exact same score as another team "The Ensemble", but submitted its solution 10 minutes earlier, and thus Netflix declared it the winner. Furthermore, both teams were "superteams" that had formed by combining two teams that had posted high scores at the time of a mid-contest progress checkpoint. Some final perhaps interesting facts: the seven-person BellKor Pragmatic Chaos team included people from four countries, boasted some AT&T research engineers, and had never met in person before meeting to accept the prize.[35]

DEATH OF BLOCKBUSTER

In 2008, after two years of razor-thin operating margins, Blockbuster posted negative operating profit. Despite this performance, when asked if the company's struggles were due to Netflix, Blockbuster CEO Jim Keyes stated "I've been frankly confused by this fascination that everybody has with Netflix . . . Netflix doesn't really have or do anything that we can't or don't already do ourselves." In 2009, Blockbuster's losses increased, despite its introduction of Blockbuster Express, a kiosk system launched to compete with Redbox, an emerging kiosk-based DVD rental company. In March 2010, Blockbuster began promoting that it released movies 28 days faster than did Netflix, while also reintroducing late fees, which it expected to be worth $300 million of annual revenue.[36]

That month, in its 2009 annual report, Blockbuster stated that the company could be forced into bankruptcy because of its lack of cash relative to its $1 billion debt load. In order to save cash, the company began closing stores by the hundreds and discontinuing its international operations.[37] By July, Blockbuster's market capitalization had remained less than $75 million for 30 consecutive days, and as a result, the New York Stock Exchange delisted the company. However, when asked about Blockbuster's future, the company's head of digital strategy stated "we're strategically positioned better than almost anybody out there."[38]

On September 23, 2010, Blockbuster filed for bankruptcy. Although it had closed nearly 1,000 stores since 2008, the company still had 3,000 stores in operation. On April 5, 2011, Dish Network acquired Blockbuster for $320 million.

RISE OF REDBOX

Redbox started as a concept developed by McDonald's, which began putting DVD rental kiosks in some of its restaurants in the early 2000s. In 2005, Redbox became a stand-alone company, and Coinstar, an operator of financial-related kiosks, invested in the company. Over the next few years, Redbox dramatically increased its presence, rolling out kiosks to grocery, convenience, and wholesale stores. In 2009, Coinstar acquired the remaining stake of Redbox, which had by then achieved a 17 percent stake in the DVD rental market. In 2010, Redbox rented its billionth DVD, achieved $1 billion in rental revenues, and increased its share of the DVD rental market to 30 percent. As a result of its performance, *Advertising Age* named it one of America's hottest brands.[39]

COLLABORATION WITH ELECTRONICS COMPANIES

During the two and a half years following Roku's product launch in early 2008, many of the large electronics companies launched products that allowed for streaming Netflix shows onto TV sets. Microsoft, Sony, and Nintendo made it possible to view Netflix shows on their gaming devices in 2008, 2009, and 2010, respectively. In 2010, Apple entered the mix. First, Apple released the iPad tablet. The iPad allowed streaming of Netflix shows through a downloadable application.[40] Then, Apple released the second-generation Apple TV. Perhaps surprisingly, this device also allowed streaming of Netflix TV shows in addition to viewing of TV shows and movies rented from the Apple library.[41] Therefore, although Apple was competing with Netflix in one respect, it was collaborating with the company in another. In late 2010, Amazon, one of the world's largest online retailers, launched a tablet of its own, the Kindle Fire. This device too allowed for Netflix streaming.

MORE COMPETITION FOR NETFLIX'S STREAMING BUSINESS

Throughout 2010, the video on-demand market began to significantly heat up. In November 2010, Netflix released its first streaming only plan (at a price of $7.99 per month) and increased the prices of its streaming plus DVD rental plans[42], thus taking a major step in moving away from its DVD rental business. Around the same time, two new competitive forces entered the market.

Hulu Plus

In June 2010, Hulu launched Hulu Plus, a premium portion of its Hulu website that users could access for a fee of $9.99 per month. Hulu Plus offered "season tickets" to every episode of every TV show on ABC, NBC, and Fox, on-demand, from the current season as well as past seasons. Hulu Plus also offered viewing of many movies.[43] In November 2010, Hulu dropped the price of Hulu Plus to $7.99 per month and finalized a partnership with Roku. Under the partnership, the Roku device added a channel that provided for streaming of Hulu shows onto TV sets.[44] Within the next year, Hulu partnered with Microsoft and Sony that also provided for streaming of Hulu onto TV sets, and Apple and Amazon to allow streaming of Hulu on tablets.

Amazon Prime Instant Video and Amazon Instant Video Store

In February 2011, Amazon launched a streaming website of its own. Amazon Prime Instant Video became available to members of Amazon's "Prime" membership category, which came at a cost of $79 per year. At the time of launch, Amazon Prime Instant Video only boasted about 5,000 TV shows and movies in total, whereas Netflix's catalog included approximately 20,000 such offerings.[45] Amazon, like Hulu Plus, also partnered immediately with Roku to allow streaming of Amazon Prime Instant Video to TV sets.[46] Amazon did not initially partner with any other electronics companies, but in late 2011, it released its own tablet, the Kindle Fire. Amazon also launched a streaming website "Amazon Instant Video Store" that allowed for rental of movies for a per movie fee.

EIGHTEEN GLORIOUS MONTHS

The year and a half from January 2010 through June 2011 were months of legendary success for Netflix. After beginning 2010 at a price of $53 per share, Netflix stock price more than tripled and ended the year at a price of $179 per share. CNN/Fortune named Hastings 2010 Businessperson of the Year, touting "Already his software is a must-have for the 200-plus device makers who want to brag about having Netflix inside. Now when deals are made in media, the increasingly important question is, 'What's the Netflix piece?'"[47] Netflix stock continued its meteoric rise in 2011, climbing to nearly $300 per share by the close of the June quarter.

UNPOPULAR DECISIONS AND PR TROUBLES

However, after a year and a half of incredible success, everything changed for Netflix on July 12, 2011. On that date Netflix announced that it would separate its DVD and streaming plans. The separation was to be immediate for new customers and effective September 1, 2011 for existing customers. Netflix set the price of each separate plan at $7.99 a month, and the price of streaming plus DVD plans at $15.99, a 60 percent increase from the prior $9.99 price.[48] The price hikes were instantly met with significant backlash from customers. Over 12,000 subscribers publicly renounced the company and announced their cancellations on its blog, including one customer who wrote:

> Dear Netflix,
> Nice work, [Dorito bags]! I used to love Netflix and have recommended it to all of my friends and family. What is the justification for raising my cost by 60% and passing it off as "a terrific value"? Time for me to check out the competition. How dare you? Your Once Loyal Customer.[49]

As a result, Netflix's stock price began a razor-sharp decline, falling to $169 by mid-September.

On September 18, 2011, Hastings apologized for the price increases but did not retract them. Additionally, Netflix announced that it was going to split itself into two separate companies—Netflix for streaming, and "Quickster" for DVD rental—because of the difference in streaming and DVD rental business models. Therefore, subscribers were going to have to access separate websites for streaming and DVD rental.[50] This announcement was also met with severe backlash from the public—and stock market, which saw the stock price fall further to $130 per share.[51]

On October 10, Netflix retracted its plan to split itself into two entities but watched its stock price drop yet further to $108 per share.[52]

Two weeks later, with a stock price of $77 per share (its lowest since April 2010), it announced that it had lost 800,000 customers (about 3 percent of its customer base) during the July–September quarter.[53] In addition to pricing issues, Netflix also had problems arise regarding content. In June 2011, Netflix had to stop offering a large number of Starz movies because Netflix had reached the cap on the number of subscribers who could watch Sony movies online as specified in the Netflix–Starz agreement. (Starz was a pay TV channel that primarily showed Sony films.) Furthermore, analysts began to realize that Netflix would be running into trouble with other media networks in the near future. One analyst, Michael Pachter, stated:

> Netflix has another year or two on most of these contracts, and then the game completely changes . . . The content owners realize they can't give Netflix all the leverage . . . Netflix had the power when they were the only bidder. But you don't have as much leverage when you suddenly have competition.

Pachter estimated that the cost of Netflix's licensing contracts could increase tenfold from $180 million to nearly $2 billion when Netflix renewed them.[54]

In November 2011, Netflix announced plans to raise $400 million through debt and equity. The move further raised fears about Netflix's financial strength and future prospects.[55]

BATTLES FOR CONTENT

By 2012, Netflix, Hulu, and Amazon were in a battle for subscribers, and with that, a battle for video content. In fact, the companies were fighting two battles for content: one for "unoriginal" content (content available through the companies' websites after being shown by the media companies on national TV or in movie theatres) and one for original content (content available solely on the companies' websites). Fights for TV content were generally fiercer than for movie content, though the companies competed for both types of content.

Unoriginal Content

In 2012, ten networks or organizations comprised the majority of TV programming, with five networks (NBC, CBS, ABC, Fox, and the CW) comprising the "Big Five" of programming. After Hulu ironed out a deal with CBS in November 2012, Netflix, Hulu, and Amazon all had contracts with the Big Five networks. However, the nature of the content secured by the companies differed from one to another. Netflix's library of TV shows was much vaster than Hulu's and Amazon's as it included many shows no longer on the air. However, Hulu's library of TV shows offered shows the day after NBC, ABC, and Fox aired them on TV, whereas Netflix generally did not offer TV shows until the media companies completed showing the full seasons on TV. Netflix's children's TV show library was also much stronger than those of Hulu and Amazon.[56] Netflix and Amazon did not show commercials during TV shows whereas Hulu did so. Also to note about Amazon, its Instant Video Store library was significantly more extensive than its Prime library.

In February 2012, Netflix failed to renew its contract with Starz, and as a result lost Disney and Sony content, which was about 8 percent of its library. Netflix reportedly offered Starz more than $300 million a year to keep the content available, but Starz said it was not enough and demanded that Netflix charge an additional fee to users for Starz's content access.[57] Similarly, in August 2012, Netflix allowed its contract with pay TV channel Epix to expire, causing it to lose many Paramount, MGM, and Lions Gate movies; Amazon picked up this content.[58] In September 2012, Netflix did not renew its contract with TV network A&E. In turn, Amazon signed a contract with A&E.[59] In February 2013, Amazon secured exclusive rights to PBS's period drama *Downton Abbey* and CBS's heavily hyped sci-fi drama *Under the Dome*, created by legendary director Stephen Spielberg and based on a novel by popular author Steven King.[60] In May 2013, Netflix let certain contracts with MGM (movies), Warner Bros. (TV and movies), NBC (TV) expire, causing a loss of over 1,500 titles. That same month, Netflix failed to renew its contract with Viacom (operator of many popular channels, including reality and music channel MTV, children's channel Nickelodeon, and Comedy Central), causing it to lose more content; Amazon picked up this content in its biggest single deal as of the time.[61]

However, Netflix was not solely allowing contracts to expire. In December 2012, it signed an exclusive agreement with Disney that will become effective in 2016. Under this agreement, Netflix would have first-run rights to Disney movies. This contract marked the first instance that a major film studio sold first-run rights to a streaming company, not a TV network.[62]

Original Content

The battle for original content was a battle unlike any before in the media industry. Netflix, Hulu, and Amazon were media distributors but did not have content creation capabilities. However, they desired to distribute exclusive content, and thus all three entered the media creation space. Hulu and Netflix hired renowned writers to produce their shows, while Amazon solicited pilot scripts from the general public.[63]

In August 2011, Hulu became the first of the companies to show original content by premiering a celebrity reality documentary, *A Day In the Life*.[64] In February 2012, Hulu premiered a political campaign sitcom, *Battleground*.[65] That same month, in an unusual move for the TV industry, Netflix premiered the entire season of a show *Lillyhammer*. Experts hypothesized that releasing a full season of a show helped Netflix recruit top writers.[66] A few months later, Hulu premiered a second season of *A Day in the Life*.[67] In February 2013, Netflix again premiered an entire season of a show, this time a government drama, *House of Cards* that cost the company approximately $50 million to produce. The show was instantly met with critical acclaim and became the most watched show for Netflix subscribers.[68] In April 2013, Amazon entered the original content competition in a fashion never seen before in the TV industry. Amazon released fourteen pilot episodes of shows and asked viewers to rate and give feedback on the shows in order to determine which shows it would further develop into full season shows.[69]

Finally, in May 2013, to the pleasure of many decade-long TV fans, Netflix released the entire fourth season of a comedy show *Arrested Development* that Fox had shown for three seasons in the early 2000s.[70] While the reviews of the new season were mixed, fans of the show welcomed Netflix's revival of it. As of mid-2013, all three companies' calendars boasted launch dates of more original TV shows.

In June 2013, Netflix signed its biggest deal ever for original content. Under this contract, DreamWorks agreed to create over 300 hours of programming to be exclusively shown on Netflix.[71]

OTHER INDUSTRY DEVELOPMENTS

In 2012 and 2013, aside from the developments in the battles for content, a number of other significant happenings occurred in the video streaming industry. In February 2012, Comcast, by far the largest pay TV operator in the United States, launched a premium streaming service, "Streampix," as a complement to its traditional on-demand service, creating a threat to Netflix and its competitors.[72] In October 2012, Roku instituted a universal search feature that allowed users to search the Netflix, Hulu, and Amazon libraries together for shows, decreasing a differentiation opportunity between the three companies.[73] In March 2013, Redbox (by then a $2 billion per year company) and Verizon jointly launched "Redbox Instant", a streaming plus DVD service, thus adding another competitive force to the fray.[74] That same month, Facebook began including a Netflix application in its users' "timelines" so that users could show others what Netflix videos they had watched or wanted to watch.[75] In April 2013, rumors of development of a TV streaming box by Amazon began circulating.[76] An Amazon-only streaming device would present a new situation in the industry. Finally, and perhaps most significantly, in spring 2013, some of the large media companies began offering their own streaming websites.[77] Clearly, the possibility of viewers being able to watch TV shows and movies without the use of Netflix, Hulu, or Amazon was one that would be troublesome for the three companies. Finally, Hulu's owners were considering a late 2013 sale of the company to DirectTV, AT&T, or another large organization that had resources to grow and possibly change Hulu.[78] Clearly, the video streaming industry was in a very active state in 2013.

NETFLIX'S DECISIONS

In mid-2013, Netflix was playing in a much different and more complicated space than it was playing in when it was founded sixteen years earlier. Having initially set out to take on a brick-and-mortar movie rental company, Netflix had found itself now in a pool of competition that included three of the Big Five television networks (in a joint venture), the US's largest online retailer, a kiosk-based DVD rental company, the large pay TV companies, and the large TV and movie studios. Furthermore, Netflix was having its services delivered to its customers by telecom and electronics companies. Regarding content, in its April 2013 earnings release, Netflix stated, "As we continue to focus on exclusive and curated content, our willingness to pay for non-exclusive, bulk content deals declines."[79] Clearly, Netflix had become a very significant player—perhaps the most significant player—in the overall media industry. Despite gains made by Hulu and Amazon, the company still had an estimated 89 percent market share in the streaming space.[80] And Netflix's stock price had nearly recovered from its steep decline a year and a half earlier, as it closed the second quarter of 2013 at a price of $250 per share.

However, Netflix had a number of important decisions to make about the future. Should it continue to narrow its unoriginal content offerings? Should it continue to develop original content? Should it focus on TV shows or movies or both? Should it focus on TV shows, should it continue to release full seasons at once? Should it continue to have a subscription revenue model? Should it fear any of its competitors more than others?

NOTES

1 A history of home video. Idealink.org website. Retrieved July 21, 2008.
2 A history of home video. Idealink.org website. Retrieved July 21, 2008.
3 Ault, S. Rental stores stock more niche titles. Retrieved July 21, 2008, *Video Business.*
4 Datamonitor. June 2006. Global recorded DVD and video industry profile.
5 Blockbuster Annual Report, 1999.
6 IbisWorld. May 8, 2007. IbisWorld Industry Report: Video tape and disc rental in the U.S.
7 O'Brien, J.M. The Netflix effect. 1 December 2002. *Wired.*
8 Andrews, P. Videos without late fees, Reed Hastings, digital entrepreneur. December 21, 2003. *US News.*
9 Netflix consumer press kit. (2007). Retrieved July 21, 2008, from www.netflix.com/MediaCenter?id=5379
10 Leohardt, D. What Netflix could teach Hollywood. *New York Times,* June 7, 2006.
11 Dornhelm, R. Netflix expands Indie film biz. Marketplace.Publicradio.org website. Retrieved July 21, 2008.
12 Netherby, J. Three's company in online rental. October 21, 2002. *Video Business.*
13 Netherby, J. Three's company in online rental. October 21, 2002. *Video Business.*
14 Lieberman, D. Movie rental battle rages. April 20, 2005. *USA Today.*
15 Kipnis, J. On the video beat. September 4, 2004. *Billboard.*
16 Daikoku, G., & Brancheau, J. Blockbuster Moves to Capture Online DVD Rental Business. August 12, 2004. *Gartner G2 Analysis.*
17 Wasserman, T. Category wars: Blockbuster to hit replay on ads for online service; Service still trails rival Netflix by 3 million subscribers. December 19, 2005. *Brandweek.*
18 Sweeting, P. Blue turns to distributors for online product. February 28, 2005. *Video Business.*
19 Oestricher, D. Blockbuster's new initiatives produce mixed results in 1Q. May 5, 2005. *Dow Jones Newswires.*
20 Wasserman, T. Category wars: Blockbuster to hit replay on ads for online service; Service still trails rival Netflix by 3 million subscribers. December 19, 2005. *BrandWeek.*
21 Wasserman, T. Category wars: Blockbuster to hit replay on ads for online service; Service still trails rival Netflix by 3 million subscribers. December 19, 2005. *BrandWeek.*
22 Blockbuster (video store). Wikipedia website. Retrieved June 10, 2007.
23 Blockbuster online. Blockbuster website. Retrieved June 10, 2007.
24 Blockbuster announces new lower prices subscription plans for online subscribers. B2I website. Retrieved June 12, 2007.
25 Kirkpatrick, M. Amazon Unbox goes live. September 7, 2006. *TechCrunch.*
26 Anderson, N. Netflix offers streaming movies to subscribers. January 16, 2007. *Ars Technica.*
27 Riley, D. Netflix offers unlimited streaming as iTunes rental spoiler. January 13, 2008. *TechCrunch.*
28 Apple introduces new Apple TV Software & Lowers Price to $229. January 15, 2008. *Apple.*
29 Carr, A. Inside Netflix's Project Griffin: The forgotten history of Roku under Reed Hastings. January 23, 2013. *Fast Company.*
30 Falcone, J. Look out, Apple TV: The $100 Netflix Player has arrived. May 19, 2008. *CNet.*
31 Melanson, D. More details emerge on Netflix's abandoned hardware effort, Project Griffin. January 23, 2013. *Engadget.*
32 Gannes, L. Hulu debuts to meet foes and find friends. October 28, 2007. *Gigaom.*
33 Arrington, M. Here comes Hulu mania. Again. March 8, 2008. *TechCrunch.*
34 Van Buskirk, E. Winning teams join to qualify for $1 Million Netflix prize. June 26, 2009. *Wired.*
35 Van Buskirk, E. BellKor's pragmatic chaos wins $1 million Netflix prize by mere minutes. September 21, 2009. *Wired.*

Exhibit 3.1 Netflix and Blockbuster financial information

	2012	2011	2010	2009	2008	2007	2006	2005	2004	2003
Netflix										
Streaming and rental revenue*	$3,609	$3,204	$2,163	$1,670	$1,365	$1,205	$997	$682	$507	$272
Gross profit	27%	36%	37%	35%	33%	35%	37%	32%	45%	45%
Operating expenses (% of revenue):										
General and administrative	3%	4%	3%	3%	4%	4%	4%	5%	18%	19%
Marketing	13%	13%	14%	14%	15%	18%	23%	21%	19%	18%
Research and development	9%	8%	8%	7%	7%	6%	5%	5%	5%	7%
Operating profit	1%	12%	13%	11%	9%	8%	7%	0%	4%	2%
Blockbuster										
Rental revenue			$1,816	$3,086	$3,787	$4,082	$4,029	$4,161	$4,427	$4,533
Merchandise sales revenue			$296	$956	$1,247	$1,400	$1,432	$1,489	$1,532	$1,282
Gross profit: Rental			64%	63%	62%	61%	65%	66%	72%	70%
Gross profit: Merchandise sales			23%	21%	21%	23%	25%	22%	22%	20%
Operating expenses (% of revenue):										
G&A and R&D			32%	51%	47%	49%	51%	52%	51%	49%
Marketing			1%	2%	2%	4%	3%	4%	4%	3%
Operating profit			–6%	–9%	–6%	1%	1%	–7%	–21%	–14%

***Note:**
Netflix began disclosing streaming and rental information separately in 2012. Such results are as follows:

Revenues:
Domestic streaming $2,185
International streaming $287
  Total streaming $2,472
Base rental $1,137
  Total $3,609

Gross profit:
Domestic streaming 29%
International streaming –66%
  Total streaming 18%
Base rental 48%
  Total 27%

Source: Netflix, Inc., Blockbuster, Inc. 10-Ks

Exhibit 3.2 Netflix plans

	DVDs at a time	DVDs/month	Streaming hours/month	Price/month
January 2007 Plan				
	1	2	5	4.99
	1	Unlimited	10	9.99
	2	Unlimited	15	14.99
	3 and up	Unlimited	18 and up	17.99 and up
August 2007 Plan				
	1	2	5	4.99
	1	Unlimited	9	8.99
	2	Unlimited	14	13.99
	3 and up	Unlimited	17 and up	16.99 and up
January 2008 Plan				
	1	2	Unlimited	4.99
	1	Unlimited	Unlimited	8.99
	2	Unlimited	Unlimited	13.99
	3 and up	Unlimited	Unlimited	16.99 and up
November 2010 Plan				
	0	0	Unlimited	7.99
	1	Unlimited	Unlimited	9.99
	2	Unlimited	Unlimited	14.99
	3 and up	Unlimited	Unlimited	19.99 and up
September 2011 Plan				
	1	2	0	4.99
	1	Unlimited	0	7.99
	2 and up	Unlimited	0	11.99 and up
	0	0	Unlimited	7.99
	1	Unlimited	Unlimited	15.98

Source: Casewriter

Exhibit 3.3 Summary of Blockbuster total access movie rental plans, 2007

Plan	Maximum rentals per month	Price per month	Add'l in-store movie or game rentals per month	Mail only price (in-store rental or return)
4 DVDs at-a-time	Unlimited	$23.99	1	$22.99
3 DVDs at-a-time	Unlimited	$17.99	1	$16.99
2 DVDs at-a-time	Unlimited	$14.99	1	$13.99
1 DVDs at-a-time	Unlimited	$9.99	1	$8.99
1 DVDs at-a-time	Limit 3	$7.99	1	$6.99
1 DVDs at-a-time	Limit 2	$5.99	1	$4.99

Source: Blockbuster web site, 2007

Exhibit 3.4 Plans that allow for unlimited streaming or online movie rental without DVD rental

	Price	Limitations
End of 2008 Plans		
Hulu	Free	
End of 2009 Plans		
Hulu	Free	
Cable/Telecom/Satellite on-demand	Variable>	Traditional package subscribers only
End of 2010 Plans		
Netflix	$7.99/mo	
Hulu	Free	
Hulu Plus	$7.99/mo	
Amazon Prime Instant Video	$79/yr*	
Amazon Instant Video Store	$1.99-3.99 per rental	
Cable/Telecom/Satellite on-demand	Variable>	Traditional package subscribers only
End of 2011 Plans		
Netflix	$7.99/mo	
Hulu	Free	
Hulu Plus	$7.99/mo	
Amazon Prime Instant Video	$79/yr*	
Amazon Instant Video Store	$1.99-3.99 per rental	
Cable/Telecom/Satellite on-demand	Variable>	Traditional package subscribers only
Dish-Blockbuster	$2.99-3.99 per rental	
Dish-Blockbuster Movie Pass	$10.00/mo	Dish subscribers only
End of 2012 Plans		
Netflix	$7.99/mo	
Hulu	Free	
Hulu Plus	$7.99	
Amazon Prime Instant Video	$79/yr*	
Amazon Instant Video Store	$1.99-3.99 per rental	
Cable/Telecom/Satellite on-demand	Variable>	Traditional package subscribers only
Comcast Streampix	Free** or $4.99/mo	Comcast subscribers only
Dish-Blockbuster Movie Pass	$10.00/mo	Dish subscribers only
RedBox–Verizon	$8.00/mo	

*Price of Amazon Prime membership, which allowed for retail purchasing benefits, as well as Instant Video
**Certain Comcast cable packages included Streampix
>Price of on demand service varied depending on cable package. Additionally, some movies cost additional fees.

Source: Casewriter

Exhibit 3.5 Timing of integration of streaming with TV sets and portable devices

	TV set devices			Portable devices			
	Roku	**Apple TV**	**Xbox 360**	**Sony PS 3***	**Nintendo Wii**	**Apple iPad**	**Amazon Kindle Fire**
Netflix	Spring 2008	Summer 2010	Fall 2008	Fall 2009	Spring 2010	Spring 2010	Fall 2010
Hulu Plus	Fall 2010	Summer 2012	Spring 2011	Fall 2010	Winter 2012	Summer 2010	Fall 2011
Amazon	Winter 2011	n/a	Spring 2012	Spring 2012	Winter 2013	Summer 2012	Summer 2011

*Most commonly used device for Netflix streaming in 2012

Source: Casewriter

Exhibit 3.6 Pay TV subscriptions, March 2013

	Number of subscribers	Net adds in past year
Cable companies		
Comcast	21,935	(359)
Time Warner	12,100	(553)
Charter	4,124	(217)
Cablevision	3,191	(66)
Other	9,694	(364)
Total	51,044	(1,559)
Satellite TV companies		
DirecTV	20,105	139
Dish	14,092	21
Total	34,197	160
Telephone companies		
Verizon	4,895	542
AT&T	4,768	777
Total	9,663	1,319
Total pay TV subscriptions	**94,904**	**(80)**

Sources:
The Companies and Liechtman Research Group, Inc.
Roettgers, Janko. Pay TV is hurting, and even skeptics now admit cord cutting could be at fault. Giagom website. May 20, 2013.

Exhibit 3.7 Netflix subscriptions and subscribers

Subscriptions	2013	2012				2011	
	4/1	1/1	10/1	7/1	4/1	1/1	10/1
Streaming							
US*	29.2	27.2	25.1	23.9	23.4	21.7	21.5
International	7.1	6.1	4.3	3.6	3.1	1.9	1.5
Total	36.3	33.3	29.4	27.6	26.5	23.5	22.9
DVD (US only)*	8.0	8.2	8.6	9.2	10.1	11.2	13.9
Total*	44.3	41.5	38.0	36.8	36.6	34.7	36.9
Total US	37.2	35.4	33.7	33.2	33.5	32.8	35.4
Net adds:							
Streaming							
US*	2.1	2.1	1.2	0.5	1.7	0.2	
International	1.0	1.8	0.7	0.6	1.2	0.4	
Total	3.0	3.9	1.9	1.1	3.0	0.6	
DVD (US only)*	(0.2)	(0.4)	(0.6)	(0.9)	(1.1)	(2.8)	
Total*	2.8	3.5	1.2	0.2	1.9	(2.2)	
Total US	1.8	1.7	0.5	(0.3)	0.7	(2.5)	

*Number of subscriptions, not subscribers. Some US customers subscribe to both Streaming & DVD plans. Information on unique subscribers not available.

Subscribers	2011		2010				2009				2008			
	7/1	4/1	1/1	10/1	7/1	4/1	1/1	10/1	7/1	4/1	1/1	10/1	7/1	4/1
US	24.6	22.8	19.5	16.8	15.0	14.0	12.3	11.1	10.6	10.3	9.4	8.7	8.4	8.2
International	1.0	0.8	0.5	0.1	–	–	–	–	–	–	–	–	–	–
Total	25.6	23.6	20.0	16.9	15.0	14.0	12.3	11.1	10.6	10.3	9.4	8.7	8.4	8.2
Net adds:														
US*	1.8	3.3	2.7	1.8	1.0	1.7	1.2	0.5	0.3	0.9	0.7	0.3	0.2	8.2
International	0.2	0.3	0.4	0.1	–	–	–	–	–	–	–	–	–	–
Total	2.0	3.6	3.1	1.9	1.0	1.7	1.2	0.5	0.3	0.9	0.7	0.3	0.2	8.2

Source: Netflix quarterly earnings releases

36   Carr, Austin. Blockbuster bankruptcy: A decade of decline. September 22, 2010. Fast Company website.
37   Poggi, J. Blockbuster's rise and fall: The long, rewinding road. September 23, 2010. *The Street.*
38   Carr, A. Blockbuster bankruptcy: A decade of decline. September 22, 2010. *Fast Company.*
39   The history of Redbox. Redbox website. Retrieved July 14, 2013.
40   Lawler, R. Netflix, ABC to Release Apps for iPad Launch. April 1, 2010. *Gigaom.*
41   Overhauled Apple TV unveiled. September 2, 2010. *Media Spy.*
42   Stevens, T. Netflix formally launches $7.99 streaming-only plan, bumps unlimited DVD plans by a buck or more. November 22, 2010. *Engadget.*
43   Van Buskirk, E. Hulu Plus launches: Three networks, zero real-time shows. June 29, 2010. *Wired.*
44   Savov, V. Hulu Plus drops price to $7.99 a month, adds Roku support for official launch. November 17, 2010. *Engadget.*
45   Lawler, R. Amazon Prime instant videos isn't a Netflix killer — yet. February 22, 2011. *Gigaom.*
46   Burns, M. Amazon Prime instant video now streaming free to prime dubscribers. February 22, 2011. *TechCrunch.*
47   Copeland, M. Businessperson of the Year. November 19, 2010. *CNN Money.*
48   Netflix price hike fallout: A timeline of events. December 22, 2011. *Huffington Post.*
49   Gilbert, J. Netflix price hike's one year anniversary: A look back at one of the great tech blunders. July 12, 2012. *Huffington Post.*
50   Netflix price hike fallout: A timeline of events. December 22, 2011. *Huffington Post.*
51   McMillan, G. Cheat sheet: How bad are things for Netflix? October 26, 2011. *Time.*
52   McMillan, G. Cheat sheet: How bad are things for Netflix? October 26, 2011. *Time.*
53   McMillan, G. Cheat sheet: How bad are things for Netflix? October 26, 2011. *Time.*
54   Pepitone, J. Netflix's vanished Sony films are an ominous sign. July 11, 2011. *CNN Money.*
55   Netflix price hike fallout: A timeline of events. December 22, 2011. *Huffington Post.*
56   Holly, R. Netflix vs. Hulu Plus: Who best fits your video streaming needs? May 31, 2013. *Geek.*
57   Ludwig, S. Netflix will lose Starz' incredible trove of streaming content in early 2011. September 1, 2011. *Venture Beat.*
58   Liedtke, M. Amazon gets Epix video rights to challenge Netflix. September 4, 2012. *Yahoo Finance.*
59   Maurer, B. Amazon gobbles up more lost Netflix content. January 7, 2013. *Seeking Alpha.*
60   Gardner, E. CBS, Amazon make deal to stream "Under the Dome". February 1, 2013. *The Hollywood Reporter.*
61   Chozick, A. In Viacom deal, Amazon scoops up children's shows." *New York Times,* June 4, 2013.
62   Liedtke, M. Netflix, Disney contract: Service outbids Pay TV for rights to stream new films. December 4, 2012. *Huffington Post.*
63   Summers, N. What Hulu's original programming means for TV. May 22, 2012. *The Daily Beast.*
64   Chozick, A. ,& Stetler, B. An online TV site grows up. *New York Times,* April 16, 2012.
65   Summers, N. What Hulu's original programming means for TV. May 22, 2012. *The Daily Beast.*
66   Chozick, A. , & Stetler, B. An Online TV Site Grows Up. *New York Times.* April 16, 2012.
67   Pepitone, J. Netflix's $100 million bet on must-see TV. February 1, 2013. *CNN Money.*
68   Ingraham, N. Redbox and Verizon hope to follow in Netflix's footsteps and launch original programming. March 9, 2013. *The Verge.*
69   Farber, D. Amazon studios debuts 14 pilots for free viewing. April 19, 2013. *CNet.*
70   Pepitone, J. Netflix's $100 million bet on must-see TV. February 1, 2013. *CNN Money.*
71   Barnes, B. DreamWorks and Netflix in deal for New TV shows. *New York Times* June 17, 2013.
72   Cheredar, T. Comcast launches 'Netflix-like' Streampix to complement expensive cable packages. February 21, 2012. *Venture Beat.*
73   Lawler, R. Roku Adds Universal Search For Netflix, Amazon, Hulu Plus, Crackle, Vudu, and HBO to its streaming devices. October 29, 2012. *TechCrunch.*
74   Silbert, S. Redbox Instant exits private beta and launches to the public. March 14, 2013. *Engadget.*
75   Sparks, D. Facebook rolls out new timeline and deepens Netflix integration. March 13, 2013. *The Motley Fool.*
76   Stone, B. Here Comes Amazon's Kindle TV set-top box. April 24, 2013. *Bloomberg Businessweek.*
77   Atkinson, C. Netflix sees media giants start own streaming services. *New York Post,* May 2, 2013.
78   Mitchell, D. Conflicted Hulu owners face tough choices. July 10, 2013. *CNN Money.*
79   Pepitone, J. Amazon Prime scores Viacom shows after Netflix deal expires. June 4, 2013. *CNN Money.*
80   Solsman, J. Hulu, Amazon nibbling at more of Netflix's streaming-TV pie. June 4, 2013. *CNet.*

Case 4

THREADLESS IN CHICAGO

In 2000, Jake Nickell, a multimedia and design student at the Illinois Institute of Art, and Jacob DeHart, an engineering student at Purdue University, entered an online T-shirt design contest, which Jake won. However, both of them went away with the idea that having someone else compete to design T-shirts for them could lead to something interesting. They kept in touch and worked together on a few projects before starting their own T-shirt company in 2000, with $1,000.[1] Their company, Threadless, would make and sell T-shirts with colorful graphics.[2] They were venturing into the colorful T-shirt—a so-called hit-and-miss product. Traditionally, to be successful with such a product, a firm needed to have the right distribution channels and its fingers on the pulse of fast-changing trends.[3] A firm needed to have the right market research and forecasting abilities to do well. The two founders added creative director Jeff Kalmikoff later. They also took venture capital money from Insight Venture Partners, not so much because they needed the money, but because they could, well, obtain some insights from the venture capitalist firm.

THE COMMUNITY DESIGNS AND MARKETS

Threadless had a community of registered members that in 2004 was 70,000 strong and mushroomed to 700,000 by 2008. Anyone with a valid email address could join free. Each week, members of the community—largely artists—uploaded hundreds of T-shirt designs to the community site. (In 2007, the firm received 150 submissions per day.) Visitors to the site then voted for their favorite designs by scoring them on a scale of 0 to 5.[4] Each design remained available for voting for seven days. From the scoring, the best six designs were chosen from the hundreds of submissions. Creators of the winning designs were awarded prizes. In 2007, these prizes were worth $2,000 per design: $1,500 in cash, $300 in a gift certificate, and a subscription to Threadless T-shirts.[5] By 2008, the prize had climbed to $2,500. However, to many artists, there was something bigger than the cash prize. "It was how cool it was to get your shirts printed,"[6] remarked Glen Jones, a 2004 winner. The name of the designer (winner) was put on the label of the T-shirt.[7] Threadless retained the rights to the design.

To help the artists with the design process, Threadless sent digital submission kits—complete with HTML code and graphics to each potential submitter. With these kits, artists could create advertisements for their designs that looked very professional. The artists not only spent weeks seeking advice from other community members and perfecting their designs, they posted links to their submissions to their personal websites, any online design forums that they frequented, MySpace pages, or blogs, asking their friends to vote for them and buy if and when they won.[8] Effectively, the artists not only designed the shirts for Threadless, they also pre-marketed them, adding to the brand. Some of the members who participated in voting for designs saw the process as one of exploring the latest in designs and learning. In effect, the firm committed financially only to T-shirt designs that many of its customers approved of.

Some Results

The company printed the winning designs and sold them to the very community that had competed to create the designs and voted to decide the winning design. By 2008, it had printed 1,000 designs[9]—all online. The T-shirts usually sold out. It had no professional designers, used no fashion photographers or modeling agencies, had no sales force, did not advertise, and, except for its retail store in Chicago, it had no distributors.[10] Members of the community socialized, blogged, and chatted about designs. It even had an official fan site: www.lovesthreadless.com. In 2007, its shirts cost about $4 each to make and sold for about $15.[11] The company sold 80,000–90,000 shirts a week.[12] Revenues were growing at 500 percent a year. The company did all this without the help of big retailers like Target who had come knocking but been turned down by Threadless.

A Retail Store?

Threadless opened its first offline retail store in September 2007, in Chicago.[13] Why would an online company build an offline store when it could keep its margins even higher by avoiding brick-and-mortar costs? Threadless offered several reasons.[14] First, the firm wanted a building that reflected the Threadless culture in which design classes could be offered, galleries with Threadless artists' work hosted, and real-world group interaction and critics facilitated. Second, the company's products changed every week and most retailers were not equipped to handle such changes. Third, there was a story behind each of their T-shirts and the person who created it, how it was created, scored and selected for print that needed to be told. Such a story would be lost in a traditional retail outlet. With the retail store, they could tell the story their own way. Of the 1,000 designs that had been created since its inception, about 300 of them were still in stock. The firm only displayed 20 designs for sale. The rest could be obtained from its website. Designs were released in the offline retail store before online.

Other Holdings

Threadless had a parent company called SkinnyCorp, also run by Nickell, DeHart and Kalmikoff. In June 2008, the other units under the SkinnyCorp umbrella were Naked and Angy, Yay Hooray, and Extra Tasty.

NOTES

1   Brabham, D. C. (2008). Outsourcing as a model for problem solving: An introduction and cases. *Convergence: The International Journal of Research Into New Media Technologies*, 14(1), 75–90.
    Gilmour, M. (2007, November 26). Threadless: From clicks to bricks. *Business Week*.

2   Ogawa, S., & Piller, F. T. (2006). Reducing the risk of new product development. *MIT Sloan Management Review*, 47(2), 65–71.

3   Ogawa, S., & Piller, F. T. (2006). Reducing the risk of new product development. *MIT Sloan Management Review*, 47(2), 65–71.

4   Weingarten, M. (2007, June 18). 'Project Runway' for the T-shirt crowd. *Business 2.0 Magazine*.

5   Kawasaki, G. (2007). Ten questions with Jeffrey Kalmikoff, Chief Creative Officer of skinnyCorp/Threadless. Retrieved June 17, 2008, from blog.guykawasaki.com/2007/06/ten_questions_w.html

6   Chafkin, M. (2008, June). The customer is the company. *Inc. Magazine*. Retrieved July 21, 2008, from www.inc.com/magazine/20080601/the-customer-is-the-company.html

7   Boutin, P. (2006). Crowdsourcing: Consumers as creators. Retrieved June 26, 2008, from www.business week.com/innovate/content/jul2006/id20060713_755844.htm

8   Chafkin, M. (2008, June). The customer is the company. *Inc. Magazine*. Retrieved July 21, 2008, from www.inc.com/magazine/20080601/the-customer-is-the-company.html

9   Threadless Chicago. (2008). Retrieved June 17, 2008, from www.threadless.com/retail.

10 Chafkin, M. (2008, June). The customer is the company. *Inc. Magazine*. Retrieved July 21, 2008, from www.inc.com/magazine/20080601/the-customer-is-the-company.html

11 Weingarten, M. (2007, June 18). 'Project Runway' for the T-shirt crowd. *Business 2.0 Magazine*.

12 Kawasaki, G. (2007). Ten questions with Jeffrey Kalmikoff, Chief Creative Officer of skinnyCorp/Threadless. Retrieved June 17, 2008, from blog.guykawasaki.com/2007/06/ten_questions_w.html

13 Threadless Chicago. (2008). Retrieved June 17, 2008, from www.threadless.com/retail

14 Threadless Chicago. (2008). Retrieved June 17, 2008, from www.threadless.com/retail

Case 5

ZYNGA*

INTRODUCTION

Best known for its hits like *FarmVille* and *Mafia Wars*, the social video game company named Zynga accumulated more than 230 million active players in the three years following its debut on Facebook in 2007.[1] Perhaps even more surprising than the number of players that Zynga attracted were the market segments that it penetrated. In 2010, the average player of a Zynga game was a 43-year-old woman who played for at least an hour per day: a far-cry from the classic image of a "hard-core gamer."[2] In late 2010, valuations for the privately held company were estimated to be $5.5 billion, versus the long-time industry incumbent, Electronic Arts, which was valued at $5.2 billion.[3] Annual revenues for Zynga were approximately $500 million in 2010, with a $1 billion projected revenue for 2012.[4] Without original storylines, impressive graphics, or any other characteristics that typically predicated the success of video games, how did Zynga make this rapid rise to the top of its industry?

SOCIAL GAMES

Social games refer to games played online between multiple users. Typically, these games create a virtual world, and players assume different characters within this world. As these characters gain new experiences and achieve certain tasks, the players win points and earn higher statuses. Social interactions take place within the game as players form co-operative or competitive relationships with one another. A common characteristic of social games is that even when the player logs out, the game keeps going. This perpetual nature of social games tends to make them more addictive than typical video games, as users feel a sense of urgency to frequently log in to see how the game is progressing.

---

* This case was written by Shana Anderson, Christina Bosch, Fiona Huang, and Daniel Rich under the supervision of Professor Allan Afuah as a basis for class discussion and is not intended to illustrate either effective or ineffective handling of a business situation.

History of Social Games

By 2010, "social games" were most often associated with social networks such as Facebook or MySpace, but their history actually dates back to the 1970s. That is when Multi-User Dimension (MUD) games first arrived on Essex University's network. In the first social games, players engaged in online forms of *Dungeons & Dragons*.[5] For the two decades following, games such as *World of Warcraft*, *EverQuest*, and *Lineage* joined millions of concurrent users over the Internet, and became known as Massively Multiplayer Online Role-Playing Games (MMORPGs).

The most popular games were those that featured creative and complex storylines—usually based upon science fiction or fantasy worlds. Players enjoyed the games' rich graphics and customizable features. The traditional revenue model for a social game was the sale of the initial software (approximately $20), followed by an online monthly subscription rate ($13–$15 per month), which was needed to play the game with other people.[6] Players often made friends through the game's subscription network, thus making social connections an important part of the game. In 2010, *World of Warcraft* by Blizzard Entertainment became the most popular MMORPG with over 12 million subscribers.[7]

SOCIAL GAMES MEET SOCIAL NETWORKS

In January 2007, Mark Pincus started the social video game company Zynga, naming it after his late bulldog Zinga. At the time, the social network Facebook was just beginning to move mainstream with approximately 100,000 new users joining the network every day.[8] Additionally, it was in May 2007 that Facebook first launched "Facebook Platform" which enabled third-party developers like Zynga to create applications for the network.[9] Another trend at the time was the growing popularity of online gambling. Sites like PokerStars.com and FullTilt.com featured both real-money and play-money poker games.[10]

It was at the cross-section of the Facebook Platform and the online gambling trend that Zynga released its first game *Texas Hold 'Em* in 2007, which was played between Facebook friends for virtual currency. Unlike MMORPGs, where players met other people through the game network, Zynga offered games to people who were already connected through Facebook. Pincus compared Facebook to a cocktail party where friends and family showed up but had nothing to do; so he created a company where these people could interact by playing games together.[11]

Zynga players were encouraged to actively recruit more Facebook friends to join the game and were rewarded with virtual currency to do so. Facebook users were bombarded with spamlike advertisements every time one of their friends played a Zynga game or achieved a certain level within the game. This encouraged people to play online with each other, invite more people to join, chat about the games, as well as post their progress to Facebook.

In some games collaboration, or making a move that "helped a friend," players earned points. For example, in *FarmVille*, Facebook friends appeared on the screen as "farm neighbors" who helped with labor and exchanged gifts. Consequently, recruiting more friends to play the game helped a player access special gifts and advantages that improved his/her performance.

Users could also convert real money into virtual money to help their standing. Since accomplishments within the game were published to the users' Facebook accounts, players felt social pressure to spend real money to help them progress.[12]

Virtual Transactions

Unlike traditional video games, Zynga games were completely free to play. Zynga's revenues, which were speculated to be around $500 million in 2010, were derived 90 percent from the sale of virtual goods.[13] Virtual goods were items that had no tangible value and could only be used in the game setting. For example, in *FarmVille*, players managed a virtual farm. Players accumulated "farm coins" by harvesting the crops that were planted on the farm. Crops could only be harvested after a predetermined amount of time had passed. If too much time passed, the crops wilted, rendering them useless. However, a player could spend real money to purchase the use of a virtual biplane that would instantly rejuvenate the crops. Costs of virtual goods were low: generally $2 to $5.[14]

For some, the idea of spending real cash on a completely intangible good was difficult to comprehend. However, once a player was immersed in the game, buying virtual goods became second nature. The widespread acceptance of virtual goods in the marketplace was confirmed in 2010 when American Express began allowing its Membership Rewards holders to spend their points to buy Zynga virtual goods.[15] Citi quickly followed suit by allowing its Thank You Rewards recipients to do the same.[16] In return, Zynga created exclusive goods for Citi users.[17]

With estimated first-year revenues of $100 million[18], Zynga proved that selling intangible products to Facebook users offered a lucrative opportunity. In 2009, the market represented $835 million. Social game companies closed 2010 with $1.6 billion of revenue, and were expected to increase the market size to $2.1 billion (40 percent) by 2011.[19]

Characteristics of Zynga's Games

After the successful launch of *Texas Hold 'Em* in 2007, Zynga continued to release major blockbuster games like *Mafia Wars* in June 2008, *FarmVille* in June 2009, *Café World* in October 2009, and *CityVille* in November, 2010.[20] Other Zynga games included *TreasureIsle*, *FishVille*, and *FrontierVille*. Exhibit 5.1 shows the top ten rankings for Zynga's games on Facebook in 2010.

Within three years of its first release, the company had 20 games: from puzzle and card games to role-playing and fantasy world games.[21] As a result of its abundant and diverse portfolio, Zynga was well positioned to capture value from the immense Facebook universe. The easy-to-grasp concepts on which Zynga games were based—such as playing cards, farming, and tending fish aquariums—were immediately appealing to younger kids, older women, and many others who did not typically play video games. By developing Web-based games, Zynga's target market included anyone with Internet access and a social network account, versus other video game companies that targeted young males who purchased manufacturer-specific consoles, devices, and software.

Reports showed that by 2010, 52 percent of video games were played on computers and 12 percent were played on mobile phones.[22] According to the NPD Market Research group, in 2010, an estimated 56.8 million Americans played social games, which was equivalent to one in five people aged six and older.[23] Exhibit 5.2 shows top-ranked online games by monthly active users in 2010.

Surprisingly, in 2010, Facebook data revealed that most of Zynga's users were middle-aged females.[24] Based on a survey conducted in the US and the UK, more than 55 percent of players of social network games were women.[25] This demographic shift closely coincided with trends seen on the Facebook platform. From 2009 to 2010, Facebook users age 35 and older increased from approximately 8 million people to nearly 40 million people; and in all age groups on Facebook, the number of females exceeded males.[26] Additionally, because Zynga gained new users through social connections rather than from video game features, people began playing video games simply because their friends and family members were playing them. The number of players was not trivial: in 2010, *FarmVille* alone had over 80 million monthly active users (MAUs) with more joining each month.[27]

Imitation Versus Innovation

Ironically, even though Zynga was the most successful online video game company, it lacked two of the most important traditional characteristics of game developers: creativity and graphic design capabilities. One industry analyst actually stated of Zynga's graphics, "We've never before seen this kind of deliberate unconcern for the aesthetics of the experience."[28] While other video games were moving to high-definition, characters in Zynga games were generally cartoonlike and pixilated.

Likewise, Zynga represented the antithesis of "creativity"—as the company became better known for *stealing* games. Often accused of using the "Microsoft Approach" to development, Zynga admitted to its strategy of identifying already-created successful products and recreating them with superior marketing and distribution channels.[29] Exhibit 5.3 shows a table of successful Zynga games and the predecessors on which they were based. After a competitor's game was released, it was often only a matter of months before Zynga released their own version of the same game.

This predatory business model was effective for Zynga because users of the other games could seamlessly transfer over to Zynga's platform to have a similar experience. Although it was useful in attracting new players, this method was not without legal issues. In 2009, Zynga faced a lawsuit from David Maestri, the creator of *Mob Wars*, who alleged that Zynga had infringed his copyright with their creation of *Mafia Wars*.[30] Both games had similar characters, interfaces, and strategies. The lawsuit settled outside of court for $10 million, which, by comparison, was approximately 7–10 days of Zynga's revenue.[31,32]

Other Zynga games had undeniable similarities with competitors' versions. One intellectual property attorney remarked of *FarmVille*, "I'm surprised there hasn't been litigation, because from what I've seen, they did copy [*Farm Town*]."[33]

Some insiders asserted that Zynga's CEO, Mark Pincus, fully expected intellectual property lawsuits and built them into the company's business model.[34] Evidence of this came directly from the website, where Zynga proactively informed competitors of how to contact them about copyright infringement. Their page titled "Copyright Notices/ Complaints" provided potential victims with information about their rights, and directed them to Zynga's representing agent for intellectual property issues.[35]

Financially speaking, these legal issues were hardly a deterrent for Zynga—as the original content creators were generally small companies who were likely to settle outside of court. In an article published in the *San Francisco Weekly*, interviews with anonymous Zynga employees revealed that the company was not shy about its "replicate success" strategy, and programmers were often told to model games after existing ones. However, employees asserted that Zynga did not intentionally break any laws, and that stealing concepts for games and mimicking certain mechanics and designs did not alone constitute infringement.[36]

Growth and Market Position

Zynga raised investments almost as fast as it released games. With an initial round of $10 million in early 2008, Zynga earned a second round of $28 million in Series B funding led by Kleiner Perkins later that year.[37] Series C funding of $180 million led by Digital Sky Technologies and other firms such as Andreessen Horowitz in 2009 enabled Zynga to grow quickly and leave potential competitors falling short.[38] Rumors also circled that Google had invested $100–200 million in the company in September 2010.[39] Combined with funding from Softbank, investments in 2010 were estimated to be at least $300 million, bringing the total funding for the company to $519 million.[40]

The several rounds of funding enabled Zynga to recruit more programmers and advertise aggressively. In 2010, employee headcount quadrupled over the previous year's to 775.[41] Zynga's strategy was to spend millions of dollars on social media advertising whenever a new game was released. The abundance of advertising made it difficult for rivals to compete.

Further limiting competition, the company's growth strategy included several acquisitions. It picked up YoVille in 2008, and accelerated its acquisitions in 2010 with Serious Business (social game developer), XPD Media (Chinese social gaming company), Challenge Games (social game company), Bonfire Studios (PC and Xbox 360 game developers), Unoh (leading Japanese social game developer), Conduit Labs (social games company), and NEWTOY (developer).[42] Exhibit 5.4 shows the top ten game developers on Facebook, where Zynga held over 50 percent of the market. Electronic Arts was previously the incumbent, but only held 12 percent while other competitors such as Playdom and Slashkey held less than 10 percent each.

Zynga and Facebook

Zynga primarily released its multiplayer games on Facebook. In several attempts to expand operations, Zynga also extended its distribution to the iPhone and Android universe, as well as to MySpace, Yahoo, Bebo, and Hi5; however, Facebook's 500-million-user network was the main channel by which Zynga expanded its base.

Facebook proved to be an important marketing channel for Zynga. Less than two weeks after its launch of *CityVille*, Zynga executives reported that 17 million people had played the game on Facebook.[43] By way of comparison, *CityVille* had acquired 5 million more players in 14 days than the number accumulated by *World of Warcraft* after six years on the market.[44] Mark Pincus said in a 2010 press release, "Facebook was a pioneer in opening their platform in 2007 and in just three years tens of millions of Facebook users play our games every day, from *FarmVille* and *Café World* to *Treasure Isle* and *Mafia Wars*."[45]

In exchange for Facebook's user base, Zynga gave Facebook advertising revenue (about $8 million per month).[46] But Facebook also wanted a share of Zynga's virtual goods revenue, and it planned to capture this by forcing Zynga players to buy goods with Facebook Credits, a proprietary virtual currency.[47] The new service made Facebook competitive with PayPal.[48] Since Zynga was the second biggest client for Paypal (after eBay), this move placed Zynga in a precarious position. Some speculated that the co-dependency of Zynga and Facebook was what led to their May 2010 announcement regarding a five-year partnership and the use of Facebook Credits for Zynga games.[49] This arrangement was estimated to provide Facebook with up to 30 percent of Zynga's virtual goods revenue.[50]

Possible Problems for Zynga

While Zynga appeared to be on the top of the world, negative media coverage about the addictive nature of Zynga games began casting shadows upon the company's success. In October 2010, 22-year-old Jacksonville mother Alexandra Tobias was so engrossed in a *FarmVille* game that she shook her infant son to death when he disturbed her.[51] Tobias pled guilty to the murder of her child, a tragedy that occurred as a result of playing a Zynga game.[52] A similar case was reported in January 2011 when another mother, Shannon Johnson, allowed her one-year-old son to drown in the bathtub while she played Zynga's *Café World*.[53] While these cases were tragic and extreme, they highlighted the intensity of social game addiction, and made many question the merits of Zynga.

Other concerning issues for Zynga included intellectual property matters. However, this time they found themselves on the other side of the lawsuits. In 2010, Zynga sued the start-up company Playdom for unfair competition when some of Zynga's former employees were hired away and asked to reveal trade secrets.[54] Zynga, the company best known for stealing ideas, now had to defend its own intellectual property rights.[55]

Conclusion

In just three years, Zynga had taken the social gaming market by storm. With over 45 million active daily users, and skyrocketing estimated revenues, the company had established itself as the leader in this new space.[56] Its success had not been without issues. Competitors claimed plagiarism, and Facebook users were sick of being bombarded with Zynga ads. They responded by creating groups like "I don't care about your farm, or your fish, or your park, or your mafia!"

How would Zynga be able to keep other companies from replicating its success in the future? Would Facebook change the rules and limit Zynga's key distribution channel? Would the company be blamed for the bad behavior of addicted users?

Exhibit 5.1 Top ten Zynga games on Facebook

Game	Monthly active users	Fans	Release date	Application rating (out of 5)
FarmVille	74,806,786	16,022,479	June 19, 2009	4.1
Café World	30,304,588	4,228,008	October, 2009	3.1
FishVille	24,488,757	24,924,751	2009	3.7
Zynga Poker	24,810,241	1,505,323	September, 2007	4.0
Mafia Wars	24,174,812	1,594,810	June, 2008	3.8
PetVille	17,970,006	2,360,821	December, 2009	4.2
YoVille	14,872,748	3,391,251	2008 (acquired)	3.6
Roller Coaster Kingdom	7,822,440	2,028,684	–	2.6
Vampire Wars	3,184,952	463,454	–	3.8
Street Racing	1,144,774	120,921	Closed, November 30, 2010	3.6

Sources: Top 10 Zynga Games on Facebook. Weblog post. Retrieved from: www.associatedcontent.com/article/2634521/top_10_zynga_games_on_facebook.html?cat=19. January 26, 2010. Web; Zynga.com; and insidesocialgames.com; engagedigital.com

Exhibit 5.2 Top ten ranked online games by monthly active users in 2010

Game	Developer	Rank	Monthly active users (millions)
FarmVille	Zynga	1	83.2
Café World	Zynga	2	30.3
Texas Hold 'Em	Zynga	3	39.7
Mafia Wars	Zynga	4	25.3
Happy Aquarium	CrowdStar	5	23.3
FishVille	Zynga	6	22.1
PetVille	Zynga	7	21.2
Pet Society	Electronic Arts	8	19.7
Restaurant City	Electronic Arts	9	16.0
Country Life	Country Life	10	9.3

Source: www.secondshares.com/wp-content/uploads/2010/04/Zynga-Report.pdf

Exhibit 5.3 Selection of Zynga's top-rated games and the predecessor games on which each was based

Zynga games	Competition
Name: *Mafia Wars* Developer: Zynga Users: 23,256,287 Release date: November 2008	Name: *Mob Wars* Developer: Psycho Monkey Users: 1,205,879 Release date: September 2008
Name: *FarmVille* Developer: Zynga Users: 74,008,714 Release date: June 2009	Name: *Farm Town* Developer: Slashkey Users: 14,104,459 Release date: April 2009
Name: *FishVille* Developer: Zynga Users: 24,460,783 Release date: November 2009	Name: *Fish World* Developer: TallTree Games Users: 7,607,655 Release date: October 2009
Name: *Café World* Developer: Zynga Users: 29,967,961 Release date: September 2009	Name: *Restaurant City* Developer: Playfish Users: 15,009,117 Release date: April 2009
Name: *PetVille* Developer: Zynga Users: 17,944,083 Release date: December 2009	Name: *Pet Society* Developer: Playfish Users: 20,042,566 Release date: September 2008

Source: Nick Saint. Zynga's secret to success: steal great ideas! *Business Insider.* January 19, 2010.

Exhibit 5.4 Top ten game developers on Facebook

Developer	MAU	Rank
Zynga	237.1	1
Electronic Arts	53.3	2
CrowdStar	49.2	3
Playdom	37.1	4
Rock You (Games)	23	5
Mindjolt Games	21.4	6
Pop Cap Games	10.7	7
Slashkey	9.6	8
Country Life	9.3	9
Meteor Games	7.6	10

Source: Lou Kerner, Eli Halliwell, and Jay Gould for Track.com and SecondShares.com. April, 2010. Retrieved from: www.secondshares.com/wp-content/uploads/2010/04/Zynga-Report.pdf

NOTES

1   McGarvey, Robert. Zynga draws record VC funding. June 28, 2010. Retrieved from: www.internetevolution.com/author.asp?section_id=852&doc_id=193697&f_src=internetevolution_gnews

2   2010 Social gaming research. *PopCap Games: Information Solutions Group*. Retrieved from: www.infosolutionsgroup.com/2010_PopCap_Social_Gaming_Research_Results.pdf

3   Levy, Ari. Zynga tops electronic arts as social games spread. *Bloomberg Businessweek*. October 26, 2010. Retrieved from: www.businessweek.com/news/2010-10-26

4   Zynga $5 billion valuation: BUY – Early Leader in Social Gaming is Printing Money. *Second Shares*. April 6, 2010. Retrieved from: www.secondshares.com/2010/04/06

5   Mulligan, Jessica, & Patrovsky, Bridgette (2003). *Developing Online Games: An Insider's Guide*. New Riders. p. 444.

6   Retrieved from: www.costhelper.com

7   World of warcraft subscriber base reaches 12 million worldwide. October 7, 2010. Retrieved from: http://us.blizzard.com/en-us/company/press/pressrelease.html?101007

8   Arlington, Michael. Facebook launches Facebook Platform; They are anti-MySpace. *Tech Crunch*. May 24, 2007. Retrieved from: http://techcrunch.com/2007/05/24

9   Arlington, Michael. Facebook launches Facebook Platform; They are anti-MySpace. *Tech Crunch*. May 24, 2007. Retrieved from: http://techcrunch.com/2007/05/24/

10 Crowson, Arthur. Millions hooked on Facebook Hold 'em. *PokerListings*. Retrieved from: www.pokerlistings.com/millions-hooked-on-facebook-holdem-4406512.

11 Inside Zynga: Now the creators of CityVille. *ABC Nightline Exclusive Interview*. Retrieved from: http://abcnews.go.com/Nightline/inside-zynga-creators-farmville/story?id=12169767

12 Kohler, Chris. Farm wars: How Facebook games harvest big bucks. *Wired*. May 19, 2010. Retrieved from: www.wired.com/gamelife/2010/05/farm-wars/3

13 Sherman, Chris. Pincus says no IPO for Zynga. *Engage Digital*. April 22, 2010. Retrieved from: www.engagedigital.com/2010/04/22

14 Buckman, Rebecca. Zynga's gaming gamble. *Forbes Magazine*. November 16, 2009.Retrieved from: www.forbes.com/forbes/2009/1116/revolutionaries-technology-social-gaming-farmville-facebook-zynga.html

15 Morrison, Chris. American Express offers Zynga virtual goods as a member reward. *Inside Social Games*. November 30, 2010. Retrieved from: www.insidesocialgames.com/2010/11/30

16 Ashby, Alicia. Citi adds Zyngs Virtual Goods to Thank You Rewards. *Engage Digital*. December 7, 2010. Retrieved from: www.engagedigital.com/2010/12/07

17 Ashby, Alicia. Citi adds Zynga virtual goods to thank you rewards. *Engage Digital*. December 7, 2010. Retrieved from: www.engagedigital.com/2010/12/07

18 Crowson, Arthur. Millions hooked on Facebook Hold 'em. *PokerListings*.Retrieved from: www.pokerlistings.com/millions-hooked-on-facebook-holdem-44065

19   Helft, Miguel. Virtual goods expected to grow by 40% next year study says. *New York Times.* September 28, 2010. Retrieved from: http://bits.blogs.nytimes.com/2010/09/28/virtual-goods-expected-to-grow-by-40-percent-next-year-study-says

20   Zynga. Retrieved from: www.zynga.com/about/timeline.php

21   Zynga. Retrieved from: www.zynga.com/games/

22   2010 social gaming research. *PopCap Games: Information Solutions Group.* Retrieved from: www.infosolutionsgroup.com/2010_PopCap_Social_Gaming_Research_Results.pdf

23   NPD Group. 20 percent of the population, or 56.8 Million U.S. consumers, reports having played a game on a social network. *Press Release.* August 23, 2010. Retrieved from: www.npd.com/press/releases/press_100823.html

24   Shipman, Claire, Kelly Hagan and Suzan Clarke. Betting the farm: FarmVille soars in popularity. *ABC Good Morning America.* September 6, 2010.Retrieved from: http://abcnews.go.com

25   2010 social gaming research. *PopCap Games: Information Solutions Group.*Retrieved from: www.infosolutionsgroup.com/2010_PopCap_Social_Gaming_Research_Results.pdf

26   Retrieved from: www.istrategylabs.com/2010/01/facebook-demographics-and-statistics-report-2010

27   Retrieved from: www.socialtimes.com

28   Jamison, Peter. FarmVillians: Steal someone else's game. Change its name. Make millions. Repeat. *San Francisco Weekly.* September 8, 2010. www.sfweekly.com/2010-09-08/news

29   Saint, Nick. Zynga's secret to success: Steal great ideas!" *Business Insider.* January 19, 2010. Retrieved from: www.businessinsider.com/how-zynga-is-just-like-microsoft-2010-1?slop=1

30   Jamison, Peter. FarmVillains. *San Francisco Weekly.* September 8, 2010. www.sfweekly.com/2010-09-08/news/farmvillains/2

31   Ashby, Alicia. Zynga and Playdom settle lawsuit. *Engage Digital.* November 23, 2010. Retrieved from: www.engagedigital.com/2010/11/23/zynga-and-playdom-settle-lawsuit

32   Carlson, Nicholas and Kamelia Angelova. Chart of the day: FarmVille-maker Zynga's revenues reach $600 million fueled by social obligation. *Business Insider.* April 26, 2010. www.businessinsider.com/chart-of-the-day-monthly-active-users-of-various-widgets-on-facebook-2010-4

33   Jamison, Peter. FarmVillains. *San Francisco Weekly.* September 8, 2010. Retrieved from: www.sfweekly.com/2010-09-08/news/farmvillains/2

34   Jamison, Peter. FarmVillains. *San Francisco Weekly.* September 8, 2010. Retrieved from: www.sfweekly.com/2010-09-08/news/farmvillains/2

35   Retrieved from: www.zynga.com/about/dmca.php

36   Jamison, Peter. FarmVillains. *San Francisco Weekly.* September 8, 2010. Retrieved from: www.sfweekly.com/2010-09-08/news/farmvillains/2

37   Zynga Blog »2008» July. *Zynga Blog.* Web. December 16, 2010. Retrieved from: http://zblog.zynga.com/?m=200807

38   Zynga. Retrieved from: www.zynga.com/about/timeline.php

39   Kushner, David. Why Zynga's success makes game designers gloomy. *Wired Magazine.* September 27, 2010. Retrieved from: www.wired.com/magazine/2010/09/pl_games_zynga/

40   O'Dell, Jolie. Startups that bucked the recession. *Forbes.com.* August 31, 2010. Retrieved from: www.forbes.com/2010/08/31/groupon-zynga-twitter-technology-startups.html

41   MacMillan, David. Zynga and Facebook. It's complicated – BusinessWeek. *BusinessWeek.* April 22, 2010. Retrieved from: www.businessweek.com/magazine/content/10_18/b4176047938855.htm

42   Zynga Press Room and Zynga Blog. Retrieved from: www.zynga.com/about/blog.php

43   Winda, By. Zynga's new Strategy Turns CityVille into boom town. *Technology.* December 14, 2010. Retrieved from: http://technolog.msnbc.msn.com/_news/2010/12/14/5649599-zyngas-new-strategy-turns-cityville-into-boom-town

44   World of warcraft subscriber base reaches 12 million worldwide. October 7, 2010. Retrieved from: http://us.blizzard.com/en-us/company/press/pressrelease.html?101007

45   Facebook and Zynga enter into five year partnership, expand use of Facebook credits. *TechCrunch.* May 18, 2010. Retrieved from: http://techcrunch.com/2010/05/18/facebook-and-zynga-enter-into-five-year-partnership-expand-use-of-facebook-credits

46   MacMillan, David. Zynga and Facebook. It's Complicated. *BusinessWeek.* April 22, 2010. Retrieved from: www.businessweek.com/magazine/content/10_18/b4176047938855.htm

47   McGarvey, Robert. Zynga draws record VC funding. June 28, 2010. Retrieved from: www.internetevolution.com/author.asp?section_id=852&doc_id=193697&f_src=internetevolution_gnews

48   Facebook now takes PayPal. *TechCrunch.* February 18, 2010. Retrieved from: http://techcrunch.com/2010/02/18/facebook-now-takes-paypal

49 Facebook and Zynga enter into five year partnership, expand use of facebook credits. *TechCrunch*. May 18, 2010. Retrieved from: http://techcrunch.com/2010/05/18/facebook-and-zynga-enter-into-five-year-partnership-expand-use-of-facebook-credits

50 McGarvey, Robert. Zynga draws record VC Funding. June 28, 2010. Retrieved from: www.internet evolution.com/author.asp?section_id=852&doc_id=193697&f_src=internetevolution_gnews

51 Jacksonville mom shakes baby for interrupting FarmVille, pleads guilty to murder. *Jacksonville.com*. October 27, 2010.

52 Jacksonville mom shakes baby for interrupting FarmVille, pleads guilty to murder. *Jacksonville.com*. October 27, 2010.

53 Shannon Johnson admits playing Facebook game as son drowned. *Huffingtonpost.com*. January 14, 2011. Retrieved from: www.huffingtonpost.com/2011/01/14/shannon-johnson-facebook-game_n_809170.html

54 Ashby, Alicia. Zynga and Playdom Settle Lawsuit. *Engage Digital*. November 23, 2010. Retrieved from: www.engagedigital.com/2010/11/23/zynga-and-playdom-settle-lawsuit

55 Ashby, Alicia. Zynga and Playdom settle lawsuit. *Engage Digital*. November 23, 2010. www.engagedigital.com/2010/11/23/zynga-and-playdom-settle-lawsuit

56 Parr, Ben. Zynga has more than 45 million daily active users. December, 2010. *Mashable/Social Media*. Retrieved from: http://mashable.com/2010/12/09/zynga-has-over-45-million-daily-active-users

Case 6

MINUTECLINICS

INTRODUCTION

Waking up with a sore throat was the last thing that Amber needed to start her workday. Worried that her condition might be strep throat, she called her doctor's office, but the after-hours answering service informed her that she would have to call back after 8:00 a.m. to make an appointment. When she finally got through to the receptionist, she was put on hold for five minutes, only to find out that the soonest available time slot was four weeks away! By then, her illness may have subsided—or worsened. And with only minor symptoms, going to the emergency room seemed like an expensive and unnecessary alternative. But what if she needed antibiotics or some other type of prescription to get better?

As of 2010, Amber's experience demonstrated the typical inconveniences faced by Americans when trying to handle routine medical issues. Even if an appointment could be scheduled, one- to two-hour waiting times in the lobby were a common occurrence.

Consequently, people were excited about the concept of "mini-clinics"—places where they could walk in, without any appointment, and get minor ailments treated at low cost. Known by names such as in-store clinics, walk-in clinics, retail clinics, convenience care clinics, onsite clinics, and "McClinics," this new option solved some of the most frustrating aspects of the patient experience.

MINI-CLINICS

Each mini-clinic was staffed by either a nurse practitioner or a physician assistant, not a doctor. No appointments were needed and most insurers covered the appointment costs. People could receive treatment for simple minor medical problems such as colds, ear infections, sore throats, bronchitis, or rashes. These clinics also administered immunizations and completed employment physicals. Nurse practitioners received physician oversight through routine chart reviews, consultations, and clinical protocols.

Unlike hospitals, mini-clinics did not treat any serious illnesses or injuries. Problems that required advanced procedures—such as taking X-rays, setting broken bones, or performing surgery—were still reserved for more well-equipped emergency rooms or urgent care centers.

The prices for services were transparent and were displayed on the websites and on the clinic walls, much like at a fast-food restaurant. The average price for a visit was $50 to $65, less than half of most Americans' co-pay to see their primary care physician, and less than a quarter for an emergency room visit. Mini-clinics did not necessarily compete directly against physicians, but rather worked with them. Conditions that were beyond the scope of services were referred to local doctors. Mini-clinics kept electronic records which could be given to the patient, or to the patient's doctor. Patients without a primary care doctor were given a list of neighborhood physicians who were accepting new patients.

Location and Hours

Mini-clinics were located in retail pharmacies, grocery stores, big-box discount stores, employer sites, and airports.[1] Those that were located in pharmacies had the additional benefit of allowing patients to have their prescriptions filled at that same location. Those that were located in retail stores had the advantage that patients could also run errands while there for their visit. People who had to wait could shop with a beeper in their hand to let them know when it was time for their consultation.

Most clinics were open 12 hours per day during the workweek and 8 hours per day during the weekend. Thus, they performed some of the same services that were once available only during business hours in physicians' offices. Since costly specialized capital-intensive equipment such as CAT scans, MRIs, and ultrasounds were not needed, mini-clinics required only a low-cost computer, diagnostic software, and rented furniture in a pre-existing retail space to get started. Most mini-clinics operated in less than 150 square feet.[2] No special additions or modifications to buildings, such as lead-lined walls, were needed. Thus, in 2007, starting a mini-clinic cost only $75,000–$100,000.[3]

Customer Response

Several studies confirmed what many patients already knew: the cost of using retail clinics was considerably lower than existing alternatives of primary care physicians or emergency rooms. One study showed that for the comprehensive treatments of five basic illnesses (sore throat, urinary tract infection, inflammation of the middle ear (otitis media), conjunctivitis, and acute sinusitis), a retail clinic visit cost $51 less than a trip to a primary care physician, and $279 less than a trip to the emergency room.[4] Another study, published in the *Annals of Internal Medicine* in 2009, compared the cost and quality of care given to patients with a urinary tract infection, pharyngitis, or otitis. They found that the cost of treatment for episodes initiated at mini-clinics was $110 compared to $166 at physician offices, $156 at urgent care centers, and $570 at emergency departments.[5] The quality score for mini-clinics was 63.6 versus 61.0 percent for physician offices, 62.6 percent for urgent care centers, and 55.1 percent for emergency departments.[6]

In a 2009 survey of healthcare consumers, the Deloitte Center for Health Solutions found that 12 percent of the respondents had used mini-clinics in the past 12 months, and 30 percent of those who responded would use mini-clinics if the cost of doing so was less than that of seeing their doctors.[7]

Not surprisingly, many customers, especially the uninsured, liked mini-clinics. Insurance companies also liked mini-clinics because they were less expensive than the other physician- and hospital-based alternatives. Some insurance companies went as far as waiving the co-pays for its members who used designated mini-clinics. In 2008, Blue Shield of Minnesota waived co-pays for using retail clinics, after realizing that going to the retail clinic instead of a primary care physician saved both the employer and insurance company money.[8] Because mini-clinics saved both time and money, many employers liked them too. In fact, as employee healthcare costs escalated, some firms began bringing mini-clinics on-site for their employees.

Opposition

Effectively, mini-clinics offered predictable services with many benefits including transparent prices, low costs, convenience, on-site pharmacies, and electronic medical records. However, there were still skeptics, especially from the established medical community. The American Medical Association (AMA), an association of medical doctors, argued that medical symptoms that looked trivial could actually be a signal of a serious problem, and therefore should not be left in the hands of a nurse practitioner or physician assistant. Some even went as far as arguing that nurse practitioners at mini-clinics attached to pharmacies might have an incentive to prescribe medicines unnecessarily to boost pharmacy sales. In some states, regulators argued that mini-clinics were a "compromise" to safe and effective care, and therefore did not accept them or limited the scope of their activities. As of 2010, mini-clinics operated in only 32 states.

However, rather than seeing them as a threat, some hospitals saw them as a tool to reduce their own costs. By law, emergency rooms could not turn uninsured patients away; therefore, mini-clinics could stop some simple problems that may otherwise have required emergency-room care and resources.

DISRUPTIVE INNOVATION? HEALTHCARE IN THE US

By one estimate, the US spent 17.3 percent of its GDP or $2.5 trillion ($8,047 per person) on healthcare in 2009, an increase of 6.8 percent from 2008. Yet, according to the World Health Organization (WHO), the quality of service was not the best in the world. Exhibit 6.1 shows the spending distribution. With growing concerns about the rising costs of medical care in the United States, some advocated that new, less expensive innovations were the solution. Innovations such as mini-clinics, General Electric's $1,000 handheld electrocardiogram and $15,000 personal-computer-based ultrasound machine, generated a lot of enthusiasm for those focused upon cutting costs. Thus, the slow-down in the number of new clinics seemed to curtail progress. In July 2009, there were 1,107 mini-clinic outlets in the United States compared to 960 a year earlier.[9] Exhibit 6.2 shows the number of clinics opened in the United States since 2006.

MINUTECLINICS

The first MinuteClinics, formerly known as QuickMedx centers, opened their doors in May 2000 in Cub Foods stores in the Minneapolis–St. Paul area. The idea for the centers had come to co-founder Rick Krieger a year earlier when he took his sick son to an urgent care center in Minneapolis for a strep throat test and had to wait for two hours on a weekend in winter. In 2002, Rick and his co-founders, Douglas Smith (MD), Steve Pontius and Kevin Smith (RN, FNP) changed the name of their treatment centers to "MinuteClinics." In 2006, the company was bought by CVS Caremark Corporation, the parent company of CVS/pharmacy and Caremark Pharmacy Services.

Staffing

As of August 2010, MinuteClinic had 500 walk-in clinics inside CVS pharmacy stores in 26 states and Washington, DC.[10] Each clinic was staffed by a physician assistant or nurse practitioner. A physician assistant was a person who was licensed to practice medicine under the supervision of a physician. With a few exceptions, physician assistants had master's degrees in Physician Assistant Studies (MPAS), Health Science (MHS), or Medical Science (MMSc). Some had the Doctor of Science Physician Assistant, or DScPA. A nurse practitioner was a registered nurse who completed an accredited master of science in nursing (MSN) program and passed a national certification exam. See Exhibit 6.3 for the list of activities that physician assistants and nurse practitioners were qualified to perform.

Operations and Pricing

MinuteClinics were located primarily at CVS pharmacies. They were open seven days a week, typically 8 am to 8 pm Monday through Friday, 9 am to 6 pm on Saturdays, and 10 am to 5 pm on Sundays. No appointments were necessary and a typical examination took 10 to 15 minutes. Their activities were transparent. The conditions treated and their prices, as well as the procedures followed during a visit, were clearly displayed on their website (Exhibit 6.4).[11] Electronic medical records were maintained on each patient so that there was continuity of care to the next stage, be it the primary physician, emergency room, or any other type of care requested by the patient.

Insurance and Miscellaneous

In Q4 2009, over 80 percent of MinuteClinic's business was third-party-paid, while CVS Caremark's investment in the MinuteClinic business was $0.05– $0.06 per share.[12] In the second quarter of 2010, the company saw a 36 percent rise in patient visits compared to the same period in 2009.[13] In April 2010, MinuteClinic became the first mini-clinic to start monitoring patients who had been diagnosed with asthma, diabetes, high blood pressure, and high cholesterol levels. The clinics performed lab tests and exams to monitor these conditions for patients between visits to their primary care physicians or for those patients who did not regularly receive care.

Competitors

In 2009, MinuteClinic had a 41 percent market share. Main competitors in the mini-clinic industry included: Take Care (31 percent), The Little Clinic (9 percent), Target Clinic (3 percent), Wal-Mart (3 percent), RediClinic (2 percent), and other one-off locations (11 percent).[14] All competitors offered similar services and fee schedules, and even advertised the same consumer benefits, such as the lack of waiting and affordability, on their websites and marketing materials.

As of 2010, the industry was still fairly new and not yet established nationwide. Accordingly, each company was best differentiated by their locations rather than by their services. Some brands operated only within a few states or in affiliation with a particular store. For example, Take Care Clinics operated within Walgreens, while The Little Clinic operated in different grocery store chains, such as Publix and Kroger, within a handful of states. Similarly, RediClinic only operated in Texas in affiliation with the HEB grocery store chain. Interestingly, Wal-Mart Clinics were branded under the Wal-Mart name, but all of their mini-clinics were owned by independent health care providers based on the location.

THE FUTURE OF LOW-COST HEALTH CARE

As more people and organizations looked for alternatives to traditional primary care physicians, new health care solutions became potential competitors for mini-clinics. For instance, in 2009, Hawaii became the first state to launch Online Care.[15] Launched as a partnership between American Well and Hawaii Medical Service Association (HMSA), this new service offered Hawaii residents all-hours access to physicians over the Internet.

Members of HMSA's insurance could have an online Web session with a doctor for only $10, while non-members paid $45.[16] Unlike mini-clinics where the care provider was a physician assistant or nurse practitioner, Hawaii's online medical services linked patients to doctors in specialties including general practice, family practice, cardiology, psychiatry, and more.[17] If the patient's issue could not be resolved over the Internet session, the patient was referred to a doctor for an in-person visit.

Conclusion

As the US population continues to age and the country faces a number of critical healthcare issues, the concept of mini-clinics becomes an even more attractive alternative to congested, slow, and expensive primary care physicians. By scaling back the patients' experience to expedite the steps from diagnosis to treatment; mini-clinics have cured the major pain points for Americans dealing with everyday medical ailments.

But will the opposition from physicians curtail the success of mini-clinics? Will state legislations prevent mini-clinics from further expanding? Will even cheaper online alternatives undercut the success that mini-clinics have enjoyed?

NOTES

1   Big-box stores are supercenters, superstore, and megastore. These are the physically large retail establishments such as Wal-Mart, Carrrefour, Target, etc.
2   Sturm, Arthur C., Jr. Miniclinics: trend, threat, or opportunity? All Business. January 1, 2006. Retrieved on January 16, 2011 from www.allbusiness.com/marketing/channel-marketing/857114-1.html
3   McGirt, Ellen. 2007. Fast-Food medicine. Fast Company.com, December 19, 2007. Retrieved on August 15, 2010 from www.fastcompany.com/magazine/118/fast-food-medicine.html
4   Thygeson, M., Van Vorst, K.A., Maciosek, M.V., and Solberg L. 2008. Use and costs of care in retail clinics versus traditional care sites, *Health Affairs*, 27(5): 1283–1292.
5   Mehrotra Ateey (MD) et al. 2009. Comparing costs and quality of care at retail clinics with that of other medical settings for 3 common illnesses. *Annals of Internal Medicine*, 151: 321–328.
6   Authors used well-established quality measures used in the medical field. See Mehrotra Ateey (MD) et al. 2009. Comparing costs and quality of care at retail clinics with that of other medical settings for 3 common illnesses. *Annals of Internal Medicine*, 151: 321–328.
7   Keckley, P.H. Underwood, H.R. Ganhi, M. 2009. Retail clinics: Update and implications. Deloitte Center for Health Solutions. Retrieved August 14, 2010 from www.deloitte.com/assets/Dcom-UnitedStates/Local%20Assets/Documents/us_chs_RetailClinics_111209.pdf
8   Enrado, P. 2008. Blues plan supports retail health use. *Healthcare Finance News*, August 27, 2008. Retrieved August 15, 2010 from www.healthcarefinancenews.com/news/blues-plan-supports-retail-health-use

9   Keckley, P.H. Underwood, H.R. Ganhi, M. 2009. Retail clinics: Update and implications. Deloitte Center for Health Solutions. Retrieved August 14, 2010 from www.deloitte.com/assets/Dcom-UnitedStates/Local%20Assets/Documents/us_chs_RetailClinics_111209.pdf

10   CVS Caremark Press Release. August 2, 2010. Retrieved August 14, 2010 from http://investor.cvs.com/phoenix.zhtml?c=99533&p=irol-newsArticle&ID=1455064&highlight

11   For services, see www.minuteclinic.com/services/ and for pricing, see www.minuteclinic.com/services

12   CVS Caremark Corporation Q2 2010 Earnings Call Transcript, July 29, 2010. Retrieved August 14, 2010 from http://seekingalpha.com/article/217241-cvs-caremark-corporation-q2-2010-earnings-call-transcript

13   CVS Caremark Corporation Q2 2010 Earnings Call Transcript, July 29, 2010. Retrieved August 14, 2010 from http://seekingalpha.com/article/217241-cvs-caremark-corporation-q2-2010-earnings-call-transcript

14   CVS Caremark Corporation Q4 2009 Earnings Call Transcript, February 8, 2010. Retrieved August 15, 2010 from http://seekingalpha.com/article/187379-cvs-caremark-corporation-q4-2009-earnings-call-transcript

15   Lott, Laura. Hawaii launches online health care through HMSA. Hawaii Health Guide.com January 17, 2009. Retrieved January 15, 2011 from http://hawaiihealthguide.com/healthtalk/display.htm?id=726

16   Wicklund, Eric. Hawaii debuts new online care service for all residents. *Healthcare IT News*. January 16, 2009. Retrieved January 20, 2011 from www.healthcareitnews.com/news/hawaii-debuts-new-online-care-service-all-residents

17   Lott, Laura. Hawaii launches online health care through HMSA. Hawaii Health Guide.com January 17, 2009. Retrieved January 15, 2011 from http://hawaiihealthguide.com/healthtalk/display.htm?id=726

Exhibit 6.1 Healthcare spending in the US

Item	Share of spending %
Hospital care	31
Physician services	21
Pharmaceuticals	10
Nursing homes	8
Administrative costs	7
Diagnostic and laboratory testing, pharmacies, medical device manufacturers, etc.	23

Source: Wikipedia. (2010). Health care in the United States. Retrieved August 18, 2010 from http://en.wikipedia.org/wiki/Health_care_in_the_United_States

Exhibit 6.2 Number of mini-clinics in the US

Month	Mini-clinics	Month	Mini-clinics
October 2006	202	February 2009	1,185
April 2007	424	March 2009	1,188
July 2007	521	April 2009	1,111
October 2007	710	May 2009	1,118
December 2007	868	June 2009	1,111
April 2008	964	July 2009	1,107
July 2008	969	August 2009	1,125
August 2008	981	September 2009	1,110
September 2008	1,028	October 2009	1,142
October 2008	1,066	November 2009	1,154
November 2008	1,104	December 2009	1,172
December 2008	1,135	January 2010	1,183
January 2009	1,175	February 2010	1,197

Source: Merchant Medicine. Retrieved from: www.merchantmedicine.com/home.cfm

Exhibit 6.3 What nurse practitioners and physician assistants are qualified to do

- Diagnose and treat common illnesses and minor injuries.
- Prescribe medication.
- Obtain medical histories.
- Perform physical assessments and examinations.
- Perform and interpret diagnostic and laboratory studies.
- Counsel and teach health and nutrition.
- Screen and refer patients to specialists and other health care providers.
- Provide education to allow patients to make decisions about their own health.

Source: MinuteClinic's website: www.minuteclinic.com/en/USA/About/Quality/Qualified-Clinicians.aspx

Exhibit 6.4 MinuteClinics' services and costs, August 19, 2010

Minor illness exam ($69 except where indicated)	Allergy symptoms Body aches Cough Earache Ear wax removal $59	Flu-like symptoms $69–$129 Itchy eyes Motion sickness prevention Nasal congestion	Pink eye Sinus symptoms Sore throat $69–$122 Urinary tract infection symptoms $69–$84
Minor injury exam ($69 except where indicated)	Blisters Burns Bug bites and stings Corneal abrasions	Jellyfish stings Lacerations Splinters	Sprains (ankle, knee) Suture and staple removal Wounds and abrasions
Skin condition exam ($69 except where indicated)	Acne Athlete's foot Chicken pox Cold and canker sores Infections (minor) Lice	Oral/mouth sores Poison ivy Rashes (minor) Ringworm Scabies	Shingles Styes Sunburn (minor) Swimmer's itch Wart treatment $69–$109
Wellness and prevention $19– $104	Asthma screening $69–$102 EpiPen refill $49 Pregnancy evaluation $69–$89 Smoking cessation $19–$29 TB (Tuberculosis) testing $27	Health screening package $94–$104 Cholesterol screening $59 Diabetes screening Glucose $44 Diabetes screening HbA1c $54 Blood pressure screening $29 Weight evaluation $29	Physical exams Camp physical $35 (reg. $69) College physical $35 (reg. $69) DOT physical $84 Sports physical $35 (reg. $69)
Vaccinations $29.95–$147	DTaP (Diphtheria, tetanus, pertussis) $82 Flu (seasonal) $29.95 Hepatitis A (adult) $117 Hepatitis A (child) $97	Hepatitis B (adult) $102 Hepatitis B (child) $102 Meningitis $147 MMR (measles, mumps, rubella) $116	Pneumonia $77 Polio (IPV) $96 TD (tetanus, diphtheria) $76 Tdap (tetanus, diphtheria, pertussis) $92
Health condition monitoring $69– $114	Asthma monitoring $102 Diabetes monitoring $69–$114 High blood-pressure monitoring $69–$99 High cholesterol monitoring $69–$99		

Source: MinuteClinics website: www.minuteclinic.com/services retrieved August 19, 2010

Case 7

SWATCH: THE BATTLES OF TIME*

INTRODUCTION

Nicolas George Hayek, the former CEO and chairman of the Swatch Group, passed away on June 28, 2010. In the 1980s, Hayek created a new-game business model under the name brand "Swatch" that saved the Swiss watchmaking industry from being overtaken by Japanese competition.

In 2010, the economic crisis again threatened the Swiss watchmaking industry. Without Hayek's visionary leadership, many were left wondering if the Swiss's prized industry would be able to survive.

THE SWISS WATCH INDUSTRY BACKGROUND

Geneva, Switzerland, was long known as the center of the jewelry industry. In the mid-16th century, a provision known as the "Ordonnances Ecclésiastiques" banned the wearing of jewelry. As a result, most of the goldsmiths who possessed the knowledge and skill of jewelry making changed their profession to watchmaking.[1]

For the Swiss, the two important standards for manufacturing and assembling watches were the aesthetics of the exterior elements as well as the accuracy and reliability of the timepieces. Therefore, producing a Swiss watch required a high level of mechanical skills, precision, and craftsmanship. A typical watch consisted of more than one hundred components, and jewels were used to accentuate the watch and later became a sign of quality.[2] For the Swiss, possessing a watch demonstrated status and prestige. Therefore, buying a watch was considered to be a financial investment, as a good watch could be handed down for several generations.

Through the mid-19th century, Swiss watches were sold exclusively through jewelry stores and up-scale department stores.[3] Watch repair was also an ongoing source of

---

* This case was written by Xiaoqi Wang, Achariya Leevanichayakul, Jing Cao, Koji Nakajima, and Shana Anderson under the supervision of Professor Allan Afuah as a basis for class discussion and is not intended to illustrate either effective or ineffective handling of a business situation.

revenue for retailers.[4] The prestigious Swiss brands such as Rolex, Omega, Movado, Piaget, and Longines appeared in the watch market during the 18th and 19th centuries.[5] Exhibit 7.1 shows the value chain for Swiss watchmaking. By 1945, the Swiss brands dominated the watch industry and acquired around 80 percent of global market share.[6]

QUARTZ REVOLUTION BY JAPANESE WATCH COMPANY "SEIKO"

From the 1950s until around the 1970s, Swiss watchmakers enjoyed their domination of the global market. In 1969, a Japanese watch company, Hattori-Seiko (later known as Seiko Corporation), created the world's first quartz wristwatch, named the Quartz Astron.[7]

The early quartz watches were considered inferior technology to Swiss standards in both their aesthetic and functional aspects. The electronic circuits were power hungry, which resulted in short-lived batteries. Moreover, the watches lacked durability, and therefore became unreliable from wear and tear. In 1976, the return rate for quartz watches was as high as 30 percent.[8]

However, Japanese watch manufacturers continuously improved their technology by responding to customer dissatisfaction. By 1976, quartz technology was regarded as the most accurate timekeeping technology available to customers.[9] Moreover, compared with mechanical Swiss watches, quartz watches had fewer components. This simplicity offered an additional benefit: people could easily clean and repair quartz watches, and could therefore handle them more aggressively than Swiss ones.

Perhaps the greatest differentiator between Swiss watches and quartz watches was their prices. Quartz watches were significantly cheaper. Whereas the making of mechanical watches required sophisticated craftsmanship, quartz watches could be mass produced, and as the demand for quartz watches increased, manufacturing costs declined even further.

Ironically, Swiss companies had experimented with quartz technology even before the Japanese.[10] However, Swiss watchmakers had hesitated to adopt quartz technology because they feared it would dilute the reputation of luxurious and mechanical Swiss watches. Their reluctance to consider quartz hurt their position in the market, and they were quickly overtaken by Japanese low-cost newcomers like Seiko.

Established in 1881, Seiko was one of the leading Japanese watchmakers. The company name, Seiko, means both "success" and "high quality" in Japanese. Its name echoed its philosophy: "Offering good quality products and services with the consistent emphasis placed on a customer-oriented approach."[11]

Seiko marketed its quartz watches by emphasizing affordability via huge marketing campaigns. With the increased competition from quartz watchmakers, Switzerland lost its leader position and was no longer able to compete with Seiko and other incoming watchmakers, including those in Hong Kong.[12]

OVERTHROW OF THE SWISS WATCH INDUSTRY

During the two decades following the entrance of Japanese competition in the watchmaking industry, the Swiss faced further declines. The Swiss worldwide market share declined from 80 percent in 1946 to 42 percent in the 1970s (and fell even further thereafter), whereas the global demand for watches kept rising.[13] The classic "innovator's dilemma" almost killed the Swiss watch industry.[14]

The Swiss continued to resist the movement to quartz technology for fear that it would cannibalize their existing product lines. Additionally, the high fragmentation within the Swiss market further challenged their ability to cohesively adopt new technology. Two companies, ASUAG and SSIH, dominated the market; however, these two companies represented more than one hundred separate brands.[15] In total, over 1,600 firms crowded the Swiss watchmaking industry.[16] The lack of a consistent strategy and the decentralized research and development, marketing, and manufacturing of each brand made it impossible to compete with the Asian competitors that focused on high-volume production.

Without any response to Japanese competitors, the global market share of Swiss watch companies kept shrinking. In order to maintain their profit margins, the Swiss regularly increased prices, while their foreign competitors established large market shares in low- and mid-price ranges. As a result, Swiss companies were forced to abandon those two segments and remain isolated at the high-end segment of the market, which was declining due to its reliance on traditional craftsmanship.

The reluctance of the Swiss companies to adopt quartz technology almost affected the financial viability of the whole industry in the late 1970s to early 1980s. The export of watches shrank from 94 million in 1974 to 43 million in 1983, and the worldwide market share also shrank from 43 percent to less than 15 percent during the same period.[17] The number of firms declined from over 1,600 to around 600 due to bankruptcies.[18]

RENAISSANCE OF THE SWISS WATCH INDUSTRY: NO TIME TO LOSE

In 1983, both SSIH and ASUAG faced insolvency and were taken over by Swiss creditor banks.[19] The banks almost sold prestigious Swiss brand names to Japanese competitors.[20] Nevertheless, Nicolas Hayek, the chief advisor of the nation's watch industry and the CEO of Hayek Engineering, a consulting firm based in Zurich, assessed the chances of survival of these two companies and recommended the merger of SSIH and ASUAG.[21] Hayek became the CEO of the merged entity named Société Suisse de Microélectronique et d'Horlogerie (SMH).

The New Swiss Strategy: Swatch

Under Hayek's management, the strategy of SMH was shifted to create a portfolio of global and profitable brands in every product segment, particularly in the low-end segment. Hayek stated that if the Swiss could not have a strong position in the low-end, they could not control the quality and cost in other segments.[22] Realizing the importance of the low-end market, Hayek executed his strategy under the brand name "Swatch."

Swatch ("Swiss"+ "Watch") was a real revolution, breaking Swiss tradition. Swatch was the low-end product equipped with quartz technology. It was designed to strip off several attributes of the classic Swiss watch to reduce the manufacturing costs to Asian levels. This mass-market product was encased in cheap plastic. Swatch was priced as low as $40.[23] In spite of these characteristics, Swatch distinguished itself from other low-end commodity products by focusing upon "design and image." As Hayek told The New York Times, "We were convinced that if each of us could add our fantasy and culture to an emotional product, we could beat anybody. Emotions are something that nobody can copy."[24] Swatch infused the idea of youthful individualism into its watches. Thus, customer self-image became entwined with the design, engaging owners with its product. In addition, the reputable "Swiss Made" label allowed Swatch to sell at a premium relative to its low-end competitors.

In 1983, the first Swatch watches were launched with immediate success. They became popular fashion accessories for the masses. In 1985, 70 million units were sold, accounting for 80 percent of SMH's total unit sales.[25] Most of Swatch's fans were young people who had never shown interest in watches before. Moreover, with the bright colors, endless creativity, affordable prices, and unique designs with 70 models each year, the Swatch watch became an instant collectible.[26]

In 1990, the company created a Swatch Collector Club, which attracted more than 50,000 members within the first year. With an annual membership fee of $90, the members received an exclusive collector Swatch watch each year, as well as the "Swatch Street Journal" which provided the latest news about Swatch and pop-culture trends.[27]

Swatch Design

We have no set routines to come up with ideas. We travel constantly, all over the world. We go to the big fashion shows. We go to the opera, to art exhibitions. You can't imagine how many books and magazines we read, how many painters we study. We steep ourselves in the culture of life. And then things happen.

(Franco Bosisio, the head of the Swatch design lab)[28]

It was the design of the Swatch that differentiated it from its competitors. The Swatch's great success came from the definition of the watch as a fashion accessory as much as a timekeeping device. Built inside a brightly colored and stylish body, the plastic watch touched the heart of young customers who desired to distinguish their own unique personalities.

Swatch updated the collection and models frequently. Every year, two collections with 70 models each were offered to customers. All the models were designed in a lab located in Milan, Italy, the center of fashion. Coming from different backgrounds and different countries, the designers in the Milan lab inspired numerous popular models. To stay on top of leading trends in fashion, designers were rotated through the Swatch lab frequently and few of them worked there for more than two years.[29]

Manufacture

If we can design a manufacturing process in which direct labor accounts for less than 10% of total costs, there is nothing to stop us from building a product in Switzerland, the most expensive country in the world. Nothing.

(Nicolas Hayek, CEO of Swatch Group)[30]

More than two decades ago, the original Swatch team asked a crazy question: "Why can't we design a striking, low-cost, high-quality watch and build it in Switzerland?" Yes, "build" in Switzerland—where the junior secretary cost more than the senior engineer in Thailand and Malaysia. The strategy was highly suspect to banks, investors, and even suppliers. Yet, the company did it.

Given the high cost of Swiss labor, Swatch could achieve this objective only by making radical changes in the product itself and the production process. First, Swatch used plastic instead of traditional metal and leather for cases and belts, respectively. Second, Swatch adopted quartz movement, replacing older mechanical movement. Third, the engineers simplified the inner design of the watch, slashing the number of required parts from 91 to 51.[31] Fourth, newer and cheaper assembly techniques were developed. Instead of screws, the watch was sealed by using ultrasonic techniques. Taking all the improvements together, the company was able to produce the Swatch on a fully automated production line, which reduced the ratio of direct cost to total costs from 30 to 10 percent.[32] Considering that most of the customers preferred the "Swiss Made" label and were willing to pay a 10 percent premium for it, the disadvantage of high labor costs in Switzerland was no longer an obstacle.[33]

Marketing and Distribution

Everything we do and the way we do everything sends a message.
(Nicolas Hayek, CEO of Swatch Group)[34]

Realizing that accurate time-keeping was no longer the most important differentiator between watches, the Swatch team decided to focus on creating artistic and emotional products. Hayek believed that Swatch's ability to capture emotions could not be duplicated by competitors.[35] However, in addition to fanciful design, the company still needed to convey that their watches were high-quality, low-cost, provocative, and exuberant.

In the upstream marketing activities, the trendy and fashion-forward image was achieved by linking Swatch product launches to fashion shows and celebrity endorsement programs. The company also sponsored high-profile special events to promote the brand. For example, Swatch was listed in the *Guinness Book of World Records* for the 13-ton 500-foot high Swatch at the headquarters of Commerzbank in Frankfurt, Germany.[36]

On the retail and distribution side, the company vertically integrated downstream by opening hundreds of Swatch shops. In department stores, the company set up shop-in-shop systems that focused exclusively on the Swatch brand. The company also focused on travel by putting kiosks in main airports. Exhibit 7.1 summarizes the company's value chain.

A DECADE LATER: THE NEW CHALLENGE

As mentioned earlier, the 21st century brought new challenges, including a large worldwide economic recession. Almost all watchmakers have encountered a large drop in sales revenue. The Swatch Group's sales revenues dropped by 9.4 percent in 2009.[37] Overall, export growth of Swiss watches dropped by almost 30 percent, especially in the high-end segment. In 2010, Marc Alexander Hayek, the grandson of Nicolas George Hayek, was appointed as the new CEO of the Swatch Group. The question became whether Swatch Group would be able to gain victory in this new type of battle.

Exhibit 7.1 Value chain of Swiss watch industry before the quartz crisis

Technology	Product design	Manufacturing	Marketing	Distribution	Service
Micromechanical technology Jewelry maker	Durable Luxurious Craftsmanship	More than 100 parts Craftsmanship Precious metal case Jewelry ornament Fragmented suppliers all over the country	Discreet promotion Targeting upscale demographic "Swiss Made" advantage	Jewelers Upscale department stores	After-service Repair Maintenance

Source: Case writers' estimates.

Exhibit 7.2 Value chain of Swatch

Technology	Product design	Manufacturing	Marketing	Distribution	Service
Quartz technology Electronics technology	Simple Disposable Fashionable	Reduced to 51 parts Automatic line Direct labor costs < 10% Plastic case Ultrasonic seal Vertical integration	Fashion shows Celebrity endorsements Special events Collector's club	Shop-in-shop Swatch stores Travel sectors	1-year warranty No repair No maintenance

Source: Case writers' estimates.

NOTES

1 Ram Mudambi. 2005. Branding time: Swatch and global brand management. The Richard J. Fox School of Business and Management.
2 Cyril Bouquet. 1999. Swatch and the global watch industry. Richard Ivey School of Business.
3 Cyril Bouquet. 1999. Swatch and the global watch industry. Richard Ivey School of Business.
4 Cyril Bouquet. 1999. Swatch and the global watch industry. Richard Ivey School of Business.
5 Youngme Moon. 2004. The birth of Swatch. Harvard Business School.
6 Youngme Moon. 2004. The birth of Swatch. Harvard Business School.
7 Seiko Quartz Astron 35SQ. The watch that revolutionized horological history. December 1969. Retrieved from: http://global.epson.com/company/milestones/05_35sq.htm
8 Carlene Stephens and Maggie Dennis. 2000. *Engineering Time: Inventing the Electronic Wristwatch.* Cambridge University Press.
9 Carlene Stephens and Maggie Dennis. 2000. *Engineering Time: Inventing the Electronic Wristwatch.* Cambridge University Press.
10 Ram Mudambi. 2005. Branding time: Swatch and global brand management. The Richard J. Fox School of Business and Management.
11 Seiko company website "About Us" retrieved from: www.seiko.co.jp/en/corporate/philosophy/index.php
12 Ram Mudambi. 2005. Branding time: Swatch and global brand management. The Richard J. Fox School of Business and Management.
13 Case study on Swatch. Retrieved on November 26, 2010 from www.scribd.com/doc/35656270/Swatch-Watch-A-Case-Study
14 Clayton M. Christensen. 1997. *The Innovator's Dilemma When New Technologies Cause Great Firms to Fail.* Harvard Business Press.

15 Youngme Moon. 2004. The birth of Swatch. Harvard Business School
16 Cyril Bouquet. 1999. Swatch and the global watch industry. Richard Ivey School of Business
17 Gabor George Burt. 2009. Getting the Blue Ocean strategic sequence right. Retrieved November 29, 2010 from http://blueoceanstrategy.typepad.com/creatingblueoceans/2009/04/blue-ocean-strategy-strategic-sequence-step-four.html
18 Ram Mudambi. 2005. Branding time: Swatch and global brand management. The Richard J. Fox School of Business and Management.
19 Ram Mudambi. 2005. Branding time: Swatch and global brand management. The Richard J. Fox School of Business and Management.
20 Ram Mudambi. 2005. Branding time: Swatch and global brand management. The Richard J. Fox School of Business and Management.
21 Ram Mudambi. 2005. Branding time: Swatch and global brand management. The Richard J. Fox School of Business and Management.
22 Ram Mudambi. 2005. Branding time: Swatch and global brand management. The Richard J. Fox School of Business and Management.
23 Cyril Bouquet. 1999. Swatch and the global watch industry. Richard Ivey School of Business.
24 Ram Mudambi. 2005. Branding time: Swatch and global brand management. The Richard J. Fox School of Business and Management (p. 5).
25 Cyril Bouquet. 1999. Swatch and the global watch industry. Richard Ivey School of Business.
26 Youngme Moon. 2004. The birth of the Swatch. Harvard Business School. Note: the annual membership fee in 2010 was $24.
27 Cyril Bouquet. 1999. Swatch and the global watch industry. Richard Ivey School of Business.
28 Robert Howard. 1993. *The Learning Imperative: Managing People for Continuous Innovation.* Harvard Business Press.
29 Robert Howard. 1993. *The Learning Imperative: Managing People for Continuous Innovation.* Harvard Business Press (p. 65).
30 Robert Howard. 1993. *The Learning Imperative: Managing People for Continuous Innovation.* Harvard Business Press (p. 60).
31 Robert Howard. 1993. *The Learning Imperative: Managing People for Continuous Innovation.* Harvard Business Press.
32 Robert Howard. 1993. *The Learning Imperative: Managing People for Continuous Innovation.* Harvard Business Press.
33 Robert Howard. 1993. *The Learning Imperative: Managing People for Continuous Innovation.* Harvard Business Press.
34 Robert Howard. 1993. *The Learning Imperative: Managing People for Continuous Innovation.* Harvard Business Press (p. 68).
35 Ram Mudambi. 2005. Branding time: Swatch and global brand management. The Richard J. Fox School of Business and Management.
36 Ram Mudambi. 2005. Branding time: Swatch and global brand management. The Richard J. Fox School of Business and Management.
37 Wright Comparative Business Analysis Report, report date: October 29, 2010.

Case 8

ESPERION: DRANO FOR YOUR ARTERIES?*

Dr. Roger Newton sat in his car after leaving the office for the day, and paused before turning the ignition and heading home. It was late November in 2003, and Esperion Therapeutics, the company Dr. Newton founded, had just received an offer from Pfizer to buy the company for $1.3 billion. He smiled a little, remembering several years earlier when he was recognized by Warner-Lambert (which was later purchased by Pfizer) for developing the world's most successful drug—Lipitor. Along with the award, Dr. Newton was provided with a cash prize: $20,000. Times had certainly changed, and the award for guiding Esperion through the development of several novel cardiovascular compounds had obviously grown significantly. Dr. Newton and his team invested time, money, and a great deal of thought and effort into Esperion, and while the financial offer from Pfizer was significant, he worried whether now was the right time to be acquired. Esperion had just announced very positive clinical data for its lead candidate, and its novel method of addressing high cholesterol was generating interest in both the scientific and business communities. Was now the right time to sell, or should Esperion push on and build itself into a fully integrated biotech company? Was Pfizer the right suitor, or was there another company that could better help continue Esperion's success? And what would happen to Esperion if it was acquired—to the people who had founded and built the company, and developed the molecules so highly regarded today? Dr. Newton turned his key and pulled out of Esperion's parking lot. He had several weeks to evaluate Pfizer's offer, and would need the time to fully think through his options.

CHOLESTEROL

Cholesterol is a natural substance used in the body for a variety of purposes from cell membrane formation to the makeup of hormones. The liver makes most of the cholesterol

---

* This case was written by Brian Levy, Melissa Vasilev, Jess Rosenbloom, Scott Peterson, and Patrick Lyon under the supervision of Professor Allan Afuah as a basis for class discussion and is not intended to illustrate either effective or ineffective handling of a business situation.

a person needs; however, it is also found in many foods and is an inherent part of many diets. Cholesterol levels result from both genetic and dietetic influences. While genetic influences are beyond an individual's control, lifestyle choices that are marked by fatty foods and a lack of exercise serve to increase cholesterol levels for many people.

Cholesterol is transported through the bloodstream when it is coupled with special carriers called lipoproteins. Low-density lipoprotein (LDL), often referred to as "bad" cholesterol, transports cholesterol from the liver to the body's cells for use. High-density lipoprotein (HDL), often referred to as "good" cholesterol, removes cholesterol and other lipids (fats) from arterial walls and other tissues, transporting them to the liver where they are eliminated from the body.

Complications from Cholesterol

Excessive levels of LDL can lead to the buildup of cholesterol and other fats in the walls of arteries, a condition known as atherosclerosis, causing a progressive narrowing of arterial walls. If unchecked, these deposits can eventually form a plaque. If a plaque ruptures and a clot forms, potentially blocking an artery, a heart attack can result. A heart attack may also result if excessive amounts of plaque form in the arteries that deliver blood to the heart, known as coronary arteries, slowly starving the heart muscle of oxygen needed to function. This set of complications is also collectively known as coronary artery disease and is the number one cause of death in the United States (Exhibit 8.1).

High LDL also increases the chances of stroke. Like dislodged plaque blocking a coronary artery of the heart, if a clot cuts blood flow to the brain, serious nervous system damage or even death may occur. Further, increased blood pressure from high LDL also poses the risk that sensitive arteries near the brain may burst, resulting in nervous system damage or death.

Treatment Options

To treat high LDL levels and reduce the likelihood of the associated health risks doctors had several options at their disposal. Base recommendations always included diets that were low in saturated fat and an increase in physical exercise. However, lifestyle changes alone were rarely enough to reduce more elevated patient LDL levels. Physicians often chose from the following options to further reduce the risks posed by cholesterol:

Pharmaceuticals (statins)—If LDL levels had not dropped enough after 6–12 months of lifestyle changes, physicians recommended a drug called a statin that works to reduce LDL levels. Statins interfere with the liver's ability to produce cholesterol and, depending upon the particular patient, some statins may actually serve to increase HDL production slightly.

Angioplasty—For patients with more advanced and potentially acute atherosclerosis, a doctor may have elected for an invasive solution to counter the effects of plaque in arteries. An angioplasty is a surgical procedure in which a surgeon inserts a small tube or balloon at the spot of arterial blockage. The balloon is inflated, expanding the artery allowing for greater blood flow.

Stents—If an angioplasty was done on coronary arteries, standard procedure included the placing of a stent. A stent is a small metal scaffold that expands and supports the arterial wall to allow for greater blood flow. Stents are left in the patient after the angioplasty procedure to ensure greater long-term blood flow. Some stents, called drug-eluting stents, are coated with specialized pharmaceutical compounds to prevent future blockages, a condition known as restenosis.

THE CARDIOVASCULAR DRUG MARKET

The cholesterol drug market in 2003 was the world's largest pharmaceutical market, generating $17 billion annually and expected to grow at a 5 percent compound annual growth rate (CAGR) through 2010.[1] While the market comprised three therapeutic classes—statins, resins, and fibrates—the statin class dominated treatment, comprising 90 percent of dollar volume. Within the statin market, an oligopoly competed fiercely: Pfizer, Bristol-Meyers Squibb, and Merck promoted Lipitor, Pravachol, and Zocor against each other, generating $8, $2.2, and $5.5 billion (respectively).[2] With each drug having a similar efficacy and safety profile, companies utilized their significant cardio-vascular experience to apply large sales forces, high marketing spend, and exhaustive post-approval clinical trial strategies to differentiate drugs to cardiologists.

While heavy market development was helping to grow the hypolipemic market, several additional characteristics were expected to contribute to the market's growth. Recent updates to treatment guidelines encouraged physicians to pursue lower target lipid levels in their patients, causing upward titration in statin dosage. Additionally, the first combination product—Zetia—had recently been launched, offering a complementary treatment to be added to ongoing statin use to increase efficacy (raising the overall cost of treatment), and additional combination treatments were expected. Lastly, patient demographics were expected to contribute to growing the incidence of cardiovascular diseases worldwide: aging populations, and increasingly unhealthy eating habits in the US and Europe were driving the overall number of possible patients significantly.[3]

While patient populations and new therapeutic guidelines were growing the hypolipemic market, two issues did threaten the market's growth. Zocor, Pravachol, and Lipitor all faced patent expiry by 2010, and the entrance of generic forms of these drugs (typically at 10–20 percent of branded patent prices) would erode branded sales of these drugs significantly. Additionally, patient compliance with statin regimens was a continuing issue. Because statins were prescribed as a preventative measure (prior to a heart attack or other major health event), patients often did not recognize the importance these drugs played in continuing their health—they often did not adhere to the recommended treatment frequency that physicians recommended, adversely affecting sales.

THE PHARMACEUTICAL DEVELOPMENT PROCESS

With several well-entrenched, well-performing statins already on the market in 2003, few statins were in trials or expected to be developed in the future.[4] Instead, new classes of drugs were being developed to either complement or improve upon the treatment success of the statins. New molecules in development faced tremendous difficulty reaching the market, however, due to significant regulatory and financial requirements (Exhibit 8.2).

Financial requirements for pharmaceutical research and development are extremely high, with research costs for each new approved drug compound reaching as high as $850 million. Additionally, once the decision to pursue a drug target is made, the probability of passing through each trial and successfully reaching the market is very small. Of the compounds that are chosen to exit preclinical trials, only 8 percent will be approved by the Food and Drug Administration (FDA) (Exhibit 8.3).

The large expenses of drug development, and the large risk associated at each trial stage, represent significant decision points for companies engaging in drug development. Because of these factors, alliances between healthcare companies are frequent: small companies with novel compounds are often partnered with larger sales and marketing-focused "big pharma" companies to help defray development costs and provide a commercial outlet for drugs. In fact, in the post-bubble year of 2002, biotech companies raised $10.5 billion in financing from venture capital, IPOs, and other financing mechanisms. However, the biotech sector pulled an additional $7.5 billion through 411 partnering revenues—representing 42 percent of all funding for the year and yielding an average of about $18 million per agreement.

COMPETITION

In 2003, there were three major cholesterol drug makers: Merck, which pioneered the statin drug category, Pfizer, and Bristol-Myers Squibb. Pfizer's Lipitor had a 46 percent share of the market, Merck's Zocor had 32 percent, Bristol Myers Squibb's Pravachol had 13 percent and the remaining 9 percent was split among other statin and non-statin drugs.[5] The project market for cholesterol drugs that these firms were vying for, a summary of their financials, and their costs of capital are shown in Exhibits 8.4, 8.5 and 8.6, respectively.

Pfizer

Founded in 1849, Pfizer grew to become the world's largest pharmaceutical company. The firm, based in New York, focused on discovering, developing, marketing and delivering medications for both humans and animals. Pfizer led the statin market with Lipitor, the most popular drug in the world. In addition to Lipitor, Pfizer's internal development of a cholesterylester transfer protein (CETP) inhibitor called Torcetrapib stood to strengthen the company's hold on the cardiology market. Pfizer focused Phase III studies on the combination of Lipitor and the new Torcetrapib based on promising Phase II studies. The planned Phase III trials would be the largest for any drug of any type. Torcetrapib was not only one of the most promising drugs in Pfizer's pipeline, but also within the entire spectrum of CETP-Inhibitors.[6] Pfizer backed Lipitor and other drugs with the strongest sales and marketing spending in the industry.

Merck

Merck & Co., Inc. (Merck) was a global pharmaceutical company based in New Jersey and founded in 1901. It had two statins on the market: Mevacor and Zocor. Mevacor, launched in 1987, was one of the first statins to launch. Mevacor experienced tremendous success, which built high expectations for Merck's second-generation statin, Zocor, and by 2002 Zocor had replaced sales of Mevacor.[7] Zocor's popularity made it the top-selling drug for Merck and the number two cholesterol medication in the world.[8] Historically, Merck's drug pipeline created numerous successes for the company across several treatment categories, but by 2002, several Phase III setbacks called its pipeline into question. Merck continued to develop promising arthritis and diabetes drugs in its pipeline, but its cardiovascular pipeline was relatively weak.[9] The most promising cardiovascular drug was based on a joint venture between Merck and Schering Plough. They co-developed a combination Zocor–Zetia drug that they thought might be more effective than Zocor alone through attacking cholesterol from different approaches.[10]

Bristol-Myers Squibb

Bristol-Myers Squibb (BMS), based in New York, was founded in 1914. In 2002, BMS generated $18.1 billion in revenue, 81 percent of which came from pharmaceuticals.[11] BMS is responsible for the third most successful statin in the world, Pravachol. Pravachol was expected to lose share over the next few years as its patent expired in 2006.[12] Pravachol was expected to be BMS's only cholesterol drug success given the company's poor drug development track record in recent years. Two new products, Questran and Pravigard Pac, were launched in 2003, although neither was projected to generate significant revenue. A cholestyramine, Questran, targeted a non-statin method of cholesterol reduction, but its market was much smaller than the statins. Pravigard Pac was simply a combination package of Pravachol and aspirin for patients requiring both medications.[13]

Other Competitors

London-based AstraZeneca launched a new statin in 2003, Crestor. On the surface, Crestor appeared to face an already saturated market; however, Crestor also demonstrated that it could be "unquestionably"[14] the most effective statin on the market, including the wildly successful Lipitor. One analyst projected that Crestor could own 30 percent of the cholesterol drug market within seven years.[15] Such promising potential for Crestor could undermine the current statin oligopoly and drive current players to seek out new cholesterol treatment solutions.

In addition to large pharmaceutical companies, over 35 companies were marketing or developing lipid therapeutics that were in some stage of clinical trials. It is unknown how many additional companies were researching solutions.[16] Most of the new drug development was centered on increasing the amount of HDL through a variety of new avenues, rather than lowering LDL with traditional statins.

ESPERION THERAPEUTICS

Company History

Esperion Therapeutics was founded in July 1998 with $16 million in capital provided by four venture capital firms and several undisclosed investors.[17] Based in Ann Arbor, Michigan, the firm focused on conducting large molecule research on cardiovascular drugs with a specific emphasis on cholesterol medication.

The driving force behind Esperion was its President and CEO, Dr. Roger Newton. At the time of Esperion's founding, Newton was already a well-established name in the cardiovascular pharmaceutical industry. Newton was most famous for his work as a lead scientist at Warner-Lambert, where he was instrumental in the development of Lipitor.[18] After his experience developing Lipitor, Newton spurred the founding of Esperion to further drive development in cholesterol drugs. He was considered one of the leading thinkers in cholesterol therapy.

Esperion made its first significant move only a month after its founding by licensing an HDL-raising drug from Pharmacia called ETC-216.[19] The research behind ETC-216 first appeared in a 30-year old study of a group of rural Italian villagers with surprisingly long life spans. The research uncovered a genetic anomaly in the villagers, forming the basis for ETC-216's development.[20] Once licensed from Pharmacia, the drug provided the cornerstone for Esperion's cholesterol research. The HDL-raising potential of ETC-216 offered a dramatic departure from the statins that target lowering LDL. Backed by the promise of ETC-216 and research on similar HDL-raising drugs (e.g. ETC-588 also showed significant promise), Esperion made an initial public offering in August 2000. The company raised $58 million despite never having generated a single dollar of revenue.[21] Since its founding, Esperion managed to raise $200 million through venture capital and stock offerings.[22]

Esperion used the money raised in its initial public offering (IPO) to drive forward clinical trials of its HDL drugs over the next several years. In June 2003, Esperion announced significant progress in the development of ETC-216. A Phase II clinical study revealed that ETC-216 successfully reduced the heart plaque in study participants. Although the study contained only 47 patients, too few for a statistically meaningful sample, the effectiveness and rapidity of the treatment created a buzz across the pharmaceutical industry.[23] Furthermore, the reputation of Newton in the cholesterol industry continued to grow with ETC-216's success. Esperion's stock price reached a 52-week high after the June announcement.[24]

Challenges

Despite excitement over ETC-216's Phase II clinical trials, Esperion faced a steep uphill battle. Many biopharmaceutical companies with promising early stage clinical trials had faced serious setbacks in later stages.[25] Esperion would not be immune to this statistic.

In addition, Esperion was a new biopharmaceutical firm and did not have the capabilities of its larger competitors. It currently had no way of commercializing its therapies, and therefore, had to rely heavily on the money earned from its IPO as well as venture capital funding to support its clinical trial efforts. If any of Esperion's drugs were capable of making it through clinical trials and earned FDA approval, Esperion did not have the infrastructure to commercialize its product candidates. Esperion would again have to rely on third parties to successfully bring its new drug to market.

Current Pipeline Portfolio

Esperion's pipeline of products looked to replace both statin treatments as well as surgical procedures. According to preliminary results for clinical trials, Esperion's product candidates were able to raise levels of HDL. This fostered the removal of plaque from the artery walls as well as its movement to the liver for expulsion from the body. In addition, there were also signs that the damaged arteries were able to repair themselves. If Esperion could get one of the four products in its pipeline through clinical trials, it could revolutionize the way doctors treated cardiovascular disease.

- *ETC-216 (AIM):* ETC-216 was being developed as an infused treatment for patients with acute coronary syndrome.[26] The properties of ETC-216 allowed it to mimic naturally occurring HDL as well as improve HDL's function. Initial pre-clinical studies as well as Phase I and II clinical trials illustrated positive results for ETC-

216 and proved its capabilities. ETC-216 was now poised for Phase III trials. Esperion hoped ETC-216 would be a major success in the industry. As of 1999, there were already 47 drugs in the market with greater than $500 million in US sales.[27]

- *ETC-588 (LUV):* treatment for acute coronary syndromes.[28] When introduced in the ETC-588 was also being developed as an infused human bloodstream, the biopharmaceutical served as a "sponge" for cholesterol. Pre-clinical animal studies showed that ETC-588 did remove cholesterol from the arteries and helped arteries regain their flexibility and function. ETC-588 was beginning Phase II trials.

- *ETC-642 (RLT Peptide):* Esperion continued to develop RLT Peptide for the treatment of acute coronary syndromes.[29] ETC-642 had similar biological properties to ETC-216 and ETC-588 in mimicking HDL, preventing the accumulation of cholesterol on the artery walls. The completion of Phase I trials in the first half of 2002 indicated that RLT Peptide was safe and well tolerated at several different dose levels. The trials also illustrated evidence of rapid cholesterol mobilization and increased HDL-cholesterol levels.

- *ETC-1001 (HDL Elevating/Lipid Regulating Agents):* Esperion was "pursuing the discovery and development of oral small organic molecules that could increase HDL-C levels and/or enhance the RLT pathway." [30] Pre-clinical studies not only showed an increase in HDL-C molecules in animals, but also suggested that these molecules might also have "anti-diabetic and anti-obesity properties." Esperion hoped to file an NDA for ETC-1001 and begin Phase I clinical trials in 2003.

Pfizer Inc. Company Background
Strategic Overview

Pfizer fueled its growth in research and products in three primary ways: internal R&D, mergers and acquisitions, and agreements and alliances. Given this structure, Pfizer had hundreds of subsidiaries throughout the world. Despite pressures to develop drugs at a faster rate than witnessed in recent years, the industry had experienced a significant reduction in mergers and acquisitions (M&A) activity from $23 billion in the first half of 2001 to just $3 billion in the second half of 2002. When considering transactions, buyers were becoming more cautious, and started relying more heavily on licensing deals.[31] The actions of Pfizer proved to be exceptions to this rule, as the firm undertook two significant mergers: Warner-Lambert in 2000 (the largest hostile takeover ever) and Pharmacia in 2003. Placing pressure on competitive firms to consolidate, Pfizer boasted the industry's largest pharmaceutical R&D organization with a library of more than 700 major active collaborations and a 2003 R&D budget of $7.1 billion.[32] Pfizer's pipeline acceleration strategy was expressed through the comments of Dr. LaMattina, president of Pfizer Global Research and Development:

Pfizer's strength is its ability to maximize opportunities from our internal programs and through partnerships. Our scale and R&D breadth are obvious advantages that we secure with very strict attention to our goals. Some of our competitors believe the term 'research management' is an oxymoron, but we don't think so at Pfizer. True, it's hard to predict when discoveries will occur. The process can be managed to maximize the chances of discoveries happening . . . Before we closed the acquisition of Pharmacia, we conducted extensive due diligence and understood the value of the pipeline, and the way it complemented the R&D efforts under way at Pfizer. There were very few surprises and we have retained the great majority of projects.[33]

Proper management of acquisitions, combined with links to more than 250 partners in academia and industry, strengthened Pfizer's position on the cutting edge of science by providing access to novel R&D tools and key data on emerging trends.

Marketing

Capitalizing from the US Food and Drug Administration's 1997 decision to loosen restrictions on consumer advertising of prescription medications, Pfizer recruited a new senior media director in 1999 to establish Pfizer's first consumer media unit and form a company approach on how to use the fledgling direct-to-consumer (DTC) medium.[34] Two years later, Pfizer was regarded as being in the front tier in DTC brand building with hits such as Zyrtec and Viagra. By using consumer ads to drive sales of prescription drugs, Pfizer became a major player in the annual TV upfront season. Over the first six months of 2001, Pfizer became the second largest DTC spender with about $76 million.[35]

Manufacturing and Distribution

For decades, the manufacturing component of the pharmaceutical industry had been highly inefficient with manufacturing expenses accounting for 36 percent of the industry's costs. The top 16 drug companies spent $90 billion on manufacturing in 2001.[36] With inefficiencies resulting in lower quality and product recalls, the FDA updated its manufacturing regulations for the first time in 25 years in 2003. In response, Pfizer applied funding towards manufacturing research and developed a fast and accurate new way to test drugs. This technology was being tested in a few of Pfizer's plants around the world.

Pfizer had the distribution capability to launch a product simultaneously in dozens of markets around the world. As of 2000, Pfizer's US sales force consisted of 5,400 representatives in nine divisions. Pfizer's rigorous training and ongoing education programs were unmatched in the industry, yielding best in class sales representatives who consistently communicated advances in the understanding and treatment of diseases to millions of healthcare providers.[37] In 2002, Pfizer's pharmaceutical sales organization placed first overall in a survey of US physicians in nine core specialty groups for the seventh consecutive year.[38]

Pfizer and the Cholesterol Drug Market

Pfizer obtained the rights to the blockbuster drug Atorvastatin (Lipitor) after the acquisition of Warner-Lambert in 2000. Prior to the acquisition, Pfizer had entered into a marketing agreement with Warner-Lambert to help successfully launch the drug in 1996.

Warner-Lambert faced a number of setbacks in bringing Lipitor to market. The firm had recently dealt with a series of drug recalls of some of its major products. Furthermore, Warner-Lambert's sales force was much smaller in size relative to its competitors with established cholesterol drugs already in the market. Given these circumstances, the firm signed a co-marketing alliance with Pfizer. Pfizer agreed to cover a significant portion of the upfront expenses of launching Lipitor as well as use its extensive networks of sales representatives to bring the drug to market.[39] In exchange, Pfizer would receive payments based on Lipitor's sales targets.

On November 5, 1999, American Home Products Corporation announced a $70-billion dollar merger agreement with Warner-Lambert. Such a deal left a great amount of uncertainty regarding the future status of marketing rights to Lipitor and the alliance between Pfizer and Warner-Lambert. Lipitor's billions in sales represented a large portion of Pfizer's drug sales portfolio. Therefore, before the co-marketing alliance came to an end, Pfizer placed its own hostile bid of $82.4 billion for Warner-Lambert. The two companies eventually merged in 2000, giving Pfizer full rights to Lipitor.[40] With Lipitor secured as a Pfizer product and Torcetrapib entering Phase III trials, Pfizer was poised to strengthen its hold on the cholesterol drug market.

Pfizer's Offer

In November 2003, Esperion published the official results of its ETC-216 study in the *Journal of the American Medical Association*. The article indicated that its drug-reduced buildup of fatty plaque in arteries by over 4 percent in patients who were given weekly injections of the experimental medicine over a course of only five weeks during the Phase II trial.[41] According to John LaMattina, Director of Research at Pfizer, ETC-216 would have to be tested on "hundreds, possibly thousands (of people), and would have to be shown to significantly reduce the risk of a second heart attack" before the Food and Drug Administration would approve it. This type of clinical trial would require a significant investment.[42]

After the trial results appeared in the *Journal of the American Medical Association*, Newton publicly announced that the company would be looking for a partner to develop and market the drug. Pfizer acquired first bidding rights to co-develop and commercialize ETC-216 through its acquisition of Pharmacia.[43]

On December 21, 2003, Pfizer announced its intent to purchase Esperion Therapeutics for $1.3 billion. Pfizer made an all-cash tender offer to acquire shares of Esperion's common stock at $35 per share.[44] This price represented a 54 percent premium over Esperion's average closing share price over the 20 trading days prior to the acquisition.[45] At the time of the offer, Newton owned 890,000 shares of Esperion stock.

The Decision

Newton had to decide if Esperion would benefit from a buyout by a major pharmaceutical company. Dr. Newton knew that his company faced an uphill battle with the continued development of ETC-216. Phase III trials would prove incredibly expensive for Esperion and they would again have to look to venture capital funding and potential stock offerings for additional cash. Dr. Newton knew that despite positive Phase II results, Phase III results could always be negative and ETC-216 might never make it to FDA approval. If, however, the ETC-216 Phase III trials proved successful, Esperion would have to look for a partner to help launch and commercialize the product.

Dr. Newton had a lot to consider. He had started Esperion so that he could create an entrepreneurial environment for drug discovery, in which the scientists received the rewards for their research. If he sold out to Pfizer would he be giving up everything he had worked so hard to create? Would Esperion be able to maintain the entrepreneurial identity that had brought about the discovery of a new line of cardiovascular pharmaceuticals? Would Newton be giving up control over the development of ETC-216 and the other promising drugs in Esperion's pipeline? In addition, how would his employees react to working for a major pharmaceutical company?

Exhibit 8.1 Selected disease statistics, US, 2003

People who have one or more forms of cardiovascular disease (CVD)	71,300,000
High blood pressure	65,000,000
Coronary artery disease	13,200,000
Myocardial infarction (heart attack)	7,200,000
Angina pectoris (chest pain)	6,500,000
Stroke	5,500,000
Deaths from cardiovascular disease	910,614
Deaths from coronary artery disease	479,305
Deaths from cancer (all types)	554,642
Deaths from accidents	105,695

Source: Cardiovascular disease statistics, 2003, American Heart Association.

Exhibit 8.2 Drug development process

The Food and Drug Administration (FDA) regulates drug development and requires progression through testing stages to ensure the safety and efficacy of potential drugs.

- *Drug Discovery* is the first step in development, and is conducted in order to test a potential molecule's effect on a disease target *ex vivo* (not in a live subject). Once a basic understanding of a disease is established, scientists will screen thousands of compounds in order to determine one or several "lead" compounds which seem to have an effect on the disease mechanism and which warrant testing *in vivo* (in a live subject).
- *Preclinical Studies* are done in animals, to determine the effect of a new molecule on a living organism. Scientists monitor the drug's safety in the animal and also monitor its effect on the target disease, attempting to understand whether the molecule has potential benefit in humans. Preclinical studies typically take three to six years.
- *Phase I Studies* typically involve 20–100 healthy volunteers, and are conducted in order to gauge basic characteristics of a potential new drug in humans: how the drug is absorbed, distributed, metabolized and excreted, as well as its pharmacokinetics (how long the drug is active in the body). Phase I studies typically take six months to one year to complete.
- *Phase II Studies* typically involve 100–500 volunteers who have the target disease. In this phase, companies attempt to establish "proof of concept:" that the potential new drug actually has a beneficial effect on its target disease. Scientists monitor the drug's effect on the disease as well as potential side effects, and attempt to determine the appropriate dose for the new drug. Phase II studies typically take six months to one year to complete.
- *Phase III Studies* typically involve 1000–5000 sick patients, and are conducted in order to provide statistically significant proof that the potential new drug is effective against its target disease. Physicians monitor patients at regular intervals and test for side effects. Phase III trials can take from one to four years to complete. At the end of Phase III trials, companies will submit a NDA (New Drug Application) to the FDA in order to gain approval to launch and market the drug commercially.
- *Phase IV Studies* are clinical trials required after the drug has been approved (in this case, drugs are often said to have received "conditional approval") in order to provide the FDA with further data regarding the drug or more long-term evidence of its use. Companies are required to fulfill these data requirements, but may do so after launching the drug commercially. Studies can range in both years and expense.

Source: Clinical trials. Retrieved July 22, 2008, from http://en.wikipedia.org/wiki/Clinical_trial.

Exhibit 8.3 Drug trial expenses per approved compound

	R&D	Animal	Phase I	Phase II	Phase III	TOTAL
Cost ($millions)	358.0	12.5	42.9	117.8	325.8	857.0
Time (months)			21.6	38.0	56.5	116.1
Success rate			69%	38%	15%	8% (FDA approval)

Source: Joseph Dimasi, Ronald Hansen, and Henry Grabowski, The price of innovation: new estimates of drug development costs, *Journal of Health Economics*, 2003. Bain and Co., 2003.

Exhibit 8.4 Total hypolipemic market sales and expectations

Year	2000	2001	2002	2003E	2004E	2005E	2006E	2007E	2008E	2009E
Revenues ($M)	13,937	15,830	17,210	19,845	21,990	24,232	25,390	26,725	27,680	29,115

Source: CDC IXIS Securities, Cholesterol: The battle rages on, February 24, 2003.

Exhibit 8.5 Select pharmaceutical company financial information ($000s), 2002

	$	$	Pfizer $
Sales	18,119	51,790	32,373
COGS	6,388	33,054	4,045
Marketing, sales, and admin.	5,218	6,187	10,846
R&D	2,218	2,667	5,176
Other costs	1,648	(331)	510
Total costs	15,472	41,577	20,577
Pre-tax income	2,647	10,213	11,796
Taxes	613	3,064	2,609
Net income	2,034	7,149	9,187

Source: Firm 10-Ks.

Exhibit 8.6 Nominal and real cost-of-capital (COC) for the pharmaceutical industry, 1985–2000

	1985 %	1990 %	1994 %	2000 %
Nominal COC	16.1	15.1	14.2	15.0
Inflation rate	5.4	4.5	3.1	3.1
Real COC	10.8	10.6	11.1	11.9

Source: Dimasi, 2003, Tufts Center for the Study of Drug Development.

Dr. Newton had to decide whether Esperion's future lay as an independent biotech company, a wholly owned subsidiary, or an integrated part of "big pharma."

NOTES

1   CDC IXIS Securities. (February 24, 2003). Cholesterol: The battle rages on.
2   CDC IXIS Securities. (February 24, 2003). Cholesterol: The battle rages on.
3   CDC IXIS Securities. (February 24, 2003). Cholesterol: The battle rages on.
4   Two drugs are notable exceptions. Crestor (AstraZeneca) was expected to be launched in 2003 with a better safety and efficacy profile than any currently marketed statin. Additionally, Novartis/Sankyo's Pitavastin was a statin currently in Phase IIb trials in Europe expected to be launched in 2007.
5   CDC IXIS Securities. (February 24, 2003). Cholesterol: The battle rages on.
6   Deutsche Bank Securitiers. (December 22, 2003). Pfizer Inc.: Building cardio dominance.
7   How far we've come. (August 1, 2006). *Pharmaceutical Executive.*
8   CDC IXIS Securities. (February 24, 2003). Cholesterol: The battle rages on.
9   UBS Investment Research. (November 21, 2003). Merck & Co.
10 Harper, M. (2003). Merck's troubles, Schering's solution. Retrieved December 6, 2006, from www.forbes.com/2003/11/21/cx_mh_1121mrk.html
11 Bristol-Myers Squibb Co. (2002). 10-K.
12 Bristol-Myers Squibb Co.: Where's the growth? Oppenheimer Equity Research. November 19, 2003.
13 Bristol-Myers Squibb Co. (November 19, 2003). Where's the growth? Oppenheimer Equity Research.
14 CDC IXIS Securities. (February 24, 2003). Cholesterol: The battle rages on.
15 CDC IXIS Securities. (February 24, 2003). Cholesterol: The battle rages on.
16 Frost & Sullivan. (November 10, 2005). U.S. lipid therapeutics market. (Section 2.6.1).
17 Thomson Financial Venture Economics. (September 27, 2006). Esperion Therapeutics, Inc. Company Report (VentureXpert).
18 Rozhon, T. (2003, December 22). Pfizer to buy maker of promising cholesterol drug. *New York Times.*
19 Datamonitor Company Profiles. (January 24, 2004). Esperion Therapeutics – History.
20 Winslow, R. (2003, November 5). New HDL drug shows promise in heart study. *The Wall Street Journal.*
21 PR Newswire. (October 31, 2000). Esperion Therapeutics, Inc. announce results for third quarter 2000.
22 Rozhon, T. (2003, December 22). Pfizer to buy maker of promising cholesterol drug. *New York Times.*
23 Winslow, R. (2003, November 5). New HDL drug shows promise in heart study. *The Wall Street Journal.*
24 Braunschweiger, A. (2003, June 26). Esperion shares surge on study of heart-plaque treatment. *Dow Jones Business News.*
25 Esperion. (2002). 10-K.
26 Esperion. (2002). 10-K.
27 Dimasi, J., Hansen, R., & Grabowski, H. (2003). The price of innovation: New estimates of drug development costs. *Journal of Health Economics,* 22(2), 151–185.
28 Esperion. (2002). 10-K.
29 Esperion. (2002). 10-K.
30 Esperion. (2002). 10-K.
31 Young, P. (2002, September 18). Troubling times for Pharma. *Chemical Week.*
32 Pfizer.com. (March 2004). Press release.
33 Pfizer.com. (March 2004). Press release.
34 Goetzl, D. (2001, October 1). Media mavens: Donna Campanella. *Advertising Age.*
35 Goetzl, D. (2001, October 1). Media mavens: Donna Campanella. *Advertising Age.*
36 Abboud, L., & Hensley, S. (2003, September 3). Factory shift: New prescriptions for drug makers; update the plants – after years of neglect, industry focuses on manufacturing; FDA acts as a catalyst; the three story blender. *Wall Street Journal.*
37 Physician survey ranks Pfizer sales force first in industry for fifth consecutive year. (2000, January 20). *PR Newswire.*
38 Pfizer sales force most esteemed by US doctors. (2002, February 18). *Marketletter.*
39 Mintz, S.L. (2000). What is a merger worth? Retrieved October 12, 2006, from www.cfo.com/article.cfm/2988576
40 Morrow, D.J., & Holson, L.M. (1999, November 5). Warner-Lambert gets Pfizer offer for $82.4 billion. *New York Times.*
41 Pfizer to buy maker of promising cholesterol drug. (2003, December 22). *New York Times.*

42   Ibid.
43   Ibid.
44   Pfizer to acquire Esperion Therapeutics to extend its research commitment in cardiovascular disease. (2003, December 21). *Pfizer Press Release.*
45   Pfizer to buy Esperion for $1.3bn. (2003). Retrieved October 10, 2006, from www.cnn.com/2003/BUSINESS/12/21/us.pfizer.reut

Case 9

PIXAR: CHANGING THE RULES OF THE GAME*

On June 29, 2008, on the first anniversary of the release of *Ratatouille*, a former Pixar Animation shareholder wondered if Pixar had done the right thing selling itself to Disney. *Ratatouille* had grossed more than $600 million worldwide with an undisclosed amount from merchandising. What was even more amazing than the revenues was the fact that *Ratatouille* was the eighth straight hit for Pixar, in an industry where every other movie risked crashing. Why had Pixar been so successful? Would the success continue under Disney? Should Pixar have stayed as a separate company in a continued alliance with Disney or parted ways and found another partner? Eight straight hits with most of them grossing more than half a billion dollars!

PIXAR'S DIGITAL TECHNOLOGY ROOTS

University of Utah Days

Pixar's technical roots date back to 1970, when Ed Catmull joined the computer science program at the University of Utah as a doctoral student.[1] Given the program's notoriety and leadership in computer graphics, several young stars were attracted to Utah. John Warnock was one of those early pioneers; he would later found Adobe Systems and create a revolution in the publishing world with his PostScript page description language. Jim Clark, another alumnus, would later start Silicon Graphics and then lead Netscape Communications.

During the 1970s, the program made significant headway into the development of computer graphics. Catmull himself made a significant advance in computer graphics in his 1974 doctoral thesis, which focused on texture mapping, z-buffer and rendering curved surfaces. In 1974, interest in the work of the Utah program came from an

---

* This case was written by Catherine Crane, Will Johnson, Kitty Neumark, and Christopher Perrigo under the supervision of Professor Allan Afuah as a basis for class discussion and is not intended to illustrate either effective or ineffective handling of a business situation.

unexpected source, Alexander Schure, an eccentric millionaire and founder of the New York Institute of Technology (NYIT), who wanted to use the story from a children's record album called *Tubby the Tuba* to develop an animated film. From the ranks at Utah, Dr. Catmull recruited a team of talented computer scientists and began experimenting with computer-generated animation.

The Lucasfilm Years: 1979—1986

While Catmull's group struggled at NYIT, Hollywood was beginning to see the benefits of computer graphics for production. One early Hollywood pioneer was George Lucas, whose *Star Wars* had been a stunning special effects achievement. With this blockbuster under his belt, Lucas became interested in using computer graphics for image editing and producing special effects for his next movie, *The Empire Strikes Back.* Lucas worked with an outside computer graphics production house, Triple I, to create the effects for *Empire*, but in the end these effects were not used. However, the experience had proven that photorealistic computer imagery was possible, and Lucas decided to assemble his own computer graphics division within his special effects company, Lucasfilm.

In 1979, Lucas discovered Catmull's group at NYIT. George Lucas extended an offer to the team to come to Northern California to work as part of Lucasfilm; the team was more than happy to accept. Dr. Catmull was named Vice President and, over the next six years, the new computer graphics division of Lucasfilm would assemble one of the most talented teams of artists and programmers in the computer graphics industry.

PIXAR IS BORN (1984—PRESENT): CREATIVE DEVELOPMENT

Enter the Story Man: John Lasseter

Like Ed Catmull, John Lasseter had long envisioned the future of computer graphics animation. Lasseter had worked on Disney's first major foray into computer-aided production—*Tron* (1981). *Tron* required nearly 30 minutes of film quality computer graphics and was a daunting task for computer graphics studios at the time. The computer-generated imagery of *Tron* was technologically dazzling, but the underlying story was an unappealing cyber-adventure. Disney sank about $20 million into the picture, but it bombed at the box office. The resultant financial loss alone served to all but kill Disney's interest in the computer graphics medium.

Despite the commercial failure of *Tron*, the film was an epiphany for Lasseter. Watching what fellow animators were doing with computer graphics imagery, he started to see the possibilities of full-scale computer animation: "the minute I saw the light-cycle sequence, which had such dimensionality and solidity," Lasseter recalls, "it was like a little door in my head opening to a whole new world."[2]

Lasseter and fellow animator Glen Keane (who went on to make *Beauty and the Beast*) tried to interest Disney in the medium by animating 30 seconds of Maurice Sendak's *Where the Wild Things Are,* using standard animation drawings in computer-generated settings. But Disney, who was struggling to rejuvenate itself after years of lackluster box office performance, was not interested in further experimentation with untried computer animation. In 1984, a disappointed Lasseter left Disney. Ed Catmull, a friend of Lasseter, convinced him to come to Lucasfilm to experiment for just a month. John Lasseter liked what he found and never left.

Born in the "Next" Generation: Steve Jobs

While the computer graphics division of Lucasfilm was strengthened with the addition of Lasseter in 1984, George Lucas's interest in the project waned. Although Catmull saw tremendous further potential in the technologies being developed, Lucas viewed the project as complete and began looking for a buyer of the computer division. An early potential buyer of the division was a partnership between the behemoth General Motors's Electronic Data Systems (EDS) and a unit of the Dutch conglomerate Phillips NV. Much to Catmull's relief, the sale fell through.

Steve Jobs, then CEO of Apple Computer, heard about Lucas's intended sale of the computer division. Jobs thought the situation provided a strong acquisition opportunity for Apple, but unfortunately, Apple's Board disagreed. When Jobs left Apple in 1985, Pixar remained a division of Lucasfilm.

Ironically, it was the ousting of Jobs that ultimately permitted the sale of the computer division. With a personal net worth of more than $100 million resulting from his sale of Apple stock, Jobs approached Lucas and reiterated his interest in the division. In 1986, at a price of $10 million, Lucas sold the division to Jobs. Steve Jobs considered the idea of absorbing the group into his other firm, NeXT Computer, but instead decided to incorporate Pixar as an independent company, installing himself as Chief Executive Officer and Ed Catmull as Chief Technical Officer.

Along with Catmull and Lasseter, Jobs viewed the ultimate goal of the company as producing computer animated cartoons and full-length films. However, there were still several intermediate steps required to meet this objective. One of the most important of these hurdles was developing and refining software tools that would enable the creation of the films the team envisioned.

"Innovate or Not to Innovate?"—That is Not the Question!

Pixar developed groundbreaking software systems—Marionette, RingMaster and RenderMan, and a laser recording system for film—Pixarvision. Marionette was an animation software system for modeling, animating, and lighting simulation capabilities (see Exhibit 9.1 for an animation value chain)[3]. RingMaster was a production management software system for scheduling, coordinating, and tracking computer animation projects. Pixarvision was a laser recording system for converting digital computer data into images on motion picture film stock with unprecedented quality. These three products helped to provide a considerable competitive advantage to Pixar, as they were critical to the production of high quality 3D graphics and comparable tools were simply not available on the market.

Unlike these software systems which remained proprietary to Pixar, RenderMan software system was commercialized and quickly became a significant source of revenue, so that in 2001 approximately 10 percent of Pixar's total revenue came from software licensing. Released for commercial use in 1989, RenderMan, a rendering software system for photorealistic image synthesis, enabled computer graphics artists to apply textures and colors to surfaces of 3D images on-screen. Pixar licensed the tool to third parties and eventually sold upwards of 100,000 copies. RenderMan quickly became an industry standard and was used extensively to augment live action films. Over a ten-year period, the software had been used to create eight out of the ten films that won an Oscar for Best Visual Effects—*The Matrix, What Dreams May Come, Titanic, Forrest Gump, Jurassic Park, Death Becomes Her, Terminator 2,* and *The Abyss.* However, the true testimonial to RenderMan and the people who created it was in 2001 when the Academy of Motion Picture Art & Science Board of Governors honored Ed Catmull, the President of Pixar, Loren Carpenter, Senior Scientist, and Rob Cook, Vice President of Software Engineering, with an Academy Award of Merit (Oscar) "for significant advancement to the field of motion picture rendering as exemplified in Pixar's RenderMan."

Developing the Creative Side of Pixar

In the early 1990s Steve Jobs realized that sales of RenderMan and other tools alone would not be able to fund Pixar's technology research and internal projects, including film development. "The problem was, for many years, the cost of computers to make animation we could sell was tremendously high."[4] Jobs put Pixar technology to use in developing TV commercial campaigns for a variety of clients. As the company evolved into a successful animation studio producing TV ads for Listerine, Lifesavers, and others, John Lasseter, the director of the ads, became Pixar's big breadwinner. The company won a Gold Medal Clio Award for its LifeSavers "Conga" commercial in 1993, and another Gold Clio Award in 1994 for Listerine "Arrows" commercial.

A second successful creative outlet for Pixar was short film. In 1986, Pixar's first short movie, *Luxo Jr.*, earned an Academy Award nomination for Best Short Film (Animated). In 1988, another of Pixar's short films, *Tin Toy*, became the first computer-animated film to win an Academy Award for Best Short Film (Animated). John Lasseter, who had directed both films, had established a well-deserved reputation as one of the leading animators in the industry. Indeed, Lasseter's reputation set the creative foundation for Pixar. Meanwhile, Lasseter's success did not go unnoticed. Disney's Michael Eisner and Jeffrey Katzenberg tried to woo the director back, but Lasseter declined. "I was having too much fun," he said. "I felt I was on to something new—we were pioneers."[5]

A TALE OF FOUR ANIMATED FILMS

Teaming Up to Break New Frontiers: Disney and Pixar

In 1991, John Lasseter reviewed Pixar's work in short films and commercials, and was confident enough in the company's progress to propose the idea of producing an hour-long animated TV special. He pitched the idea to his previous studio, Disney, with the hope that the two companies could collaborate on the project. He was also hoping that Disney would be able to provide part of the money necessary to fund the idea.

The timing was just right. Unlike his pitch for *Toaster* in 1984, Disney in 1991 was riding high on the phenomenal success of its animation department. With smashes in *The Little Mermaid* (1989) and *Beauty and the Beast* (1991)—both had utilized computer animation to some extent—Disney was ready to invest in new technology. Although Disney CEO Michael Eisner and film chief Jeffrey Katzenberg rejected the TV project, they countered with a deal Lasseter and Pixar could hardly have hoped for: Disney proposed a full-length movie, which it would fund and distribute.

In July 1991, Pixar signed a three-film deal. The deal stipulated that Disney would fund the production and promotion costs, and Pixar would earn a modest percentage of box-office and video sales gross revenues. Pixar's share in the deal was estimated to amount to approximately 10–15 percent of the film profits, depending on the sales levels achieved. Pixar was required to pay a portion of the costs over specified budget levels, as well as provide the funding for the development of any animation tools and technologies necessary to complete the films.

In return for taking the lower cut of box office and video profits, Pixar gained access to Disney's marketing and distribution network, as well as creative advice from Disney's veterans. However, a substantially higher share of revenues was not the only price Disney extracted from the deal. In addition, Disney retained all ownership to the characters appearing in the films. Disney also maintained sole licensing rights to the films and characters, including very lucrative ancillary merchandise such as toys and clothing. Pixar was only able to retain the rights to any direct-to-video sequels, as well as the data files and rendering technologies employed to develop the films.

When asked about the agreement signed, Steve Jobs remarked that if the first movie was "a modest hit—say, $75 million at the box office—we'll both break even. If it gets $100 million, we'll both make money. But if it's a real blockbuster and earns $200 million or so at the box office, we'll make good money, and Disney will make a lot of money."[6]

1995—Film 1: Toy Story

With the deal signed, Pixar now had to prove it could deliver on its technology and creativity. In 1991, with a staff of only a few dozen people, Pixar had to quickly gear up to begin design and production of the first of the three films. By the end of 1992 all of the key ingredients were in place—screenplay was approved by Disney, character voices, led by Tom Hanks as Woody and Tim Allen as Buzz Lightyear, were signed, and the staff of animators was ready to turn a tale about the rivalry between a toy cowboy, Woody, and a plastic spaceman named Buzz Lightyear, to life.

Pixar completed *Toy Story* with a staff of 110, roughly one-sixth the number Disney and other studios typically use to make animated productions.[7] Of the staff, 27 were animators, compared to the 75 or more animators required for previous animated Disney films. With animators earning $100,000 or more each, the total cost savings amounted to more than $15 million over a three-year production for the movie.

Toy Story opened in US theaters over the Thanksgiving weekend of 1995 with great fanfare and extensive media publicity. During the five-day Thanksgiving Weekend, *Toy Story* box office receipts totaled $39.1 million, a record debut for the weekend and, by the end of 1995, it had become the highest grossing film of the year, making over $192 million in domestic box-office receipts and $358 million worldwide.

1998—A New Contract and A Bug's Life

In December 1997, riding high on the success of *Toy Story*, but making only an estimated $45 million from the release of the film, Pixar renegotiated its contract with Disney. Pixar agreed to produce five original computer-animated feature-length theatrical motion pictures for distribution by Disney. Pixar and Disney agreed to co-finance production, co-own, co-brand, and share equally the profits from each picture, including revenues from all related merchandise.

The first original picture released under the new agreement was *A Bug's Life*, which opened in theaters in November 1998. The story, derived from the fable *The Ant and the Grasshopper* revolved around an ant colony, led by a rebel ant named Flick, and its quest to fight off the grasshoppers who stole the ants' food every winter. *A Bug's Life* broke all previous US Thanksgiving weekend box-office records, becoming the highest grossing animated release in 1998 and making over $163 million domestically in box office receipts and $362 million worldwide. After only one week of international release, *A Bug's Life* captured the No. 1 spot in six international markets, including Thailand, Argentina, and Australia.

Computer technology had advanced to a point where the computing power used in *A Bug's Life* was ten times the power used in *Toy Story*. The results were images that were more real-life than ever before. Additionally, Pixar used Pixarvision (its laser recording system) for the first time, to convert digital computer data into images on motion-picture film stock, achieving not only faster recording time, but also higher quality color reproduction and sharper images.

1999 – 2012 : More Blockbuster Years

A Bug's Life was followed by *Toy Story 2*, which was released on November 19, 1999, and became the first film in history to be entirely mastered and exhibited digitally, and the first animated sequel to gross more than its original. It won a Golden Globe award for the Best Picture, Musical or Comedy. This was followed by *Monsters, Inc., Finding Nemo, The Incredibles, Cars* and *Ratatouille*—all of them blockbusters (Exhibit 9.2). Planned for release the following years were *WALL-E* (2008), *Up* (2009), *Toy Story 3* (2010), *Newt* (2011), *The Bear and the Bow* (2011), and *Cars 2* (2012).

COMPETITORS

Pixar had competitors, chief among them, Disney, DreamWorks PDI/SKG, Fox Studio, and Lucasfilm. In fact, two of the top five spots on the all-time grossing animation movies were occupied by PDI/DreamWorks, not Pixar (Exhibits 9.3 and 9.4).

PONDERING PIXAR'S FUTURE—WHERE TO NEXT?

In 2004, Steve Jobs and his team went to Disney for renegotiation of their agreement, confident that their strong record of six blockbusters would be enough to seal a new deal. However, Michael Eisner, Disney's CEO did not see eye-to-eye with Steve Jobs and no deal was reached.[8] On October 1, 2005, however, Bob Iger was appointed CEO of Disney to replace Eisner. Iger reopened talks with Pixar. On January 24, 2006, Disney announced that it had agreed to purchase Pixar for $7.4 billion in an all-stock deal.[9] The deal was completed on May 5, 2006, after approval by Pixar shareholders.[10] However, there were still some Pixar shareholders and analysts who wondered if Pixar had done the right thing. Should the firm have remained single?

Exhibit 9.1 An animation movie value chain

Financing, purchasing, human resources, etc.

Creative development	Production	Post-production	Marketing *and* merchandising	Distribution
Story and characters development	Modeling	Sound process		
	Layout	Picture process		
	Animation	Sound effects		
	Shading	Musical score		
	Lighting	Etc.		
	Rendering			
	Film recording			

Source: Case writers' estimates.

Exhibit 9.2 Pixar full-length animation movies

Movie name	Released	1st weekend	US gross	Worldwide gross	Budget
Toy Story	11/22/95	$29,140,617	$191,796,233	$356,800,000	$30,000,000
A Bug's Life	11/20/98	$291,121	$162,798,565	$358,000,000	$45,000,000
Toy Story 2	11/19/99	$300,163	$245,852,179	$485,828,782	$90,000,000
Monsters, Inc.	11/2/01	$62,577,067	$255,870,172	$525,370,172	$115,000,000
Finding Nemo	5/30/03	$70,251,710	$339,714,978	$864,614,978	$94,000,000
The Incredibles	11/5/04	$70,467,623	$261,437,578	$631,437,578	$92,000,000
Cars	6/9/06	$60,119,509	$244,082,982	$461,782,982	$70,000,000
Ratatouille	6/29/07	$47,027,395	$206,445,654	$617,245,654	$150,000,000
Pixar Short Film Collection – Volume 1	11/6/07				
WALL-E	6/27/08				$180,000,000
Up	5/29/09				
Toy Story 3	6/18/10				
Newt	8/31/11				
The Bear and the Bow	12/31/11				
Cars 2	8/31/12				
	Totals		$1,907,998,341	$4,301,080,146	$866,000,000
	Averages		$238,499,793	$537,635,018	$96,222,22

Source: The Numbers. Retrieved June 21, 2008, from www.the-numbers.com/movies/series/DigitalAnimation.php.

Exhibit 9.3 Top 12 grossing animation movies

Animation movie	Release date	Firm	Worldwide gross
Shrek 2	2004	PDI/DreamWorks	$920,665,658
Finding Nemo	2003	Pixar	$864,625,978
Shrek the Third	2007	PDI/DreamWorks	$798,957,081
*The Lion King**	1994	Walt Disney	$783,841,776
Ice Age: The Meltdown	2006	Fox	$647,330,621
The Incredibles	2004	Pixar	$631,436,092
Ratatouille	2007	Pixar	$617,245,650
Monsters, Inc.	2001	Pixar	$529,061,238
Madagascar	2005	PDI/DreamWorks	$527,890,631
Aladdin	1992	Walt Disney	$504,050,219
Toy Story 2	1999	Pixar	$485,015,179
Shrek	2001	PDI	$484,409,218
Cars	2006	Pixar	$461,782,982

Source: The Numbers. Retrieved June 21, 2008, from www.the-numbers.com/movies/series/DigitalAnimation.php.
* *The Lion King* was also estimated to have brought in $1 billion in profits from merchandising, theme park attractions, TV rights and videos.

Exhibit 9.4 Competing animation movies

Digital animated movie	Date released	Firm	Worldwide gross
Antz	1998	PDI	$152,457,863
Shrek	2001	PDI	$484,409,218
Shrek 2	2004	PDI/DreamWorks	$920,665,658
Madagascar	2005	PDI/DreamWorks	$527,890,631
Shrek the Third	2007	PDI/DreamWorks	$798,957,081
Ice Age	2002	Blue Sky Studios/Fox	$382,387,405
Robots	2005	Blue Sky Studios/Fox	$260,700,012
Ice Age: The Meltdown	2006	Blue Sky Studios/Fox	$647,330,621
Horton Hears a Who!	2008	Blue Sky Studios/Fox	N/A

Source: The Numbers. Retrieved June 21, 2008, from www.the-numbers.com/movies/series/DigitalAnimation.php.

NOTES

1   Hormby, T. (2007). The Pixar Story: Dick Shoup, Alex Schure, George Lucas, Steve Jobs, and Disney. Retrieved June 21, 2008, from www.the-numbers.com/movies/series/Pixar.php

2   *Toy' Wonder*. (1995). Retrieved June 29, 2008, from www.ew.com/ew/article/0,,299897,00.htm

3   From "Toy Story" to "Chicken Little." (2005, December 8). *The Economist*.

4   Schlender, B., & Furth, J. (1995). Steve Jobs' amazing movie adventure Disney is betting on Computerdom's ex-boy wonder to deliver this year's animated Christmas blockbuster. Can he do for Hollywood what he did for Silicon Valley? Retrieved June 21, 2008, from http://money.cnn.com/magazines/fortune/fortune_archive/1995/09/18/206099/index.htm.

5   *Toy' Wonder*. (1995). Retrieved June 29, 2008, from www.ew.com/ew/article/0,,299897,00.html.

6   Schlender, B., & Furth, J. (1995). Steve Jobs' amazing movie adventure Disney is betting on Computerdom's ex-boy wonder to deliver this year's animated Christmas blockbuster. Can he do for Hollywood what he did for Silicon Valley? Retrieved June 21, 2008, from http://money.cnn.com/magazines/fortune/fortune_archive/1995/09/18/206099/index.htm

7   Hormby, T. (2007). The Pixar story: Dick Shoup, Alex Schure, George Lucas, Steve Jobs, and Disney. Retrieved June 21, 2008, from www.the-numbers.com/movies/series/Pixar.php

8   Face value: Finding another Nemo. (2004, February 5). *The Economist*.

9   Disney: Magic restored. (2008, April 17). *The Economist*.

10 Kafka, P. (2006, January 23). Mickey's big move. *Forbes*.

Case 10

LIPITOR: WORLD'S BEST-SELLING DRUG (2008)[1]

Jeff Kindler, CEO of Pfizer, pondered over sales of Lipitor. The drug had brought in $12.7 billion in revenues in 2007.[2] This blockbuster belonged to a group of drugs called statins that reduce the level of cholesterol in the body by inhibiting the process by which the body produces cholesterol. What was it about Lipitor and Pfizer that had enabled the drug to do so well? Could Pfizer or any pharmaceutical company ever repeat such a feat?

CORONARY ARTERY DISEASE

In 2008, it was believed that coronary artery disease was the leading cause of death in the US, where more than a million people suffered a heart attack every year. A leading cause of coronary artery disease is the buildup of plaque in the blood vessels, which can lead to blockage of these arteries, heart attacks, and strokes. Frequently, this plaque buildup results from excessive cholesterol levels, especially of the bad cholesterol called low-density lipoprotein (LDL). High levels of triglycerides also have the same negative effect. However, high levels of so-called good cholesterol—high-density lipoprotein (HDL)—have the opposite effect as they return LDL to the liver for elimination, thereby reducing harm to people. Cholesterol is a natural substance in the body that is used in the formation of cell membranes, gastric juices, and some hormones. However, like most good things, too much of it is bad. The liver makes most of the cholesterol that the body needs but cholesterol can also be ingested directly from food.

ROLE OF STATINS

Before statins, high levels of cholesterol were treated with drugs that break down cholesterol or absorb it irrespective of whether it was naturally produced by the body or from ingested food. These therapies were somewhat effective but for many patients, the reductions in LDL levels were just not good enough. Moreover, the therapies caused

318

many side effects, including stomach pain and nausea. All that changed when Merck introduced Mevacor, a statin, in 1987. Statins work by inhibiting a key enzyme in the body from enabling the production of cholesterol. Rather than wait for cholesterol to be produced by the body and then try to eliminate it the way earlier drugs did, statins directly intervene in the process that the body uses to produce cholesterol. Bristol Myers and Novatis soon joined Merck in offering statin cholesterol drugs. The market shares for the statins available just prior to the launch of Lipitor are shown in Exhibit 10.1.

LIPITOR RESEARCH & DEVELOPMENT

The decision by Warner-Lambert to go on with the development of Lipitor was not very popular because the drug was regarded as a me-too drug since it was going to be the fifth drug in the statin family. However, a Phase I study conducted in 1992 showed that the drug reduced LDL levels much better than existing statins (see Exhibit 10.2 for the different phases through which a drug has to go before approval by the FDA). So Warner-Lambert decided to go ahead with the development of Lipitor. To reduce the time that it takes to review the data to approve or reject a new drug application (NDA) from the average of 12 months at the time, Warner-Lambert ran trials for a fatal hereditary condition called familial hypercholesterolemia that results in exceptionally high cholesterol levels. The idea was to take advantage of a law that encourages the FDA to expedite new drug applications for any new drug that treats a serious or life-threatening condition or addresses an unmet medical need. This worked as Lipitor was approved by the FDA six months after receiving Warner-Lambert's application for approval.

At the request of its marketing group, Warner-Lambert took the unusual step of carrying out so-called head-to-head clinical trials in which clinical data are collected on competing drugs and compared. Fortunately, the data showed Lipitor to be superior to all the other statins. Lipitor reduced LDL levels by 40–60 percent and reduced triglycerides by 19–40 percent. Zocor, the best of the other statins decreased LDL cholesterol by only about 40 percent.[3, 4, 5]

After arriving at Warner-Lambert in 1988, Ron Cresswell, head of R&D, had increased emphasis on biotechnology, integrated regulatory affairs and clinical research into the R&D unit, and sought to involve marketing earlier in the new drug development process. He also sought to establish closer links to manufacturing.

Warner-Lambert was granted FDA approval for Lipitor in December 1996, one year ahead of most analysts' expectations.

Bringing Lipitor to Market

To launch the drug, Warner-Lambert executives sought a partnership with a company that had the marketing and sales resources. Pfizer, which had a large sales force but no cholesterol drug was considered the best candidate. Pfizer liked the idea and promptly paid $205 million up front and future payments for the rights to sell Lipitor. Warner-Lambert positioned Lipitor as a therapeutically superior drug but set its price lower than that of market leaders (Exhibit 10.3).

At the launch of Lipitor, the combined sales force from Warner-Lambert and Pfizer numbered more than 2,200 sales representatives that called on about 91,000 physicians made up of cardiologists, internists, and general and family practitioners with a track record of prescribing cholesterol-lowering drugs.

Exhibit 10.1 US market shares of cholesterol-lowering drugs, January 1997

Drug name	Manufacturer	Launch year	Market share %
Mevacor	Merck	1987	14
Pravachol	Bristol-Myers Squibb	1991	21
Zocor	Merck	1992	32
Lescol	Novartis	1994	14

Source: C. Seiden (October 8, 1997). Pfizer, Inc., JP Morgan.
Note: Market shares are based on the entire cholesterol-lowering drug market (not only statins).

Exhibit 10.2 The drug development process in the US

To insure the safety and efficacy of drugs sold in the United States, drugs have to go through Phases I, II, and III, and the results of the testing scrutinized before the drug is approved by the Food and Drug Administration (FDA) for marketing. Phase IV studies are undertaken after FDA approval to further understand the long-term effects of a drug.

Within one year of its launch in January 1997, Lipitor reached $1 billion in domestic sales, beating estimates of $900 million in worldwide sales (see Exhibit 10.4 for more estimates). On June 19, 2000, Pfizer bought Warner-Lambert. Direct-to-consumer (DTC) marketing of statins by all competitors continued. In 2005 Bristol-Myers Squibb conducted its own head-to-head testing to compare its Pravachol against Lipitor. The tests showed that Lipitor, not Bristol's Pravachol, was better. Poor Bristol!

CEO Kindler wondered what would become of Pfizer. Had he done the right thing in closing down the R&D facility in which Lipitor had been developed? What would he have to do to get another Lipitor?

Preclinical Studies

As their name indicates, these are the studies that take place before a firm can start the actual clinical trials on a drug. Preclinical studies are undertaken *in vitro* (that is, in test tube or laboratory), and *in vivo* (in animal populations) to determine the effect that the drug in question has on living organisms. In these studies, scientists monitor the drug's efficacy, toxicity, and pharmacokinetics (how well the drug is absorbed, distributed, metabolized and excreted) to determine whether to proceed with the clinical testing or not. Preclinical trials take 3-6 years.

Phase I

This is where the first testing on human beings starts. A small group of 20–80 healthy volunteers is selected to participate in the studies. These studies are conducted to determine the basic characteristics of a potential new drug in humans—in particular, to determine its safety, safe dosage range, and identify side effects. Emphasis here is to make sure that the drug is safe before it can be tried on patients with the target disease.

Phase II

If the safety of the drug is confirmed in Phase I, Phase II trials are performed on larger groups (100–300) of volunteers who have the target disease. The idea here is to establish that the drug is effective and to further establish its safety. Thus, the testing tries to establish that the drug has a beneficial effect on the disease that it targets, and to continue the proof of safety partially proven in Phase I. The drug fails Phase II trials if it fails to work as expected or has toxic effects. That is, the drug fails when it does not demonstrate efficacy and safety. Phase II studies take 6 months to a year to complete.

Phase III

These are multi-center, randomized controlled studies undertaken on large groups (1,000–3,000) of patients that have the disease that the drug is supposed to treat. The idea here is to establish statistically significant proof that the potential new drug is effective in treating the disease that it is earmarked for. Patients are monitored at regular time intervals for progress in treatment and side effects. At the end of phase III trials, the pharmaceutical firm submits a New Drug Application (NDA) to the FDA for approval. If the FDA is satisfied with the application, the pharmaceutical firm is granted approval to launch and market the drug. This approval is often referred to as conditional approval since it can be withdrawn after Phase IV trials.

Phase IV

Also known as Post Marketing Surveillance Trial, Phase IV trials are designed to provide more data on safety and to monitor technical support of a drug after its owner receives permission (through FDA approval) to market and sell the drug. The studies offer more long-term data on the drug's effects on larger samples of patients, including the drug's risks, benefits, and optimal use. The results of Phase IV trials can result in the withdrawal of a drug from the market or its uses being restricted.

Sources: Understanding clinical trials. 2008. Retrieved July 22, 2008, from http://clinicaltrials.gov/ct2/info/understand. Clinical trials. 2008. Retrieved July 22, 2008, from http://en.wikipedia.org/wiki/Clinical_trial.

Exhibit 10.3 Statin average prescription pricing structure

Drug name	1997 Average prescription price $	1999 Average prescription price $
Lescol	52	50
Lipitor	84	91
Pravachol	93	105
Zocor	95	125
Mevacor	125	137

Source: IMS. (January–December 1997). National Prescription Audit. Price Probe Pricing History Report, 1992–1999.

Exhibit 10.4 Lipitor worldwide sales projections (1997)

Year	1997	1998	1999	2000	2001	2002	2003
Revenues ($ billion)	0.9	2.2	3.4	4.6	5.6	6.7	7.7

Source: ING Baring Furman Selz, LLC, April 12, 1999.

NOTES

1   This mini-case draws heavily on the case Leafstedt, M., Marta, A., Marwaha, J., Schallwig, P., & Shinkle, R. (2003). Lipitor: At the heart of Warner-Lambert. In Afuah, A. N. (2003). *Business Models: A Strategic Management Approach.* New York: McGraw-Hill/Irvin (pp. 356–370).

2   Loftus, P. (2008). Pfizer to protect Lipitor sales until November 2011. Retrieved June 20, 2008, from www.smartmoney.com/news/ON/index.cfm?story=ON-20080618-000684-1151

3   Grom, T. (May 1999). Reaching the goal. *PharmaBusiness.*

4   Mincieli, G. (June 1997). Make room for Lipitor. *Med Ad News.*

5   Lipitor. (March 1997). *R&D Directions.*

Case 11

NEW BELGIUM:
SOCIALLY RESPONSIBLE BREWING*

On June 11, 2008, InBev—a Belgium-based Brazilian-run, and world's second largest brewer—made a $46 billion bid for Anheuser-Busch.[1] While some Anheuser-Busch managers wondered what would happen to them if their firm were bought, many New Belgium Brewery (NBB) employees knew how they would vote if such a large brewer with an unknown environmental sustainability record wanted to buy them—no! Kim Jordan and her husband Jeff founded NBB in 1991 to turn their passion for good quality beer into a business they could work at and feel good about themselves at the end of the day. By 2008, it was not unusual for the firm to be mentioned as an example of a firm that did some socially responsible things that not only differentiated it but also kept its costs low.

THE US BEER INDUSTRY

In 2008, Anheuser-Busch (AB) alone held more than 50 percent of the US beer market share.[2] The next three firms held about 40 percent. The remaining 8 percent was held by many small brewers, many of them so-called microbrewers. At 59 percent, input materials for production and packaging, such as barley, hobs, bottles and cans, were a brewer's largest cost (Exhibit 11.1). Profit margins of 15 percent were not uncommon. In many states in the US, the sale of beer was restricted to certain areas, days and hours. The legal drinking age was 21. Brewers had to sell their beer to distributors who, in turn, sold it to consumers. Distributors often maintained exclusive contracts with one of the major breweries, carrying only beer from the brewer.

---

* This case was written by Ali Dharamsey, Lei Duran, Claudia Joseph, Steve Krichbaum, and Shama Zehra under the supervision of Professor Allan Afuah as a basis for class discussion and is not intended to illustrate either effective or ineffective handling of a business situation.

CRAFT BEERS

Craft beers were high-end premium beers that were distinguished from other beers by their quality, price and ingredients. In the early 2000s, the craft beer segment grew at an annual rate of 40 percent. While the mainstream beer segment had single digit growth, craft beers were produced in small batches, allowing the brewers to produce what customers perceived as better tasting beer, relative to the beers produced in a larger scale. Each brewer tried to market its beer as being distinct from the next, given the uniqueness of its own small batch process. For instance, Pete's Brewing (Pete's Wicked Ale), one of the larger craft beer makers, sought to establish an image of hard, bold flavors for customers "with an edge". This image was highlighted throughout its packaging, flavors, and website.

1991: FORT COLLINS, DENVER

Jeff Jordan became passionate about brewing beer during their bicycle trips through Europe. Back in Colorado, Jeff brewed some beer for their consumption, and his friends liked it. Kim became interested in commercializing Jeff's home-brewed beer when she noticed that nothing she tasted from outside was as good as Jeff's. After brainstorming, they agreed that the name of their venture would be New Belgium since Jeff's brewing process had been heavily influenced by the Belgium style of brewing. They called their first commercial beer "Fat Tire."

Kim was the CEO. She and Jeff knew that above all else, they wanted to build a company whose values and products supported their own personal core values. After more brainstorming, they decided that their firm's values would be anchored on three main tenets: philanthropy, ownership, and sustainability. She believed that these core values would attract new employees that shared their goal of creating a business that left the world a better place. They could then make products that would set them apart from other brewers in the eyes of customers. She would later be quoted as saying "The beautiful part of it is we believe in what we're doing."[3]

Sustainability

New Belgium designed its headquarters in 1995 with an emphasis on eco-friendly practices. The headquarters housed two "Steinecker" brew houses, four quality assurance labs and a wastewater treatment facility that allowed them to cleanse their process waters and create their own energy. Additionally, their operations were also entirely wind powered, an option chosen in the wake of an employee-owner vote (see Ownership section for more information). Kim and Jeff constantly focused efforts on innovations that would help New Belgium reduce its environmental footprint. New Belgium hired a sustainability director, Hillary Mizia, who noted, "We're closing energy loops. That's the principle behind everything we do."[4]

New Belgium was the first brewery, among both major players and Craft, within the USA to become entirely wind powered. In 2006, it was also still the brewery with the largest wind consumption in the country.[5] This use of wind power saved 3,000 tons of coal from being burned, thus reducing CO_2 emissions by some 5,700 tons. This, however, was one of the few energy initiatives that failed to provide an economic return because of the premium of around 1 cent per kilowatt (2006) that New Belgium paid for receiving wind-powered versus standard power energy.[6] "Our efficiency projects have to make good business sense," said Hillary Mizia, New Belgium's sustainability outreach coordinator. "The social and environmental impacts are as important as the financial impact, but the financial impact is what keeps us in business."[7]

New Belgium treated its windows with low-emission glaze that reflected heat rays from sunlight to reduce heat during the summer, thereby requiring less air-conditioning. The windows were retrofitted with light shelves that were made of perforated metal and painted white similar to a window sill. The windows were retrofitted on the south-facing side to provide up to 50 percent additional daylight into a space, thus reducing energy needs for lighting.[8] Lastly, additional modifications were made to further reduce energy costs. These included windows that opened automatically to cool rooms, and motion-sensor lights to ensure that lights were on only when a room was in use. Through these actions, New Belgium reduced its energy consumption by 40 percent (compared to the average American brewer), per barrel of beer.[9] New Belgium's attempt to build a green roof to further reduce energy expenditures was not as successful. However, that made Kim even more determined. "It's a gratifying way to use money, to try and push the envelope and the practice of alternative energy," she said. "It's our goal to completely close that loop, so all our energy use comes from our own waste stream." [10]

The third initiative was the purchase of a $5 million system that collected methane from brewing wastewater and used it to fire a 290-kilowatt electric generator (Exhibit 11.2). When the generator was running, for an average of 10–15 hours a day, it created up to 60 percent of the brewery's power. This amounted to savings of $2,500–3,000 a month. New Belgium Brewery also conserved electricity by capturing the heat created by brewing tanks and piping it back to heat water.[11] Renewable heating and cooling systems such as steam stack heat exchangers were also utilized. By treating its own wastewater, the company was able to reduce the load on the city's facilities. By recovering energy in the form of biogas and reusing water in non-brewing processes they were also able to create processes that support holistic sustainability. In 2006, New Belgium used 4.75 liters of water for every liter of beer brewed (there are 119 liters per barrel, which is the standard measure of beer sales).[12] These 4.75 liters were far less than the industry standard of 20 liters. New Belgium's goal was to reduce its usage down to 3 liters. The combination of reduced water consumption and the generator system created the largest savings by assisting New Belgium avoid steep fees that would be assessed by Fort Collins to treat the brewery's nutrient rich wastewater. It would have cost the firm $4.43 million to build a system that would reprocess the used water before releasing it into the public water system, as required by local laws.

Ownership

New Belgium was a privately held company that allowed its employees to take shares in the company and serve as employee-owners. The company had, on average, an employee ownership of 32 percent and employees enjoyed equal voting rights on all company issues.[13]

The firm's books were opened to employees, consistent with "trust and mutual responsibility."[14] Private ownership also enabled New Belgium to keep its strategies, company data, performance figures, etc., from complete public disclosure. In 2006, the firm had no public debt outstanding. The collective employee culture extended beyond ownership with additional perks to increase moral. Employees were provided generous benefits including health, dental and retirement plans. Lunch was free to employees, every other week. Employees were also entitled to a free massage (at a salon) every year. Kim and Jeff encouraged employees to bring their children and even dogs to work. Those employees that had been with the company for over five years were given an all expenses-paid trip to Belgium to understand "Beer Culture." Employees from all departments within the organization were also given roles on the Philanthropy Committee which decided how to spend the company's social and charitable fund (see Philanthropic section for more information). Lastly, New Belgium enjoyed a fairly decentralized management structure that enabled employees to be readily involved. Employees were also encouraged to understand, guide, and take responsibility for corporate decision making.

Philanthropy

New Belgium gave $1 of every barrel of beer sold to local causes such as care for kids with learning and developmental disabilities.[15] From its inception to 2006, New Belgium Brewing had donated more than 1.6 million dollars to local charitable organizations in the communities where the company conducted business. The donations were divided between states in proportion to their percentage of overall sales.[16]

Funding decisions were made by the Philanthropy Committee, made up of owners, employee owners, area leaders, and production workers. New Belgium targeted non-profit organizations that demonstrated creativity, diversity, and an innovative approach to their mission and objectives. The Philanthropy Committee also looked for groups that involved the community in reaching their goals. Past recipients included Volunteers for Outdoor Colorado and The Larimer County Search & Rescue team.

Marketing

Like most craft beer makers, NB spent twice as much per barrel on advertising as non—craft beer makers. The primary focus was to highlight "experience" and awareness of taste and brand. With Fat Tire being the flagship product and with a clear idea of the core values, Kim moved forward in bringing the positioning to life with a statement that appeared on all New Belgium product packaging:

> In this box is our labor of love. We feel incredibly lucky to be creating something fine that enhances people's lives. Know that we think about you as we're making it-enjoying Trippel by the fire, splitting Fat Tire with a friend, offering Abbey Ale as a present. Enjoy! And stop by to let us know how it was. We'd love to see you!

Kim's success in bringing New Belgium's character to life could be seen not only through Beer Aficionados's avid enjoyment of the product but more importantly through the alignment of brand champions/evangelists/ambassadors with the products and company.[17] As noted by just one set of evangelists on numerous Beer Aficionado targeted sites, Shannon and Adam, October 10, 2005 (in reference to the Abby product):

> Ever since we tried this beer it has been THE favorite. (We even had it kegged in for our wedding . . .) Keep bugging your local merchants to get it in their stores, it really deserves more shelf space. And thank goodness Coors lost.[18]

Exhibit 11.1 Average cost of goods sold for US brewery

Item	Cost (%)
Purchases	59.0
Wages	7.6
Depreciation	4.5
Utilities	1.5
Rent	0.4
Others	12.0
Profit	**15.0**

Source: IBS World.

Exhibit 11.2 Cost implications of generator purchase

Cost of new water treatment facility	$5,000,000
Estimated cost of discharge water treatment facility	$4,430,000
Electricity costs	
Energy use charge	$0.0164 per KWh
Fixed demand charge	$4.31 per KWh
Coincident peak demand charge	$11.62 per KWh (plus other misc.)
Estimated electricity savings per month	$2,500–$3,000
Water costs	
Cost of water per gallon, Denver, CO	$0.001
Liters per gallon	3.79
Liters in a barrel of beer	119
New Belgium: liters of water per barrel of beer produced	4.75
Industry average: liters of water used per barrel of beer produced	20
New Belgium: estimated barrels of beer produced per year	330,000

Source: Case writers' estimates using company sources.

The sentiments of these consumers highlighted their passion for New Belgium and furthermore an understanding of the competitive environment in which their products competed. The call to action by other loyalists by rallying and demanding for higher distribution showed the alignment that Kim had sought to achieve between her customers and New Belgium.

Future for New Belgium

Kim Jordan and Jeff Lebesch had grown their company into the third-largest American craft beer maker (after Sierra Nevada and Sam Adams). They had grown their employee base to more than 260 employees.[19] Sales had grown to more than 330,000 barrels, and New Belgium was now the fastest-growing craft brewer in the US. Annual revenues had exceeded $70 million—with its corporate soul intact. As Kim and Jeff looked to the future, they could not help but wonder what more they could do for their community and New Belgium, while still staying true to their core values.

NOTES

1   A bid for Bud. (2008, June 19). *The Economist.*
2   A bid for Bud. (2008, June 19). *The Economist.*
3   Inc. staff. (2006). Bringing fundamental change to everyday life. And, for that matter, death. Retrieved July 22, 2008, from www.inc.com/magazine/20061101/green50_integrators.html
4   Kessenides, D. (2005, June). Green is the new black. *Inc Magazine,* 27(6), 65–66.
5   The brewery with the big green footprint. (2003). *In Business,* 25(1), 16.
6   Raabe, S. (2005, June 1). Brewery supplements profits with energy savings. *Knight Ridder Tribune Business News* (p. 1).
7   Retrieved from: http://fcgov.com/utilities/wind-power.php.
8   Kessenides, D. (2005, June). Green is the new black. *Inc Magazine,* 27(6), 65–66.
9   Raabe, S. (2005, June 1). Brewery supplements profits with energy savings. *Knight Ridder Tribune Business News* (p. 1).
10 Cohn, D. (2006). This green beer's the real deal. Retrieved July 22, 2008, from www.wired.com/news/technology/0,70361-0.html
11 Kessenides, D. (2005, June). Green is the new black. *Inc Magazine,* 27(6), 65–66.
12 Retreived from: www.paulnoll.com/Oregon/Canning/number-liters.html
13 Liquid – metric to non-metric. (n.d.). Retrieved July 22, 2008, from www.paulnoll.com/Oregon/Canning/number-liters.html
14 Brewing up fun in the workplace. (n.d.). Retrieved July 22, 2008, from www.e-businessethics.com/NewBelgiumCases/NBB-BreweryFun.pdf
15 Armstrong, D. (2006, November 28). Philanthropy gets serious for some companies: Growing number are making donations from revenue, not from profit. Inc.com.
16 Retrieved from: www.newbelgiumbrewery.com/philanthropy
17 Brand evangelists/ambassadors/champions are consumers that feel so strongly connected with the brand that they spread the word of the brand and attempt to help the brand succeed.
18 Retrieved from: www.mylifeisbeer.com/beer/bottles/bottledetail/293
19 Inc. staff. (2006). Bringing fundamental change to everyday life. And, for that matter, death. Retrieved July 23, 2008, from www.inc.com/magazine/20061101/green50_integrators.html

Case 12

NINTENDO Wii

The Microsoft investor could not believe the news. Seven years after entering the video game console business, Microsoft was still losing money in its video game business. Its Xbox, launched in 2001, had lost billions, and the sophisticated Xbox 360 did not appear to be making much money. Sony's even more sophisticated PS3 was also losing money. In contrast, demand for the Nintendo Wii had been so strong during the 2007 Christmas season that Nintendo had been forced to issue rain checks to customers. In fact, it was not unusual for eager Wii customers to pay prices well above Nintendo's suggested retail price of $249 in live online auctions. Why had the Nintendo Wii performed so well? Why had Microsoft done so poorly in video games? Why had Sony started doing so poorly following its initial success in video games? The Microsoft investor wondered if Microsoft had learned from the Nintendo Wii.

COMPETING FOR GAMERS: THE EARLY YEARS

Although the invention of the video game may date back to as far as 1947 with the patenting of a "Cathode Ray Tube Amusement Device"[1] by Thomas T. Goldsmith Jr. and Estle Ray Mann, Atari is usually credited with introducing the first successful video game to the home. In 1975 it offered a dedicated home version of its popular arcade game *Pong* called the Sears Tele-Game System and 150,000 units of it sold that Christmas.[2] Many other firms entered the home video game console business but Atari reigned until Nintendo introduced its Nintendo Entertainment System—a so-called third-generation system—in 1985. Nintendo's leadership position would be challenged by Sega when it introduced its Sega Mega Drive (called the Sega Genesis in the US) in 1989. The Sega Genesis was a so-called fourth-generation console. Although Nintendo fought back, Sega would emerge as the new leader until Sony's entry.

THE MARKET THAT WII WOULD FACE

The Products

Sony entered the home video game business by introducing the Playstation in Japan in 1994 and in the US in 1995. Sega and Nintendo fought back but Sony emerged as the winner. Sony's success would attract Microsoft, which introduced the Xbox in 2001, one year after Sony introduced the Playstation 2. The world's number one software company was rumored to have spent $2 billion to develop the Xbox and another $500 million to market it. In 2001 when the Xbox was introduced, Microsoft officials knew that they were going to lose money on each console but hoped to make up for the losses with software (game) sales. (In the video console industry, platform owners such as Sony were paid royalties by game developers who sold games to be played on the platform.) It was expected that each Xbox customer would buy three games in his/her first year of owning an Xbox console, and buy one game per year thereafter. Exhibit 12.1 shows Xbox forecasted sales, costs, and prices when it was launched. In November 2005, barely four years after introducing the Xbox, Microsoft introduced the Xbox 360 in the US market. One year later, Sony introduced the Playstation 3.

Riding the Technological Progress Envelope

The microchip technological revolution that put a cell phone in most hands, a computer on many laps and desks, an ATM at most corners, etc., and that gave us the iPod, iPhone, Blackberry, etc., was the same technology that drove the video game industry. Microchip technology pushed the technology envelope and video console makers exploited the frontier. Each new generation of consoles was driven by a new generation of faster microprocessors and graphic processors with even more graphical detail. For example, the Xbox was powered by an Intel microprocessor that ran at 733 megahertz and graphics processor that delivered about 300 million polygons per second, more than three times the graphics performance of the Playstation 2, the previous generation console that Microsoft hoped to displace.[3] The Xbox 360, which Microsoft introduced four years after the Xbox, used a 3.2-gigahertz processor, an order of magnitude faster than the Xbox while delivering 500 million polygons. The PS3 also used a 3.2-gigahertz processor and the firm's new much-touted blue-ray DVD technology.

These advances in technological innovation also created more options for software (game) developers to design games for each generation of consoles that were even more lifelike and appealing to core gamers than those designed for previous generations. However, in tracking the technology frontier, console makers incurred very high console costs. Console makers had to develop custom chips dedicated to their consoles or use the fastest and best chips available in the market. The result was that each console cost so much that its maker sold it at a loss, and hoped to make money from the royalties collected on software sales and from selling accessories.

Effectively, each new generation of consoles delivered outstanding technological performance, images that were more lifelike than those from previous generations, and appealed to core gamers. Each new generation was also more complex than previous generations and many games took hours, if not days, to play. Virtual violence also became more common with each generation. Moreover, playing many of these games required players to master complicated combinations of buttons on each console's complex controls, and lots of gaming know-how and expertise.[4] Each new generation of consoles rendered the previous generation technologically obsolete and out of style as far as core gamers were concerned. Additionally, most games developed for new consoles often rendered previous games obsolete. The product cycle time—the time from when the first product in a new generation was introduced to the time when the first product in the next generation was introduced—was also decreasing.

THE Wii

Nintendo introduced its Wii video console in the Americas on November 19, 2006, only about a week after Sony had introduced its PS3 console on November 11, but one year after Microsoft had introduced its Xbox 360. The Wii had a simpler design than the Xbox 360 and PS3 to appeal to the casual or lapsed gamer, or non-core gamers who had neither the time (hours or days) to dedicate to a game, nor the expertise to handle the complexity of existing console controls and games.[5] It had easy-to-use controls and its games sought to offer real-life, rather than escapist scenarios. According to Jeffrey M. O'Brien of Fortune, the Wii differed from the Xbox 360 and PS3 in other ways:

> Nintendo used off-the-shelf parts from numerous suppliers. Sony co-developed the PS3's screaming-fast 3.2-gigahertz "cell" chip and does the manufacturing in its own facilities. Nintendo bought its 729-megahertz chip at Kmart. (Not really. But it might as well have.) Its graphics are marginally better than the PS2 and the original Xbox, but they pale next to the PS3 and Xbox 360. Taking this route enabled the company to introduce the Wii at $250 in the U.S. (vs. $599 for the PS3 and as much as $399 for the 360) and still turn a profit on every unit.[6]

The Wii also had no hard disk, no DVD, and no Dolby 5.1. Its video RAM was 24 MB compared to 256MB for the PS3 and up to 512MB for the Xbox 360.

However, the Wii had some innovative features that its high-tech competitors did not.[7] It had a remote (motion) wand-like control that resembled a TV remote control compared to the complex button-strewn controller carried by the PS3 and Xbox 360.[8] The wand-like control enabled a gamer's movements and actions to be directly mapped into the video game. For example, to swing a tennis racket or golf club, the player literally swung the remote controller as if it were a racket or club. The swing would be remotely detected by the Wii processor, and the player would get some exercise together with more of a sense of playing tennis or golf from the swing. Contrast this with having to be adept and knowledgeable enough to hit the right complicated combination of buttons on the PS3 or Xbox 360's control at the right time. The other distinguishing feature was the Mii. A Mii was a digital character that a player could create on the Wii. Once a character had been so created, it could be used as participating characters in subsequent games. It allowed players to capture different personalities and caricatures including their own. According to Saturo Iwata, President of Nintendo when the Wii was introduced, the idea for the control and shorter simpler games had been developed and tested on Nintendo's handheld device called the Nintendo DS. The Wii was also connectible to the DS so that the latter could be used as the input to the former.

Beyond the remote control stick and the Mii, the Wii had other features such as backward compatibility with all official GameCube software, and the WiiConnect24 which enabled the Wii to receive information such as news and weather over the Internet while in standby mode.

Despite the initial success of the Wii, some incumbents did not see it as much of a threat to Sony and Microsoft. Remarks such as the following from Sony Computer Entertainment of America's Jack Tretton, were not uncommon:[9]

> You have to give Nintendo credit for what they've accomplished . . . But if you look at the industry, any industry, it doesn't typically go backwards technologically. The controller is innovative, but the Wii is basically a repurposed GameCube. If you've built your console on an innovative controller, you have to ask yourself, Is that long term?[10]

The Microsoft investor wondered how long the Wii would continue to do well. Should he have invested in Nintendo instead of Microsoft? Why hadn't Microsoft followed a Nintendo type strategy when it entered the video game console market in 2001? Was it too late to follow a Wii-type strategy?

The estimated costs, wholesale prices and suggested retail prices for the Wii, Xbox 360 and PS3 are shown in Exhibit 12.2, while the forecasted number of units are shown in Exhibit 12.3.

Exhibit 12.1 Xbox forecasted sales, costs, and prices, 2001

	FY2002	FY2003	FY2004	FY2005	FY2006
Console forecasted sales (no. of Xbox units)	4	10	11	12	13
Retail price per console ($)	299	249	249	249	199
Wholesale price ($)	209	174	174	174	139
Production cost	350	300	250	250	250
Retail price per game unit sold ($)	49	49	49	49	49
Production cost of each game unit ($)	36	36	36	36	36

Source: Microsoft forecasts and analysts' estimates.

Exhibit 12.2 Costs, retail and wholesale prices

Product	Year introduced	First year			After first year		
		Cost ($)	Suggested retail price ($)	Wholesale price ($)	Cost	Suggested retail price ($)	Wholesale price ($)
Xbox360	2005	525	399	280	323	399	280
Sony PS3	2006	806	499	349	496	399	280
Nintendo Wii	Late 2006	158.30	249	199	126	200	150

Sources: Company reports. Various sources including: R. Ehrenberg (2007). Game console wars II: Nintendo shaves off profits, leaving competition scruffy. Retrieved September 8, 2007, from http://seekingalpha.com/article/34357-game-console-wars-ii-nintendo-shaves-off-profits-leaving-competition-scruff

Exhibit 12.3 Forecasted console and game sales (in millions of units)

	2005	2006	2007	2008	2009	2010
Console						
Xbox360	1.5	8.5	10	10	5	
Sony PS3		2	11	13	13	7
Nintendo Wii			5.8	14.5	17.4	18.3
Games						
Xbox360	4.5	25.5	30	30	15	
Sony PS3		6	33	39	39	21
Nintendo Wii			28.8	66.5	114.3	128.8

Sources: Company and analysts reports. HSBC Global Research. 2007. Nintendo Co. (7974). Telecom, Media & Technology Software. Equity–Japan. July 5, 2007.

NOTES

1   Video game. (2007). Retrieved December 25, 2007, from http://en.wikipedia.org/wiki/Video_games.
2   Afuah, A. N., & Grimaldi, R. (2003). Architectural innovation and the attacker's advantage from complementary assets: The case of the video game console industry. Working paper. Stephen M. Ross School of Business at the University of Michigan, Ann Arbor, MI.
3   Megahertz is a crude measure of the speed or power of a processor. The higher the megahertz, the faster the processor is supposed to be. The "number of polygons" is a measure of the graphical detail in the resulting images.
4   Playing a different game: Does Nintendo's radical new strategy represent the future of gaming? (2006, October 26). *The Economist*. Gapper, J. (2007, July 13). Video games have rediscovered fun. *Financial Times*.
5   Playing a different game: Does Nintendo's radical new strategy represent the future of gaming? (2006, October 26). *The Economist*. Gapper, J. (2007, July 13). Video games have rediscovered fun. *Financial Times*.
6   O'Brien, J. M. (2007). Wii will rock you. Retrieved December 27, 2007, from www.mutualofamerica.com/articles/Fortune/June%202007/fortune2.asp
7   Turott, P. (2007). Xbox 360 vs. PlayStation 3 vs. Wii: A technical comparison. Retrieved December 27, 2007, from www.winsupersite.com/showcase/Xbox 360_ps3_wii.asp.
8   Gapper, J. (2007, July 13). Video games have rediscovered fun. *Financial Times*.
9   Bird D., Bosco N., Nainwal S., & Park E. (2007). The Nintendo Wii. Working case. Stephen M. Ross School of Business at the University of Michigan, Ann Arbor, MI.
10 O'Brien, J. M. (2007). Wii will rock you. Retrieved January 2, 2008, from http://money.cnn.com/magazines/fortune/fortune_archive/2007/06/11/100083454/index.htm

INDEX